Robin & Lucienne Day

Pioneers of Contemporary Design

Robin & Lucienne Day

Pioneers of Contemporary Design

Lesley Jackson

MITCHELL BEAZLEY

For Ian, my family and my much-loved
sister Sue (1959–2007)

In memory of Robin Day (1915–2010)
and Lucienne Day (1917–2010)

An Hachette UK Company
www.hachette.co.uk

First published in Great Britain in 2001 by Mitchell Beazley,
a division of Octopus Publishing Group Ltd
Revised edition published in 2011
Endeavour House
189 Shaftesbury Avenue
London
WC2H 8JY

ISBN: 978 1 84533 634 9

A CIP record for this book is available from the British Library

Set in Helvetica Neue
Colour reproduction by Fine Arts Repro House Co. Ltd
Produced by Toppan Printing Co. (HK) Ltd
Printed and bound in China

10 9 8 7 6 5 4 3 2

Executive Editors	Mark Fletcher, Alison Starling
Deputy Art Director	Vivienne Brar
Managing Editor	Anthea Snow
Designer	June Fraser
Editor	Kirsty Seymour-Ure. Stephanie Milner
Picture Research	Christine Crawshaw
Production	Nancy Roberts
Index	Hilary Bird

Page 2
Robin and Lucienne Day, 1956
The Days are shown sitting by the
fireplace of their home at Cheyne
Walk in Chelsea. They decorated the
interior in the "Contemporary" style
during 1952–3.

Contents

Above
Polypropylene chairs
Tens of millions of these robust
plastic shell chairs have been
manufactured over the last four
decades since the launch of
the original stacking chair in
1963. The armchair was
introduced in 1967, and the
white version dates from 1970.

Preface

Author's Foreword

The deaths of Lucienne Day and Robin Day within a year of each other in 2010 marks the end of a heroic era in British design. This book was originally published in 2001 to accompany a major retrospective exhibition at the Barbican Art Gallery in London celebrating their achievements. It was a privilege to curate that show and to collaborate with them on this book. I am gratified for their sakes that they lived to see their work being appreciated again for a second time.

The book documents their wide-ranging activities from their early days as pioneers of 'Contemporary' design to their later years as design legends. It highlights their astonishing energy, their tireless creativity and, above all, their integrity. For the Days, good design was a mission, not an occupation. It brought them international fame and earned them worldwide respect, but it never turned their heads. They remained completely focused and true to their ideals right to the end.

This book is not a biography but it reflects the character of its subjects. They selected the designer (their friend and former colleague, June Fraser) and approved the layout and contents. I am deeply indebted to them for cooperating so fully with my research. We spent many long hours together discussing their careers in their Cheyne Walk living room and studio, and they generously gave me free rein to trawl through their archives. The book reflects the richness of these resources.

Design played a huge role in their lives, but the Days both had other great passions - Lucienne for gardening, Robin for mountaineering. They were just as enthusiastic about these activities as they were about design. The gardens Lucienne made, first on the roof-terrace at Cheyne Walk, then in woodland soil at their West Sussex cottage, provided another, more intimate, outlet for her love of natural beauty. Robin's incredible feats of long-distance walking, ski-touring, and climbing were fondly recalled by his daughter Paula and his mountaineering friends at his funeral.

The Days had long, full and rewarding lives. Lucienne was 93 when she died; Robin was 95. Although they worked independently most of the time in their own respective fields, there is a real harmony between their designs, in spirit, purpose and aesthetic. Lucienne's textiles and Robin's furniture, although of their time, have a timeless quality which will continue to make a positive impact in the world for many years to come, although they themselves have gone.

Lesley Jackson, January 2011

Preface to the First Edition

Teamwork, specialization and large offices are now usual in the design profession. This book is about two designers who have taken a different road, working independently and across many different fields of design.

With careers that span more than half a century and embrace numerous disciplines, we have witnessed many changes in design practice. The difference between the design scene today and that of fifty years ago is so great that it is difficult to remember how it was when we emerged, within a few years of each other, from the Royal College of Art, newly qualified and hoping to make our careers in design.

Not only was the practice of design virtually unknown, but we were also faced with the restrictions imposed by war. Most manufacturers of textiles, for instance, had been forced to close or to transfer their production to materials needed specifically for the war – not an auspicious beginning.

In the 1950s we both participated in the surge of modern design that was released by the ending of the war and material restrictions. There was a growing feeling of optimism and an anticipation of the emergence of a bright new world and we thought that progressive design could contribute to the quality of people's lives. We were both supported by our mutual desire to produce designs that would overcome the dreariness of the previous decade, and make it possible for the many – rather than the few – to enjoy pleasant surroundings at a reasonable price.

The Festival of Britain in 1951, which brought the resounding success of Calyx and the wonderful invitation to design the seating for the Royal Festival Hall, marked perhaps the most important stage in our early careers. This was the time of Robin's success in the Museum of Modern Art's International Low-Cost Furniture Design Competition, resulting in the remarkable Day/Hille association which attained international status for several decades, producing many award-winning furniture designs including what was probably the world's best-selling chair. At the same time Lucienne's textile designs for Heal's developed and prospered, assisted by the Award to Calyx from the American Institute of Decorators in 1952, the first time this prize had been awarded outside the USA. From 1962 to 1987 our design consultancy for John Lewis added a new dimension to our work.

We have had good fortune – enterprising clients and many awards and honours – and, best of all, our busy working lives have been spent in challenging but highly enjoyable and fulfilling work. Although we have worked separately for all these years, it has been wonderful to have the support of each other's enthusiasm and enduring commitment to modern design.

Robin and Lucienne Day

CHAPTER ONE

1930-45

THE THIRTIES AND THE WAR YEARS: SCHOOL, COLLEGE AND TEACHING

Robin Day: Early Life in High Wycombe

Born in the furniture-making town of High Wycombe in
Buckinghamshire on 25 May 1915, the second of four boys,
Robin Day grew up surrounded by timber yards and cabinet-
making workshops. Although his family had no connections with
the local industry, the fact that he spent his formative years in a
town with such strong furniture associations was undoubtedly
significant in his choice of future career. His father, Arthur Day,
was a police constable. His mother, Mary, was very practical
and was particularly skilled at dressmaking, and it may have
been from her that Robin inherited his manual dexterity. His
natural gift for drawing was apparent from an early age, and
during his teens he began to paint landscape watercolours. His
other great passion was for the countryside, and as a youth he
spent every spare moment walking and climbing trees in the
beech woods around High Wycombe.[1]

Although chronic asthma affected Robin's attendance at
primary school, his parents, realizing that his artistic talents
were exceptional, enrolled him as a junior day technical student
at High Wycombe Technical Institute in 1928, where he won the
drawing prize each year. Three years later he won a scholarship
to study as a senior art student at the adjoining High Wycombe
School of Art (now Buckinghamshire New University). One of his
teachers was a man called Bill Cutler, who combined a career
in teaching with design work for local furniture factories. Cutler
was good at recognizing the potential of his students, and it
was he who later encouraged Robin to apply to the Royal
College of Art (RCA).

Although the syllabus at High Wycombe included life
drawing and still life drawing, tuition was mainly geared towards
training draftsmen to work in the drawing offices of local
furniture factories. It was here that Robin developed his skills in
perspective, technical drawing and illustration, all of which he
would later utilize not only as a furniture designer, but also in his
work in graphics, exhibitions and interior design. Practical tuition
was focused on three main areas, cabinet-making, chair-making
and metalwork, which provided a solid grounding for the future.
Design awareness at the school was low, however, as the local
factories concentrated mainly on reproduction furniture.

In 1933 Robin took a job in the drawing office of a local
furniture factory, George Large & Son, while continuing to attend
night classes at art school. Although useful from a practical point
of view, on a personal basis the job was unsatisfactory as the
firm specialized in cheap dining suites and "fireside" chairs in
pseudo-historical styles that were not to his taste at all. His
work mainly consisted of making alterations to existing designs,
producing full-scale working drawings, and issuing hardware,

Opposite top
**Robin Day's family home,
High Wycombe**
Robin's first home (now
demolished) was the second
house from the right. High
Wycombe in Buckinghamshire,
where Robin grew up, was a
traditional furniture-making centre.

Opposite bottom left
**Arthur Day, Robin's father
(centre)**
Arthur Day originally worked on
the railways, and later became a
police constable in High Wycombe.

Opposite bottom right
**Robin Day, Royal College
of Art, 1937**
Robin won a three-year
scholarship to the RCA in 1934.
He is shown here on the day he
received his Diploma, after which
he was awarded a Continuation
Scholarship for a further year.

Left
**Robin Day and Lucienne
Conradi, c. 1940**
The couple met at a dance at the
RCA in 1940 during Lucienne's
final year, and were married two
years later.

such as screws and hinges, to the workmen. Although there was no opportunity for genuine design innovation, one positive result of this early hands-on experience of working in industry was that Robin developed an intuitive sense of how to design furniture that would be commercially viable. This, combined with his familiarity with the day-to-day running of a factory and his ease in communicating effectively with the workmen, would prove invaluable later on in his relationship with Hille.

Around this time Robin was offered a job as a designer by Lucien Ercolani, founder of one of the most famous High Wycombe factories, Ercol. However, by then he had been awarded a Royal Exhibition Scholarship by the RCA, and in 1934 he moved to London to pursue his studies. In any case, tempting though the prospect of working for Ercol must have seemed, after the sobering experience of working in a factory, the seeds had already been sown in Robin's mind for the idea of practising independently as a freelance designer.

Robin Day: Royal College of Art

Robin had high expectations of the RCA, but the reality was very disappointing. During the 1930s there was a strong art bias at the college (the two principals, William Rothenstein and Percy Jowett, were both painters), and design tuition was of an extremely general nature. Consequently, although Robin had gone to the RCA hoping to specialize in industrial and interior design, when he arrived he found that none of the staff had any expertise in these areas. "At this time the Royal College was not equipped or staffed as now for the study of woods, metals and plastics," explained the designer Milner Gray in a profile of Robin in 1952. "His studies were thus fortuitously deflected to other fields, including mural painting, publicity design, display and interior design, enabling him to acquire skills which in later practice have served him well." Robin's own recollections are somewhat less benign. "The RCA was a great let-down. I felt lost, isolated and confused. My tutor, Professor Tristram, was a specialist in the restoration of medieval frescoes. There was tuition in fine arts and craft design, but nothing for product design, furniture design and interior design, and there were no workshops other than for textiles and pottery. After a year, I went to Professor Tristram with some sketches of interiors done tentatively on my own, and he said, 'Well my boy, you obviously know more about this than I do'."

As a result, Robin was almost entirely self-taught, and his interest in modern design developed quite independently outside his formal education, largely as a result of his own curiosity and enthusiasm. He spent a great deal of time poring over books and magazines in the libraries at the Victoria and Albert Museum (V&A) and the Royal Institute of British Architects (RIBA), for example, and he regularly attended exhibitions.[2] Trade fairs such as the British Industries Fairs and the British Furniture Federation Fairs were also important, and, in addition, he frequented progressive shops such as Heal's and Dunn's of Bromley, and visited furniture showrooms such as Gordon Russell.

For his diploma show in 1937 Robin designed several items of furniture, which were made by a craftsman in High Wycombe.[3] The most striking piece was a sideboard with a plain rectangular macassar ebony case and laminboard doors veneered in figured burr ash.[4] His stand also included a series of montages of modern interiors, and the college was so impressed by his efforts that, on the basis of this display, he was awarded a Continuation Scholarship for a fourth year. During this time Robin was asked to make a sculptural feature to promote a student art exhibition at the RIBA. Responding with characteristic inventiveness, he created a surreal figure with a drawing board for its body, T-squares for arms, and an artist's palette for its head. The display skills he demonstrated in his diploma show, combined with the creativity and ingenuity of his RIBA sculpture, presaged his flair for exhibition design, a talent he utilized extensively the following decade.

After leaving the RCA, Robin's aim was to earn a living through design, but owing to the outbreak of war it took nearly a decade to get established. Early commissions included making drawings and models for architects, signwriting, and producing showcards for fashion boutiques.[5] In addition, to supplement his income, he took a series of part-time teaching posts, initially at Croydon School of Art, where he taught technical drawing and lettering, and subsequently at Beckenham School of Art. When he started at Beckenham he taught perspective and presentation drawing, which included techniques such as collage and photomontage.[6] John Cole, the headmaster, was so enthusiastic about Robin's teaching methods that he invited him to prepare a new preliminary course in three-dimensional design. The hands-on approach that he pioneered on this course proved extremely popular, and Cole was particularly impressed by the way Robin's students were introduced to product design by making small constructions out of wood, wire and plastic. Soon, demand for his course was so great that he had to be given an assistant, and this was how he came to meet Clive Latimer, with whom he would later collaborate on the prize-winning entry to the International Low-Cost Furniture Competition held by the Museum of Modern Art in 1948.[7]

Lucienne Day: Early Life in Croydon

Born at Coulsden in Surrey on 5 January 1917, Désirée Lucienne Conradi was the youngest of four children, and the only girl in a family of boys. Her father, Felix Conradi, was a Belgian reinsurance broker who had moved to London during the early 1900s to establish a branch of an Antwerp firm. Her mother, Dulcie, who was English, took great pride in the decoration and furnishing of the family home, and although their tastes were very different, Lucienne grew up in an environment that fuelled her awareness of interior design. Her mother was also a keen gardener, and it was through her that Lucienne developed an early love of plants. In 1919 the Conradi family moved to Croydon, where Lucienne spent her childhood. Initially she was educated at home, but from the age of nine she went to Woodford School in Croydon, and from 1929 to 1934 she attended the convent boarding school of Notre Dame de Sion in Worthing. As a child she was always drawing, and showed exceptional natural talent from an early age. At school she enjoyed both art and English, and excelled equally in both.

Left
Lucienne and her mother Dulcie Conradi, early 1920s
Born of an English mother and a Belgian father, Lucienne was the youngest of four children.

Below
Lucienne's family home in Croydon, 1933 (now demolished)
The Conradi family moved to Croydon in Surrey in 1919.

Bottom
RCA Theatre Group, c.1938
Lucienne, a keen actor while at college, played the lead in Gorky's *Yegor Bulichoff* (front, far left).

Eventually, though, she opted for the former, after being encouraged to apply to art school by her art mistress, Mrs Kinaston.[8]

Lucienne enrolled at Croydon School of Art at the age of seventeen. There she experimented with a wide range of media before finding her *métier* in printed textiles. Her tutor was Reginald Marlowe, a highly respected studio potter, who although committed to a craft ethos in his own work, fully appreciated the importance of industrial design. Also influential at this date was a student teacher, Peter Werner, who became a close friend. Werner introduced her to the work of the Bauhaus, and was a great enthusiast for Swedish design. Closer to home Lucienne admired the work of the interior decorator Duncan Miller, the furniture of Betty Joel, and the bold simplicity of the textiles of Marion Dorn.

Lucienne Day: Royal College of Art

In 1937 Lucienne won a place in the Design Department at the RCA, having been encouraged to apply by Reginald Marlowe. Her course included general subjects such as architecture, calligraphy (considered good for developing a flowing hand), and museum studies, which involved studying historical textiles and making drawings in the neighbouring V&A. The textile department was divided into printed and woven textiles, and although Lucienne could have spent time studying both areas, she chose to concentrate exclusively on printed textiles from the outset, somewhat to her regret later on. Craft workshops, where students gained hands-on experience in techniques such as block-printing and screen-printing, were located in the Imperial Institute Galleries on Exhibition Road.

An influential figure in the textile department at this time was Reco Capey, a pioneer industrial designer who worked as art director for the cosmetics firm Yardley's. Initially, when Lucienne started, Capey was a visiting lecturer, but in 1938 he became the RCA's first Industrial Liaison Officer. By this date the college was just starting to address its responsibility to train industrial designers, after a series of damning reports on its inadequacies in this respect. Capey's job was to arrange placements for students within industry, and it was as a result of this scheme that Lucienne was sent on a two-month placement to the firm of Sanderson during her second year, where she worked in the large wallpaper studio at Perivale. At this date Sanderson were associated with traditional floral patterns and made no attempt to produce forward-looking designs. The reality of working in a factory was an eye-opener for Lucienne, who, with her growing taste for modern design, found it hard to adapt to the conservative style of the company.[9]

Shortly after leaving college Lucienne was contacted by Nicholas Sekers of Sekers Fabrics, following a recommendation from Madge Garland, Professor of Fashion at the RCA. Sekers was keen for her to design for his company, and although the factory specialized in jacquard woven silk fabrics rather than prints, swayed by his enthusiasm she agreed to start supplying him with sketches for patterns. However, the relationship came to an abrupt end after Sekers refused to allow one of her designs to be displayed under her own name in an exhibition.

At this date designers were still expected to work anonymously, and it was unusual for them to receive any acknowledgment from their client. It was only after Lucienne teamed up so successfully with Heal Fabrics during the 1950s that manufacturers began to realize the advantages of promoting the work of "named" designers. These unsatisfactory early experiences at Sanderson and Sekers led to Lucienne's decision to practice as a freelance designer, and account for her reluctance to work under contract for a particular firm.

Robin and Lucienne Day: RCA Diploma Show

Although Robin's final year at the RCA during 1937–8 overlapped with Lucienne's first year, the college was split across so many sites that they never actually met at the time. They were finally introduced at a college dance in March 1940, almost two years after Robin had left. What drew them together from the outset was their passion for modern design, a subject they spent hours tirelessly discussing, right from the evening they first met. Idealistic and ambitious, they were united in their commitment to establishing a new, clean-lined, modern style. Kindred spirits, their relationship gave them both confidence, strengthening the determination of each to make a career in design. Such a degree of commitment was highly unusual, particularly for women, at a time when the majority of art school graduates went into teaching rather than into practice. "I doubt very much, if I hadn't met Robin, whether I would have gone on with the same determination," Lucienne later acknowledged. "Robin has helped me to follow my own ideas. He has provided a sort of 'climate', an atmosphere of originality and exploration. Early on I know I was very much influenced by Robin's attitude towards furniture and interior design."[10]

The first fruits of their creative partnership were manifested in Lucienne's diploma show in 1940, where Robin's display skills were called upon in the setting up of her stand. It was his suggestion that she should combine furnishing fabrics with furniture to demonstrate how her fabrics might be used, and the display included an armchair produced to his design by Heal's, upholstered with Lucienne's block-printed fabric, Bushmen, inspired by French cave paintings.[11] Also noteworthy was the inclusion of ceramics decorated by Lucienne with simple linear patterns, incised through overglaze enamels using the sgraffito technique. Although at this date Lucienne had no aspirations to become a ceramic designer, later she would collaborate for more than a decade with the German company Rosenthal.

A measure of how highly Lucienne's textiles were regarded is that one of her printed fabrics – a design showing a horse's head, inspired by a Chinese sculpture in the V&A – was acquired by the museum's Circulation Department in 1939. This pattern was one of several prompted by Lucienne's regular study sessions in the museum, including a screen-printed fabric called Peacocks.[12] Other patterns had a more overtly contemporary edge and contained imagery that would recur in her work in years to come, such as stylized leaves. One of the most striking patterns, called Signs of the Zodiac, featured astrological symbols printed in alternating squares in a grid.

Left
RCA diploma show, 1940
Lucienne hand block-printed and screen-printed the fabrics shown here in her diploma show, which included Peacocks (far left) and a pattern with horses' heads (second from left). Robin designed the layout of the stand and also the chair, which is upholstered with Lucienne's Bushmen fabric.

Below left
Lucienne Day, c.1941
This portrait was taken shortly before the couple's marriage in 1942.

Below right
Horse's head fabric, 1940
This screen-printed linen, inspired by a Chinese sculpture in the Victoria and Albert Museum, was bought by the V&A's Circulation Department in 1940. It can also be seen (second from left) in the photograph of Lucienne's diploma show (left).

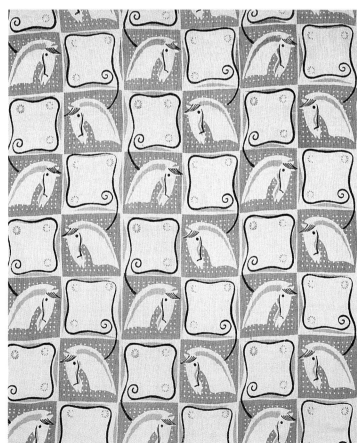

In 1950 Lucienne was invited by the BBC to present two radio programmes about pattern design as part of a series of school broadcasts for young children called *Looking at Things*. In a programme called "All over patterns", broadcast on 20 October 1950, she explained: "The easiest way [to make a pattern] is to draw a row of motifs side by side, and one below the other. This is called a 'square arrangement'. The motifs can all face the same way, or one row can look to the left and the next to the right, all down the page. Another way is to draw the motifs first looking one way and then the other, all along the line. This sort of pattern is called a 'turn over'. Another way of making a repeat pattern is called the 'brick' arrangement, because it looks like a brick wall. A third arrangement is the 'half-drop', where the motifs are drawn in columns, and each column is 'dropped' so that the top of each motif is level with the middle of the motif in the column before. This arrangement is like a 'brick' plan turned on its side. This is a very good arrangement for all kinds of patterns and many of the most successful designs are based on it."

In her student designs a decade earlier, Lucienne was just starting to find her feet as a textile designer. The fabrics in her diploma exhibition show her exploring varied sources of imagery, traditional and modern; experimenting with colourways and the impact of light on dark and dark on light; testing out her ability to work on different scales; and getting a feel for the repertoire of pattern repeats. The war meant that she had plenty of time to hone her skills as a designer before establishing herself in private practice in 1946. Frustrating though this must have seemed at the time, ultimately it may have been beneficial. When she finally came to design for production, she was much more accomplished than she might otherwise have been.

Although Lucienne was offered a Continuation Scholarship at the RCA on the basis of her diploma show, the war made it impossible for her to take this up. Instead, she was called up for national service and spent the next eighteen months working as a telephonist in the Auxiliary Fire Service at Croydon; poor working conditions made her so ill that she was eventually invalided out. Since her mother's death in 1936, she had been keeping house for her father in Croydon, and she felt unable to combine these domestic duties with further study. Instead, she took a teaching job at Beckenham School of Art, alongside Robin, an activity she combined with fire warden duties during the Blitz.

One of the courses she devised at Beckenham was on the subject of colour theory, an area of design that greatly interested her. This involved teaching students about the spectrum and the relationships between different colours, and included exercises in applying colours to isometric drawings of rooms. In the days before standardized colours, the ability to mix paints to exactly the right colour was essential for a textile designer. Lucienne's thorough mastery of this skill later stood her in good stead as a pattern designer and as a colour consultant, and accounts for her confidence and accomplishment in this field of interior design.

Robin and Lucienne Day: Markham Square

After their marriage in 1942, the Days set up home in a one-bedroom maisonette at 33 Markham Square in the Chelsea district of London. As Robin's asthma had ruled him out for active service, they both continued teaching throughout the war, although they viewed this as a temporary stopgap until circumstances permitted them to embark on their chosen careers. Their apartment was fairly spartan, partly by circumstance, partly by design. Lucienne's textiles were used as curtains and cushion covers, but initially their only furniture consisted of three Alvar Aalto bentwood stools, a wedding gift from a friend. Because furniture was in such short supply during the war, Robin made what they needed using whatever materials he could lay his hands on. A dining table was created from an old door covered with black linoleum, its legs made from iron gas pipes sheathed in copper tubes. The dining chairs were primitive precursors of his later Hillestak chairs, their seat backs created from plywood bent by hand using steam from a kettle. The most ambitious pieces were the two easy chairs: one with flat wooden armrests, the seat padded and upholstered in Lucienne's Signs of the Zodiac fabric; the other with a curved wooden frame strung with woven canvas webbing, inspired by the Swedish designer Bruno Matthsson.[13]

Some of the features in the apartment were later described by Robin in the form of decorating tips in an article for *Vogue*.[14] Suggestions included altering the scale of a room by painting a high ceiling in a dark colour, and painting the walls in pale blue or grey to make them recede. "Robin practises what he preaches," observed a visiting journalist a few years later; "the effect of dramatizing a portion of a room by changing the colour or material of the walls."[15] If coloured paint was in short supply, Robin suggested adding poster paint to white distemper to create interesting new shades. "Lack of sun can be compensated for by the glow of yellow and clear strong colours," he advised, and a warm inviting terracotta was recommended for the wall behind a sofabed to increase the feeling of refuge. "Colours and fabric must depend on the situation," he explained. "I like strong colours in small quantities among neutral ones such as greys and whites."[16]

The make-do-and-mend ethos of the period was apparent in many of Robin's recommendations, such as the idea of using coloured felt instead of carpet, and covering an ugly fireplace with a screen of wooden laths. Most of his suggestions were based on his experiments at Markham Square, including his proposal for a low glass-topped cabinet positioned at right angles to the wall. For clothes storage he suggested creating "a low horizontal and contemporary line" by cutting down large chests of drawers, and as a final touch, perhaps at Lucienne's instigation, he urged the introduction of houseplants to add "variety and life" to the room.

The experience of wartime austerity had a lasting effect on Robin's psyche, and when he was finally given the opportunity to design furniture for production, economic considerations were always at the forefront of his mind. Even during the affluent 1960s, when standards of living were so much higher, he never became self-indulgent, and refused to allow himself to be distracted by the superficialities of mere style. Significantly, when after ten years the Days moved into a larger house in Cheyne Walk, their approach to interior decoration and furnishing was similarly disciplined and restrained.

Left and below
Markham Square flat, c.1942
After their marriage in 1942, the Days set up home in Chelsea. Because of wartime shortages, Robin made most of their furniture, including the bookcase, armchair and coffee table (left), and the dining table and chairs (below). The bookcase uses broomsticks, scrap timber and glass. The dining chairs, with their bent plywood seat backs, are precursors of his later Hillestak chairs (see page 33). The armchair is upholstered with Lucienne's Signs of the Zodiac fabric. On the floor next to the lamp is a rug designed by Robin for his diploma show in 1937. The standard lamp itself is made with a bamboo pole and a silk shade.

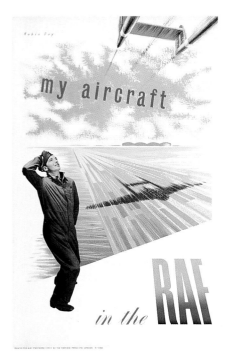

my aircraft

in the **RAF**

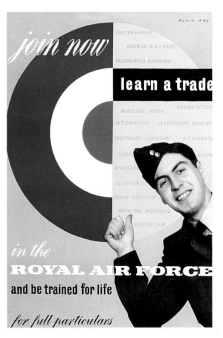

join now

learn a trade

PHOTOGRAPHER
GUNNER (R.A.F.REGT.)
TELEPRINTER OPERATOR
WIRELESS FITTER RADAR FITTER
W.T.OPERATOR INSTRUMENT REPAIRER
EQUIPMENT ASSISTANT R.T.OPERATOR
COOK CLERK
ARMOURER
TELEPHONIST
RADAR OPERATOR
WIRELESS MECHANIC
ELECTRICIAN

in the
ROYAL AIR FORCE
and be trained for life

for full particulars

they rely on me

in the **RAF**

JOIN THE **WOMEN'S ROYAL AIR FORCE**

and give your ambition wings

APPLY TO **VICTORY HOUSE, KINGSWAY, LONDON**
OR TO YOUR NEAREST RECRUITING OFFICE

do a grand job
in your spare time

JOIN THE RAF AUXILIARIES OR VOLUNTEER RESERVE

on the ground or in the air

LOOK TO THE FUTURE

in the **RAF**

overseas

in the **RAF**

CHAPTER TWO

1946-50

THE FORTIES: FLEDGLING DESIGNERS

Robin Day: Exhibition Design and Posters

Shortly after the war, Robin took up the post of assistant teacher of interior design in the School of Architecture at the Regent Street Polytechnic (now the University of Westminster). Although he carried on teaching at Beckenham for several years as well, this new appointment was much more satisfying because it gave him the opportunity to teach three-dimensional design and furniture design, the two areas in which he was most interested. Another advantage was that it brought him into contact with architects, notably Peter Moro, a fellow lecturer in the School of Architecture until 1947. Half-Slovenian, half-Austrian, Moro had arrived in Britain in 1936 after studying in Germany and Switzerland, and initially worked with Berthold Lubetkin. In 1947 he joined Leslie Martin in the Architects Department at London County Council (LCC), where he was given the task of designing the interiors of the Royal Festival Hall, and he set up in private practice in 1952. Day and Moro got on extremely well, and there was a close affinity between them. They subsequently worked together on a number of projects, and Moro was the only designer with whom Robin was ever in partnership.

When they first met, Moro was working with the Design Research Unit (DRU), and had recently designed an exhibition about post-war reconstruction for the Central Office of Information (COI). The years between 1945 and 1951 were a great era for government-funded public information exhibitions, organized by the COI on behalf of other ministries. Knowing Robin's interest in typography, Moro invited him to collaborate on subsequent COI exhibitions. Thus their partnership came about, with Moro planning the basic exhibition layout, while Robin designed the graphics and the detailed display. Their first exhibition, *Jet*, was staged on the forecourt of Charing Cross Underground station from 16 December 1946 until 3 January 1947. Organized on behalf of the Ministry of Supply, the exhibition was about gas turbine engines and the impact of their recent discovery on the aeronautical industry. The aim was to bring this technical subject alive to the general public, and one of the ways in which this was achieved was by evoking the aerodynamic qualities of jet propulsion within the display. At the entrance, visitors were confronted with a revolving impellor (the heart of a gas turbine), framed dramatically within a streamlined cross-section of a jet engine, with sweeping arrows indicating airflow. Within the main display, a series of jet airplane models suspended from the ceiling indicated the direction of visitor circulation, while photographs of actual planes in flight formed a dynamic high-level frieze. The evocative whine of jet engines was relayed at intervals, and diagrams were used extensively, with bubbles of text elucidating key facts. Graphics were mounted on

fin-shaped panels, suggesting aerofoils, and the lettering used for the exhibition title was louvred to evoke speed.

Robin also designed the poster for this exhibition, which showed four stylized jets darting across the sky, with the title in flowing script as if drawn by trails of smoke from their engines. Although he had never formally trained as a graphic designer, Robin had always displayed a natural gift for drawing, and over the years he taught himself the necessary typographic skills to design both posters and exhibition graphics.[1] His flair for creating powerful visual images that conveyed a message simply and directly was immediately recognized by the COI, leading to a commission to design seven recruitment posters for the Royal Air Force, which were displayed on thousands of hoardings around the country between 1948 and 1950. The seriousness with which Robin approached this high-profile commission is indicated by an article in *The Royal Air Force Review* in April 1949, which explained: "To get the atmosphere of the Air Force and understand the function of airmen in the pattern of the Service, he spent much time visiting airfields and flying. For his poster of an airman giving R/T instructions from the Control Tower to an aircraft landing at night, he spent many hours night-flying in an Anson, eventually landing with one engine feathered." Photomontage was adopted to inject a note of plausibility and sincerity into the design, and a distinctive feature was the use of images of servicemen and -women looking purposefully into the sky. Simple typographic messages and bold primary colour highlights also contributed to the strong visual impact of these posters. "They could not be too abstract," the designer recalled. "They had to be more literal than the *Jet* poster. The strong painted forms, combined with the photographs, were intended to give them an immediate effect."[2]

Although Robin was not actively seeking to specialize in graphic design, he received several commissions during the late 1940s and early 1950s for posters, magazine covers and book jackets. These included the dust-jacket for a book called *Ardil – The Protein Fibre* produced by Imperial Chemical Industries Ltd (ICI), and the cover of a magazine called *Furnishings from Britain*, in which Robin and Lucienne's work was regularly featured.[3] He also designed a poster for an exhibition called *Building Science*, held at Caxton Hall, Westminster, in January 1947, organized jointly by the Incorporated Association of Architects and Surveyors and the Department of Scientific and Industrial Research. Although Robin was not involved in the exhibition itself, the commission came about once again through his association with Peter Moro. The poster depicted images of modern houses, apartments and a school, suspended in glass capsules against a graph.[4]

Following the success of *Jet*, Day and Moro were invited to design another exhibition for the Ministry of Supply a few months

Right and below
Jet exhibition, 1946
This exhibition about jet propulsion was the first in a series co-designed by Robin Day and Peter Moro for the Central Office of Information. Note the aerodynamic features of the title board and display panels (right), and the assured use of photomontage in the graphics (below).

Opposite
Poster for *Jet* exhibition, 1946
This was the first poster that Robin designed. It led to the commission from the RAF for a series of recruitment posters (see page 16).

later called *British Scientific Instruments – Precisely Yours*. Like its predecessor, it was held at Charing Cross Underground station, and once again Robin designed the accompanying poster, which consisted of an image of a radar and drawings of dials, charts and gauges, framed in elliptical and free-form borders. The purpose of the exhibition was to demonstrate the importance of precision instruments in the making and testing of everyday goods, and the display consisted of a central turntable supporting a female mannequin holding a bicycle, surrounded by an undulating screen into which seventeen recessed display cases were set. Each case contained a different type of tool or instrument, from spirit-levels and calipers to complex pieces of tool-making equipment, viewed through irregular organic windows. Both the exhibition and the poster had a quasi-surreal flavour reminiscent of some of the displays in the *Britain Can Make It* exhibition of 1946, where fluid amoeboid shapes had been a leitmotif.[5]

Another commission from the COI was an exhibition stand for the General Post Office (GPO) at Radiolympia in 1947. This was another public information exhibition, its aim being to explain the range of activities in which the GPO was engaged, such as radio and telephone transmission, and to attract high-calibre recruits to the profession. As in his RAF posters, Robin made strategic use of photomontage to highlight the importance of workers within the industry. The display also featured technical gadgets, such as valves, bottom-lit like works of art, and dramatic photo-enlargements, such as views of radio masts taken from unusual angles so they looked like sculptures.

In 1947 Day and Moro designed an exhibition about atomic energy for the Atomic Scientists' Association. Installed in two railway coaches which toured the country during late 1947 and early 1948, the exhibition explained the theory and practical applications of nuclear power. "The first and largest section, which deals with the theory of nuclear energy, contains a number of 'live' experiments and working models," explained the *Architects Journal* on 13 November 1947. "The second section deals with the atomic bomb and is illuminated through a number of photographic transparencies showing explosions and casualties. Ceilings and walls here are black. In contrast, the last portion deals with the brighter side, and enumerates the benefits mankind can derive from atomic energy. Much light and warm colours are used to create an appropriate atmosphere. The exhibition ends with a 'ghost change' showing the choice between construction and destruction." Robin interpreted the material in an imaginative but accessible way through a combination of three-dimensional models, diagrams and photomontage. Arresting images included a human hand contrasted with the hand of a skeleton, and Benvenuto Cellini's *Perseus* holding up the head of Medusa.

Two other smaller COI projects from the early post-war period were a display on fuel-saving for the Ministry of Fuel and Power at the Women's Fair at Dorland Hall, and an exhibition called *The Miner Comes to Town*, co-organized by the Ministry and the National Coal Board in 1947, where Day and Moro designed a section about the byproducts of coal. Both displays were strongly diagrammatic and made use of stretched cord, a device influenced by the sculptures of Naum Gabo, which became something of a leitmotif of Robin's early post-war

Right
Precisely Yours exhibition,
1947
Co-designed by Robin Day
and Peter Moro, this exhibition
about scientific instruments
was displayed in the forecourt
of Charing Cross Underground
station in London.

Below
Atomic Energy exhibition, 1948
Robin was responsible for most
of the graphics in this exhibition,
co-designed with Peter Moro. It
was installed in a train that toured
Britain during 1948 and 1949.

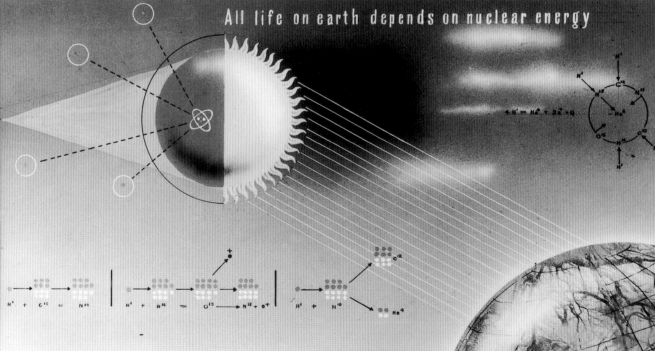

exhibition design.[6] He and Lucienne had visited the sculptor while on holiday in St Ives, and Gabo's work clearly had an impact on them both. Robin would later exploit stringing effects as a device for lowering the ceiling in the dining room at Cheyne Walk, but Gabo's influence was most apparent in a sculptural feature created for the Rayon Design Centre in January 1949. Made from perspex sheet, aluminium rod, spools and stretched rayon thread, this braced demountable structure provided the ideal vehicle for Robin's youthful exuberance and technical prowess.[7]

As Peter Moro became increasingly preoccupied with his work for the LCC, and as Robin established a growing reputation as an exhibition designer, he began to take on commissions independently. For example, in 1949 he designed part of a COI exhibition at Charing Cross called *British Transport*, celebrating the first year of the British Transport Commission. His section of the display, called "Working together for the first time", featured five small models of vehicles in circular display cases, supported on a tubular steel frame. Each mode of transport was represented by a symbol, demonstrating his ability to encapsulate the essence of an idea in a simple visual motif.[8]

Robin's most significant commercial client in the field of exhibitions was ICI, at that date one of the largest and most powerful companies in Britain. He designed innumerable exhibition stands for ICI between 1946 and 1962, some promoting the work of the group as a whole, but most focusing on the work of individual divisions, including General Chemicals, Paints, Metals, Plastics, Leathercloth, and Plant Protection. His first ICI commission was a display at the *Whither Chemistry Exhibition*, designed as early as 1946.[9] This was followed by part of a virtuoso stand for ICI at the British Industries Fair in 1947, co-designed with the architect Basil Spence, which highlighted the company's role as a scientific pioneer. In the centre was a tentlike structure created from tension wires housing a model of a factory, while around the perimeter was a translucent frieze decorated with molecular structures. The centrepiece of Robin's contribution to the display consisted of a large wire and perspex globe pinpointing ICI's activities around the world.

The annual British Industries Fairs (BIF) were one of the main venues for Robin's ICI stands over the years. Others relating to the construction industry were designed for the National Building Exhibition, while those about agriculture, or Plant Protection as it was euphemistically called by ICI, were mounted at the Royal Show. The first Royal Show pavilion, constructed using the demountable Punt system developed by Ove Arup, was created in 1952. Each year for the next decade the pavilion was re-erected, and Robin supplied perspective drawings indicating new colour schemes and modifications to the decoration of the central tower.

The stands for ICI's other divisions were geared towards a specialist audience, and the exhibits were usually of a highly technical nature. Their purpose was to alert manufacturers to the application of new products by mounting eye-catching displays of raw materials or semi-finished goods. Thus in a display for ICI Metals at the British Industries Fair in 1953, one section, focusing on wrought titanium, illustrated samples of the material in bar, sheet, tube, wire, cast and forged form. Clarity and directness

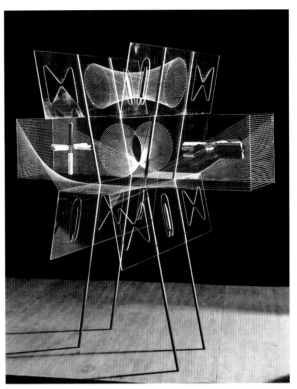

Left
Sculpture for Rayon Design Centre, 1949
Made from aluminium rod, perspex sheet and rayon thread, this demountable sculpture was commissioned by the British Rayon Federation for their new London showroom.

Below
Exhibition stand for ICI Metals, British Industries Fair, 1953
ICI was an important early commercial client, and Robin regularly designed exhibition stands for different divisions of the company between c.1946 and 1962.

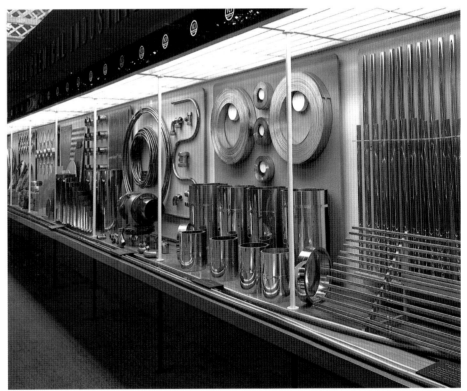

were the aim of these displays, the designer's role being to communicate a complex technical message as succinctly as possible. Working within these constraints, Robin still managed to create some extremely striking displays, sometimes through the arrangement and massing of materials, such as metal pipes or tubes, at other times through special display features, such as title panels incorporating the materials themselves.

Although Robin created many impressive stands for ICI Metals, it was the Plastics division whose work provided him with the opportunity to create the most imaginative displays. Plastics were one of the most exciting areas of new technology during the early post-war period, and all sorts of new materials, including perspex, nylon and polyethylene, were being introduced that were affecting everyday life. Polyethylene, marketed under the name Alkathene, was used for domestic items such as buckets, washing-up bowls and babies' baths, and a display of these products formed the centrepiece of one of Robin's stands. By the 1950s ICI Plastics had spawned another branch called ICI Leathercloth, which produced two different types of plasticized fabric, Rexine for wall decoration and Vynide for upholstery; displays of these were featured in a stand designed by Robin at the National Building Exhibition in 1951.

Robin's exhibition stands for ICI were in a different league from those of other manufacturers, and must have glowed like beacons within these trade fairs. However technical or mundane the subject, his displays were characterized by minute attention to detail. Each photograph was thoughtfully selected, each object strategically positioned, each display case meticulously designed and carefully lit. In 1952 Milner Gray wrote: "It is in the field of exhibition design that perhaps the widest variety of design skills are brought together into one complete and inseparable whole; and it is as an exhibition designer that Robin Day first made his mark. Planning, structural design, lighting, two-dimensional display and typography, generally the work severally of experts working as a team, are handled personally by Day in his exhibition work, resulting in a particularly well coordinated and personal effect." [10]

Apart from ICI, the other firm that benefited most regularly from Robin's talents as an exhibition designer was the radio manufacturer Ekco. Well known as makers of Bakelite radios during the 1930s, including some stylish circular sets designed by Wells Coates, Ekco expanded into a wider spectrum of plastics manufacture after the war. Robin created a series of stands for the company for various radio shows and plastics exhibitions, starting with a display at Radiolympia in 1949 and continuing until the Interplas exhibition at Olympia in 1961.[11] Like his later pavilions for ICI at the Royal Show, Robin's Ekco stands had a sleek rectilinearity, and were constructed using a prefabricated modular system of fine tubular steel posts. Distinguished from the more superficial, jazzy displays of Ekco's competitors, Robin's stands had a controlled architectural quality that reflected the company's growing commitment to modern design. A recurrent feature was the use of the company's name in giant letters, slanting inward, above the stand. To project the impression of continuity, Ekco's displays followed a similar formula from year to year and were designed as variations on a theme. Within this framework, nonetheless, there was scope for variety. For the

National Radio Show at Earls Court in 1952, co-designed with his assistant Sylvia Reid, radios and televisions were displayed in a series of room settings furnished by Heal's,[12] and on other occasions Robin incorporated his own furniture on Ekco's stands.

Robin Day: Low-Cost Furniture Competition, 1948

By 1948 Robin was well established as an exhibition designer, and apart from his teaching, this area of activity occupied virtually all his time. As the scale of his output demonstrates, he worked phenomenally hard during the late 1940s and was immensely productive. Like many whose careers had been put on hold during the war, the relief of finally being able to practise as a designer gave him limitless energy and enthusiasm. However, although he demonstrated a natural talent for exhibition design, in the longer term his ambition was still to design furniture. Consequently, when Clive Latimer, his colleague at Beckenham School of Art, drew his attention to the International Competition for Low-Cost Furniture Design that was being organized by the Museum of Modern Art (MOMA) in New York, he leapt at the chance to enter. In 1946 Latimer had designed some experimental furniture for the *Britain Can Make It* exhibition, fabricated from aluminium sheet laminated with wooden veneers. He was equally keen to participate in the competition, and so the two men decided to collaborate.

The Low-Cost Furniture Competition was a follow-up to an earlier competition for Organic Design held by the museum in 1940, which had been won by Charles Eames and Eero Saarinen with a design for a moulded plywood shell chair. In the interim, the war, and the period of enforced economy and austerity that followed, had shifted design priorities from style to affordability. "Low-cost housing and home furnishings are among the most important factors in the national economy and the general welfare of the peoples of all countries," explained the museum's director, René d'Harnoncourt, when announcing the competition in 1947. "To serve the needs of the vast majority of people we must have furniture that is adaptable to small apartments and houses, furniture that is well designed yet moderate in price, that is comfortable but not bulky, and that can be easily moved, stored and cared for; in other words, mass-produced furniture that is planned and executed to fit the needs of modern living, production and merchandising."

The MOMA competition was tailor-made for Robin, and the announcement reads like a direct personal challenge. To date his only opportunity to design furniture had been the showpieces for his RCA diploma and the items he had constructed for the apartment at Markham Square. Shortly after the war, when the government was encouraging furniture manufacturers to make use of surplus aluminium, Robin had designed a demountable aluminium-framed side chair, but attempts to put this into production proved abortive.[13] Government-imposed Utility restrictions, combined with shortages of materials and skilled labour, meant that the British furniture industry was still struggling to get back on its feet after the war. In spite of the pressing need for good-quality, affordable, mass-produced modern furniture, therefore, opportunities to design for production were still limited.

The competition was divided into two categories, seating and storage, and the brief for the latter indicated that designs should be for multi-purpose domestic storage units. Competitors

*Opposite top*
***British Transport* exhibition, 1949**
Robin was responsible for one section of this exhibition, the rest of which was created by the Design Research Unit. Note the austere rectilinearity of the structure.

Opposite bottom and left
Sketches of exhibition stands for ICI, 1950s
In his crisply rectilinear exhibition stands for ICI, Robin strove to achieve a clean-lined architectural style. He always submitted perspective drawings to show his clients the finished look of the eventual stand.

Above
Exhibition stand for Ekco, Radiolympia, c.1950–51
Along with ICI, the radio, television and plastics manufacturer Ekco regularly commissioned Robin to design exhibition stands for trade fairs between 1949 and 1961.

were required to submit scale drawings in plan and section, and to prepare perspective or isometric drawings giving an accurate impression of the finished piece. The deadline was 31 October 1948, and in addition to d'Harnoncourt, the judges included the British furniture pioneer Gordon Russell and the architect Ludwig Mies van der Rohe. The response to the competition was overwhelming, with around 750 entrants from thirty-two different countries submitting almost 3000 designs. Well-known designers who entered the competition but who did not win prizes included Marco Zanuso, Franco Albini and Luigi Columbini from Italy; Ilmari Tapiovaara from Finland; and Jørn Utzon and Hans Wegner from Denmark. The seating category was won jointly by Don R. Knorr, a graduate from the Cranbrook Academy, and a German designer named Georg Leowald, with the second prize being shared between Charles Eames and a Chicago designer, Davis J. Pratt. In the storage section, although Ernest Race received an honourable mention, only one prize was actually awarded, and the winners, much to their amazement and jubilation, were Robin Day and Clive Latimer.

Their prize-winning entry was for a range of plywood storage units suspended on tubular aluminium frames. Supported from the side rather than below, the cabinets were designed so that they could be either set back-to-back or mounted against a wall. Tapering inward at the top, the units had solid timber ends. Their key design feature, however, was the rounded body of the carcass, made from a single sheet of plywood moulded into a tube, fabricated using the Spears lamina process developed by James Henderson for the Scottish manufacturer Matthew Spears. This technique, adopted at Latimer's suggestion, gave the highest strength-to-weight ratio of any carcass construction hitherto developed, and provided the ideal solution to the problem of low-cost fabrication. Once a former had been made, it took only three minutes for the plywood to be bent into shape, and the process was highly economical in many other respects, resulting in a 50 per cent saving in the amount of timber and a reduction in the number of joints from twenty to two.

Apart from the Spears lamina construction process, what distinguished the design was the modest scale of the system and the flexible way in which different-sized units and shelving could be combined. Two types of doors were offered: a drop-flap, which could be used as a desk; and a sliding version, made of veneered plywood or glass, which ran in an extruded aluminium groove. Latimer was particularly good at analysing function, and much careful thought went into the system's planning. This was evident in the diagrams Robin created for the presentation panels, one set illustrating the way the units could accommodate objects of different sizes at different levels, others demonstrating how the profile of the units gave maximum visibility and ease of access. Both men were meticulous in their approach to design, and Latimer was an excellent technical draftsman. Every detail was carefully worked out from a practical point of view, right through from the recessed handles to the neat interior shelves and trays.

The $5000 prize money for the competition was extremely generous, and even after it had been split two ways, it still gave Day and Latimer around £1250 each. In January 1949 they travelled to New York to receive their award, presented by Nelson Rockefeller at a special ceremony at the Waldorf Astoria Hotel.[14] The exhibition of winning designs did not take place until more than a year later, as a secondary aim of the competition was for the museum to arrange for the designs to be mass-produced. At this stage, however, the project started to falter, as it soon became apparent that the Spears lamina process could not be replicated in the US, and it would be uneconomical for the units to be fabricated in Scotland and shipped over. As a compromise, Day and Latimer agreed to redesign the cabinets so that they could be constructed using more conventional methods. Unfortunately the manufacturer, Johnson-Carper Furniture of Roanoke, Virginia, subsequently engaged an American consulting designer, Edmond J. Spence, who introduced further modifications, ostensibly to bring the furniture into line with American market requirements. Key changes included altering the sizes of the cabinets so that they were no longer standardized, and replacing the side-mounted frames with conventional legs. As a result of these alterations, the original design concept was completely lost, and the designers lamented: "The design thus changed from a flexible system, which by the choice of heights, opening components, and interior arrangement would cover all normal cabinet requirements, to a series of chests of drawers." [15] In the exhibition of Prize Designs for Modern Furniture held at MOMA in 1950, the bastardized versions were displayed in place of the originals, even though, by this date, Heal's in London had produced a set of prototypes, fabricated using the Spears lamina process, exactly as originally envisaged. Made from birch-veneered plywood shells with mahogany ends, they were displayed in an exhibition at Heal's in May 1950, held to coincide with the New York show.[16]

In spite of this disappointment, both designers benefited enormously from the award, which gave a tremendous boost to their careers. For Robin it brought high-profile recognition, and helped to pave the way for important commissions such as the Home Entertainment section of the Homes and Gardens Pavilion at the Festival of Britain. More importantly, it was the catalyst for his relationship with Hille, the manufacturer with which he would enjoy such a productive relationship for the next three decades.

Lucienne Day: Dress Fabric Designs

Lucienne's career, like Robin's, had to be put on hold during the war. Subsequently, although government restrictions were relaxed in the field of dress fabrics, they remained in place for furnishing textiles until as late as 1951. Although her long-term aim remained to design textiles for interiors, in the meantime she adapted her work to suit the fashion industry. Frustrating though this situation was, there was a positive side. Furnishing fabrics tended to be rather conservative at this date and, for a forward-looking designer like Lucienne, dress fabrics gave greater scope for artistic experimentation during the early post-war period.

The downside of working with the "rag trade" was that it was much more cut-throat than the more gentlemanly world of furnishing fabrics, and dealing with the notoriously fickle men who ran this sector of the industry required all Lucienne's stamina and fortitude. As most firms bought their designs from commercial studios abroad, they tended to treat British designers

Low-cost storage units, 1948
Two variants of the storage units co-designed by Robin Day and Clive Latimer that won first prize in the storage section of the Museum of Modern Art's International Low-Cost Furniture Competition. The photographs show the prototypes fabricated by Heal's in 1950, and illustrate the diverse applications of the system.

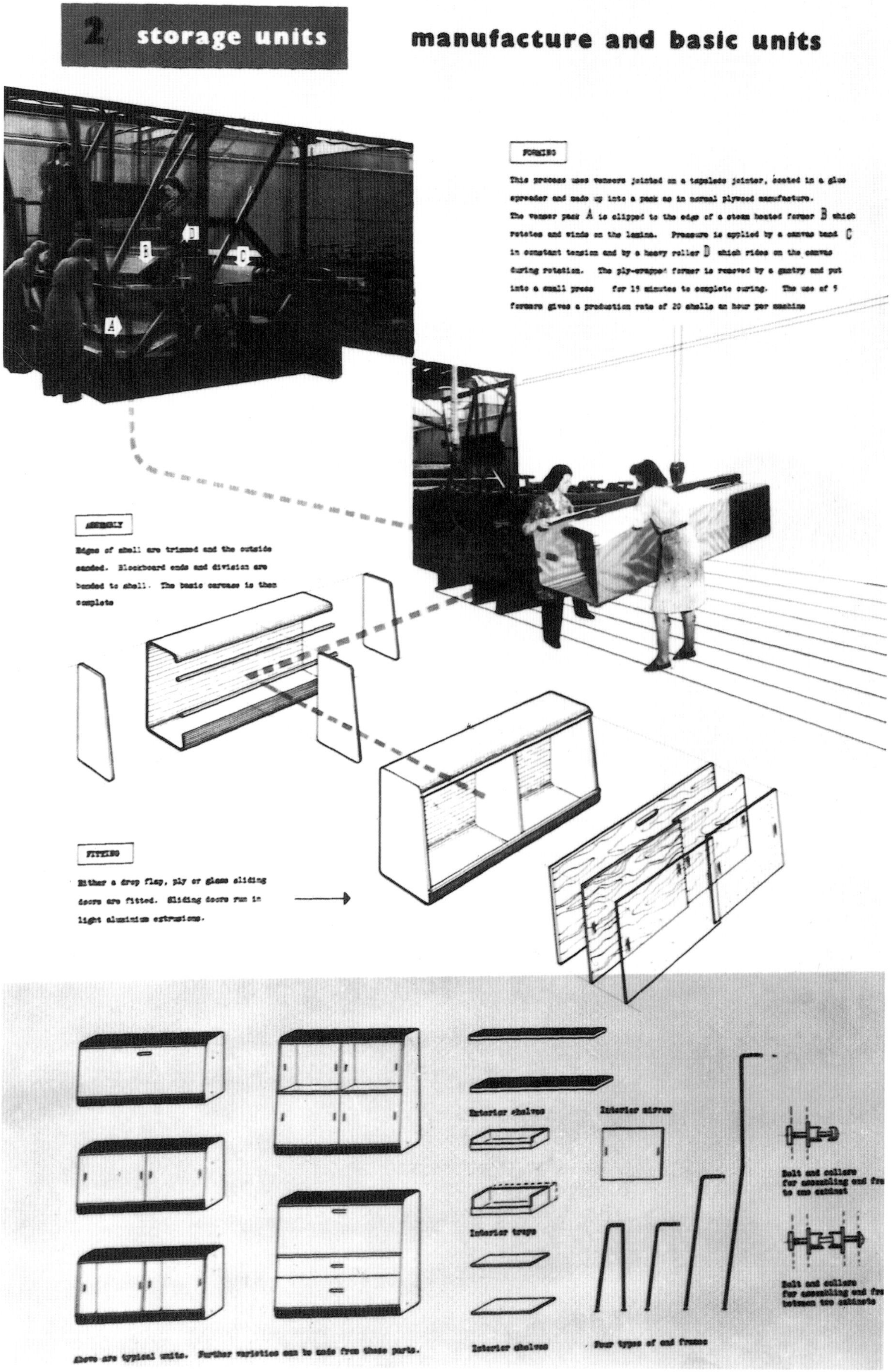

2 storage units

manufacture and basic units

FORMING

This process uses veneers jointed on a tapeless jointer, coated in a glue spreader and made up into a pack as in normal plywood manufacture. The veneer pack A is clipped to the edge of a steam heated former B which rotates and winds on the lamina. Pressure is applied by a canvas band C in constant tension and by a heavy roller D which rides on the canvas during rotation. The ply-wrapped former is removed by a gantry and put into a small press for 15 minutes to complete curing. The use of 5 formers gives a production rate of 20 shells an hour per machine

ASSEMBLY

Edges of shell are trimmed and the outside sanded. Blockboard ends and division are bonded to shell. The basic carcase is then complete

FITTING

Either a drop flap, ply or glass sliding doors are fitted. Sliding doors run in light aluminium extrusions.

Interior shelves   Interior mirror

Interior trays

Bolt and collars for assembling end frame to one cabinet

Bolt and collars for assembling end frame between two cabinets

Interior shelves   Four types of end frames

Above are typical units. Further varieties can be made from these parts.

storage units   theory and perspectives

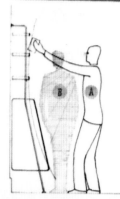

Profile is designed to give maximum visibility and ease of access (A); minimum clearance when passing units (B); storage of smaller articles at top and taller and deeper ones at bottom (C); and storage of books mainly at eye level.

Heights of units and shelves are based on: a unit 20" high for use whilst standing, including a drop-flap at 29½" (D,H and I); a unit 20" high for use from an easy chair with a top at 30", convenient when sitting and standing (F,G and K); where horizontal solutions are not practicable a more vertical solution is provided by a double height unit 36" high (J).

Length of unit of 42" is determined by room size, flexibility and cost. A length of unit is needed which is adequate for a single purpose, e.g., china storage, wine cupboard, bureau or dressing table, but not too large in combination with one or two more units. The most likely combination is a pair of single height units for the living room or a pair of double height units for the bedroom (H). This measurement of 7' seems reasonable and many rooms would permit the use of three units 10' 6" long on at least one wall (I). Previous schemes using smaller units were flexible but costly for storage provided.

Depth has been kept to a minimum of 11½" at top and either 14" for a single or 16½" for a double unit at bottom. This economises space and makes for ease of access. Internal height accommodates highest articles, e.g., bottles, leaving space above.

The design provides storage space between 10" and 60" and horizontally at intervals of 42". There are three types of

door and two depths of shelf. Internally two heights of tray and a shelf provide numerous combinations. Bookshelves are adjustable by 2¾" intervals on vertical section of frames and by 5½" on sloping section (where larger shelves are used).

The frames provide support for cabinets at two levels, and for bookshelves at all levels. The normal frame leans against the wall which makes an economy of material and provides better lateral stability than a free-standing frame (adjuster at each end of frame are rubber-faced and grip wall and floor). A further economy is the use of one frame between two units. This reduces the number of legs to a minimum and facilitates cleaning. A free-standing frame meets the requirement of units used at right angles to the wall saving the room (L,M). Back-to-back units can be used in the same way (M).

The plywood tube structure used has the highest strength-to-weight ratio of any carcass construction hitherto used. It uses 50 per cent of the timber content usual in low-cost practice. Normally there are numerous joints where strain leads to failure. The structure used has virtually two joints, one at each end. The surface area resin bonded is 50 sq. ins in each case (single height carcass). As this surface is in shear, in which it is at its most efficient, the joint is practically unbreakable. Also the light shell spans between rigid ends which take the loads. Material is distributed according to structural requirements. The designs are original but the process is already in use for low-cost furniture

Opposite and left
International Low-Cost Furniture Competition, 1948
Two of the presentation panels submitted by Robin Day and Clive Latimer as their prize-winning entry to the Museum of Modern Art competition. The panel opposite illustrates how their storage units were to be fabricated from a tube of moulded plywood using the Spears lamina process. The other panel (left) demonstrates the flexibility of the system and shows how the units were designed to be either free-standing or wall-mounted.

Right
Toro dress fabric, Stevenson & Sons, 1945
This printed rayon dress fabric was among the first of Lucienne's designs to enter commercial production. The subject was inspired by Ernest Hemingway, and the style was influenced by Picasso, who made many sketches of bullfighters.

Below
Jet dress fabric, Stevenson & Sons, c.1947
Lucienne's Jet fabric design was prompted by Robin's involvement with the *Jet* exhibition in 1946, although her design is more abstract than Robin's poster (see page 19).

Opposite top
Dress fabric, Silkella, 1948
Sold under the government-controlled Utility scheme, this design is one of Lucienne's earliest purely abstract patterns.

Opposite bottom
Artwork for dress fabric, Pasman Fabrics, c.1948
Lucienne's interest in typography is reflected in this unusual early design. The background swirls are similar to the clouds in Jet (below).

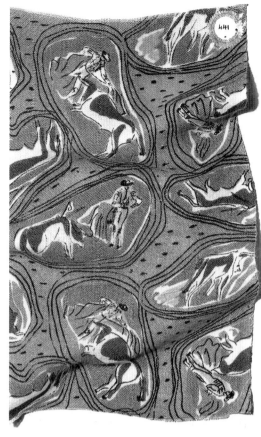

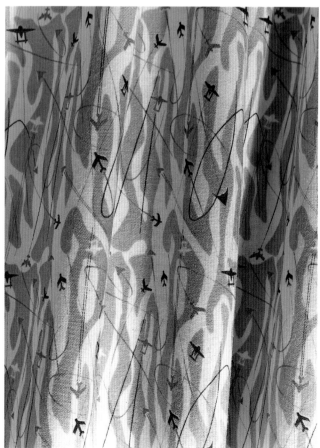

with disdain. Because Lucienne continued working under her maiden name for several years, some manufacturers only agreed to meet her because they thought she was French. Sometimes she would travel to Manchester to present her portfolio to a client, only to discover that the person with whom she had made an appointment had gone out without bothering to let her know. Very few manufacturers were prepared actually to commission a design, and it was a labour-intensive and frustrating business to sell patterns speculatively, one by one. Because she did not approve of her designs being altered, rather than just submitting preliminary sketches or *croquis* as was customary, she preferred to prepare finished artwork showing detailed pattern repeats, although this made her work more expensive than that of other freelance designers. After selling a pattern, she would rarely get the opportunity to see a strike-off, so she never quite knew how her work had turned out or even whether it had entered production.

One of Lucienne's more amenable early clients was the Irish manufacturer Stevenson & Son, whose director, Mr Millington, had an eye for unusual trend-setting designs. Stevenson were best known for their linen substitute fabric, Moygashel, made from spun rayon, which, because of restrictions on the production of linen and cotton, was extremely popular after the war. Lucienne's Moygashel patterns included English Summer, a witty design inspired by the vagaries of the British weather, and Toro, a Hemingway-inspired pattern of Spanish bullfighters, both dating from July 1945. The fine linear style with which Lucienne would later become so closely associated was already taking shape at this date, although most patterns, such as Toyshop (1946) and Jet (1947), were still based on recognizable motifs. Jet planes were still an exciting novelty at the time, and Jet, produced shortly after Robin's exhibition, showed tiny planes doing aerobatics in the sky. Breaking away from patterns in which the repeat mechanism dominated the design, Lucienne's post-war work was characterized by a new informality. Her skill as a pattern designer was in evoking the spontaneity and dynamism of scribbles and doodles in what was actually a carefully controlled and tightly structured design.

Other firms for which Lucienne designed groups of dress fabrics during the early years after the war included J.H. Birtwistle (1948), Silkella (1948) and Argand (1950).[17] More often, manufacturers only purchased single designs: Pasman Fabrics produced a one-off design based on typographic motifs, and Marks & Spencer bought a pattern of stylized leaves in 1949. For the Preston-based company Horrockses, which made printed cotton dresses in attractive modern styles, Lucienne designed a pattern of birds, leaves, flower heads and ferns in outline. Already during the late 1940s, plants had begun to emerge as the dominant imagery in her work. As well as working from actual specimens, she drew on images in natural history books, including a small German pocket book called *Das Kleine Blumenbuch*. By the early 1950s her plant forms had become less literal, and instead of depicting naturalistic clusters of flowers, she was concentrating on stylized details or isolated components, as in Calyx (1951) and Fall (1952). Lucienne brought a new freshness to the theme of nature, which she constantly reinterpreted, and plants would remain a significant source of inspiration throughout her career.

Whereas most of Lucienne's clients from the early post-war period were ephemeral, her relationship with Cavendish Textiles, a subsidiary of the John Lewis Partnership, continued on and off for more than thirty years, from 1944 to 1975. Cavendish Textiles, which produced both furnishing and fashion fabrics, were converters rather than manufacturers per se. Commissioned by the company's art director Vincent Stuart, her earliest pattern was a furnishing fabric with restrained classical imagery called Greek Wave, designed in 1944. This pattern was rather conventional, as Lucienne was concerned not to alienate her new client. However, her next two patterns were more adventurous: Chiltern Meadow (1946), a furnishing fabric decorated with sprigs of wild flowers, and Bushmen (1946), a dress fabric with a pattern of hunters, drawn in a fluid, confident, modern style.

Another important early client was Alastair Morton of Edinburgh Weavers, the progressive subsidiary of the Carlisle-based Morton Sundour. As with Cavendish Textiles, Lucienne tested the waters initially with a somewhat timid design, Martlet (1945), decorated with bird motifs, which was produced as a woven furnishing fabric. Subsequently, however, when Morton commissioned two printed furnishing fabrics, Lucienne responded more confidently with Florimel and Elysian (1949), composed of naturalistic sprigs of wild flowers. Although compared with the freedom of her later work, these early quasi-botanical patterns are still rather constrained, in creative terms they are important transitional designs. Historically, too, they have an added significance in that they attracted the attention of Anthony Heal. As a result, Heal's commissioned Fluellin (1950), and this, in turn, paved the way for the ground-breaking Calyx.

As well as being an important early patron, Alastair Morton provided Lucienne with valuable guidance on professional matters such as fees. They met through the Society of Industrial Artists (SIA), the professional body responsible for promoting the interests of designers, and Morton was the chairman of the SIA's Textile Group, to which Lucienne acted as honorary secretary from 1948 to 1953. Through this group, she met other leading practitioners, such as Jacqueline Groag, Marian Mahler, Terence Conran and Tibor Reich. As secretary, she helped to organize exhibitions by group members at venues such as the Cotton Board's Colour, Design and Style Centre in Manchester, and these helped to raise the profile of freelance designers within the textile profession.

Although many of Lucienne's early post-war designs were representational, Calyx was by no means her first abstract design. Examples of earlier abstract patterns include two dress fabrics for Silkella and a furnishing fabric for Primavera, all dating from 1948. Two of the three dress fabrics she designed for Argand in 1950 were also abstract, one a direct precursor of her Heal's fabric Allegro (1952), and the other anticipatory of her Westminster wallpaper for Rasch (1958). Lucienne's distinctive handwriting as a designer was clearly taking shape in her dress fabrics during the late 1940s. Her later abstract patterns for Heal's, Edinburgh Weavers and British Celanese marked the culmination rather than the start of a new trend. Lucienne herself acknowledges that she could not have created her "flippant and free" furnishing textiles of the 1950s without having served this at times trying apprenticeship in the dress fabric trade.[18]

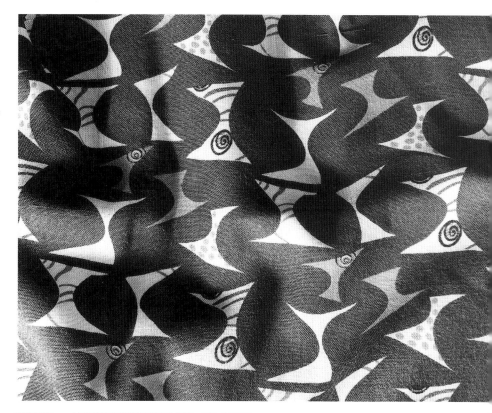

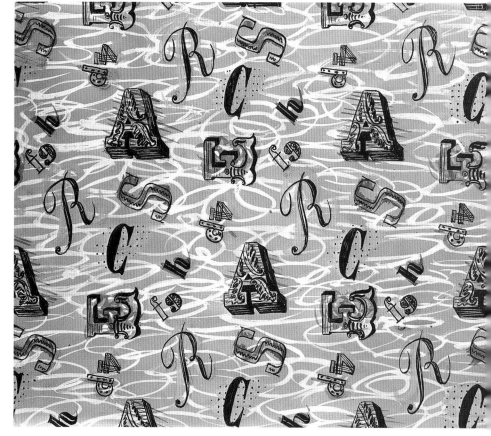

Right
Florimel furnishing fabric, Edinburgh Weavers, 1949
This stylized floral sprig design, together with another called Elysian, was the first printed furnishing fabric commissioned from Lucienne by Alastair Morton.

Far right
Artwork for dress fabric, Argand Ltd, 1950
Lucienne's earliest experiments with abstraction were through her dress fabrics. It is interesting to compare this design with a later furnishing fabric, Miscellany, 1952 (see page 81).

Below
Fluellin furnishing fabric, Heal's, 1950
The success of Florimel (right) prompted Heal's to commission their first design from Lucienne. She was specifically asked to create a pattern in a similar vein.

Furnishing fabric, Primavera, 1952
Although not produced until 1952, this screen-printed cotton was originally designed as early as 1948. There are parallels with a later pattern, Ticker Tape, 1953 (see page 86). Primavera was a small shop on Sloane Street in London devoted to modern design, owned by Henry and Pauline Rothschild.

CHAPTER THREE

1951

THE FESTIVAL OF BRITAIN

Robin Day: Hille

As well as giving a huge boost to his confidence, winning the
Museum of Modern Art's Low-Cost Furniture Competition was
crucial in announcing to the world that Robin Day, furniture
designer, had arrived. Until this point, Robin had been better
known as an exhibition designer, and although he continued to
practise in this field for another decade, the award enabled him
to refocus his energies on furniture and attracted his first serious
industrial client.

S. Hille & Co. had been founded by a Russian émigré,
Salamon Hille, in 1906. Based initially in the East End of London,
the firm made high-quality reproduction furniture in the newly
popular Queen Anne and William and Mary styles. By the 1920s
Hille employed around eighty staff, and supplied leading stores
such as Hamptons, Maples, and Waring & Gillows. In 1932
Salamon's daughter, Ray Hille, took over the running of the
company, and as well as designing historical revival furniture,
she created suites in the luxurious French-inspired Moderne
style. Having managed to keep the firm operating during the
war by undertaking repairs to bomb-damaged furniture, Ray
Hille was joined by her eldest daughter, Rosamind Julius, and
her son-in-law, Leslie Julius, in 1945. Together they set about
rebuilding the firm's depleted workforce and securing new
contracts, concentrating on the export of luxury furniture to the
United States rather than on the Utility-regulated home market.
This was a golden era for American design, and as a result of
a series of sales trips from 1946 onward, the Juliuses became
aware of the radical new trends emerging in the American
furniture industry at that time. Inspired by the work of progressive
manufacturers such as Knoll and Herman Miller, they proposed
that Hille should change direction and start producing modern
furniture. "These trips to America have shown us how necessary
change is," said Leslie Julius, "how we must keep pace and help
mould public taste." [1]

After hearing of the success of Day and Latimer in the
Low-Cost Furniture Competition, the Juliuses contacted the
designers through the agency of the Council of Industrial Design
in 1949. Following the initial meeting, Latimer was invited to
design a suite of bedroom furniture, and Robin a dining group,
both geared towards the American market, with the results to
be displayed on Hille's stand at the British Industries Fair later
that year. [2]

Robin's suite consisted of a dining table, chairs and a
sideboard. The sideboard, produced in two sizes, contained
echoes of his MOMA storage units in its tapering form and side-
mounted exterior frame, but differed in its use of wood rather
than metal for the frame. In this first design for Hille, Robin was

Opposite
Calyx, Heal's, 1951
This vibrant pattern, originally
created by Lucienne for the
Home Entertainment section
of the Homes and Gardens
Pavilion at the Festival of
Britain, revolutionized British
textile design during the 1950s.
The cupped shapes represent
flowers in abstract form.

Left
Hillestak chairs, 1950
With its beech frame and
moulded plywood seat, the
Hillestak was the first low-cost
design by Robin for Hille. The
chairs shown here have the
original U-shaped dowelled leg
joints. This feature was
modified in 1956.

anxious to make use of the cabinet-making skills of the workforce. The choice of woods such as ash, cherry and mansonia was also an attempt to achieve a degree of continuity with Hille's past. "Looking back I think now that the first things which I did for Hille were too dramatic," Robin reflected in 1964, "but at least they had some effect and some of this furniture was sold as had been hoped in America." [3] Although the British furniture trade adopted a cool or even hostile reaction to Hille's initiatives, American buyers were enthusiastic, and the company was still trying to meet its orders a year after the suite was launched in the US. "It was something of a revolution to begin the manufacture of completely contemporary furniture which owed nothing to the past," reflected Leslie Julius,[4] and although Robin's opening gambit was uncharacteristic of what he would later go on to achieve, at the time it represented a bold attempt to introduce modern furniture into an extremely conservative market.

After testing the water, the Juliuses were keen to continue the relationship with Robin, whose ability and integrity they greatly admired. With his next design, he began to pursue his private agenda to design low-cost furniture, and it was from this date onward that his true design character emerged. Having seen the potential of moulded plywood in the hands of designers such as Charles Eames and Aalto, Robin chose this material for the seat and seat back of his first low-cost stacking chair, the Hillestak (1950). Because the workers at Hille were unfamiliar with the technique of moulding plywood, Robin's input extended even to designing the jigs and formers to bend the material into shape, and this hands-on approach to design and problem-solving earned him great respect among the workforce. New techniques and materials always involve an element of risk, however. For Robin, trouble-shooting was always an essential part of the design and production process, and he was not averse to making modifications later on. In the case of the Hillestak, the original leg structure proved a weak point, and in the mid-1950s the original dowelled U-shaped joint was replaced with a spliced glued V-shaped joint.[5] As well as making the chair stronger, the revised model had the added advantage of using less timber and making the chair easier to stack.

The Hillestak chair was a great success commercially, and was widely used in schools, canteens and church halls over the next two decades, as well as being produced under licence abroad. It was followed by the Hillestak table (1950), which had the same basic leg structure as the chair, and a variant – the Hillestak desk (1950) – with a suspended drawer attachment. A little later came the Hilleon dining group (1951)[6] and the Hilleplan storage units (1952), and thus, quite soon, a pattern began to emerge of families of furniture that could be used either as stand-alone items or in coordinated groups. Robin was particularly keen to break away from the restrictive formula of the suite, an outmoded convention which he felt was unsuited to the smaller spaces in which people were obliged to live. From a commercial point of view, the key to the success of his furniture was flexibility, typified by the Hillestak chair, which served equally well as a dining chair in the home or as public seating in a hall. Robin's aim was to create practical designs in which the basic

structure, proportions and materials were so intrinsically satisfying that there was no need for superfluous ornamentation.

Ray Hille, although from an earlier generation, greatly admired Robin's talents and calmly accepted his plain designs. "He has the unusual ability to 'see' his furniture first, and then produce the drawings," she commented.[7] For his part, Robin was grateful to see his designs realized. "For a small firm like Hille, it was a major investment to put my designs in production initially, so I felt I should share the risk they were taking." [8] After his initial commission, for which he was paid a one-off fee, he chose to work purely on a royalty basis. He felt that this arrangement was fairer to both parties because if a design succeeded, they both shared the benefits, whereas if a design failed, he took responsibility as well. Although, at his instigation, Robin only ever worked as a design consultant for Hille, rather than being employed as part of the in-house team, in terms of status he was regarded as a director, and for as long as the Hille family ran the company, he was treated with the highest esteem. "A mutual agreement was entered into between Robin Day and the company," explained Leslie Julius in 1960. "No written contract passed between us and never has from that day. This relationship has tied designer and management together by bonds which go far beyond those of employer and employed, and presupposes complete trust in one another." [9] It was the integrity of this relationship between designer and client – a rare commodity in manufacturing – that accounted for the lasting success of the Day–Hille partnership.

When it came to decisions about what went into production, "the designer's word is always final," Julius noted, "but he exercises the authority with tact." [10] In Robin's account of his relationship with Hille, he confirmed: "The lines on which design development proceeded were left largely to me. I would explain my ideas to Mrs Hille and Mr Julius, and in their wisdom they not only accepted one as a specialist, but also showed tremendous interest and enthusiasm in designs which I felt must seem shockingly stark and over-simple to them." [11]

By 1954 Hille had dropped all their old-fashioned ranges and were producing only Robin's designs. Within weeks of their first meeting, he created a stylish new logo for Hille in clean-lined, attenuated, lower-case type. He believed that all visual aspects of a company should be related, and that they should express the philosophy of the firm. Consequently, for the first ten years he designed all Hille's catalogues, advertisements, exhibitions, and even their vehicle livery, without any fee. Furthermore, to ensure that his furniture was presented to good advantage in appropriate surroundings, he personally oversaw all publicity photography at his own expense. As a result of his dedication and attention to detail, within a short space of time Hille's image was revolutionized, and from 1950 onward the names Robin Day and Hille were married in the public mind.

Robin Day: Royal Festival Hall

The next group of pieces that Robin created for Hille was prompted by a major commission to design the furniture for the Royal Festival Hall. Built by London County Council (LCC) in what was described as "a frankly contemporary style",[12] the hall was

Left
Butterfly cocktail cabinet, 1951
A one-off design produced at the request of Ray Hille. The cabinet was displayed on Hille's stand at the British Industries Fair in 1951.

Centre left
US Airforce Officers' Club, Ruislip, Middlesex, 1952
Hillestak tables and chairs *in situ*, with curtains in Lucienne's Cocktail fabric for Edinburgh Weavers, 1952.

Centre right
Hillestak table and chair, 1950
The filing tray, blotter and waste-paper bin shown here formed part of a set of office accessories designed by Robin from 1957.

Bottom
Dining Group, 1949
Robin's first design for Hille, created specifically for export to the US.

significant in being the first modern public building to be erected in London after the war. Designed by a team of architects from the LCC headed by Robert Matthew and Leslie Martin, the interiors were assigned to Peter Moro, who was anxious to ensure that the furniture should be in keeping with his design. Fresh from his success in the MOMA competition, Robin was the obvious choice for the job. He, in turn, was ready for the challenge, which was "a tremendously important and exciting project", as he recalled.[13]

The hall was a large and complex building, with a central auditorium surrounded by extensive free-flowing public spaces, spread over several levels and spilling out onto terraces overlooking the Thames. Robin was asked to furnish all these areas, and his brief fell into three main categories: concert hall seating; orchestra chairs; and public seating for the restaurants, foyers and terraces.

Designing the auditorium seating required all his technical ingenuity, and was undoubtedly his greatest challenge to date. As there were so few precedents other than crude timber-framed cinema seating supported on cast-iron stanchions, he came up with a completely new concept, engineered using materials and techniques associated with the car industry. Produced by a Watford-based firm, Cox & Co., which specialized in tubular steel furniture, the chassis on which the chairs were supported was made of elliptical steel tubing, while the seat frames were fabricated from pressed steel. To deaden noise when the seat was being moved, and to improve the acoustics when it was in an upright position, the underside of the tip-up seat was padded with glass fibre concealed behind a perforated panel. Attention to detail was evident in all aspects of the design. The side panels of the leather-covered armrests were faced with figured sapele mahogany, while the seats were padded with Dunlopillo latex foam rubber, shaped to give maximum comfort and support. An inventory of the original furnishings in the Royal Festival Hall indicates that Robin also designed the seating for the boxes in the concert hall. The leather-covered chairs for the Royal Box were made by Hille; the other chairs, designed to complement the main auditorium seating, were produced by B. North & Sons of West Wycombe, and were upholstered in ribbed moquette.[14]

Robin's Royal Festival Hall orchestra, dining and lounge chairs, with their spindly steel rod legs and curvaceous moulded plywood seat backs, form a distinct family of designs. The stacking orchestra chair (later manufactured by Hille as the 661C) was the most minimal of the three, and was designed with a gap between the seat and back to accommodate the tails of the players' jackets. More generously padded than the orchestra chair, the dining chair (later produced as the 661 Small Moulded Chair) was upholstered in cream leather, whereas the orchestra chairs were covered in a new woven plastic fabric called Tygan.[15] However, the main distinguishing feature of the lounge and dining chairs was the organic form of the seat back with its integral sprouting arms. Moulded from a single sheet of plywood, the original seat backs had two-tone colouring, veneered on the inside in walnut and on the outside in lighter-coloured birch. Upholstered in lemon woven fabric with copper-plated legs, the lounge chair (later produced as the 658 Large Moulded Chair) was more generous in proportion, and marked a natural progression from the dining chair. Set at a reclining angle, its back was partially padded and its seat lower, and its wide flat armrests extended outward like wings.

The complex double curvature of these seat backs had been made possible by the development of urea formaldehyde glues during the war. These new resin-based adhesives, originally used on the Mosquito aircraft, bonded the plywood together so strongly that it was possible to mould a flat sheet in several different directions at once. By adopting modern materials such as steel, plywood and latex foam, Robin was able to pare his designs down to a minimum, so that they seemed to float off the ground. These chairs had a sprightly presence that perfectly suited the light, open character of the spaces for which they were created. Stylish but comfortable, they were equally successful individually and en masse.

Apart from a dumb waiter for the restaurant, Robin's two other main contributions to the hall were his dining tables and outdoor chairs. The tables, produced in square and circular versions, had tubular steel legs and thick plywood tops, which contrasted birch lippings with walnut veneer. The terrace chair was another robust but spidery design, its seat constructed from a ladder of narrow wooden bars, painted white, set on a curved steel plate. These items were fabricated not by Hille but by a West Bromwich firm called Kingfisher Ltd, which also made the original orchestra chairs. Although it had been envisaged that Hille would make this furniture, an abortive attempt to build a new factory at Hainault resulted in serious production problems, with the result that several other contractors had to be brought in at short notice to produce the furniture on time.[16] In the event, the only furniture made by Hille, apart from the Royal Box chairs, was the lounge chairs. The plywood seat backs of the dining chairs were moulded by Alesbury Brothers of Maidstone, while the chairs were fabricated by Dare-Inglis of Harrow.

Robin was particularly proud of his Royal Festival Hall auditorium seating, which is still in use sixty years after its introduction. However, the speed at which the rest of the furniture had to be produced threw up a number of technical glitches that could be ironed out only later on. This explains why the Hille production versions of the lounge and dining chairs differ in certain details from the original pieces. The 661C orchestra chair enjoyed a long life and was produced in several different plywood and upholstered versions until at least 1966. The 661 dining chair, although manufactured for more than ten years, was overtaken by a more successful and flexible design, the 675 chair, from 1952. The 658 lounge chair was replaced during the mid-1950s by a more practical variant, the 700 armchair, whose wooden armrests, instead of floating, were attached directly to the sides of the seat. Nonetheless, given the pioneering nature of the technology that Robin was exploiting, the Festival Hall furniture was remarkably successful and, in visual terms, admirably well suited to the building. Although some teething troubles were encountered, these were an inevitable consequence of the rush to get all this revolutionary new furniture produced on time.

Far left
Robin Day, c.1949
Winning the International Low-Cost Furniture Competition in 1949 established Robin as one of Britain's most promising young furniture designers, and prompted his alliance with Hille.

Left and below
Royal Festival Hall auditorium seating, Cox & Co., 1951
Robin adopted materials and techniques associated with the car industry to fabricate the steel frame used on this seating. The underside of the seat was padded with glass fibre. This and the pierced panel improve the acoustics in the hall.

Royal Festival Hall, 1951
The building was designed by
Leslie Martin and a team of
architects from London County
Council, with interiors by Peter
Moro. Robin's auditorium seating
proved so successful that it has
remained in use for sixty years.

Right
Royal Festival Hall dining chair, 1951
The original chairs made for the hall were fabricated by a firm called Dare-Inglis. This model was subsequently manufactured by Hille as the 661 Small Moulded Chair.

Below
Royal Festival Hall lounge chair, 1951
The lounge chair was a lower and more expansive version of the dining chair (right). Hille supplied the original chairs, later marketed as the 658 Large Moulded Chair.

Opposite
Royal Festival Hall restaurant, 1951
Robin's dining chairs and tables *in situ*, showing how well they complemented the architecture of the building.

Robin Day: Homes and Gardens Pavilion at the Festival of Britain

The Festival of Britain, held in 1951 on the riverside site directly adjoining the Royal Festival Hall and on other sites around London and Britain, played a key role in establishing the link between scientific progress, social welfare and modern design. A godsend for architects and designers, the Festival was an extremely ambitious project, providing unparalleled opportunities for the creation of adventurous buildings and imaginative displays. For Robin and Lucienne it provided another crucial benchmark in their careers.

Robin was involved from the outset, as one of twelve designers invited to submit ideas for the Festival symbol. His proposal showed the British Isles encircled by a pennant, but the panel eventually selected Abram Games's Britannia and bunting logo instead.[17] Among the other shortlisted designers was Milner Gray from the Design Research Unit, and he and Robin were subsequently given responsibility for the signage on the Festival site. Working with a team of associates, including Kenneth Lamble, John Messenger, Peter Werner and Sylvia Reid, they developed a coordinated scheme consisting of a combination of typographic and pictographic signs. Consistency and clarity were the primary aims of the signage, one of the first examples of systematic design coordination over a large exhibition site. A bold, capitalized, sans serif typeface was chosen for all the pavilion signs, while services were indicated by pictograms, produced in low relief on perforated plastic board. Colour-coding was used to indicate upstream and downstream attractions, and directional signs were screen-printed on aluminium sheet, attached to walls or mounted on free-standing conical posts.

Milner Gray subsequently praised Robin as "a designer of marked individuality as well as wide versatility", noting that he "preferred to work in many fields of design, believing that experience gained in one industry can be of value in another, and that freshness and originality can result from diverse design activities".[18] For the Festival organizers, Robin was an ideal designer, being so flexible that his talents could be deployed wherever required. Initially he was assigned to work on a pavilion called "The Land of Britain",[19] but by 1949 he had become part of the team working on the South Kensington-based Exhibition of Science.[20] Although his experience of designing scientific displays for ICI would have made him ideal for this project, ultimately this exhibition was assigned to another designer, Brian Peake, and Robin became involved instead with the Homes and Gardens Pavilion. A legacy of his involvement in the Exhibition of Science was the poster he created to advertise the display. Imaginative and dramatic but at the same time serious, it showed atoms orbiting the earth, along with constellations and a swarm of meteors, illuminated against the night sky.

Partly on the basis of his track record as an exhibition designer and partly as a result of his growing reputation as a furniture designer, Robin was invited to design three room settings for the Home Entertainment section of the Homes and Gardens Pavilion in 1949. The aim of the pavilion as a whole was to tackle the issue of shortage of space, and Robin was one of six design teams that were asked to present their solutions for space-saving furnishings, each focusing on a different theme. The brief for the Home Entertainment section was to design a multi-purpose living room with storage facilities, which could accommodate a range of traditional leisure activities such as reading, sewing and music-making, along with new technology in the form of radio, television and gramophone. Robin created three room settings, including a low-budget and a high-budget interior incorporating furniture he had designed.[21] Although the brief did not stipulate the inclusion of dining facilities, Robin considered dining an important aspect of home-entertaining, and took it upon himself to create flexible dining-living rooms. His third interior, devoted to the theme of lighting, was furnished with the work of manufacturers from a Council of Industrial Design-approved list, and included furniture by E. Gomme and Morris of Glasgow, and lighting by Merchant Adventurers and Troughton & Young. Functioning as a demonstration chamber, parts of this room were variously illuminated in sequence, while a voiceover explained the benefits of the different forms of lighting on show.[22]

Although clearly differentiated by cost and size, the challenge for Robin in both his high-budget and his low-budget interiors was to create rooms that appeared uncluttered and spacious while accommodating a number of apparently conflicting activities. The low-cost room was smaller and more compact, featuring a dining table with steel rod legs complemented by four 661C chairs. One wall was decorated with Lucienne's Provence wallpaper, and the floor was laid with mats of unspun jute and cane by Mourne Textiles. Heal's seem to have acted as the unofficial sponsors of this interior, which they illustrated in a leaflet called "Heal & Son at the Festival of Britain".[23] It was they, rather than Hille, that manufactured the low-level Utility storage units designed by Robin for this display, variants of which were later sold through their store.[24] Made of mahogany and ash, and supported on thin steel legs, these simple cabinets were designed on a basic modular plan. One section of the two-tier, three-bay system housed a built-in television, radiogram and speaker. Another, with a drop-flap door, served as a drinks cabinet, and the remaining units were fitted with a variety of shelves and drawers.

Like his entry to the MOMA competition, Robin's low-cost units for the Homes and Gardens Pavilion were created in direct response to pressing issues of the day. In 1948 a Council of Industrial Design report, prepared as a policy document for the Festival, had concluded that many people were now living in servantless houses, small apartments, and temporary dwellings, often bed-sitting rooms. In response, it recommended that standardized unit furniture should be developed and that individual items should be smaller, more flexible, and preferably dual-purpose, to save space.[25] All this made perfect sense to Robin, whose low-cost storage units for the Festival met each of these criteria. Learning from his earlier experience at MOMA, however, he abandoned curved and tapered forms in favour of simple rectangular boxes. Later these ideas were refined and consolidated in Hilleplan (1952), his first mass-produced Hille storage range.

Royal Festival Hall foyer, 1951
With their thin steel rod legs
and their fluid moulded plywood
seat backs, Robin's Royal Festival
Hall chairs were radically different
from anything else on the market
at the time. They set the trend for
what became known as the
"Contemporary" style.

Royal Festival Hall terrace tables and chairs, Kingfisher Ltd, 1951
This range of outdoor furniture was designed to complement the moulded plywood chairs used in the restaurant and foyers. Unlike the orchestra, dining and lounge chairs, this terrace furniture did not subsequently enter production.

Robin's higher-budget interior, although more generously proportioned, was similarly clean-lined and restrained. Divided into two free-flowing sections, one for dining, one for relaxation and music-making, the room was separated by a divider in the form of floor-to-ceiling glass shelves. Fabricated by the Scottish firm Wylie & Lochead, this shelving system was ingenious from a technical point of view, with the shelves being supported on rudder-like mahogany columns, held in position with brass rods and tension cables.[26] Six 661 dining chairs were arranged around a table in one half of the room, which was dominated by a two-tier storage system, arranged in four bays in a continuous bank along a luxurious fossil marble-clad wall. Based on similar principles to the low-cost version, but larger in scale, the high-price storage system, made by Hille and later sold in the US,[27] was supported on a framework of square-section tubular steel. The cabinets themselves were plain and flush, faced with rich decorative veneers. In addition, shelves, drawers and a magazine rack all formed part of the system, which, because it was flexible, could be asymmetrically arranged. To avoid a blocky appearance, the structure allowed for sections to be left empty, thus enabling larger objects, such as sculptures and ceramics, to be displayed. These were all personally selected by Robin, and included works by Barbara Hepworth and Reg Butler, which complemented the aesthetic of his furniture designs.

The other half of the high-price room focused on home entertainment, and featured a gramophone and a cabinet for storing records, along with a cluster of 658 lounge armchairs. Above this was a platform intended for music-making, containing a cello, a piano and a 661C chair. Two tripod floor lamps, co-designed with the architect John Reid, were positioned in this area to provide localized lighting. The wall was decorated with a mural of a violin, against which various other instruments were suspended, highlighting the theme of music-making and injecting an element of visual ingenuity and fun.

Lucienne Day: Calyx

As well as providing the ideal showcase for Robin's recent furniture, the Homes and Gardens Pavilion provided a favourable setting for three new wallpapers by Lucienne, and acted as the catalyst for her revolutionary new furnishing fabric, Calyx. Displayed at the entrance to the Home Entertainment section, Calyx was designed at Robin's request, and manufactured, at Lucienne's instigation, by Heal's. [28] According to Marilyn Hoffman: "He wanted something modern and in keeping with his own furniture designs. His wife was the one who understood best what he needed." [29] Of all her work at the Festival, it was Calyx that made the greatest impact on public taste, and that exerted the most dramatic and long-lasting effect on industrial design. Heal's later referred to it in their publicity as "a revolution", and Calyx not only opened up the road to modern design for them but electrified the whole of the British textile industry, as well as sending out shock waves abroad.

Although Lucienne had made inroads into modern design during the late 1940s through the agency of her dress fabrics, as yet she had not managed to persuade any of her clients in the furnishing trade to take what she considered a truly progressive

Opposite top
Festival of Britain symbol, 1950
Robin was one of twelve designers invited to submit ideas for a logo for the Festival. The British Isles motif recurs in the poster opposite bottom.

Opposite bottom
Exhibition of Science poster, 1951
This exhibition was held at the Science Museum in South Kensington, London, to complement the main Festival of Britain on the South Bank. Robin's virtuoso graphic skills are evident in the evocation of the night sky.

Left
Festival of Britain signage, 1951
Robin designed this free-standing direction post as part of an overall signage scheme for which he and Milner Gray were jointly responsible. Skylon is to the left, and the Transport Pavilion to the right.

design. Her first design for Heal's, Fluellin (1950), was somewhat backward-looking, composed of floral sprigs and an ivy trellis, printed on linen in muted green and brown. The reason for her initial caution was that Anthony Heal, who commissioned Fluellin, had requested a pattern in a similar vein to her two earlier designs for Edinburgh Weavers, Florimel and Elysian. Having managed to get her foot in the door at Heal's, Lucienne was now in a much stronger position. Also significant was the fact that, by this date, she had struck up a good relationship with Tom Worthington, director of Heal's Wholesale and Export.[30] Although he was sceptical about the commercial viability of Calyx, for the sake of the Festival he was at least prepared to give it a go. Lucienne realized that the Festival provided a unique opportunity to launch a bold initiative, and she was confident that the risk would pay off. With Calyx, she pulled out all the stops, refusing to allow the market to cramp her style and giving free rein to her taste for modern art.

Lucienne was always very particular about the titles of her Heal's textiles, most of which she chose personally. The word "calyx" refers to the outer covering of a flower, the part composed of sepals rather than petals. In addition, because of its similarity to the Latin word *calix*, meaning cup, calyx is often used as a generic term for cuplike structures. Both definitions are relevant to Calyx, but above all the designer has always stressed the importance of the "sense of upward movement" in the design. "I wanted it to have a sense of growth, but not to be a floral pattern," she emphasized. "It is based on plant life, although it is very abstracted."[31] Lucienne was, of course, aware of the work of artists such as Joan Miró and Paul Klee, and the generalized influence of both can be detected in the mood and character of Calyx. Later she became a great admirer of Alexander Calder, although at this stage she was unfamiliar with his work.

However, while acknowledging the positive impact of modern art on her aesthetic, Calyx still shines out as an outstandingly confident and original design. Certain characteristics, such as fine lines breaking up into dashes, and loose textural abstract effects, had been features of her dress fabrics since the late 1940s, but with Calyx she moved up a gear, injecting a new freedom and dynamism into the pattern, and dramatically increasing the scale of the repeat. Her inspired use of colour was also crucial to the success of Calyx. Lime yellow, vermilion and black on olive was the version shown at the Festival, startling not only for the combination of colours but for their distribution within the design.

One measure of the phenomenal impact of Calyx is the fact that it was so widely copied, always an indication of commercial success. In Britain it triggered off an avalanche of lookalikes, often printed on cheaper rayon fabric. Even Marian Mahler, a fellow member of the SIA's Textile Group, produced several Calyx derivatives during the early 1950s, albeit at the instigation of her client, David Whitehead, a direct competitor to Heal's. Abroad, several direct imitations appeared on the market, notably in Sweden and the US, prompting the threat of legal action by Heal's. In America, where it was sold by Greeff Fabrics, Calyx proved a great hit with interior decorators, and was sold

Opposite

Low-cost room setting, 1951
Robin created three room settings in the Home Entertainment section of the Homes and Gardens Pavilion. His low-cost room featured modular storage units made by Heal's, complete with built-in radio and television. Also shown here are his Festival Hall orchestra chairs and Lucienne's Provence wallpaper for John Line (see page 49).

Left and below

High-cost room setting, 1951
These photographs show both halves of Robin's high-cost room setting, divided by a bank of open shelving. Left is the dining area with his Festival Hall restaurant chairs, and four bays of storage units made by Hille, supported on a tubular steel frame. The music-making area below includes three Festival Hall lounge chairs, an orchestra chair drawn up to the piano, and two floor lamps co-designed with John Reid.

through many leading department stores. This led to a Citation of Merit from the American Institute of Decorators (AID), who recognized the outstanding qualities of Lucienne's pattern and awarded it their highest honour in 1952, over and above the achievements of home-grown design talents such as Alexander Girard and Ben Rose.

Reflecting six years later on the genesis of Calyx and the impact of her patterns of the early 1950s on the market, Lucienne wrote: "A great deal of thought and worry went into those early post-war designs, created by designers who knew they were offering the public something unusual, and perhaps difficult to accept at first. Many of them, though gay and unconventional, were well drawn, well organized and restrained. Unfortunately, the quality of naïveté which was inherent in this trend seemed to be superficially easy to copy, and in a year or two the market was flooded with riotously coloured 'abstracts' which were unconsidered and crude, on cheaper and cheaper cloth. A medium-sized repeat was characteristic of these patterns, designed for the one-and-a-half yard windows of flat-blocks and prefabs. While it was obviously perfectly right for producers to cater for public requirements, one got very tired of these neither-large-nor-small patterns, even if one liked the designs themselves." [32]

The success of Calyx at the Festival of Britain, together with the extensive publicity following the AID Award, acted as a springboard for Lucienne's career, and gave her the boost she needed. Now she and Robin were regarded on an equal footing, and whenever one was featured in the press the other was inevitably mentioned. During the 1950s they were regarded as a double-act, and actively boosted each other's fortunes. Being a couple gave them an added cachet, and with their growing international success, they were treated as joint ambassadors promoting the cause of British "Contemporary" design.

Lucienne Day: Festival of Britain

In addition to Calyx, Lucienne created several other designs specifically for the Festival, including a printed rayon dress fabric for Penny Mason Models (1950). A self-consciously joyful and lighthearted design, this pattern combined the word "festival", written in several different languages, with motifs such as pennants, loops and dashes. Her third textile was a woven upholstery fabric she created for the seating in the Telekinema, an auditorium designed by Wells Coates. A neat small-scale geometric abstract pattern, it was manufactured by Morton Sundour, the Carlisle firm with which she had already collaborated for several years.

Keen to have as much work as possible on display in the Festival, Lucienne took the initiative and contacted Hugh Casson, Director of Architecture, to ask whether some of her designs for wallpapers could be used in the Homes and Gardens Pavilion. Casson put her in touch with Cole & Son, which specialized in traditional flock wallpapers, but which agreed to produce two of her modern abstract designs. Stella (from stellar, meaning "of the stars") was decorated with organic free-form shapes overlaid with small linear starlike motifs. Diabolo (referring to a children's game in which a two-headed wooden top is spun, tossed and caught on a string stretched between two sticks) was decorated with rows of small hourglass motifs. Hand screen-printed in pale shades such as slate grey, beige, lemon yellow, mushroom and olive green, both of these wallpaper patterns were deliberately small and recessive, designed for a domestic environment. The fact that they were washable made them particularly well suited to use in the kitchen and nursery. Both were displayed in room settings in the Kitchens section of the Homes and Gardens Pavilion, and afterwards remained in production for several years, sold through outlets such as Heal's.

Provence, the wallpaper used by Robin in his low-cost living room, was originally commissioned by the Bowater Papers in 1950, but subsequently manufactured by John Line & Son in 1951. Marketed as part of their Limited Editions collection of work by named designers, produced to coincide with the Festival, it was block-printed in bolder tones on a coloured ground in Lucienne's characteristic graphic style. Composed of linked capsules containing a mixture of abstract and representational motifs, the linking stripes of the pattern gave it a more formal quality than her Cole wallpapers and made it better suited to use in a living room.

Robin and Lucienne Day: Milan Triennale, 1951

In the absence of any official British presence at the Milan Triennale in 1951, Robin received a personal invitation from the organizers to mount a display. The costs were borne by Hille, and Robin personally erected the display, which was a variation on the upmarket dining-living room he had created for the Festival. In the Triennale room setting, however, he dispensed with the music-making adjunct, and the interior took the form of a large rectangular room. At one end were five of Robin's 661 chairs set round a dining table, with a long length of Lucienne's Calyx resplendent as a backdrop behind. The lounge area, decorated with an unusual textural straw wallcovering and three striped rugs by Gerd Hay-Edie, was furnished with a group of 658 lounge chairs and two spindly Day-Reid tripod lamps, with accessories in the form of studio pottery by Hans Coper and Lucie Rie.

The dominant feature of the display was a long bank of storage units, similar to those at the Festival, but arranged in three tiers and spanning the full length of the room. Instead of housing electrical gadgets, a distinctive feature of the Triennale storage system was that one door was decorated with a large black and white engraving, an abstract composition by the sculptor Geoffrey Clarke. Printed on paper, bonded and sealed under a layer of plastic, this bold skeletal image complemented a large textile hanging suspended above the display, featuring a reclining figure by Henry Moore.

In 1952 Milner Gray wrote: "If asked his views on the much-discussed question of style and the need for a national idiom, Robin Day says that, however desirable, this can only come about as a natural by-product of solving contemporary design problems, and that no amount of self-conscious striving to regain the national design characteristics of the pre-Industrial Revolution era will produce a valid result." [33] Although the

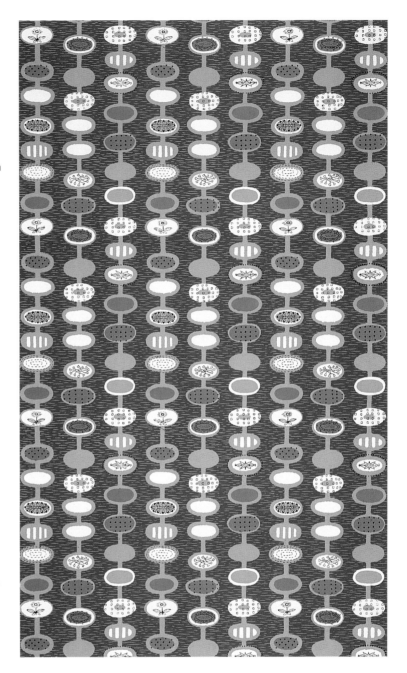

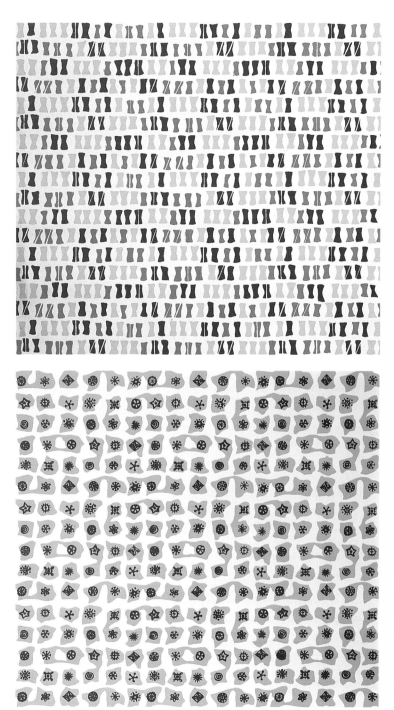

Italians, on the whole, tended to favour design of a more flamboyant nature, they were clearly impressed by Robin's Triennale ensemble, and both his room setting and Lucienne's Calyx were awarded Gold Medals.

1951 had been a frenzied year, with the opening of the Royal Festival Hall, the launch of the Festival of Britain, and the Milan Triennale all happening within the space of a few months. As a result, Lucienne's true potential as a textile designer came to light, and Robin Day's reputation as the country's most promising furniture designer was confirmed. The next decade would be spent consolidating their relationships with Heal's and Hille, and building up an extensive repertoire of designs.

Robin and Lucienne Day: Cheyne Walk

By the time the Days moved into their new house at 49 Cheyne Walk in 1952, they had had plenty of chance to experiment with hypothetical room settings, and were keen to put their interior design ideas into practice. Described by Robin as "a simple, solid and friendly house, not in any way an architectural gem",[34] the house was a tall, narrow, mid-Victorian terrace overlooking the Thames at Chelsea, with accommodation spread over five storeys. The ground floor became their studio, with two rooms being knocked into one. On the first floor was a large open-plan living room-dining room, serviced by a kitchen from above.

During the early years the house served as a laboratory for testing out their ideas about form, pattern and colour. Initially the banisters were painted alternately in black, white and yellow, with a grey haircord carpet on the stairs, while a staircase window had black and white awning canvas curtains, and the hall was decorated with a cartoon-like bird wallpaper by Saul Steinberg. "This hall will be used partly as a waiting room," Robin told a visiting journalist, "so we thought we should give visitors something amusing to look at." [35] The second-floor kitchen was described by their visitor as "the gayest room in the house". The doors on the kitchen cupboards were painted lemon and white, with grey laminate tops and a grey linoleum floor. The walls were papered with Lucienne's Diabolo wallpaper in a complementary colourway, and the lift hatch was decorated with an amusing line drawing by Saul Steinberg on a culinary theme.

As at Markham Square, Robin made some of their furniture himself during the early days, including a glass-topped table on a wire cage base, a small cube-shaped lamp, and a set of fire-irons. Later the house was used as a testing ground for his prototypes, and furniture was changed at regular intervals, particularly during the 1950s and 1960s, as new Hille designs came on the market.[36] Lucienne was less happy to have her own work around her, and the original dining room curtains, made from her newly launched Dandelion Clocks (1953),[37] were soon replaced with a plain orange vermilion fabric, complemented by restful stippled grey tweed on the lounge side of the room. "I'm the sort of designer who can't look at her own work with an unprofessional eye," she explained. "When I should be sitting at peace or listening to music I find myself holding a mental post mortem on the pattern." [38] She also pointed out that "it is wonderfully restful in the evening, after leaving the studio, where one has been wrestling with patterns for curtains, patterns for

Opposite top
Diabolo wallpaper, Cole & Sons, 1951
One of two screen-printed wallpapers created by Lucienne for the Festival, used in various room settings in the Homes and Gardens Pavilion.

Opposite bottom
Stella wallpaper, Cole & Sons, 1951
Lucienne's two simple modern abstract wallpapers for Cole & Sons introduced a completely new style onto the British market. They continued to sell for several years after the Festival.

Above
Milan Triennale, 1951
Robin's display at the Milan Triennale was similar to his high-cost room setting at the Festival (see page 47) and included his Royal Festival Hall lounge and dining chairs. The Hille storage system was also similar, although larger.

Right
49 Cheyne Walk, Chelsea
The Days leased this Victorian
house in 1952 and transformed
the interior into an icon of
"Contemporary" design.

Right
49 Cheyne Walk, Chelsea
The Days leased this Victorian
house in 1952 and transformed
the interior into an icon of
"Contemporary" design.

Below
Living room-dining room, 1954
This photograph shows the view
along the length of the large,
spacious open-plan living room.
Note the white cord stringing
below the black ceiling above the
dining area at the far end. Robin's
Hilleplan sideboard is used as a
room divider, and the furniture
also includes a glass-topped table
(centre) and a lamp (far left), both
made by Robin. The striped rug
on the floor, made by Gerd Hay-
Edie, is the one previously used in
the Milan Triennale display (see
page 51).

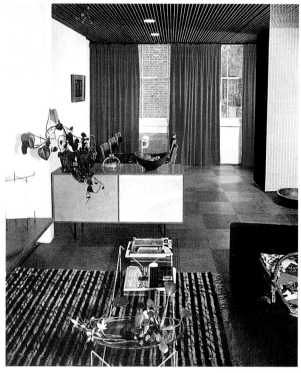

wallpapers, or patterns for dress fabrics all day, to go into this
'unpatterned' room".[39] Instead she used her fabrics as cushion
covers, strategically positioned around the interior. "I suppose
that what I really do, subconsciously, is to make a pattern of the
whole room. I set my background in white, then I go in for colour
accents in a fairly bold way. I put them in places where they can
be changed or varied fairly easily. Then, if need be, I can alter the
general pattern of the room by just moving away the purple chair
or changing the green or yellow cushion." [40]

"In dealing with the equipping and decoration of the living
room," revealed Robin, "our aim was to obtain simplicity and
a sense of space by eliminating fussy detail and establishing
clearly defined basic wall and ceiling areas, sometimes
contrasting in colour and texture." [41] Their main intervention
was to remove an unsympathetic fireplace, install a low terrazzo
ledge below, and strip the chimney-breast back to the brick.
This wall was then whitewashed; other surfaces in the room
included a wallcovering made of split bleached cane and an area
of flush walnut veneer. Instead of carpet, the floor was laid with
large birch plywood squares, softened by a striped Gerd Hay-
Edie rug. An armchair and settee were positioned around the
fireplace, with a pebble-filled trough for plants behind.

As in Robin's Festival and Triennale interiors, custom-
designed cabinets, incorporating built-in appliances and a
desk, were installed along one wall. The doors of the cabinets
were black and white, contrasting with a large yellow speaker
panel, and the units were supported on a grey square-section
tubular steel frame. A Hilleplan sideboard, decorated on one
side with a map of the river Thames at Chelsea, acted as a
drinks cabinet and room divider, later supplemented by a
suspended fine metal gauze. To create a change of mood and
level between the relaxing and the eating zones, the dining
room ceiling was painted black with white cords stretched
below and lighting above, a feature that caught the attention of
many visitors. "We prefer a living room-dining room arrangement
for a number of reasons," Robin affirmed, "the most important
being that it helps to make possible one really large room. We
think space is the greatest luxury obtainable in a living room,
and tried to preserve and increase the sense of space as
much as possible." [42]

Press coverage began as soon as work was completed,
and the house caused a minor sensation. As well as an article
by Robin in the *Ideal Home Book* and a fashion shoot by
Vogue in 1953, there were numerous other features, including
House & Garden and *Ideal Home* in 1954.[43] In addition, the
house was also frequently mentioned by newspaper columnists.
"There is a modern trend to expose the structural materials
indoors to make a pleasing broken texture to contrast with
matt walls and contemporary furniture," wrote Audrey Werge in
the *Daily Telegraph*,[44] while a columnist in the *Sunday Express*
praised the house for its '"clean, smooth colours with sweeping
lines and polished surfaces that give it tremendous space and
light". [45] Media interest in the couple and their lifestyle grew to
a frenzy during the mid-1950s, extending beyond interior
decoration to their taste in clothes, recipes and drinks, and
even to their choice of car.[46]

Left
Storage system, 1953
As in his Festival and Triennale room settings, Robin used one wall of the living room to house a built-in storage system. The cupboard doors were painted black and white, while the speaker panel (top right) was bright yellow.

Below
Living room, 1999
The Days' house was altered very little during the 48 years they lived there. This photograph shows the original whitewashed brick chimney breast with its terrazzo seating ledge below. Later furniture included Robin's Forum settees, 1964, and his 4-4000 armchair, 1970, both shown here.

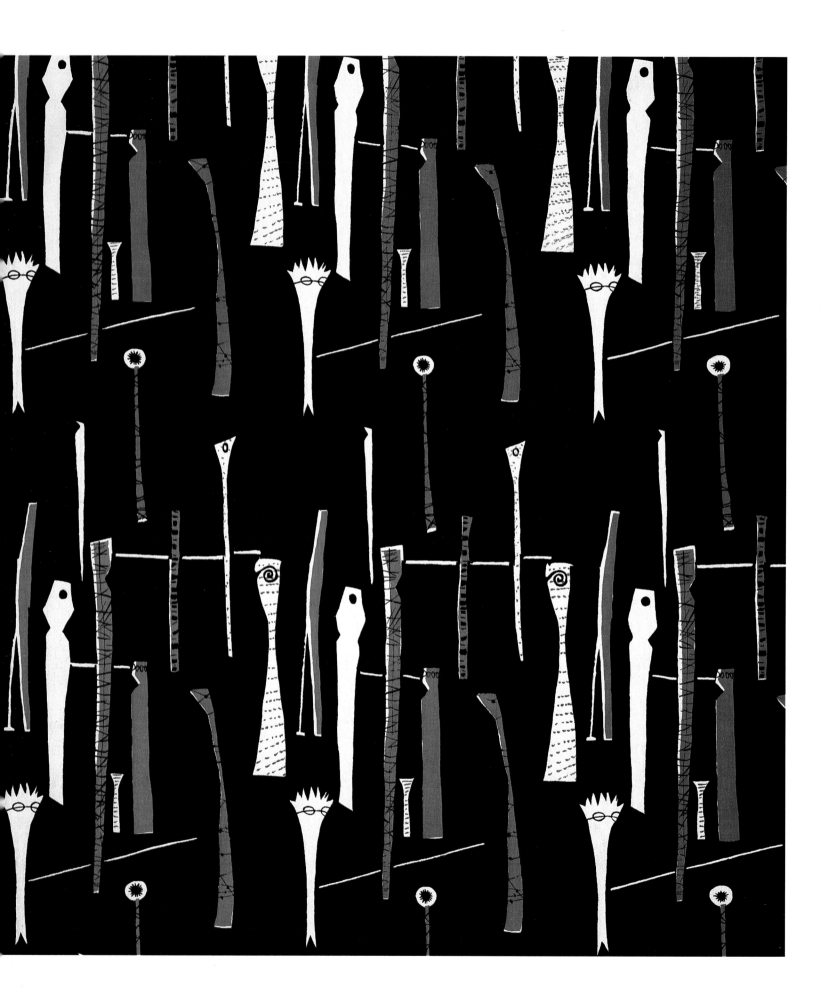

CHAPTER FOUR

1952-59

THE FIFTIES: THE TRIUMPH OF CONTEMPORARY DESIGN

Robin Day: Desks and Storage Furniture

In the aftermath of the Festival of Britain, Robin's main concern was to build on his success with Hille and to consolidate their position as Britain's leading progressive furniture manufacturer. Within the space of a few years he transformed their image, not only with his furniture, but through a complete overhaul of their corporate identity. The smart new logo he had created for them in 1949 was applied to everything from letterheads to company vans. By 1954, demand for his furniture was so great, and his repertoire so broad, that Hille stopped making reproduction furniture and devoted themselves exclusively to his designs. The previous year Robin had introduced a stylish new format for their printed catalogues, and these were now produced as slim folded leaflets with vibrant multicoloured covers. Each leaflet was devoted to a different range, illustrated with crisp black and white photographs, personally overseen by Robin using his favoured photographer, Tony Mann. Later, during the early 1960s, after Ray Hille's second daughter, Cherrill Scheer, became involved in marketing, the company established their own in-house design unit to create their printed publicity. During the 1950s, however, while Hille was still growing from small to medium size, Robin had control over all aspects of design, including advertisements, and it was not until the launch of the Status range in 1959 that a specialist graphic designer was employed.[1]

In design terms Hille was very much a blank sheet for Robin at this stage. Following his triumphant success at the Festival and the Milan Triennale, Ray Hille and the Juliuses looked to Robin to lead the way, trusting him to come up with designs that, while progressive, were commercially sound. In 1964 Robin recalled: "It seemed to me fourteen years ago that the most promising market for the sort of furniture I wanted to design would be with architects and professional people, and that this could be an expanding source of sales as there was a vast post-war programme for the construction of such buildings as business premises, airports, universities and hotels."[2] His suggestion was that, while continuing to produce domestic furniture, Hille should manufacture ranges suitable for commercial use and, instead of relying exclusively on retail outlets, they should pitch their work directly at architects, as it was through them that lucrative contracts might be secured. As restrictions eased on commercial buildings, high-rise office blocks began to appear in cities, and purpose-designed factories and company headquarters sprang up around the country at a growing rate. Modernism became the accepted idiom of these buildings, making architects – who would be actively seeking contemporary furniture to complement their modern interiors – an obvious target of Hille's marketing.

Opposite
Spectators, Heal's, 1953
This witty furnishing fabric characterizes Lucienne's spirited approach to design during the 1950s. It was one of the four textiles for which she received a Gran Premio Award at the Milan Triennale in 1954.

Above
Hilleplan desk, 1952
The top of this desk is covered in linoleum and the drawers are veneered in rosewood. In the foreground is Robin's 675 chair, also dating from 1952.

Right
Hilleplan unit J, 1952
The Hilleplan range consisted of
nine different storage units. Unit J
was a chest of drawers with a
drop-flap writing desk above.

Below
Hilleplan unit B, 1952
A distinctive feature of Robin's
early furniture was his use of
woods in contrasting colours.
Here, light-coloured elm contrasts
with darker-coloured walnut on
the handles and drawers.

The importance of commercial clients explains the special
emphasis on office furniture within Hille's range. Robin's first
design, the Hillestak desk (1950), had been little more than a
modified table. Better suited to the needs of the business world
was his next model, the Hilleplan desk (1952), with its robust
mahogany carcass and practical features such as recessed
handles, aluminium footrest and linoleum top. Intended to
complement the Hilleplan storage units, it was produced in
Junior and Senior versions with a choice of wood or metal legs,
and rosewood or ash veneer. While the Hilleplan desk was
geared to the needs of clerks, secretaries and middle-ranking
personnel, the more upmarket Executive desk (1952) was, as its
name suggests, pitched at managers and directors. This
handsome range was prompted by a commission undertaken by
Robin that year to design an executive's office in the new Time-
Life building designed by Michael Rosenauer. The commission
came from Sir Hugh Casson, who was in overall charge of the
interiors, but who delegated one office to Robin. Originally
veneered in mahogany, elm or walnut, later in luxurious figured
Rio rosewood, the Executive desk proved so enduringly popular
that it remained in production until 1980, providing many years of
work for Hille's skilled cabinet-makers.[3]

From the outset, ever since his first demountable chair,
Robin had demonstrated a commitment to the use of metal
frames for furniture. Initially he had experimented with aluminium,
but for his Festival of Britain storage units he adopted square-
section tubular steel, a device more commonly used in exhibition
stands. Square-section tubular steel, variously finished with grey
or black stove enamel or with polished or satin chrome, became
the mainstay of his desks, cabinets, tables and modular seating
for the next two decades. Because of his penchant for metal, Hille
took over a shopfitting company in Battersea during the early
1950s, and in 1957 they established their own metalwork factory
at Haverhill. As well as being extremely strong, metal frames gave
a lightness to Robin's furniture that he found particularly satisfying.
In the case of the Executive desk, for example, it enabled him to
separate the desk top from the carcass as a thin floating platform,
and to raise the pedestal units clearly off the ground. The
enforced rectilinearity of the resulting furniture complemented the
rational post-and-beam aesthetic of modern architecture. On a
more mundane level, he was also conscious of practical issues
such as cleaning. "What one needs in today's small rooms is to
see over and under one's furniture," he told a journalist in 1955.[4]

Apart from the clean-lined simplicity of its appearance,
Robin's domestic furniture was distinguished by the fact that it
was produced mainly in the form of flexible ensembles rather
than set suites. When asked to give advice on home furnishing,
Robin urged consumers to be pragmatic and to think for
themselves. "The essential thing is not to be badgered by
convention. Don't be ruled by what your friend has got – or by
what your parents have always had. Buy what you need. And
don't be afraid to look different." [5] It was this independent-
minded approach that led Robin to pioneer the introduction of
unit furniture to Britain, starting with storage and later tackling
seating. Although the resulting furniture systems looked so
different from other products on the market, contrary to the

Office in Time-Life Building, London, 1952
This photograph shows one of the executive offices designed by Robin in this showpiece modern building by Michael Rosenauer. The furniture includes his upholstered Stamford chair (far right) and Executive desk (centre), as well as several steel rod 661 and 661C chairs. On the wall is a clock that Robin designed for Gent's. The storage system (top right) was purpose-designed for this room.

Left
Junior Executive desk, 1952
The distinctive features of this handsome desk are its floating top and its neat recessed drawers. It was so successful that it remained in production until 1980.

Robin Day, 1953
The chair on which Robin is working is the Q Stak (see page 68).

expectations of the sceptical British furniture trade Robin's ideas were well received and became part of Hille's stock-in-trade.

The Hilleplan range (1952), Robin's first fully standardized storage system, embodied the fruits of all his accumulated experience in the MOMA competition and the Festival of Britain, but translated them into production form. Consisting of nine different cabinets and drawer units, denominated Units A–J, it was designed on an 18-inch (46cm) modular system so that different elements could be coordinated or aligned. Intended to house everything from books and crockery to table linen and domestic accounts, the units worked equally well in groups or as stand-alone bookcases, sideboards and chests of drawers. Their sides were made of solid agbar, a pale golden timber chosen for its anonymous and quiet character, with the rest of the carcass made from plywood veneered in walnut, cherry or elm. Bookcases had doors of clear glass, and an innovative feature for sideboards was the option of chic black or grey vitrolite for the sliding doors.[6]

The successor to the Hilleplan range was Interplan (1954), consisting of fourteen boxlike cabinets identified as Units K–Z. Like Hilleplan, it was based on an 18-inch (46cm) module, and all the basic dimensions were the same. The main differences were that it had a mahogany rather than an agbar case, complemented by rosewood or ash veneers; and that all cabinets had flush surfaces, with recessed grips on sliding doors and projecting right-angled metal handles on drawers. These features gave the range a crisp appearance, while its flexibility was emphasized by the parallel introduction of a multifunctional low slatted bench, which could be used as a table, a seat or a base for a cabinet, as an alternative to conventional legs. Displayed in this form at the Milan Triennale in 1954, Interplan was later offered with a wall-mounted tubular steel frame. This functioned in a similar way to the earlier 1951 Triennale system, with cabinets and shelving being fixed to an exoskeleton by means of brass collars and bolts.

At the end of the decade Hille launched an ambitious range of coordinated office furniture called Status (1959), which offered the widest choice of desk sizes and pedestals to date. In technical and visual terms it closely resembled Interplan, and as well as desks it included tables, cabinets and chairs. With Status, Hille sought to clinch their position as market leaders in the world of office furniture, but it also marked the culmination of eleven years of experimentation by Robin in the field of domestic storage.

Robin Day: Seating

Robin's desire to introduce modular seating into the home took rather longer to develop, and it was not until the Form Group (1960) that his ideas really gelled. Prior to this he had been constrained by traditional upholstery methods, which restricted both flexibility and form. His XU sectional seating (1952), for example, had hand-tied coiled-spring seats, and cushions with coiled-spring units embedded in rubberized hair. However, by the end of the decade Robin noted: "Rubber webbing is replacing springs for settees, divans and chairs. The lengths of webbing have a metal binding at each end and these are slipped into place on the frame. When one bit of webbing wears out, you can replace it in a matter of moments – a far simpler business than dealing with a broken spring."[7]

Hilleplan Unit J

Drawers and drop flap in either Nigerian cherry or walnut. Recessed handles. Top portion either fitted as writing desk, or with single shelf.

Length 3' 0", height 45" wood legs, 44" steel legs, depth 18".

← Wood legs and drop flap open
Steel legs and cabinet closed →

Dressing Desk

The top of this cabinet is divided into two compartments closed by two lift up lids. One of these compartments is lined with white plastic, and the lid of this compartment is fitted with a mirror. Frame of solid beech. Lift up lids veneered in walnut or Nigerian cherry.

Length 3' 0", height 29", depth 18".

677A. Table

Construction and materials as 677 table but with circular top 2' 9" diameter. A further version, the 677B table, is similar with a square top 2' 9" x 2' 9".

Hilleplan Unit G

Drawer fronts in either Nigerian cherry, walnut or elm. Recessed handles. A small cupboard (Hilleplan Unit H) is available with identical dimensions, but with hinged door and one interior shelf.

Length 1' 6", height 30" wood legs, 29" steel legs, depth 18".

Hille furniture can be seen in showrooms at
Fourth Avenue at 32nd Street, New York 16.
206/210, Chaussee D'Etterbeek, Brussels, Belgium.

The models shown in this leaflet are standard Hille designs and may be seen at the showrooms of **Hille of London Ltd., 39-40 Albemarle Street, W.1** Tel.: MAYfair 4474

The address of your nearest dealer displaying Hille furniture will be sent on request.

High quality timber is used in construction, exposed surfaces remaining in the natural colour protected by a synthetic lacquer. Moulded plywood components are resin bonded. Cases are precision built in solid timber with mitred corners, the clean plywood backs are well finished and show no fixing screw, so may be exposed if desired.

All cabinet units may be purchased with either turned beech or dark grey stove enamelled steel legs.

Dimensions of cabinets are related, and with legs removed can be banked one above the other. This provides considerable flexibility and many combinations not shown in the illustrations are possible.

S Hille & Co 134a St Albans Rd Watford Herts
Tel.: Watford 7291

Cabinets & Tables 1953-54

Contemporary furniture by

hille

London showrooms
39-40 Albemarle Street W 1

Hillestak Table

Top 4' 0" x 2' 0"
Height 28"

Beech frame and top finished in either Nigerian cherry, walnut or elm, also Warerite in a choice of colours.

Hillestak Desk

Construction dimensions and finishes as Hillestak table, the drawer unit is removable, and may be fitted on either the left or right hand side. Drawer fronts in either Nigerian cherry, walnut or elm.

Coffeestak Table

Top 2' 0" x 2' 0"
Height 1' 8"

Beech frame. Top veneered in either Nigerian cherry, walnut or elm, or Warerite in a choice of colours.

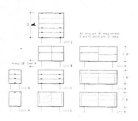

Low Table

Top 4' 0" x 2' 0"
Height 16"

Aluminium alloy legs with rubber feet. Top veneered in walnut edged with a natural beech fillet.

677. Table

Top 5' 0" x 2' 6"
Height 28½"

Laminated top veneered in either walnut, Nigerian cherry or elm. Frame of tubular steel stove enamelled dark grey.

Hilleplan Unit F

Length 3' 0"
Height 30" wood legs, 29" steel legs
Depth 18"

Drawer fronts in either Nigerian cherry or walnut. Recessed handles.

Hilleplan Unit C

Length 3' 0"
Height 30" wood legs, 29" steel legs
Depth 16"

Interior fitted with either one full length shelf or one half length shelf and four moulded ply trays. Sliding doors veneered in either Nigerian cherry or walnut.

Hilleplan Dining Table

Top 4' 0" x 2' 9"
Height 28½"

Frame of solid beech, top veneered in Nigerian cherry or walnut. A simple swivel device allows one half of the top to fold down making a 2' 9" x 2' 0" side table.

Hilleplan Unit B

Length 4' 6"
Height 30" wood legs, 29" steel legs
Depth 18"

Two exterior drawers in either Nigerian cherry or walnut. Sliding doors either veneered in elm or of black or light grey Vitralite.

Hilleplan Unit D

Length 4' 6"
Height 30" wood legs, 29" steel legs
Depth 12"

Bookcase with sliding glass doors and adjustable shelves. With legs removed this unit is frequently used standing on other units. A 3' 0" long bookcase (Hilleplan Unit E) is also available of identical construction.

Hilleplan Unit A

Length 4' 6"
Height 30" wood legs, 29" steel legs
Depth 18"

Two interior drawers and interior shelves. Sliding doors in either black or light grey Vitralite, or veneered in Nigerian cherry or walnut. Illustration shows steel legs and black Vitralite doors.

Hilleplan Unit A

Length 4' 6"
Height 30" wood legs, 29" steel legs
Depth 18"

Two interior drawers and interior shelves. Sliding doors veneered in Nigerian cherry or walnut, or of black or light grey Vitralite. Illustration shows steel legs and walnut doors.

Left and below
Hille Cabinets and Tables leaflet, 1953–4
Robin redesigned Hille's logo shortly after teaming up with the company in 1949. During the 1950s he designed most of their catalogues and advertisements. This was one of a series of folded leaflets produced between 1953 and 1962, each illustrating a different range. It features the Hilleplan storage units.

Right

Interplan storage units and slatted bench, 1954
Interplan was the successor to the earlier Hilleplan range. Cabinets could be either supported by a slatted bench or mounted on legs (see below). Also shown in this photograph are two upholstered 682 Tub armchairs and an oval occasional table, c.1955.

Below left

Interplan unit U, 1954
This small chest of drawers was one of fourteen units in the Interplan range. The case is made of mahogany and the drawers are veneered in ash.

Below right

Interplan unit K or L, 1954
The sliding doors on this sideboard were made of black vitrolite glass. Unit K had shelves inside; unit L also had interior drawers.

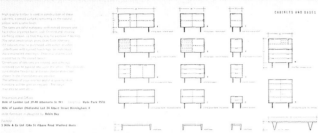

Left and below
Hille Cabinets leaflet, 1958
This leaflet illustrates the complete Interplan storage range, including a system-based version launched in 1958 with cabinets and shelves suspended from a tubular steel frame. As well as designing this leaflet, Robin supplied all the drawings and oversaw the photography.

Right and opposite
Status desks and cabinets, 1959
Original publicity photographs of
this extensive coordinated range
of office furniture deliberately
emphasize the crisp rectilinearity of
the design. The vinyl-covered chair
that appears at the forefront in
both photographs is the Stamford
chair, 1952. The photograph on
this page also includes the Q
Swivel desk chair, c.1954 (left)
and the upholstered 661C chair,
1951 (centre).

Top and above
Hille seating leaflet, 1961
Designed by Robin, this leaflet
highlights the quantity, quality
and scope of his seating designs
during the 1950s. Most were
equally well suited for domestic
or commercial use.

The Form Group, originally called Modulus, was designed in 1959 in response to a challenge from *Ideal Home* magazine for designers to create new furniture models that plugged specific gaps in current provision for the home. Robin's proposal, proudly presented to the magazine's readers in February 1960, was for a seating system consisting of banks of benches, tables and chairs, designed on a 28-inch (71cm) module. Intended to be as flexible as possible, as well as simple to construct, the basic framework was of square-section tubular steel, across which rubber webbing was stretched to support cushions, which were supplied with removable covers in mix-and-match colours. Backrests were optional, and squares of veneered wood or plastic laminate could be inserted into the frame at intervals to create benches or tables. "The long tyranny of the dreary three-piece suite has given way to adaptable seating arrangements and changing patterns even in family sitting rooms," announced *Ideal Home* triumphantly in May 1960, after the runaway success of the Form Group at the Furniture Fair that year. At the time, the Form Group was the most advanced and flexible system on the market; winning a Design Centre Award in 1961, it remained a best-seller until the mid-1970s.

The range of furniture produced by Hille grew extremely rapidly during the first half of the 1950s, although because of the experimental nature of Robin's approach, some pieces – such as the 676 demountable armchair – inevitably fell by the wayside, particularly during the early years. Later, as Hille became more familiar with their market and as Robin became more experienced at tailoring his designs to suit its needs, the number of short-lived designs diminished, and the turnover became less rapid. Nonetheless, it was sometimes only through a process of trial and error that real progress could be made. By the end of the 1950s, in addition to storage furniture, desks and modular seating, Hille's range encompassed dining tables, occasional tables, and a wide variety of seating, including side chairs, benches and easy chairs. "One of the most refreshing things about designing for Hille has always been that there has never been any pressure to design to meet short-term changes in taste," observed Robin in 1964. "We gradually built up a collection of furniture which we thought sound enough to stay on the market year after year. While other firms made annual design changes, we slowly added to the furniture types that were being made, and only discontinued designs if new and better ones which fulfilled the same requirement were thought of. Creating designs for a specific building has been one of the ways in which standard Hille furniture has come into being. Designs are also initiated in two other ways: one is when a need is felt for a piece of furniture not included in the range; the other is when I have simply had an idea I have felt like pursuing. It is perhaps interesting to note that new designs have never been the result of orthodox market research. New designs have come about because they were ones we liked and believed should be made rather than the result of what sales staff thought was commercially needed. It is tremendously satisfying to me that this seemingly uncommercial attitude, which in these days is a rare one, has proved to be commercially successful." [8]

Robin was keenly aware of the need to design chairs that were appropriate for particular tasks or activities. This was why he designed so many different types of easy chair, each with a

Left

Living room in Peter Moro's house, Blackheath, London
When Peter Moro built a house for himself in 1957, he furnished it with Robin's furniture. Shown here are four Chevron chairs around a Cheyne table, 1959.

Below

Form Group, 1960
Designed to replace the conventional three-piece suite, this was Robin's first modular seating system, and it won a Design Centre Award in 1961. Seating could be combined with tables and drinks cabinets, and cushions were supported on rubber webbing rather than springs.

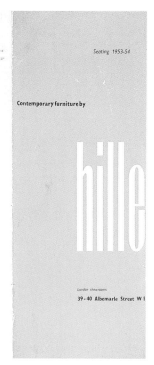

The Telesettee and the Telechair have beech legs and resilient laminated nylon supporting back-spine handled spring inset, back upholstered rubberised hair. Both are demountable for Export.

The XU settee and the XU chair have hardwood frames and beech legs, hardboard inlaid spring seats and back, base reversible seat cushions of patent coiled spring units embedded in rubberised hair. Rubber-padded arms. Covers can be all of the same colour or with contrasting seat cushions.

specific purpose, such as the Reclining chair (1952), set at an incline to encourage a relaxed posture, and the Telechair (1953), deeply padded but more upright for watching television, and with a springy back. Comfort was a key issue, as was ergonomics, and the level of Robin's awareness of this embryonic science was highly unusual among furniture designers at this date. His interest is clear from the text of a leaflet for a range of chairs with one-piece moulded plywood seats called Q Stak (1953), where he explained: "The seat and back unit common to all versions is designed to give maximum comfort with freedom from fatigue. Correct support is given to the lumbar region of the back which physiologists regard as vitally important to health and good posture, especially for anyone seated for long periods."

The Q Stak was also shaped by another significant consideration, the desire to simplify materials and construction in order to reduce costs. Robin and Lucienne were both deeply committed to making their work affordable: "I get a great kick out of seeing my fabrics rolling off the machines to sell at 10 shillings a yard," said Lucienne in 1953. "I would much rather see them in a lot of houses than in a few grand ones. My husband has the same idea for furniture, to get prices down." [9] The Q Stak was prompted by a challenge from Leslie Julius for Robin to design a chair that served a similar function to the Hillestak, but that drastically reduced the number of component parts. Simple though it looked, the Hillestak chair was, in fact, constructed from more than twenty elements. The Q Stak reduced this number to seven: the seat, the two-part tubular steel leg structure, and two pairs of nuts and bolts. Produced with either a veneered plastic laminate or an upholstered seat, the Q Stak was extremely practical and enjoyed a long production life. Typically, it was produced in several versions so that it appealed to as wide an audience as possible, including the non-stacking Q Rod with straight steel rod legs, the QW Stak with V-shaped wooden legs, and the Q Swivel, designed for office use, mounted on a rotating tubular steel pedestal base.

"A good design must fulfil its purpose well, be soundly constructed, and should express in its design this purpose and construction," observed Robin in 1962. [10] The designs that he himself considers most satisfactory from the early part of his career are those in which the structure is most clearly articulated, notably the Reclining chair, with its inverted V-shaped legs and flat wooden armrests, and the 675 chair (1952), with its simple curved plywood back. Although it could be argued that spindliness and austerity were simply part of the "Contemporary" style of the period, Robin's reasons for adopting this aesthetic arose not from a desire to be fashionable, but out of his concern to design furniture with integrity and economy, whose framework was undisguised. This explains why he so often attached metal legs to the exterior of a chair seat or arm, instead of hiding them beneath upholstery, as most designers do. It also explains why, when he used rubber webbing on his seating, as in the Chevron chair (1959) and the Gatwick chair (1958), he made no attempt to cover the rails over which it was stretched. Revealed structures were a key element of his furniture. In the Slat chair (1952) and the Cane-Back armchair (1958), for example, even the titles drew attention to the structure as the principal feature of the design.

Opposite top and bottom
Hille seating leaflet, 1953–4
Robin took great care to
ensure that his furniture was
photographed from interesting
angles to show off its form and
construction to good advantage.

Left
Reclining chair, 1952
Key features of this design are the
slimness of the chair's profile, the
angularity of its form and its clearly
articulated structure. Among his
early work, Robin considers this
to be one of his most successful
designs.

Right

Q Stak chairs, 1953

The successor to the Hillestak chair, this design used far fewer components and was therefore much cheaper to produce. An early example of ergonomic design, the contour of the plywood seat back was designed to give lumbar support.

Below

Q Rod chair, 1953

This straight-legged chair was a non-stacking version of the Q Stak chair (right). The moulded plywood seat was veneered in beech, Nigerian cherry or walnut.

Sometimes, however, in an attempt to create a structure that was practical in manufacturing terms, an awkward visual feature would result. An example of this was the Stamford chair (1952), where Robin was obliged to use upholstery to "disguise" the fact that a solid timber armrest had been fixed to the plywood seat back. The reason for combining timber and plywood in the Stamford chair was entirely practical, because the 661 and 658 chairs had exposed the difficulty and costliness of moulding plywood in two directions. The outcome, from Robin's point of view, was severely compromised, but this did not stop the Stamford range from becoming one of Hille's most commercially successful designs of the decade. An awareness of design and manufacturing issues such as these helps to explain why, of all his early chair designs, it is the 675 that Robin rates most highly. In this design he overcame the problem of forming a one-piece moulded plywood chair back with armrests, by creating a shape bent using a single rather than a double curve. The result is disarmingly simple but also highly sophisticated, and the chair's success lies in the perfect marriage of engineering, function and style.

"Acceptance of contemporary furniture is highest among younger people with less spending power," Robin observed to an American audience in 1953. "These younger people tend to live in small flats, rooms or small prefabricated houses, and are likely to move their quarters from time to time. Space-saving dual-purpose pieces help to meet these requirements." [11] To prove this point, one of his most popular pieces of domestic furniture was the Convertible bed-settee, an ingenious but stylish creation that scooped one of the first Design Centre Awards in 1957, and remained in production for more than a decade. The concept of a dual-purpose sofa that could be converted into a bed was not in itself new, but earlier solutions had all been somewhat cumbersome. Robin's achievement was in rethinking the mechanism as a piece of engineering, so that it glided rather than crashed into place, and in making the bed more comfortable by incorporating a high-quality Dunlopillo mattress supported on rubber webbing in place of metal springs. This, combined with handsome mahogany end panels and smart woven upholstery fabrics,[12] resulted in a design that served each of its applications equally well, and at the same time perfectly complemented the long low line of "Contemporary" design. "Metal for strength and lightness, rubber for comfort and efficiency, wood for touch and appearance", was how Robin himself summed it up.[13]

Robin Day: Danish and American Influences

Designers do not work in a vacuum. No matter how resourceful they are, they will inevitably be affected to some degree by the *Zeitgeist*. In Robin's case, his chief influences came from Denmark and the US, the design superpowers of 1950s furniture, his admiration for which was clearly apparent in a lecture he gave at the time: "Those countries, such as Denmark, whose traditional production and design was not disrupted by the Industrial Revolution, are evolving a fine modern style, using timber; inspired by, though not copying, handcraft. This furniture stresses the beauty of organic materials such as wood and cane, and the subtle shaping that a combination of machines and hand-work can produce. In contrast to this approach is the enterprising

Left
Q Swivel chair, c.1954
Intended as a typist's chair, this was another variant of the Q Stak, with an upholstered seat mounted on a tubular steel swivel base.

Below
Q Stak chairs, 1953
The Q Stak was widely used in schools and canteens, and remained in production until 1967, when it was finally superseded by the Polypropylene chair. Since the plywood seats could be finished in melamine, as here, this made them particularly durable.

furniture that is made in the United States, produced by advanced machine techniques, and often using synthetic materials. The best of this work displays a true machine aesthetic, stressing precision, economy of material, and a tautness of line." [14]

Danish furniture manufacturers had established a healthy export market to Britain during the early 1950s, mainly through the agency of actively Danophile wholesale import companies such as Finmar and Danasco. Robin admired the elegance and craftsmanship of Danish furniture, and respected the undemonstrative approach of designers such as Hans Wegner, Paul Kjaerholm and Finn Juhl. Although Robin did not often use teak, the wood most closely associated with Danish post-war furniture, by the mid-1950s Hille were beginning to favour the adoption of other rich dark hardwood veneers. These timbers, generically described as "rosewood", were derived from various different species of tree in Brazil and India, hence the respective terms "Rio rosewood" and "Bombay rosewood". Among the earliest pieces to be made from rosewood were the chairs, table and sideboard in the Albemarle group (1954).[15] This range was also the first in a series of designs to reflect elements of Danish styling, characterized by graceful proportions, and gently sculptural, curvilinear, bowed and tapering forms. Other Danish-inspired designs included the Cane Back armchair, the President chair (c.1957), made from mahogany or a teaklike wood called makore, and various dining groups such as Albany (1958) and Marson (1961). Although the notion of the fixed suite was something from which Robin had consciously striven to escape, during the second half of the decade he came under increasing pressure from Hille (themselves under pressure from retailers) to produce some designs that catered to this more conservative sector of the market. In contrast to other manufacturers, in Robin's hands the Danish influence was incorporated in a characteristically restrained and thoughtful way.

The American influence on Robin's work can be narrowed down to two leading firms, Knoll and Herman Miller, both with impeccable design pedigrees. An indication of how closely Hille identified with these two companies was that, as well as producing Robin's designs, they later became the British licensees for both firms.[16] Robin was particularly sympathetic to the no-nonsense, rational approach of Florence Knoll; and her use of square-section tubular steel for case furniture, tables and seating closely mirrors his own. Also significant was George Nelson, whose platform bench and modular storage systems informed the development of the Hilleplan and Interplan ranges, and whose designs for office furniture and modular seating clearly influenced the creation of Robin's Executive desk and Form Group. Charles Eames's work, while inspirational, had a less discernible impact, although his pioneering use of moulded plywood acted as a catalyst for the Hillestak and Royal Festival Hall chairs. Robin later reflected, "My early work may also show the influence of constructivist aspects of Italian designs in the use of diagonal structure."

Robin Day: Contract Furniture

In an article about furniture design in Britain during the early 1950s, Robin noted: "New schools, hostels and housing

Opposite top
Chevron chair, 1959
The way in which the steel rod legs arc attached to the exterior of the wooden seat frame on this chair is a characteristic Robin Day structural device.

Opposite bottom
Stamford chair, 1952
The curved plywood seat back of this chair is similar in form to the earlier Royal Festival Hall chairs, but here upholstery covers the hardwood arms.

Far left and left
675 chair, 1952
The shape and structure of this chair are particularly satisfying. The fact that its plywood seat back only had to be moulded in one direction made it easier to produce than the earlier Royal Festival Hall dining chair.

Below
Single Convertible bed-settee, 1957
A best-selling design, the Single Convertible bed-settee won a Design Centre Award in 1957. In the single bed version the seat back dropped down vertically, whereas in the double version the back folded down flat to increase the width of the bed.

Cane Back settee, 1958
The solid mahogany frame and
woven cane seat back gave this
design a decidedly Danish flavour.

schemes for the main post-war building programme in Britain
provide an outlet for genuine contemporary work. The rational
outlook of architects concerned with the equipping of these
buildings and the fact that the quantities required justifies
investment in enterprising production techniques, has caused
some of the most interesting work in this country to occur in this
market." [17] Hille's Contract Division, established in 1952 and run
by Rosamind Julius from the company's stylish showroom at
39 Albemarle Street, took on increasing importance as the
decade progressed, and prompted the creation of a number
of specific designs. An important early contract was to supply
furniture for the new terminal at London Airport (now Heathrow),
designed by Frederick Gibberd in 1953. The scale of the order
was considerable, and included XU settees for the passenger
handling building, Stamford armchairs for the waiting room, and
Q Stak chairs for the staff canteen. Hille became involved at the
instigation of June Lyon, a young textile designer charged with
responsibility for furnishing the interiors of Gibberd's building.
Already a great admirer of the Days, whose work she had
encountered in her previous job at Heal's, in Robin she found "an
exceptional person, whose genuine charm and modesty matched
his great talent and success as a designer". Lyon recalled that by
this date "Hille had already recognized the coming need for well-
designed contract furniture, and the partnership between this
company and Robin had been yielding the best for some time". [18]

After supplying the furniture for London Airport, Hille were
requested by the architects Yorke, Rosenberg and Mardall to
create a range of public seating for their new terminal at Gatwick
Airport. This contract resulted in the Gatwick group (1958), a
coordinated range of handsome leather-upholstered chairs and
benches, Robin's first attempt at purpose-designed foyer seating.
Subsequently manufactured as part of Hille's standard range,
Gatwick remained in production until the end of the 1960s, and
proved enduringly popular with public institutions and museums. [19]

One of the crucial advantages of Hille, from a client's point
of view, was that they produced furniture with such a wide
range of applications. For large companies, Robin's designs
encompassed low-cost utilitarian chairs and tables for behind-
the-scenes areas such as staff restaurants; functional desks
and cabinets for office workers; executive office and boardroom
furniture for senior managers; and foyer seating for reception
areas. Rather than having to liaise with several different suppliers,
therefore, clients such as the Bowater Paper Corporation, whose
headquarters at Northfleet in Kent were furnished by Hille during
1956–7, were able to buy a complete package from one firm. As
well as greatly adding to convenience, this gave them the added
assurance that all the furniture throughout the building would be
visually coherent and of a consistently high technical quality.

Although many clients were content to buy off-the-peg
furniture from Hille's standard ranges, Robin was sometimes
asked to design furniture to meet specific requirements, a
challenge he always enjoyed. A good example of this is the
heavy-duty waiting-room seating he designed for British Rail in
1955, commissioned by H.H. Powell, architect of the Eastern
Region Division, but later adopted nationwide. The brief specified
that the furniture should be extremely low maintenance and

Conference room, Bowater Paper Corporation, Northfleet, 1957
During the 1950s Robin created a number of one-off designs for boat-shaped boardroom tables, such as this one at Bowater, seen here with his President chairs.

Below
Albemarle dining group, 1954
The table and sideboard in this elegant suite were veneered in rosewood. The chair seats were supported on leather straps.

**Departure lounge,
London Airport, 1953**
Hille supplied most of the furniture
for this new building, designed by
Frederick Gibberd with interiors
by June Lyon. Shown here are
Robin's 682 Tub chairs upholstered
in stylish two-tone grey and red.

exceptionally hard-wearing, and the full family of furniture included armour-hard makore slatted armchairs and benches, vinyl-covered plywood seating, and waiting-room tables with scratch-resistant lacquered makore tops.[20] Robin's designs were severe and economical, but at the same time refined, particularly in the curvature of the bench seat, and the use of stainless steel collars on the black stove-enamelled tubular steel legs. This project demonstrated how effectively Robin rose to a demanding design challenge, although typically he played down his own achievement. "I tried to fulfil this requirement in a direct, uncomplicated and visually anonymous way," he told *Ideal Home* in June 1962, at the time of his somewhat belated Design Centre Award for this range.

Robin Day: Pye

Robin's position among the top rank of British designers was confirmed by the fact that in 1957 he won not just one Design Centre Award (for the Convertible bed-settee), but two. His second award was for a television set for the Cambridge firm of Pye, produced in two versions, in a wooden console (model CW17) and on steel legs (model CS17), with technical design by J.E. Cope. Demonstrating the same clean-lined functionalism as his furniture for Hille, and one of the first models on the market in an overtly modern style, Robin's television was praised by the judges for its "well-organized appearance" and because "the detailing of the lettering and knobs is so good that they become one of the main features of the design as a whole".[21] In a Pye publicity leaflet, Robin noted: "No attempt has been made to disguise or elaborate these sets, but instead we have tried to express their real character – that of fine electronic instruments." The leaflet also stated that, with its "simple unassertive cabinet work and clean unfussy lines, the Pye Contemporary TV has been specially created to harmonize with the new trend in good furniture design".

Robin's links with the radio and television set-making industry had begun during the late 1940s with his regular exhibition stands for Ekco. In April 1949 he wrote an article for *House & Garden* called "Make Room for Television", which offered typically down-to-earth practical tips on how these new electrical devices could be incorporated into the modern home. "Most of the day your set will sit lifeless in the room, so its looks are important," he remarked, and he suggested that televisions could be built into fittings such as a bookcase or an unused fireplace. The article includes a photograph of a television set built into the wall of a house designed by the architects Tayler and Green for Godfrey Imhof, the owner of a trend-setting electrical goods shop on London's New Oxford Street. Shortly after the war Imhof had commissioned Robin to design some packaging for record-player needles and, impressed with his professionalism, had subsequently recommended him to Pye.

Robin's first designs for Pye included a large radiogramophone and a table radio, both with wooden cabinets, illustrated in *Designers in Britain*, published by the Society of Industrial Artists in 1949. These were followed by the minimalist PE60 radio (1952), whose angular contours complement Robin's furniture of the same period, and later by one of the first transistor radios (model 444), whose sleek form and stylish aluminium casing perfectly matched the restrained elegance of

Left
Gatwick chair and bench, 1958
This range of foyer seating was specifically designed for Gatwick Airport at the request of the architects Yorke, Rosenberg and Mardall.

Below
British Rail bench and table, 1956
Commissioned by the Eastern Division of British Rail, this range of heavy-duty waiting-room furniture won a Design Centre Award in 1962. Note the rust-proof stainless steel collars on the legs, and the gap at the back of the bench to prevent dust and litter from becoming lodged.

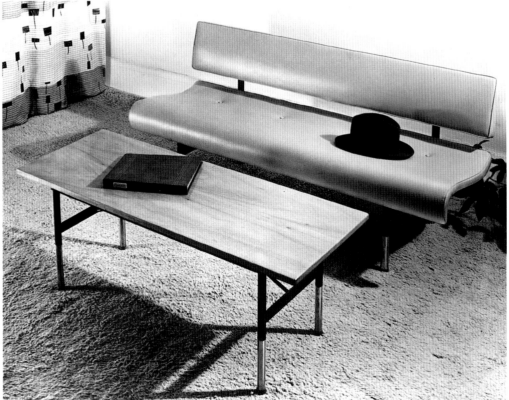

**Television (model CS17),
Pye, 1957**
With its plain case and fine steel
rod legs, this television was
designed in the same idiom as
Robin's furniture, and is pictured
here in the Days' living room.
It won a Design Centre Award
in 1957.

"Contemporary" interiors. Surprisingly, though, considering the
fast-moving technology with which they were working, Pye proved
to be one of Robin's most awkward and reactionary clients.
Although his work for the company spanned almost two decades,
commissions were spasmodic, and there were lengthy intervals
between the first appearances of his various designs. In spite
of the fact that he had been brought in by the management
specifically to provide a fresh approach, he found it difficult to
persuade the engineers of the merits of adopting a more modern
style, and several of his proposals failed to progress beyond the
prototype stage. According to Alan Bednall, Robin's assistant
during the early 1950s, "Robin's work for Pye was erratic because
of sales resistance to such innovative and up-to-date designs. He
was always thinking way ahead of public taste and found it difficult
to come to terms with sales demands for traditional designs." [22]

In spite of these difficulties, Robin's work for Pye was highly
distinguished, and reached a peak of sophistication in the radio,
television and stereogram he designed in conjunction with Douglas
Jones, head of Pye's advanced development department, in
1964–5. With their teak cabinets, anodized aluminium control
panels, and black or grey speaker grills, these pieces were
meticulously detailed but deliberately understated in character, and
shared the long, low lines of modern furniture. The stereogram
(a stereo record player, model 1207) resembled a sideboard, and
was housed in a rectangular box with a lift-up lid. The radio (in
mono and stereo versions, models 1111 and 1108) was slim-line
and economical, its satisfying minimalism reflecting the fact that
the chassis and body had been designed in tandem. The television
(model 24) was similarly unobtrusive and low-lying, its function
neither over-exaggerated nor over-disguised. "Until now, TV sets
have been designed to look important and expensive," observed
Robin. "But with people more used to them, they can take their
place calmly and serenely in a room. I have tried to express clearly
and simply what the various parts of these instruments do. In the
TV cabinet, for instance, the control and speaker grill are clearly
differentiated from the screen, but assertive knobs have been
avoided as there should be minimal visual disturbance near the
screen." [23] Robin's success in achieving these aesthetic goals was
acknowledged when his radio received a Design Centre Award in
1966, his second for Pye, and his sixth overall. Shortly afterwards
Pye were taken over by Philips, by which date, however, his
relationship with the company had already come to an end.

Robin's views on design remained remarkably consistent
over the years, and the hopes he expressed in an American
magazine in 1953 are as valid today as they were six decades
ago. "It seems that the creation of new furniture has sometimes
become almost entirely a vehicle of self-expression for the designer,
or a seasonal quick-change act for the marketing requirements
of manufacturers. No one would pretend that material, technical
needs and function were the sole dictates of form, but it is evident
that in some of the finest furniture of our time, technology on the
one hand and superlative craftsmanship on the other, have played
a major role. I think that general acceptance of modern furniture
depends largely on sincerity of design. If designers accept this
responsibility, and if manufacturers allow them to do their best
work, the movement should eventually mature." [24]

Left
Robin Day, early 1960s
On his drawing board is a design
for a radiogram. This was one of
many proposals for Pye that never
came to fruition.

Centre
Radio (model 1108), Pye, 1965
This radio, which won a Design
Centre Award in 1966, has the
same low-slung rectilinear form as
Robin's storage units of the period
(see page 113).

Bottom left
**Stereogram (model 1207),
Pye, 1964**
With its teak cabinet, vinyl-
covered front and linen speaker
covers, this stereogram has a
highly sophisticated and stylish
modern appearance.

Bottom right
Television (model 24), Pye, 1965
During the 1960s Robin's furniture
designs became increasingly
minimal and understated, a trend
reflected by this television.

Lucienne Day: Heal Fabrics, 1952

The overwhelming success of Calyx, and in particular the American Institute of Decorators Award, convinced the initially doubtful Tom Worthington, director of Heal's Wholesale and Export, that Lucienne's fresh and fearless approach to pattern design was the way forward for Heal's. "At first he knew very little about modern art," she recalls, "but he was open-minded and receptive, and we developed a good rapport." [25] From this date, although never formally under contract, Lucienne produced up to six designs a year for Heal's, and on a professional basis became integrally linked with the company's identity in the public mind. Throughout the 1950s she was promoted as their flagship designer, culminating in a prestigious solo exhibition at the store in 1958.

In the aftermath of the Festival of Britain, the immediate task was to capitalize on the success of Calyx by putting more patterns into production of a similar style. Because the scale of Calyx was unusually large, however, Tom Worthington specifically requested some patterns with smaller repeats suitable for houses and apartments of a more modest size. Also, to balance the range, other fabrics were needed with a paler background, to cater for customers who preferred a lighter overall effect. "I think the answer for small windows lies, not so much in scaling down every pattern to an accepted norm, as in getting away from formal boxiness and traditional pattern repeat plans," said Lucienne.[26] Flotilla (1952), with its suggestion of brightly coloured buoys, and its textural painterly background evoking the choppy sea, was her first attempt to fulfill these requirements.[27] Rig (1952), with its hint of portholes and taut stretched rigging, also had a loosely nautical theme. However, it should be stressed that Lucienne's approach to pattern-making was lateral rather than literal, and often a title, with its specific associations, would only emerge on completion of a design. Strata (1952), for example, had nothing to do with geological rock formations; the name was simply chosen because the design was structured in clear layers.

For the motifs in Strata, Lucienne drew on a similar vocabulary to that of Stella and Provence, two of her Festival wallpapers from the previous year. Over the years she developed a pool of imagery, consisting of her own personal family of leitmotifs. When creating a new pattern, she might draw upon motifs from this reservoir, but use them in a different context or combine them with new elements, so that the results, although sometimes self-referential, were always fresh. This recycling and reworking of familiar imagery was a key factor in establishing her instantly recognizable version of the "Contemporary" style. Conversely, some of her designs had no parallels, and emerged as complete one-offs. This was the case with Small Hours (1952), with its suggestion of surrealism and the world of dreams, and its imagery of nocturnal creatures including owls, spiders and moths. Small Hours was unusually complex and multilayered. As well as reaffirming her interest in nature, it reflected her awareness of the work of contemporary British sculptors such as Reg Butler, Eduardo Paolozzi and Lynn Chadwick.

Lucienne was a perfectionist and did not like her designs to go into production unless she felt she had got them absolutely right. However, after the Festival, her work was suddenly in such demand, and she was under such pressure from so many clients, that one design for Heal's went into production that she would later regret. This was Allegro (1952). With hindsight she felt that the ribbon of colour running between the kitelike strings of triangular motifs was too dominant and gave the pattern an unbalanced effect. Yet the perceived failings of one pattern provide useful pointers by which the success of others may be gauged. Miscellany (1952), a screen-printed rayon designed the same year for British Celanese, offers an illuminating contrast. Like Allegro it consists of strings of linear motifs, here arranged vertically rather than horizontally and complemented by circles of colour rather than stripes. While equally dynamic, Miscellany achieved a sense of balance and control that Allegro lacked.

Lucienne Day: British Celanese, Edinburgh Weavers, Liberty and Mölnlycke, 1952–4

Although Lucienne preferred cotton and linen, during the early 1950s she was prepared to experiment with some of the cheaper synthetic fibres coming on to the market in an attempt to reach consumers from lower-income brackets. "Lucienne is working now to get her designs into more low-cost fabrics, particularly for those adventurous young people who are furnishing new homes and must do it on a shoestring," noted Marilyn Hoffman in 1952.[28] The initiative that Hoffman referred to was a commission from British Celanese for six furnishing fabrics, produced in lightweight acetate rayon taffeta and Travacel slub rayon chintz. Fired by the prospect of introducing "Contemporary" design to a wider audience, Lucienne created an exceptionally exciting and dynamic group of patterns for British Celanese, which stand out as a high point in her early career. In addition to Miscellany, the first batch included a quartic abstract pattern called Quadrille (1952), and Palisade (1952), composed of rows of spindly seed pods and flowers. The second series of Celanese designs, launched in 1953, included Climbing Trees, suggesting thrusting plant forms, and Travelogue. The latter was inspired by a long bus journey from Norway to Sweden. Of all the Celanese patterns, the most joyful and dynamic was Perpetua (1953), directly inspired by the mobiles of Alexander Calder and, even more so than Calyx, embodying the vigour and energy of plant life. The collection, marketed by Sanderson, was commercially successful and critically acclaimed. "These patterns are not stepping stones bridging the gulf between the historical and the contemporary, nor half-way houses between the traditional and the experimental. They are boldly original and advanced," enthused Paul Reilly in *Design* magazine.[29] By 1952 Lucienne was so busy that she took on an assistant, Colleen Farr (who later became a successful textile designer in her own right and head of Textiles at the Central School), to help prepare her finished drawings.

Her third major British client during the early 1950s was Edinburgh Weavers, the company that, through Alastair Morton, had helped her to get a foothold in the furnishing trade. In 1952 she created four new designs for Edinburgh Weavers, Acres, Foreshore, Fall and Cocktail.[30] Each pattern was quite different. Prompted by the designer's recent trip to America, the starting point for Acres was an aerial view of fields as seen from a plane;

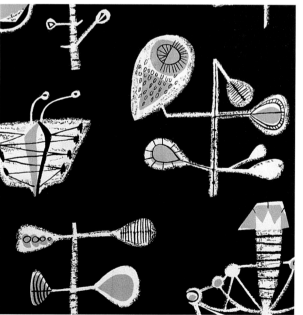

Top left
Flotilla, Heal's, 1952
The motifs in this furnishing fabric suggest buoys floating on the sea. It was produced as a follow-up to Calyx, but designed on a smaller scale.

Top right
Lucienne and Robin Day, 1952
This photograph shows the Days in their original studio at Motcombe Street shortly before they moved to Cheyne Walk.

Bottom left
Rig, Heal's, 1952
Like Flotilla, this design has a nautical title. Stringing motifs also appear in Robin's work at this date, such as his sculpture for the Rayon Design Centre, 1949 (see page 21).

Bottom right
Small Hours, Heal's, 1952
The title refers to nocturnal creatures such as moths, owls and spiders, all of which are depicted in this unusual design.

Right
**Climbing Trees, British
Celanese, 1953**
One of a range of six screen-
printed acetate rayon taffeta
furnishing fabrics designed by
Lucienne for British Celanese
during 1952–3, four of which
are illustrated here.

Below
**Palisade, British Celanese,
1952**
The spidery linear style that
characterized Lucienne's work
during the early 1950s reached
its apogee in her designs for
British Celanese.

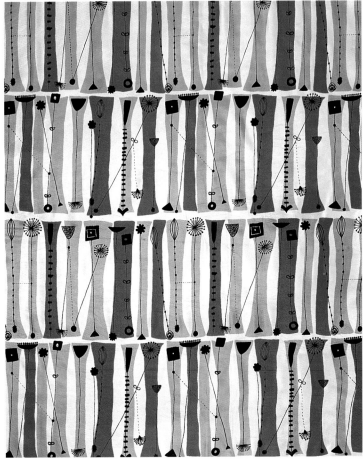

Foreshore suggested boat forms; Fall depicted the skeletal forms
of leaves, viewed as if under a microscope, and drawn in outline
with a fine-nibbed pen; and Cocktail was a small-scale abstract.
These fabrics demonstrate the expert way in which, without
diluting her identity, Lucienne adapted her work to suit the needs
of different clients; and their confident modernity shows how far
she had progressed since Elysian and Florimel five years earlier.

By 1953 the significance of Lucienne's breakthroughs in
pattern design was widely appreciated, and she was rightly
credited with introducing a new creative freedom into British
textile design. The extent of her renown was evinced by the
number of clients seeking to work with her. Even Hille, which
did not usually upholster their furniture with patterned fabrics,
asked her to produce a printed textile, Eclipse (1953), for use
on Robin's new Telechair.[31] Lucienne also began to receive
commissions from foreign companies, an indication of her
growing international influence. A trip to Scandinavia in 1952
resulted in two commissions, one from a Norwegian wallpaper
firm called Vallo Tapetfabrik,[32] and another from a leading
Swedish textile company, Mölnlycke. The four furnishing fabrics
she designed for Mölnlycke, one of which became a best-seller,
combined stylized botanical plant motifs with bold blocks and
stripes of colour. Designed to complement the simplicity and
restraint of contemporary Swedish interiors, they were more
consciously architectural than her designs for the British market.

While respecting Lucienne's desire to remain independent,
Tom Worthington became increasingly concerned about her
working for Heal's competitors. The issue came to a head after
Lucienne was approached by Liberty, asking her to design a
linen dress fabric to celebrate the Coronation in 1953. The
resulting pattern, Tudor Rose (also known as Coronation Rose),
led to a request from Arthur Stewart of Liberty for a furnishing
fabric: this elicited a screen-printed linen, Fritillary (1954), a
striking composition based on butterflies. Subsequently, Tom
Worthington came to an arrangement with Liberty, whereby
Heal's agreed not to commission designs from Liberty's designer,
Robert Stewart, as long as Liberty stopped working with
Lucienne. From this date onward, Lucienne's clients were in
complementary areas of manufacturing, notably dress fabrics,
wallpapers, carpets, ceramics, table linen and bedding.[33]

Lucienne Day: Heal Fabrics, 1953–6

Heal's astuteness in commissioning new work from Lucienne
on an annual basis, and of promoting her as a star designer by
printing her signature on the selvedge of their fabrics, proved
to be fully justified. Each year her work went from strength to
strength, and the more designs that went into production, the
more solid the relationship between designer and client became.
Lucienne was given an unusual degree of freedom, and the
choice of subject matter, colour and treatment were entirely her
own. Although her designs convey the impression of spontaneity,
each pattern developed slowly; they were never simply dashed off.
"When I start a design I literally begin with a blank piece of
paper," she explained. "Sometimes I sit in front of it for a long
time with absolutely nothing happening. It isn't an easy process.
It doesn't roll out. I have to work at it." [34] It annoyed her that

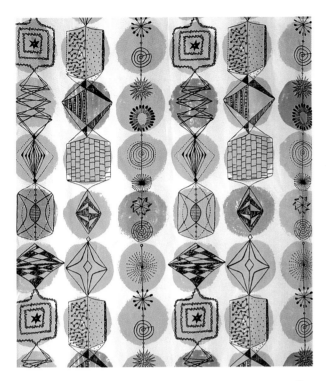

Miscellany, British Celanese, 1952
The apparently casual quality of this furnishing fabric belies the carefully controlled effects achieved by the designer, particularly the balance of colour and line.

Below
Perpetua, British Celanese, 1953
Inspired by the mobiles of Alexander Calder, this pattern embodies the youthful exuberance and dynamism of Lucienne's approach to design during the early 1950s.

Right

Acres, Edinburgh Weavers, 1952
In 1952 Lucienne flew to New York to receive her award from the American Institute of Decorators. This pattern was inspired by the aerial view of fields that she saw from the plane.

Below left

Foreshore, Edinburgh Weavers, 1952
The three furnishing fabrics illustrated on this page were all created for Edinburgh Weavers, the forward-looking Carlisle-based firm run by Alastair Morton.

Below right

Fall, Edinburgh Weavers, 1952
In this pattern skeletal leaf forms are overlaid against squares and circles of flat colour, producing an effect that is both delicate and architectural.

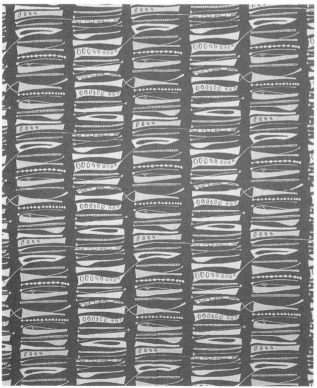

Left
Artwork for furnishing fabric, Mölnlycke, 1952
In 1952 Lucienne visited Sweden, where she was commissioned to design four textiles for a leading Swedish manufacturer, Mölnlycke. Flat triangles and squares give this design an architectural quality that appealed to the Swedish market.

Below
Fritillary, Liberty, 1954
In this furnishing fabric for Liberty the triangular shapes of the butterflies' wings are used to create an abstract geometric pattern.

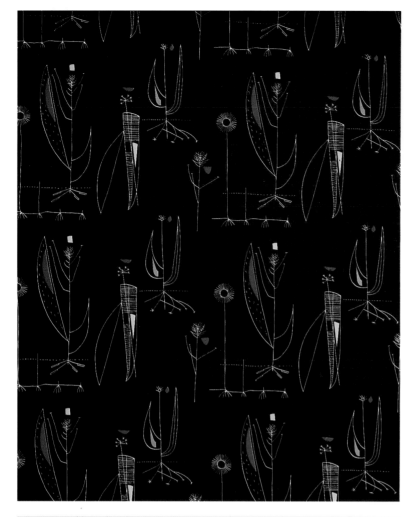

people underestimated the skill involved in designing textiles. "Someone once said to me (a graphic designer who should have known better): 'Designing a printed fabric must be very easy. You just choose a motif and then repeat it all over the cloth, don't you?' It is not enough to 'choose a motif' nor enough to 'have ideas' and be able to draw. There must also be the ability to weld the single units into a homogenous whole, so that the pattern seems to be part of the cloth rather than to be printed upon it." [35]

Lucienne's talents as a colourist were as remarkable as her skills as a pattern designer, and this was the part of the design process that she found easiest and most enjoyed. The fact that her furnishing fabrics were produced in multiple colourways – normally between four and six – gave her plenty of scope to exercise her gift, often to inspirational effect. The key to her success lay in her early grounding in the science of colour theory. "It's a fascinating subject, although complicated," she enthused. [36] Equally crucial was her fearless attitude, a reflection of her independent-minded nature and strength of character. Speaking in 1967, she recalled: "Once upon a time, orange with pink or blue with green was thought of as vulgar, and, mistakenly, they were believed to clash. In fact orange and pink (both based on red) are close together and can be the same tone, and don't clash at all... This I think is a good principle, because it can lead to all sorts of exciting colour combinations, but breaking conventions means that one has to be much more discriminating when one is choosing." [37]

Spidery and feathery plant motifs, as seen in Dandelion Clocks (1953), Flower Show (1954) and Herb Antony (1955), continued to form a significant part of Lucienne's repertoire until the mid-1950s. Dandelion Clocks was inspired by photographs of dried flowers in the house of Charles and Ray Eames; while Herb Antony, the most directly Miróesque of all Lucienne's patterns, refers to a mythical wild flower. Her preference for drawing in outline using a fine-nibbed pen has specific parallels with the graphic style of the American designer Saul Steinberg, whose work, and sense of humour, she greatly admired. Although her work became increasingly abstract as the decade progressed, she still created many patterns, such as Linear (1953) and Graphica (1953), from finely drawn lines. Graphica, inspired by the criss-crossing structure of electricity pylons, particularly appealed to the European market, [38] and subsequently led to Prisma (1954), a machine-printed wallpaper for Rasch. Other fabrics from the mid-1950s, such as Lapis (1953) and Isosceles (1955), were created from blocks or triangles of colour, sometimes with overlaid textural effects to add variety and depth. Such patterns reflected Lucienne's keen interest in contemporary architecture, flat planes of colour being frequently used on the exterior and interior of new buildings at this date.

The majority of Lucienne's mature "Contemporary" patterns were of a hybrid nature, combining linear patterns with coloured stripes or planes. Ticker Tape (1953), Springboard (1954), Trio (1954), Triad (1955), [39] Highway (1956) and Perpendicular (1956) all fall into this category. Whatever their format, whether abstract or representational, linear or planar, they all expressed the dynamism of Lucienne's lively imagination, itself a reflection of the buoyancy and optimism of the time. Energetic titles such as

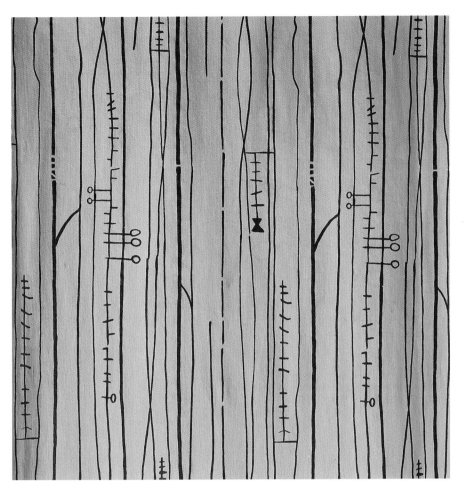

Opposite top
Herb Antony, Heal's, 1956
The use of fine white lines against a black background, combined with primary-colour highlights, emphasizes the Miróesque quality of the design.

Opposite bottom
Dandelion clocks, Heal's, 1953
Attenuated plant forms recur frequently in Lucienne's furnishing fabrics during the 1950s, particularly the feathery forms of seed heads, which suited her fine linear style.

Left
Linear, Heal's, 1953
The two furnishing fabrics on this page, along with Ticker Tape (see page 86) and Spectators (see page 54), were jointly awarded a Gran Premio at the Milan Triennale in 1954.

Below
Graphica, Heal's, 1953
Lucienne's distinctive spidery graphic style was equally well suited to stylized representational patterns (opposite) and to purely abstract designs, as here in a pattern inspired by electricity pylons.

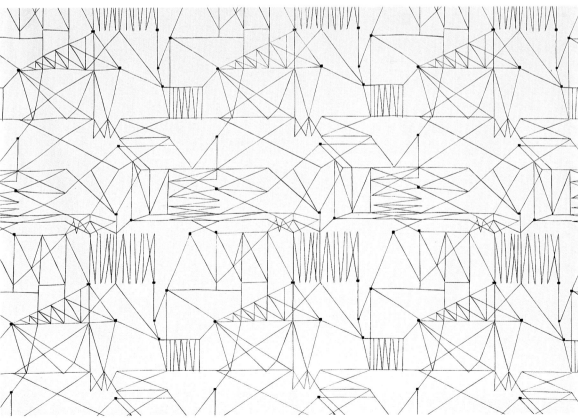

Right
Lucienne Day, 1952
The overwhelming success of Calyx cemented Lucienne's long-term alliance with Heal's, for whom she continued to design until 1974.

Far right
Lapis, Heal's, 1952
Lucienne's expert use of colour, and in particular her choice of unusual colour combinations, played a key role in the success of her designs.

Below
Ticker Tape, Heal's, 1953
The tiny hourglass shapes, dashes and knobbly lines in this pattern formed part of a repertoire of design motifs upon which Lucienne frequently drew in her work.

Opposite
Springboard, Heal's, 1954
Lucienne's designs from the early 1950s, although not over-busy, are full of energy. The title of this fabric, Springboard, hints at this dynamism.

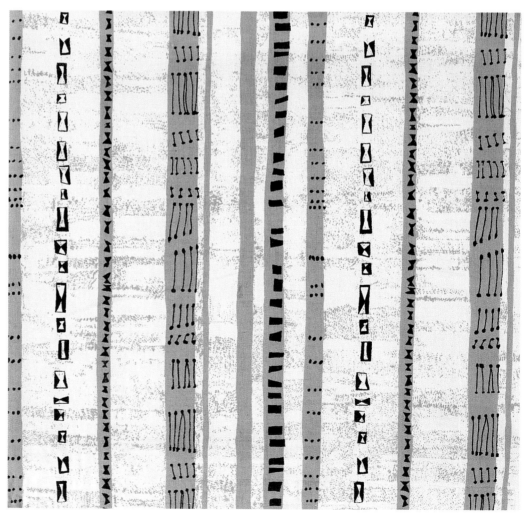

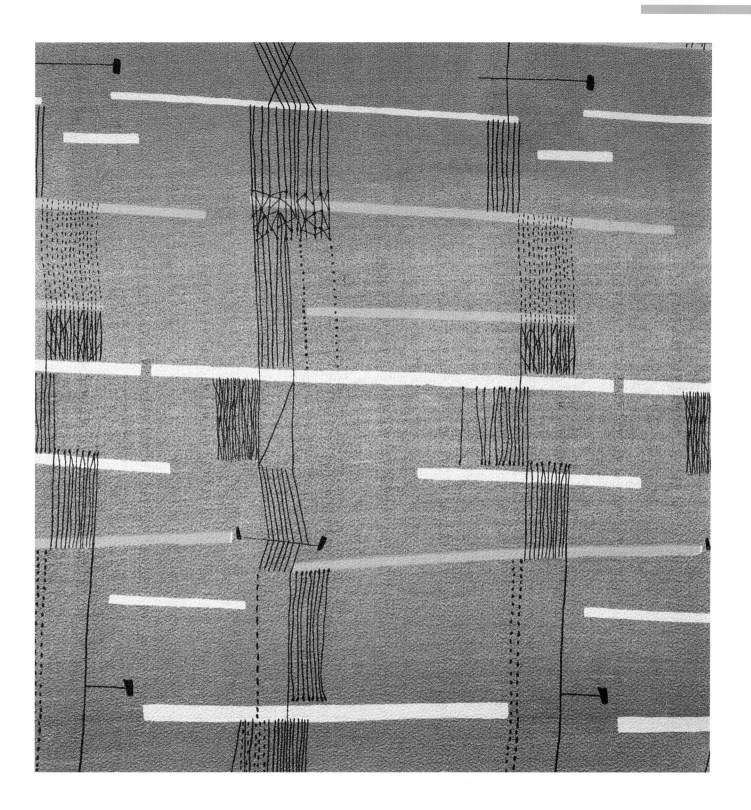

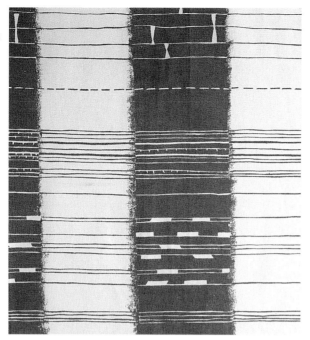

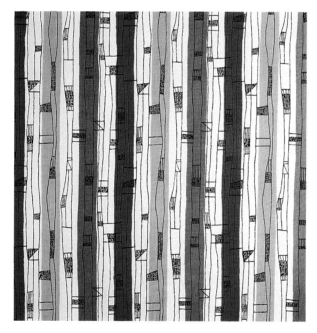

Springboard and Perpetua suggest that Lucienne herself was aware of this. Rhythm was always a crucial element of her designs, and arose out of the distribution of motifs and the way they were clustered or scattered within a pattern. Although Lucienne herself was more interested in theatre than music, the titles of several of her patterns – Trio and Triad, for example – make direct reference to music. Furthermore, these and other textiles, such as Springboard and Highway, resemble musical notation, and on an abstract level it is almost as though she were composing modern music, expressed in visual form. Related ideas were also explored in several Rasch wallpapers, notably Chelsea (1956), City (1956) and Westminster (1958). In addition, the rhythmic qualities of patterns such as Highway and Picadelli (1956), another Rasch wallpaper, suggest electrical transmissions, like surges on a television screen or pulses on a scanner.

"Laughter is never more than a couple of remarks away, and she speaks of her achievements with a buoyant freedom from care." These were the comments of a journalist from *House & Garden* in a profile of Lucienne at the time of her Heal's exhibition in May 1958. Lucienne's "Contemporary" patterns are full of *joie de vivre* and literally bubble with visual and verbal wit. The pattern that best sums up her character and aspirations is Spectators (1953), which she herself regarded as her most successful early design. Consciously indebted to Giacometti (one of her favourite artists), but replacing angst with mirth, it shows a crowd of attenuated, stylized, humanoid figures, some wearing spectacles, peering out at the viewer.[40] The abstract-comic nature of Spectators, combined with the wordplay of its title, captures the essence of her spirited approach to design.

In 1957 Lucienne wrote an article for the *Daily Mail Ideal Home Book* called "Plain or Fancy?" in which she reflected on developments in pattern design over the last decade. Her observations provide a good "on the spot" assessment of the Calyx-inspired revolution. "In the very few years since the end of the war, a new style in furnishing fabrics has emerged. Thinking back and seeing this period as a whole, I suppose the most noticeable thing about it has been the reduction in popularity of patterns based on floral motifs and the replacement of these by non-representational patterns – generally executed in clear bright colours, and inspired by the modern abstract school of painting. For a conservative country like ours, the new designs were accepted extraordinarily quickly. Probably everyone's boredom with wartime dreariness and lack of variety helped the establishment of this new and gayer trend."

Lucienne Day: Wallpapers

Although Lucienne found wallpapers more difficult to design than furnishing fabrics, because the pattern could not be softened by a drape, she built up a considerable body of work in this medium, and in both Britain and Germany she attracted commissions from some of the most progressive manufacturers of the day. The British wallpaper industry was flourishing during the 1950s, and there was a healthy interest in modern design. Trends initiated by upmarket firms such as Cole & Son and John Line at the time of the Festival of Britain were afterwards picked up and mass-produced by the hitherto conservative WPM (Wall

Left
Trio, Heal's, 1954
The rhythmical qualities of
Lucienne's early designs are
particularly evident in these two
fabrics, the titles of which both
suggest musical references.

Below
Triad, Heal's, 1955
The horizontal lines in this pattern
resemble musical bars while the
motifs suggest notes.

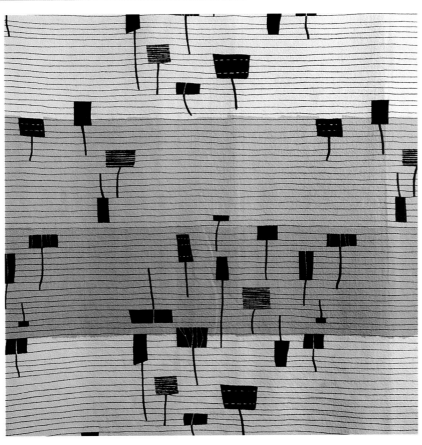

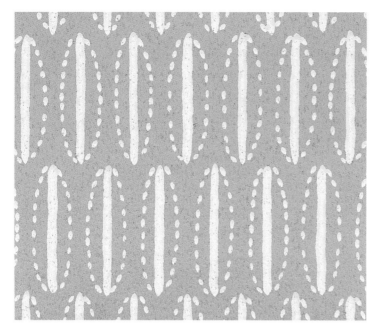

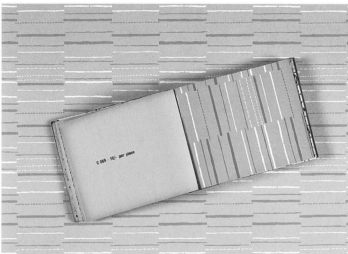

Paper Manufacturers Ltd). The WPM was a large combine whose products were marketed under the trade name Crown. Although much of its output remained ultra-traditional, the Stockport-based Lightbown Aspinall branch, under the enlightened direction of the discerning Richard Busby, pinned their flag to the mast of "Contemporary" design.

Like Hille, Busby realized that if they targeted their work at architects, this could generate significant orders and exert a knock-on effect in popularizing avant-garde design. Lucienne's early patterns formed part of *The Architects' Book of One Hundred Wallpapers*, a series of collections produced annually from 1954. One pattern was also included in the first Modus collection, which included higher-quality machine-printed patterns on a slightly larger scale. Lucienne's wallpapers were much simpler than her textiles, produced in no more than three colours and often in muted tones. Small in scale and regular in structure, they illustrated her belief that wallpaper plays a very different role in an interior from curtains and that, if it is too dramatic, it will dominate and distort a room. One pattern, dating from around 1958, was consciously architectural, composed of horizontal bands of vertical lines and broken stripes. Several wallpapers suggested letters from imaginary scripts, notably Serif (1957), which made reference to typography in its title; C-Stripe (1954), consisting of strings of tiny geometric motifs; and Yokohama Times (1956) whose criss-crossing lines evoked Japanese characters.

Lucienne's relationship with the flagship West German wallpaper company Rasch began in 1952 after she was contacted by the firm's director, Dr Emil Rasch.[41] Her first designs were created in 1953, although they did not enter production until the following year.[42] Rasch had established their reputation for progressive design in 1928, after producing a collection of textural monochrome wallpapers by designers from the Bauhaus. This minimalist collection still formed the mainstay of the firm's output after the war, but was supplemented by new decorative designs called *Künstler Tapeten*, commissioned from international artists and designers hand-picked by Emil Rasch. In addition to Lucienne, Rasch artists included Klaus Bendixen, Sigvard Bernadotte, Cuno Fischer, Margret Hildebrand, Bruno Munari and Shinkichi Tajiri. Their achievements were collectively celebrated in an exhibition called *Künstlerisches Schaffen – Industrielles Gestalten* (Artistic Creation – Industrial Design) held at the Städtisches Museum at Osnabrück from July to September 1956.

Lucienne's Rasch wallpapers, which number ten in all, spanned a six-year period from 1954 to 1960. Unlike her fabrics, their titles – apart from Prisma (1954), meaning prism, and Spindel (1956), referring to textile spindles – gave little idea of their subject. As in her ceramics for Rosenthal, London place-names were chosen by the manufacturer to emphasize English associations. As well as being marketed as part of Rasch's *Künstler Tapeten*, some of Lucienne's wallpapers were included in their *Bauhaus-Kollektion*, indicating the perceived complementarity between her designs and those of her Bauhaus forebears. Some patterns were closely related to her work for Heal's, notably Prisma, which was a variation on Graphica, and City (1956), which utilized the same kind of stringing effects as Linear. Similarly, the serrated lines of Westminster (1958) recall

Opposite top
Wallpaper (C691), WPM, 1954
This was one of the earliest designs by Lucienne for the Lightbown Aspinall branch of the Wall Paper Manufacturers (WPM). Machine-printed, they were marketed under the Crown trade name.

Opposite bottom
Wallpaper (C868 and C869), WPM, c.1958
Lucienne's Crown wallpapers were promoted through a series of pattern books called *The Architects' Book of One Hundred Wallpapers*, containing largely modern designs.

Left
C-Stripe wallpaper (C649), WPM, 1954
In her wallpapers Lucienne deliberately used a much more limited palette than in her furnishing fabrics. Many are printed in just one or two colours.

Below
Yokohama Times wallpaper (C760), WPM, c.1956
This pattern suggests Japanese characters, hence the title of the design. Unlike her Heal's textiles, however, Lucienne did not choose the names of her wallpapers for WPM or Rasch.

City wallpaper, Rasch, 1956
The wallpapers on these two pages form part of a group of ten designs created between 1954 and 1960 for the German manufacturer Rasch. This pattern has similarities to Lucienne's furnishing fabric Linear, 1953 (see page 85).

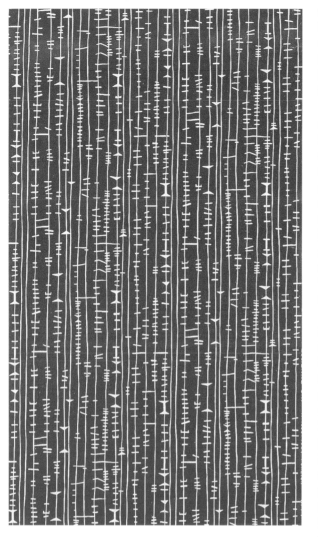

an earlier dress fabric for Argand in 1950; while the broken bands of Chelsea (1956) have visual parallels with one of her later wallpapers for Crown. Three designs, Piccadilly, Spindel and Lotura (1956), are composed of attenuated motifs overlaid with fine linear patterns. These patterns bear a loose resemblance to Spectators, although the imagery is abstract rather than humanoid.

Rasch followed the standard European arrangement of paying royalties rather than a one-off fee. This meant that Lucienne gained a clear idea of which patterns were successful, and of all her designs, the one that sold best was a wallpaper called Kleinmuster-Motiv (1958). This pattern, consisting of columns of bonelike motifs, was produced in three different versions, including one variant with enlarged shapes and another with a background of coloured stripes. Her final design, Bristol (1960), was also produced in two versions, the basic pattern resembling filaments seen under a microscope, some twisting, some running in parallel. Emil Rasch was refreshed by the "feeling for life" in Lucienne's work, and praised the "freshness, naturalness and openness" of her approach to wallpaper design.[43]

Lucienne Day: Göppinger and Rosenthal

While attending the opening of the Rasch exhibition in 1956, Lucienne was introduced to two new clients, Philip Rosenthal, director of the ceramics firm Rosenthal, and Seibert Göppinger, director of Göppinger Kaliko- und Kunstlerderwerke GmbH, which made printed plastic fabrics. After visiting Göppinger in 1957, Lucienne created five patterns for them, three of which went into production in 1958 as part of the Omnia-Kollektion 59; this also included designs by Helmut Lortz, Sibylle Kringel, Günter Hennig and Herbert Pridöhl.[44] Rather than being a woven fabric with a plastic coating, the material on which the designs were printed was a form of soft plastic sheeting. Simplicity of design was therefore essential, and feathery leaves and grasses were adopted as the subject matter for two patterns, one in outline, the other overlaid with planes of colour. The third was a mottled pattern resembling animal markings, of a type that might otherwise have formed the background to a more complex textile pattern.

While the relationship with Göppinger proved short-lived, partly because Lucienne did not feel entirely comfortable designing for this medium, Rosenthal became an important and long-standing client, and Lucienne's involvement with the company lasted for twelve years. Philip Rosenthal, the son of the founder, had only recently taken charge of the company in 1950, but had immediately initiated a programme of modernization and expansion. From 1952 onward he began to commission modern designs from leading international artists and designers, including the Finnish glass designer Tapio Wirkkala, the Danish graphic designer Bjørn Wiinblad, and the French book illustrator Raymond Peynet. The tableware that Lucienne decorated initially was the hourglass-shaped Service 2000, designed by the American industrial designers Richard Latham and Raymond Loewy, and her work, along with Rosenthal's other hand-picked design élite, was marketed separately from the firm's more traditional ranges, under the name Studio Line.

Lucienne's only previous experience of ceramics was the plates she had decorated for her RCA diploma show. However,

Left
Lucienne Day with Dr Emil Rasch (left) and Herr Rudolf, 1957
Lucienne visited Germany many times as a result of her work for Rasch at Bramsche and for Rosenthal at Selb.

Centre left
Westminster wallpaper, Rasch, 1958
In her wallpapers Lucienne often arranged her patterns into bands of short stripes, as in this design and Chelsea (bottom).

Centre right
Kleinmuster-Motiv wallpaper, Rasch, 1958
Lucienne's wallpaper designs are deliberately recessive as she believed that the patterns on wallcoverings should not dominate a room.

Bottom
Chelsea wallpaper, Rasch, 1956
This wallpaper has a decidedly textural effect, like woven fabric. To counter the liveliness of this pattern, the colours are deliberately subdued.

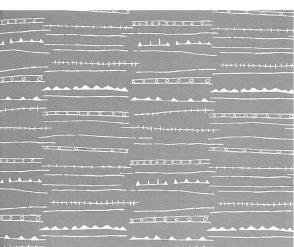

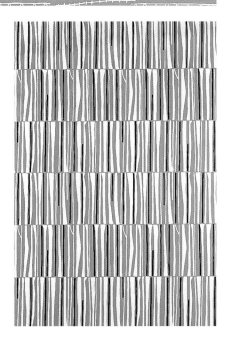

Right
**Printed plastic fabric,
Göppinger, 1958**
While working in Germany
for Rasch, Lucienne was invited
to design several patterns for
printed plastic fabrics on behalf
of a manufacturer called
Göppinger Kaliko- und
Kunstlerderwerke.

Right
**Printed plastic fabric,
Göppinger, 1958**
While working in Germany
for Rasch, Lucienne was invited
to design several patterns for
printed plastic fabrics on behalf
of a manufacturer called
Göppinger Kaliko- und
Kunstlerderwerke.

Below
**Printed plastic fabric,
Göppinger, 1958**
When designing for this
medium Lucienne deliberately
kept her patterns simple, as in
the mottled pattern (right), and
this design of black twigs and
large flat coloured leaves.

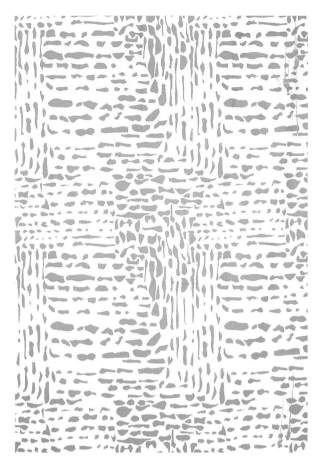

encouraged by the enthusiastic Philip Rosenthal (who had been educated in England and was a keen Anglophile), she created a large number of patterns for Rosenthal, at least fifteen of which entered production between 1957 and 1965. Her initial contract with the company was for three years, and during the first eighteen months she spent eight weeks working in the guest atelier at the factory. Once she had developed sufficient technical awareness, she undertook the bulk of her design work in her Cheyne Walk studio. Using blanks shipped over from Germany, she painted her designs directly onto the china using gouache. From these, Rosenthal would select those patterns to develop for production, and these were then used as the basis for transfer prints, mainly in coloured enamels, but sometimes etched in gold.

Bond Street (1957), her first pattern, shows how confidently Lucienne adapted to the new medium. Plates were printed with a veined leaf, derived from her earlier Edinburgh Weavers textile Fall, while vessels were decorated with a border pattern of tiny circles, suggesting leaf pores, arranged in graduated rings.[45] Her next design was a scribbly all-over abstract pattern called Columbine (1958). Printed in grey, and complemented by lids and saucers in plain pink or yellow, this proved to be her most successful pattern commercially over the years. Her most ambitious and complex design was Four Seasons, showcased at her solo exhibition at Heal's in 1958, but not manufactured until the following year. Four Seasons consisted of four colour-coded patterns, one for each season, and each season symbolized by a different stylized linear image. It was originally conceived in white on a coloured ground, but concerns about the acid-resistance of the enamels eventually prompted the decision to produce the pattern in reverse. This was the freest of all Lucienne's ceramic patterns, and although straightforward to apply on flatware, it had to be carefully adapted for use on upright vessels.

With Regent Street (1958), Lucienne adopted a different approach, but one that was equally novel. On this service, each item was decorated with a column of small geometric shapes running down the centre, printed in grey, apart from one motif picked out in red. Lucienne's early patterns for Rosenthal were all overtly experimental, and it was because she came from such a different background that she was able to tackle the medium in such a fresh and unconventional way. However, from a technical point of view, some of her designs proved difficult to execute, with the result that her later production designs became simpler in concept, with central motifs abandoned in favour of patterned bands and borders. The etched gilt border of Odyssey (1958), for example, created in response to Philip Rosenthal's request for a luxury pattern, was decorated with a quotation from Homer's epic executed in 4th-century Greek script.[46]

Lucienne Day: Thomas Somerset and Cavendish Textiles

Closely related to Lucienne's work for Rosenthal was the table linen she designed for the Belfast firm Thomas Somerset during the late 1950s. Some patterns were specifically designed to coordinate with her Rosenthal tableware, notably the Mitre tablecloth and napkins (1958), which match Regent Street, and a range of embroidered place mats that complement Four Seasons. Certain items relate tangentially to work in other media,

Left
Bond Street tableware, Rosenthal, 1957
Printed in black and pale brown, this was Lucienne's first design for Rosenthal. The leaf pattern on the plates was derived from a motif in an earlier textile, Fall (see page 82).

Below
Columbine tableware, Rosenthal, 1958
Raymond Loewy's Service 2000 was the shape on which most of Lucienne's patterns were printed. Here the linear pattern is printed in grey, while the saucers and lids are in pink and yellow.

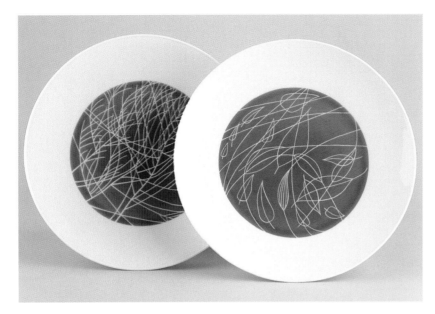

such as her Motley place mats (1957), which contain similar motifs to her fabric Talisman (1959), demonstrating her propensity for lateral thinking. The initiative behind these commissions came from Ron Crawford, Thomas Somerset's director, who had joined the company in 1953. Motivated by a desire to revive the fortunes of the declining Irish linen industry, he believed that design was the key to the achievement of this aim, and he worked closely with a London-based subsidiary, Fragonard, to market Lucienne's innovative designs.

The revitalized Thomas Somerset range was praised by Dan Johnston at the Council of Industrial Design for setting a new standard for the industry with its "bold colours and controlled patterns".[47] Crawford's masterstroke came in 1959 with the launch of three patterned glass towels by Lucienne. These designs – Black Leaf, Bouquet Garni and Too Many Cooks – won a Design Centre Award in 1960, and it was through this medium that Lucienne's work was popularized the following decade, with the release of a series of other designs. "This range of glasscloths would enliven any kitchen," commented the Design Centre judges. "The patterns are lighthearted, bold and in good colours. Designs of such quality are rare on this type of product." [48]

Although Lucienne had made a conscious shift away from the dress fabric industry after the Festival of Britain, and no longer actively sought work in this field, she continued to produce designs on occasion at the request of particular clients. In 1954 she was invited by Frank Davis from the John Lewis Partnership to design a group of six dress fabrics for Cavendish Textiles. Small in scale and tightly arranged, these patterns were designed so that the material could be cut in any direction. Some drew on motifs from her work in other fields, such as Symphony, whose leaf vein patterns were similar to Fall. Others broke completely new ground, particularly Sequence, depicting rows of tiny stylized figures, and Serenade, composed of tiny leaves and coloured stripes. Their colours, which took into account the client's suggestions about seasonal trends, were quite different from her furnishing fabrics that year.

Lucienne Day: Heal Fabrics, 1956–9

In 1954 Robin and Lucienne's daughter Paula was born, as a consequence of which her output for Heal's dipped the following year. Before too long, though, she was back in full swing, and between 1956 and 1959 she produced sixteen designs for Heal's, as well as taking on five new clients in other fields. From 1956 onward Lucienne began to explore new sources of inspiration, and her furnishing fabrics gradually took on a different character, becoming less linear and more textural. Script (1956), inspired by a 15th-century Persian manuscript in the V&A, seems to mark a turning point, and suggests that Lucienne was making a conscious attempt to take her work in new directions. In it she transcribed part of a mystical poem called *Masnawi* (1463) by Maulana Jalal Al-Din Rumi, using the lively cursive quality of the manuscript as the basis for the design.[49] The idea of patterns derived from letters, characters and symbols had already emerged as a recurrent theme in Lucienne's work and would continue for several years. It was

Opposite top

Prototypes for Four Seasons tableware, Rosenthal, 1958
This service consisted of four patterns representing the seasons. Here, winter is on the left and autumn is on the right. Originally conceived as a white line pattern against a coloured ground, when it was eventually produced the pattern was reversed, as in the examples opposite bottom.

Opposite bottom

Four Seasons tableware, Rosenthal, and table linen, Thomas Somerset, 1958–9
Each of the four patterns in this service was printed in a different colour. Spring (coffee pot) was in lime; summer (plate and cup) was in pink; autumn was in tobacco; and winter (jug and sugar bowl) was in grey-blue. Lucienne also designed a set of matching place mats, made from black linen embroidered in white.

Top left

Regent Street porcelain, Rosenthal, and Mitre table linen, Thomas Somerset, 1958
Lucienne's unconventional approach to ceramic patterns is reflected in this minimal design, printed in dark grey with one motif picked out in red. A range of coordinated table linen was also produced.

Bottom left

Odyssey and Delphi tableware, Rosenthal, 1958 and 1962
Odyssey, shown here on the cup, saucer and jug, uses a quotation from Homer's poem etched in gold in Greek script. A translation was provided on the accompanying side plate (back right). The dinner plate (back left) features a pattern called Delphi, printed in red-brown enamel on a gold border.

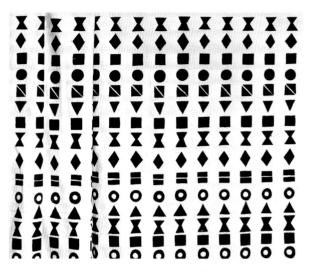

first explored through a series of wallpapers (C-Stripe, Yokohama Times and Serif), and was further developed in three patterns for Rosenthal (Odyssey, Delphi and Ilias) between 1958 and 1962. Related ideas resurfaced in her Heal's fabric Runic (1959) in which the pseudo-Viking script works as an effective rhythmic device, while the geometric motifs in Talisman (1959) suggest primitive symbols.

Another important thread running through Lucienne's work during the late 1950s and early 1960s was designs on an arboreal theme. The shift from flower and leaf patterns to tree imagery parallels the development of a more painterly textural style, and the emergence of a heightened architectural awareness in her designs. Silver Birch (1958), Tarn (1958) and Forest (1959) record the evolution from spidery to calligraphic effects. Cedar (1958), with its suggestion of rough bark, and Brushwood (1961), with its evocation of dense matted undergrowth, mark a further shift in direction, while Maquis (1959) signifies the emergence of the mature textural-architectural idiom, with strips of colour, suggesting tree trunks, juxtaposed against freely drawn thickets of shrubs.

Towards the end of the decade Lucienne's interest in the relationship between the structure and colour of her compositions and the spatial qualities of modern architecture became increasingly pronounced. Some patterns, such as Mezzanine (1958), made overt reference to buildings, while in others, such as Plantation (1958) and Linden (1960), linear motifs were juxtaposed against coloured planes in an overtly architectural way. The marriage of arboreal and tectonic themes culminated in two masterly patterns, Larch (1961) and Sequoia (1959), the latter evoking the giant redwoods of California. In these fabrics, the pattern is divided into two distinct halves, printed in contrasting colours, but the design as a whole is welded together by the bold tree silhouettes. Reflecting on these emergent trends in 1957, Lucienne commented: "In the last year or two there has been a definite move towards greater simplification and therefore more dignity; more attention to detail and to colour relationships, less colour in a single pattern, and above all for designs of a more diffuse and textural nature where the repeat is cleverly disguised, so that one is not immediately and consciously aware of it. This is largely, I think, where the skill of a good print designer lies." [50]

Lucienne Day: Carpets

By the second half of the 1950s, "Contemporary" design, once the province of a few upmarket firms, was regarded as the accepted idiom of a wide cross-section of the furnishing trade. Even carpet manufacturers were starting to produce ranges that catered to this sector of the market, and during 1956–7 Lucienne was approached by two leading firms, Tomkinsons of Kidderminster and the Salisbury-based Wilton Royal Carpets, which were both equally keen to utilize her talents. Unable to contract herself as a designer to both companies concurrently, an arrangement was struck whereby she designed patterns for Tomkinsons, while at Wilton she was employed as a colour consultant, where her role was limited to commissioning and colouring designs.

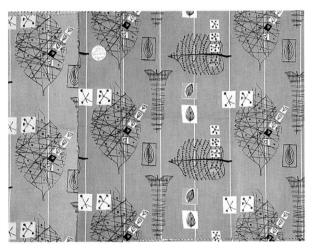

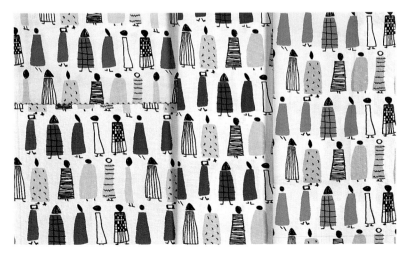

Five dress fabrics, Cavendish Textiles, c.1954
After embarking on her partnership with Heal's in 1951, Lucienne rarely designed dress fabrics. This group of patterns for Cavendish Textiles, manufactured on behalf of the John Lewis Partnership, marks a notable exception. Illustrated in various colourways, the patterns are as follows: HC 6236 (top left); HC 6237 (top right); HC 6239 (second from top); Symphony (second from bottom); Sequence (bottom). Symphony contains miniaturized motifs that relate to an earlier textile, Fall (see page 82), while Sequence bears a resemblance to Too Many Cooks (opposite centre).

Right
Script, Heal's, 1956
This design was inspired by a 15th-century Persian manuscript in the Victoria and Albert Museum. The text is from a mystical poem called *Masnawi* by Maulana Jalal Al-Din Rumi.

Opposite top left
Runic, Heal's, 1959
Whereas Script (right) is an accurate transcription of Islamic writing, Runic is merely intended to suggest ancient Scandinavian lettering. Both are used to create purely abstract rhythmic effects.

Opposite top right
Magnetic, Heal's, 1957
This roller-printed cotton furnishing fabric was produced in six colourways. Some versions were printed in two colours, as here; others used up to five different colours.

Opposite bottom left
Silver Birch, Heal's, 1958
Lucienne's designs fall naturally into families of patterns. There are similarities between Silver Birch and Tarn (opposite bottom right), for example, and Silver Birch also relates to Four Seasons (see page 96).

Opposite bottom right
Tarn, Heal's, 1958
A best-selling design, this fabric was produced in nine different colourways. The fact that it was roller-printed rather than screen-printed meant that it could be produced much more cheaply.

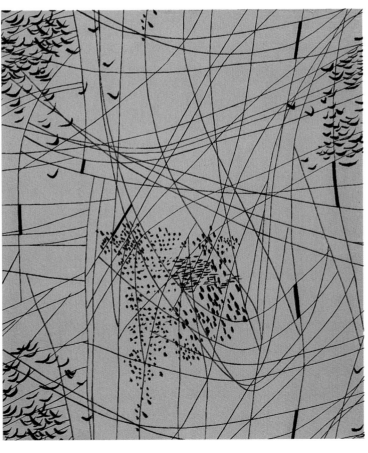

Maquis, Heal's, 1959
Maquis is a type of thicket, and this painterly design combines rough inky sketches of shrubs with strips of colour suggesting tree trunks.

Below
Plantation, Heal's, 1958
Plantation, Maquis (right) and Linden (opposite left) all make use of a similar design formula, with fine black outline motifs juxtaposed against flat planes of colour. This gives them a strongly architectural feel.

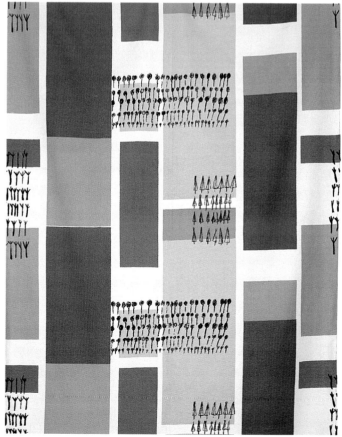

Left
Linden, Heal's, 1960
Linden is another name for the lime tree, and the pattern depicts enlarged skeletal lime leaves. Although superficially similar to the earlier fabric Fall (see page 82), Linden is designed on a much larger scale.

Below left
Sequoia, Heal's, 1959
Sequoias are the giant redwoods that grow in the forests of California. This pattern and Larch (below right) are large-scale designs intended to be hung in a long drop, which both adopt the same formula of dividing the fabric into two halves.

Below right
Larch, Heal's, 1961
This pattern marks the culmination of a series of designs on arboreal themes from 1958 onward. At this date the use of tree imagery suited Lucienne's aspiration to create simpler, bolder furnishing fabrics on an architectural scale.

Right
Lamina carpet, Wilton Royal, 1957
This best-selling pattern was designed by Philip Coombes and coloured by Lucienne, who acted as colour consultant for Wilton from 1957 onward.

Far right
Cirrus carpet, Wilton Royal, c.1958
Similar to Lamina (right) but with a more widely spaced pattern, this design was also by Philip Coombes, with colourways chosen by Lucienne.

Second from top
Furrows carpet, Tomkinsons, 1957
One of the first patterns designed by Lucienne for the Kidderminster firm of Tomkinsons, Furrows was later manufactured from 1965 by their sister company, I. & C. Steele.

Second from bottom
Tesserae carpet, Tomkinsons, 1957
This carpet, with its mosaic pattern and striking jewel-like colours, won a Design Centre Award in 1957. It was much copied subsequently within the carpet industry.

Bottom left
Forum carpet, Tomkinsons, 1959
The rectilinearity of this design presages the more geometric carpet designs that Lucienne created during the 1960s.

Bottom right
Strada, Tomkinsons, 1957
Strada is the Italian word for road, and this pattern was inspired by watching car headlights at night while on a visit to Turin.

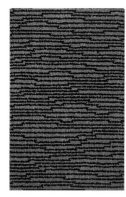
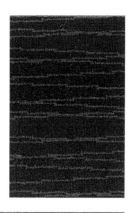

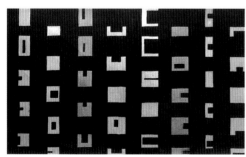
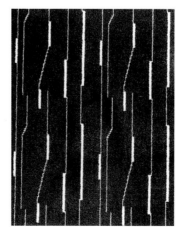

Lucienne's main contact at Wilton was their chief designer, Philip Coombes, and it was he and two other in-house designers, Norman Runacres and later Pam Golding, who created the basic patterns for which she then selected the colours. Launched at the National Carpet Show in 1958, the first range was called the Architects Collection, and initially consisted of four abstract designs, one geometric, the others linear and textural.[51] Some of these patterns bear a striking resemblance to Lucienne's own work, indicating how strong an influence she exerted over all aspects of design. Her approach to the commissioning process was clearly an active one, and a certain amount of "tidying up" seems to have gone on. For example, Lamina (1957), a disjointed linear pattern designed by Philip Coombes, was originally embellished with overlaid motifs, but to make the pattern simpler Lucienne suggested they be removed, leaving just the textural background. Her choice of colours was highly original. "I don't believe that there should be different furnishing and fashion colour ranges," she remarked in 1959. "I think I proved that last year when I used fashion colours like purple and blue in my new carpet and fabric designs."[52]

Lucienne's relationship with Tomkinsons, which specialized in Axminster carpets, slightly predated her consultancy at Wilton, and it was her work for this firm that attracted the most attention. She developed a good rapport with Michael Tomkinson, who ran the company, and the partnership was immediately fruitful, resulting in a Design Centre Award for Tesserae, a textural pattern suggesting mosaic pavements, in 1957. Tesserae was praised by the judges for "the sparkle and contemporary character of its pattern, which, on account of its scale, is admirably suited to the small-sized house. The asymmetric disposition of the pattern and its colour make this an eminently practical carpet which will not show marks or wear in general use."[53] Lucienne's skill as a carpet designer was in developing an idiom appropriate to the medium, which took into account both the constraints of the manufacturing process and the context in which the product would be used. As when designing wallpapers, she was acutely conscious of the way her carpets would interact with other furnishings, and of the potential overkill effect of large areas of pattern within a room. "In my experience the happy juxtaposition of pattern with pattern is quite difficult to achieve," she observed.[54]

Tesserae was widely copied within the industry, as were two of her other early patterns, Fandango and Strada, both dynamic, pulsating, linear designs.[55] Strada, meaning "street" in Italian, was inspired by watching the headlights of approaching cars in Turin on a recent trip to Italy, although the pattern also resembles dislocated stitching on a sewing machine. Pennant (1958), a close-knit design of stylized flags, was the last of her irregular patterns, and the emergent trend as the decade progressed was towards increasingly rectilinear designs. Patterns such as Crossways (1957), Furrows (1958) and Forum (1958) explored the interrelationship between rhythm, geometry and colour, and showed Lucienne forging an aesthetic that complemented modern buildings. Furrows was particularly successful commercially, and set the design agenda in carpets for the following decade.

Lucienne Day: Heal's Exhibition, 1958

Lucienne's status as Britain's premier pattern designer, and a figure of significant international renown, was confirmed by her prestigious solo exhibition *Lucienne Day – Designs at Home and Abroad*, held in the Mansard Gallery on the fourth floor of Heal's from 14 May to 7 June 1958. Displayed in a cool, stylish, rectilinear arrangement, the exhibition brought together examples of her work in wallpapers, furnishing fabrics and ceramics. Highlighting the consistency and complementarity of her aesthetic in different media, the exhibition drew attention to the quality and variety of her pattern-making skills in all areas.

By this date Lucienne's designs completely dominated the output of Heal Fabrics, and the launch of each new collection was treated as a media event. Their popularity with consumers meant that, instead of being produced manually, they were manufactured in large quantities by means of roller-printing and mechanised screen-printing.[56] In 1959 Lucienne told the German magazine *Gebrauchsgraphik* that by collaborating with industrial manufacturers she hoped that "the greatest possible number of people might share in the efforts towards good, modern design". By the end of the decade, with her work being mass-produced by fifteen manufacturers, she had more than achieved her ambition, and had every reason to feel proud.

Robin and Lucienne Day: European Exhibitions

Whenever the Days were interviewed, journalists remarked on how well suited they were to each other. "There is a continual exchange of artistic ideas between them," observed Marilyn Hoffman,[57] and Judy Fallon noted that "ideas are tossed from one to the other with lightning speed".[58] Frankness, always an essential part of their creative dialogue, was something the Days themselves frequently mentioned. Robin commented in 1968: "We have always had similar tastes and a reasonably sympathetic attitude towards each other's approach, although often there are individual things about each other's work we don't like. Although we work for different clients on different projects, it can be very useful to have an absolutely honest opinion without any reservations at all from someone who feels they can say just what they think." [59]

Although Robin and Lucienne practised separately during the 1950s, on a creative and psychological level they were instinctively in tandem. "I suppose each of us must have influenced the other," admitted Lucienne in 1968,[60] although sometimes it was hard for them to see this simply because they were so close. To outsiders, the visual complementarity between their work is striking, and during the 1950s it was apparent at every stage. Thus the spindly steel legs of Robin's Festival Hall furniture were paralleled by the spidery lines in Lucienne's early textiles. Later they both adopted planar rather than linear forms, and responded to developing trends in contemporary architecture, such as the move from the expressive organic shapes of the Festival of Britain to the increasingly rectilinear structures of buildings later in the decade.

The creative harmony between them was noticeable whenever their work was displayed side by side, and was

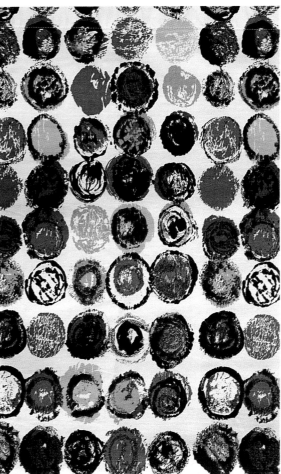

Above
Heal's exhibition, May 1958
The exhibition was called *Lucienne Day – Designs at Home and Abroad*, and it included examples of her work in ceramics, wallpapers and textiles.

Left
Ducatoon, Heal's, 1959
This roller-printed furnishing fabric, produced in five different colourways, was another high-volume seller. By the end of the decade Lucienne had created thirty-five designs for Heal Fabrics, and her work dominated the firm's catalogue.

Top
Robin and Lucienne Day, c.1963
Although the Days practised
independently, they worked side
by side in their studio, and there
are many visual correspondences
between each other's work.

Above
**British Design Today exhibition,
Frankfurt, 1958**
In this exhibition, designed by
Robin, the Days' work was
juxtaposed. Here, Robin's Interplan
storage unit, Slatted bench, High,
Wide and Handsome chair and
Pye television are shown alongside
Lucienne's Kleinmuster-Motiv
wallpaper for Rasch and her Bond
Street porcelain for Rosenthal.

particularly evident in three foreign exhibitions designed by
Robin at intervals during the course of the decade. The first,
called *Design from Britain*, was organized by the Society of
Industrial Artists (SIA), and toured to three venues in Norway –
Oslo, Bergen and Stavanger – in 1952.[61] A wide-ranging
exhibition containing 300 objects, it featured packaging, posters
and accessories, as well as furniture, furnishings, ceramics and
glass. Although it contained work by many SIA members, the
display served to highlight the "special relationship" between
Robin's 661 and 658 chairs and Lucienne's early Edinburgh
Weavers and Heal's textiles.

For the Milan Triennale in 1954 Robin again received a
personal invitation to mount a display, although this time he
shared a stand with Ernest Race. Lucienne's textiles formed a
key element of Robin's room setting, along with lighting by
John Reid and ceramics by Hans Coper and Lucie Rie. His
furniture included the Reclining chair, the Q Stak, the 675 chair,
and the Interplan range, several of which were awarded Gold
and Silver Medals. A frieze of photographs showed individual
chairs in profile, drawing attention to the spareness and
refinement of their structure. This, in turn, highlighted their
correspondence with Lucienne's fabrics, four of which –
Graphica, Linear, Ticker Tape and Spectators – won the
highest honour, a Gran Premio award. The work of each
provided the perfect foil for the other, making them both look
doubly accomplished and assured.

In 1958 Robin was invited to design an exhibition in
Germany, shown at the Göppinger Galerie in Frankfurt, called
British Design Today, for which he and Lucienne made the
selection. The initiative arose out of Lucienne's collaboration with
the manufacturer who ran the gallery, and was supported by the
Council of Industrial Design. As well as showcasing a substantial
group of work by Robin and Lucienne, the exhibition featured
lighting by Rotaflex, furniture by Race and Kandya, and fabrics
by Sanderson.[62] From his own work, Robin chose, among
others, the Executive desk, Gatwick seating, a Single
Convertible, and a Pye television. Lucienne's designs, in addition
to her Göppinger fabrics, included her Plantation and Magnetic
textiles, Kleinmotiv wallpaper, Strada carpet, and Bond Street
tableware. The display emphasized the Days' professionalism,
and showed the couple at the height of their powers. It testified
to their efforts to expand the scope of their work over the last
few years, Robin by tackling a full range of furniture types
and through his new venture into product design, and Lucienne
through the range of different media she had conquered, and
the tremendous visual diversity of her patterns.

In 1959 Robin was appointed a Royal Designer for
Industry, and three years later, he was joined by Lucienne,
making them the only married couple to share the honour.
Summing up their achievements in 1960, Gillian Naylor wrote:
"Robin and Lucienne Day, each working in their own particular
spheres, seem to be able to strike the highest common
denominator of design. They, however, have no explanations
for their success, nor do they work to a formula. But they try
never to accept compromise, and their aim has always been
to attempt to find the best solution to any design problem."[63]

Left
Alpha tables, 1959
By the end of the 1950s Robin's furniture was becoming increasingly geometric in form, a trend that continued the following decade.

Below left
Chequers, Heal's, 1954
During the first half of the 1950s Lucienne's textiles were characterized by fine linear patterns such as this. At this date her aesthetic complemented the spindly steel rod legs of Robin's early furniture.

Below right
Quarto, Heal's, 1960
By the end of the decade Lucienne's patterns were becoming larger in scale and more architectural in quality, a trend that paralleled the direction in which Robin's furniture was also moving.

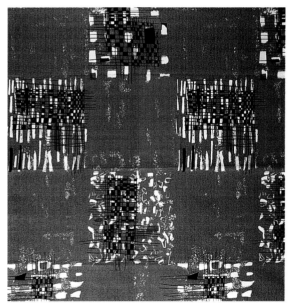

CHAPTER FIVE

1960-69

THE SIXTIES: GEOMETRIC PATTERNS AND ARCHITECTURAL FORMS

Robin Day: Foyer Seating

Robin's attitude to design has remained remarkably consistent over the years, but is perhaps best summed up in an article he wrote for the Design and Industries Association in 1964: "Designers have a responsibility which is all too often pushed aside by commercial expediency. This is to produce new designs to be better than previous ones – better in every way and with regard to the continually accelerating developments of materials and technology. In our profession a tremendous amount of time and energy goes into making changes merely to be different though not necessarily better, and into striving for a merely stylistic originality." [1]

Reflecting on trends in furniture design at the start of the 1960s, he observed: "There is a clearer division evolving between the advocates of more and more simple and austere designs, and those who prefer what one might call sinuous and sculptural shapes. There seems to me to be a psychological need for calmness at the moment, rather than for design which is too eventful and busy." [2] These observations pinpoint the differences between Robin's furniture of the 1950s and that of the 1960s, as he moved away from the exuberant curvilinear shapes of the early post-war period to a more calm and disciplined mode of expression characterized by cool restraint. "When we began, we were producing very spikey, over-vivacious, vital stuff. Designers were so excited by the new idiom that they had to try it out," he reflected in 1961. "Now we have reached a period where we know what we can do, and a sort of 'refinement' has crept in. As a designer, I am anxious to create homes that are a refuge from the tearing pace of modern life. I want rooms of calmness, space and simplicity." [3]

The people who perhaps most appreciated the refinement of Robin's furniture were architects, and a key factor in securing orders was to ensure that architects were given the opportunity to view his work in appropriately serene surroundings. Hille's new showroom at 41 Albemarle Street, which opened in January 1963, created the perfect environment, and was guaranteed to produce a favourable impression. Housed in a new building designed by Peter Moro, the light, spacious, open-plan interiors were, in the words of Leslie Julius, "a complete reflection of the Hille philosophy". The showroom interiors were designed by Robin with characteristic cool panache. His elegant, airy spiral staircase, running up through the core of the building from the basement to the second floor, was an inspired intervention. Fabricated by Hille's metals and cabinet-making divisions, it was constructed from a central steel post supporting radiating teak treads, encircled by a ring of steel tension wires. As with his

Greetings for Christmas and the New Year from Hille of London

Opposite
Polypropylene chairs, 1963 and 1967
The Polypropylene side chair was introduced in 1963 and the armchair followed four years later. They are shown here in two of their original colours: charcoal and flame red. Dark blue was introduced in 1968 and white in 1970.

Left
Hille Christmas card, 1960s
Although Hille set up their own graphic design unit in the 1960s, Robin continued to design greetings cards and invitation cards for the company at intervals over the next two decades.

Robin designed this staircase
for Hille's new showrooms at
41 Albemarle Street, which
opened in January 1963. The
teak treads were supported by
steel tension wires.

furniture, the structure of the staircase was clearly articulated, and its floating, transparent quality was a direct expression of the strength of metal.

The ground-floor reception area of the showroom, with its large floor-to-ceiling windows, provided a handsome setting for existing foyer seating such as Gatwick (1958), and new ranges such as Club (1962) and Forum (1964). Produced as armchairs and settees with coordinated low tables, these two ranges were generously proportioned, comfortable and luxurious, without being ostentatious. With their rectilinear forms and leather upholstery, both designs were strongly architectural with an overtly masculine character, although they were equally adaptable to a domestic environment. The Club chair, suggesting associations with gentlemen's clubs, gave a modern edge to a traditional genre, and its buttoned upholstery highlighted the squareness of the frame.[4] Forum, with its exposed comb-jointed structure made of afrormosia (a wood similar to teak), was also quietly iconoclastic; through this design, Robin challenged the notion that the back of an easy chair should be upholstered as well as the front. Contemporary advertisements highlighted the fact that Forum "reverses the convention of hiding the frame within the upholstery by exposing the beautifully proportioned enclosing structure into which the large cushions are slipped". Robin had already applied this principle to carcass furniture, but with Forum he took the idea one step further. The accompanying Forum table (1966) was equally confident and unusual, with its suspended plate-glass top and black PVC-covered magazine shelf.

Robin Day: Office and Restaurant Furniture

Although Hille were faced with mounting competition from specialist firms, office furniture remained an important part of their range throughout the 1960s, and during the early years of the decade, Robin designed two new models, targeted at different sectors of the business world. The Director range (1962–3), designed for senior executives, was pitched at the upper end of the market. Hand-crafted by Hille's most skilled cabinet-makers using sumptuous Rio rosewood veneers, the full collection consisted of handsome leather-topped desks with chunky stainless steel frames, along with matching tables and sleek four-door storage cabinets. These cabinets looked so sophisticated that they could easily be mistaken for sideboards, except that they were kitted out with accessories such as fittings for suspended files.

At the other end of the spectrum was the Interplan office furniture range (1962), which included a typist's chair with adjustable-height seat mechanism and ergonomically designed seat back, and a modestly sized knock-down desk and table with discreet recessed drawers. Made from afrormosia with black vinyl-covered tops, the desks were described by Hille catalogue as "sturdy, stable, handsome and well-proportioned", and were promoted from 1963 onward as a low-cost desking solution for the mass market through a series of advertisements called "Hille by the hundred".[5] In 1959 Hille entered into partnership with a firm called Acorn Products, which manufactured a range of coordinated desk and office accessories on their behalf. Specifically designed by Robin to complement his office furniture,

Desk accessories, 1959–63
These aluminium desk accessories,
manufactured by Acorn Products
on behalf of Hille, were designed
by Robin to complement his office
furniture. Subsequently, coat
stands, waste-paper bins and
pedestal ashtrays were added to
the range.

items included filing trays, blotters, pen stands and letter racks, made of steel and anodized aluminium with a black or silver finish. Larger items such as coat stands, pedestal ashtrays and waste-paper bins also formed part of this stylish but functional range.

Boat-shaped boardroom tables were another area of office furniture where Hille's craftsmanship was in demand. Initially custom-designed on a one-off basis for individual clients, from 1962 they were made in graduated sizes using a standardized template devised by Robin, which rationalized the manufacturing process, saving both money and time. In 1964 he developed a similar formula for the rectangular tables that superseded the earlier London range. Using this system, clients could select from a wide range of lengths and widths, and a choice of legs and veneers. The original London table (1959), with its deep, solid top, had proved popular as a dining table. Subsequently, the Audley table (1965) served equally well for executive meetings or for dining in the home. Produced in circular and oval versions, the table top was richly veneered with figured Santos or Rio rosewood in radiating or striped patterns, while the storage unit could be adapted for storing files or housing drinks. Flexibility of application had been a distinctive feature of Robin's designs of the 1950s, and was maintained as a principle in many of his later designs. Even an executive easy chair such as Leo (1965) was promoted for both home and office use.[6]

In addition to office furniture, the main area of the contract market targeted by Hille from the mid-1960s onward was the restaurant trade. The Polypropylene chair (1963) proved ideal for café seating, but in addition there was a growing need for heavy-duty tables with tough plastic laminate tops. The circular pedestal BT table, the demountable Disque table, the rectangular Carlton table, and the square 339 table were all designed to cater to this sector of the market around 1966. Later, towards the end of the decade, they were succeeded by the standardized, circular, square and rectangular P280, P281 and P282 pedestal range. Although this type of furniture offered limited creative scope for the designer, Robin recognized its commercial significance, and tackled it in a characteristically pragmatic, professional and effective way.

Robin Day: Domestic Furniture

Hille remained actively committed to making domestic furniture until around 1965, when commercial emphasis shifted to high-volume production for the contract market. In the domestic field the most significant area of production during the early 1960s was dining furniture, although apart from a small number of purpose-designed suites, they mainly promoted flexible groupings of coordinated items from existing standard ranges. For marketing purposes, these composite ranges were sometimes given specific titles. Hence the Welbeck Group consisted of the Status table, 661C chairs and an SKP or SLP sideboard; and the Wigmore Group comprised the 690 table, Albany chairs and Interplan Unit M storage units. Danish furniture was still very popular at this time, and its influence is apparent in several suites illustrated in Hille's Dining Groups catalogue in 1962. Among these were the Curzon Group (1960), made of oiled teak, and the Marson Group (1961), which had stretched

Top left
Director desk, 1962
This luxury desk veneered in Rio rosewood was intended for senior executives. It contrasts with the low-budget Interplan desk (centre left).

Top right
Leo armchair, 1965
During the 1960s Robin's furniture was still promoted as being suitable for both domestic and commercial use, although by this date the contract market was becoming increasingly important.

Centre left
Interplan desk, 1962
Although designed for the mass market, this knock-down desk has a handsome appearance with its black vinyl top and afrormosia-veneered drawers.

Centre right
Audley storage unit, 1966
Designed to complement the Audley table (bottom left), this long low four-door storage unit was veneered with Santos or Rio rosewood.

Bottom
Nimbus chairs, 1965, and Audley table, 1966
The Audley table, with its eye-catching striped or radiating rosewood veneer, served equally well as a meeting table in an executive office or as a dining table.

leather upholstery, with frames of rosewood or teak. Gradually, as the decade progressed, turned legs, curved arms and rounded table tops diminished in favour of less mannered forms. Domestic furniture also became heavier and squarer, a trend presaged by the cruciform base of the pedestal Curzon table, which reached its apotheosis in the Studio Group (1964).[7]

The Studio Group, designed for open-plan living room-dining rooms, was a wide-ranging coordinated collection, including accessories such as trolleys and coffee tables as well as basics such as storage cabinets, dining furniture and easy chairs. Launched at the International Furniture Show in 1965, it appears to have been produced in response to the success of the first Habitat store, which had opened in London in May 1964, showcasing the demountable pine Summa system by Conran Furniture. The Studio Group was Hille's attempt to appeal to a more youthful clientele through a pick-and-mix collection, and was characterized by greater informality than their standard ranges. Made of afrormosia with teak veneers, some pieces, such as the coffee table, adopted slab construction, and according to Hille's publicity, the range as a whole had "a simple direct design character suitable to the timbers in which it is made". Its chunky appearance - which Robin described as the "peasanty primitive" look[8] – and the ambitious scope of the items within the range, marked a departure for Hille, albeit a short-lived one. "Chair design seems to be moving in two sharply divergent directions," wrote Elizabeth Good in the *Sunday Times* on 19 May 1963. "One signpost points back to the hand-made tradition of wood, solid and square, with rustic rush seats; the other forward to streamlining in metal and man-made fibres, adapted to mass production." Although Robin dabbled with the "peasanty" look in the Studio Group and his furniture for Churchill College, Cambridge (1963–5), in the longer term he opted to move in the other direction, towards plastics and mass production.

Robin Day: Seating

Although Robin had clearly identifiable preferences in terms of materials and styles, his work for Hille never became formulaic. "My interest in the design of furniture is insatiable," he wrote in 1964. "It has so many fascinating problems and possibilities of construction and of exploiting materials and techniques, as well as important human considerations, both social and anatomical." [9] For Robin, a key part of the design process was practical experimentation, as he explained in 1968. "I scratch and scribble a lot when I am starting something new, but I am always very keen to work in three dimensions as soon as I possibly can. I have a small workshop and I start by making a quarter-scale model, and then continue with a full-size model. When the first prototype is made, I bring it up here, use it and live with it for a time. Often you find weaknesses – economic, structural, aesthetic or whatever – and unless you can modify it, you have to scrap it." [10]

Seating continued to dominate his output during the 1960s, and in stylistic terms his work falls into two main categories, rectilinear and curvilinear forms. The general-purpose Plan chair (1962), with its square seat and right-angled metal frame, provides an extreme example of the former, along with the

afrormosia-framed Mark II version of the Convertible bed-settee (1962). Square-section tubular steel continued to provide the standard framework for much of his furniture, and where wood was used it became increasingly robust and blocklike, as in the Brutus chair (1969). A modular seating system called the Plus Group (1965) typifies this aesthetic. Designed along similar lines to the Form Group, but with an African walnut or pine frame, it differed from the earlier range in that, as well as banks of seating, it included stand-alone tables and armchairs. Like the Forum chair, the Plus Group had prominent combed joints which, as well as emphasizing the rectilinearity of the overall structure, demonstrated revealed construction and provided extra strength.

Set against these blocky forms was a group of chairs distinguished by their generous curves. One of the most refined was the 41 dining chair (1962), with its sculptural wooden U-shaped back and armrest and straight tubular steel legs. Another was the Scimitar chair (1962), which became almost as widespread in its application as its all-purpose predecessor, the Stamford chair. The evocative name Scimitar was chosen because of the sweeping wrap-around back, made of moulded plywood, padded and upholstered, and raised several inches above the seat. Among its spin-offs was the robust Captain's dining chair (1964), made of makore or afrormosia, with turned legs and a cross-braced underframe. The capacious Concourse chair (1965), developed as part of a second generation of seating for Gatwick Airport, was another direct descendant, similar in structure but with a circular section tubular steel frame. While the original Gatwick seating (1958) had been limited to rectilinear formations, the Concourse chair, although equally substantial and architectural, could be placed in freer arrangements, and grouped informally around tables.

Whereas many of Robin's designs formed natural clusters, others arose as one-offs. This was the case with the demountable Axis chair, with its distinctive cast-aluminium starfish-shaped side frame. Produced on Hille's behalf by the British Aluminium Company using low-pressure die-casting techniques, the aluminium frame had an extremely fine finish, and provided structural support for the rosewood- or teak-veneered moulded plywood seat. Back in the late 1940s two Danish designers, Peter Hvidt and Orla Mølgaard-Nielsen, had created a demountable wooden chair for Fritz Hansen called the Ax. Imported into Britain by Finmar during the early post-war period, and widely advertised in architectural magazines, this chair was a wooden precursor of Axis, while another source of inspiration may have been the cast-aluminium-framed seating designed by Charles Eames. Drawing on these sources, but adding his own experience of demountable modular seating, Robin created a chair that could be used either as single unit, or in banks of two or three, using a shared frame. Although designed with the minimum number of components, its applications were characteristically diverse, and it was produced in armchair and upholstered versions with optional table attachments. Ahead of its time when it appeared on the market, the Axis chair was one of Robin's most expressive designs, and was enthusiastically promoted in advertisements headed "Knock-down assembly – Knock-out chair".[11]

Left
P280, P281 and P282 restaurant tables, c.1969
As Hille moved increasingly into the contract market, Robin was asked to design a variety of heavy-duty dining tables to complement his Polypropylene chairs.

Below left
Delphi chairs, table and sideboard, 1968
The distinguishing feature of this range of luxury office furniture was its inverted T-shaped steel legs. Hille continued to cater to both the upper and the lower end of the market.

Below
Single Convertible Mark II, 1962
The original Single Convertible proved so successful that another variant was subsequently introduced, this time with an afrormosia frame.

Right
Plus Group, 1965
This range of modular seating was designed along similar lines to the earlier Form Group (see page 65) but reflected the prevailing fashion for solid wood and chunky forms.

Below
Studio trolley and dining group, 1964
The Studio Group was a stylish coordinated range of lounge and dining furniture made from solid afrormosia and teak. The dining chairs were distinguished by their slung PVC seats, and the sideboard had rattan cane panels on its sliding doors.

Opposite top left and right
41 chair, table and sideboard, 1962
The 41 chair was unusual in the way it combined a sculptural wooden seat back with straight tubular steel legs. The wood used in this stylish range was either rosewood, as in the chair on the left, or ash, as in the dining group on the right.

Opposite bottom left
Concourse chair, 1965
This chair formed part of a range of seating and tables designed for the newly extended Gatwick Airport.

Opposite bottom right
Interplan table and Scimitar chair, 1962
Wrap-around curved seat backs were a distinctive feature of Robin's chairs during the first half of the 1960s, as shown by the photographs on this page.

Right and centre
Axis chair, 1966
Axis, seen here also in knock-down form (centre), was the first of Robin's designs to use a cast-aluminium frame. Designed to be flexible, it could either be constructed as an individual chair or in linked groups, with either moulded plywood or upholstered seats.

Bottom
Occasional table, late 1960s
Over the years Robin made various one-off pieces of furniture for the Days' Chelsea home, including this glass-topped table mounted on a perspex cruciform base.

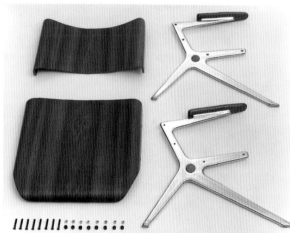

Robin also remained active in the field of auditorium seating, with new designs such as Stratford (1968), which was created for the refurbished Shakespeare Memorial Theatre in Stratford-upon-Avon and subsequently entered Hille's standard range. As during the 1950s, his most important commission of the decade originated from Peter Moro, who invited him to design the seating for the Nottingham Playhouse, completed in 1963. The challenge on this occasion was to design seats for installation in curved rows, which had a diminishing radius towards the front of the theatre. This meant that each unit had to be independent, as seats can only share arms when arranged in a straight line. Robin's solution was a one-piece moulded plywood seat back and armrest, supported on an independent steel frame, and the structure proved so effective that it, too, was offered as part of Hille's standard auditorium seating range.

Robin Day: Polypropylene Chair

Robin's most significant design of the decade was the Polypropylene chair (1963), still in production five decades later, and one of the sturdiest and best-selling chairs of all time. Polypropylene, a new type of thermoplastic, had been invented in 1954 by the Nobel prize-winning Italian scientist Giulio Natta. Four years later the British petrochemicals firm Shell acquired the rights to its manufacture, and it was as a result of being invited to judge a competition by Shell in 1960 that Robin first became aware of the remarkable properties of the material and began to realize its potential. Leslie Julius was equally enthusiastic about exploring the possible applications of polypropylene in the furniture industry, and although no one had managed to overcome the technical problems associated with its manufacture to date, he urged Robin to experiment and provided financial backing.

Light, strong, scratch-proof, heat-resistant and incredibly durable, polypropylene had many advantages over other materials commonly used in the furniture industry at that time. It was more flexible than plywood, warmer to the touch than sheet metal, less waxy and more stress-resistant than polyethylene, and more supple than fibreglass-reinforced polyester resin (the material used in Charles Eames's plastic shell chairs). As a thermoplastic, it was particularly well-suited to the technique of injection-moulding, which involves granules being softened in a heating chamber, then forced under pressure through a narrow channel into a cooled split mould. Injection-moulded plastics require very little finishing, and as a manufacturing process, it is both quick and economical, creating a minimum of waste.

The thinking behind the Polypropylene chair was clearly explained by Robin in a press release issued at the time of its original launch: "This chair arose from the need for a multi-purpose side chair at very low cost. Some of the uses we had in mind were cafés and canteens, chairs for working at a table, seating in lecture halls and assembly halls, and high chairs for use at bars and benches. The differences demanded by these functions could be achieved by various stands or leg frames carrying a mass-produced seat-and-back unit." He also elaborated on the functional and aesthetic reasons for its shape. "Considerations of posture and anatomy largely determined the sections through the shell. For the overall shape we have aimed

Nottingham Theatre seating, 1963
This seating was commissioned by Peter Moro and was designed to suit the circular layout of the auditorium. The curved seat backs were made of moulded plywood and the seats were mounted on steel frames.

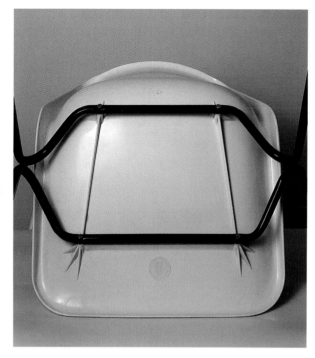

at an anonymous unflamboyant form suitable for either single or mass seating. I wanted to avoid seeing the frame fixings through the seat of the chair, and designed bosses integrally moulded with the underside of the seat. Another feature of the chair is the fully rolled-over edge which helps to give strength and stability against over-flexing." [12] Although moulding experts advised against the use of integral bosses, this device proved highly successful, and was subsequently copied by other manufacturers.

Development work began in 1960 using a specialist plastics firm called Thermo Plastics Ltd, and the mould-makers Talbot-Ponsonby, with regular testing being conducted by the Furniture Industry Research Association. The design process began with sketches and quarter-scale models, then progressed from plaster casts to fibreglass shells to epoxy resin patterns. Although polypropylene itself is cheap, the production tools are extremely expensive, as they have to be made from the high-grade steel, finished to exacting standards. The development and fine-tuning of these moulds was extremely time-consuming. Because of the pioneering nature of the enterprise, many setbacks were encountered along the way, and progress was painstakingly slow.

The challenge was to create a shell that was thin enough to make the plastic quick-setting, but thick enough to provide the requisite strength. The first shells to come out of the mould were found to be too flexible, so the design had to be altered to make the seat back more rigid. Testing also revealed weaknesses in the bosses holding the screws to the shell, which is how they came to be strengthened by a series of radiating ribs. The Mark I version of the Polypropylene chair, launched in May 1963, tackled all these glitches, but threw up further problems. Strengthening the shell had altered the chair's profile, for example, making it uncomfortable to sit on, and in addition there were problems with the roughness of the plastic surface, which snagged on people's clothes. Therefore, the decision was taken to develop a completely new model, known as the Mark II. Although this was expensive for Hille, ultimately the risk paid off. Relaunched in March 1964, the Mark II ironed out all the earlier deficiencies, and the final chair had several other advantages, including a more balanced and fluid shape, and an attractive textured surface created by means of a new photo-etching process.

The launch of the Mark I Polypropylene chair in May 1963 was handled in a particularly innovative way. Instead of simply being issued a press release, journalists were sent an actual sample, and it was on the basis of their feedback to an accompanying survey that the subsequent Mark II modifications were made. In marketing terms, this was a masterstroke, whetting media appetite and guaranteeing the maximum amount of coverage when the Mark II finally arrived. Mark I was also sent to potential clients, including architects, thereby generating significant advance orders. The *Architects' Journal* described the Polypropylene chair as "the most significant development in British mass-produced chair design since the war", and in 1965 it received the British design establishment's seal of approval in the form of a Design Centre Award. It was this design that clinched Hille's status as the most progressive furniture manufacturer in Britain, and its success stimulated a huge increase in the scale of their operations, raising their profile

Left

Polypropylene armchairs, Heathrow Airport, 1967
The Polypropylene armchair, launched in 1967, proved particularly popular in airports, where rows of shells upholstered with elasticated "aprons" could be mounted on a beam.

Below

Sports Stadium at Mexico Olympics, 1968
Mass-produced under licence in many different countries, the global triumph of the Polypropylene chair was assured when it was chosen for the main sports stadium at the Mexico Olympics in 1968.

Above
Polypropylene chairs
The Mark II chair is shown here in its three original colours: pale grey, flame red and charcoal. Tubular steel legs were either stove-enamelled in black (left) or chromium-plated (centre and right).

Right
Robin in a canoe in Botswana fitted with Polypropylene chairs, 1980s
The Polypropylene chair is so tough, light, flexible and cheap that it has proved invaluable for communities all over the world. When Robin visited Botswana he was delighted to find that the shells of his chairs had been installed in canoes.

to a truly international level. In 1968, for example, 38,000 Polypropylene chairs were installed in the newly built sports stadia at the Mexico Olympics. Since then the chair has been produced in tens of millions, and has been manufactured under licence all over the world. Sales would have been even higher but for the number of lookalikes that subsequently appeared on the market, starting with a version by PEL, produced within months of the Polypropylene chair's arrival. Over the years Robin's design was often plagiarized, sometimes through a mould being taken from the original, prompting Hille to resort to legal action on a number of occasions.

"What has 44 legs but is very light on its feet, a weatherproof shell yet wears many different covers, sometimes has arms – sometimes hasn't, works alone, or in large groups, can be seen all over the world but is only three years old?" asked a Hille advertisement in *Architectural Review* in September 1966. The basic stacking version of the Polypropylene chair was supported on bent tubular steel legs, fitted directly to the plastic shell by means of four self-tapping screws. However, because it was designed to be as flexible as possible, it was produced with an array of other bases, including skid, pedestal, swivel, cruciform and bar chair versions, and later as multi-beam seating for concourse, waiting room and auditorium use. Optional extras included linking mechanisms, armrests and writing tablets. Elasticated upholstered "aprons" were also offered, along with loose cushions and upholstered pads.

In 1967 the original side chair was supplemented by an armchair version, known as the tub. This, too, has been enduringly popular, and both shells proved ideal for mounting on other structures, and were widely installed in lecture theatres and sports stadia. Charcoal, light grey and flame red were the original colours used for the shells. Later, dark blue and white were added, while chairs sold through Hille's American agent, John Stuart International, were produced additionally in yellow ochre and olive green. Over the years the Polypropylene chair has been made in many different colours, reflecting changing fashions. An updated version, introduced by Habitat in 1999, exploited the translucency of polypropylene in its raw state.

Robin Day: Polystyrene and Polyurethane Chairs

When Robin began his career, plastics were in their infancy, but from the mid-1960s they played an increasingly prominent role in furniture design. After the success of the Polypropylene chair, Leslie Julius encouraged Robin to experiment with other forms of plastics, including polystyrene, polyurethane and ABS. The use of polystyrene, a plastic from the vinyl group, proved fairly short-lived, resulting in just one main design, the Polystyrene chair (1965), subsequently renamed Nimbus. Prior to this Hille had used moulded plywood for the shells of their upholstered furniture, but for the Nimbus chair they teamed up with a firm in Sweden that had developed a technique for making expanded polystyrene shells. However, high transport costs, combined with expensive tooling, adversely affected the viability of the original Nimbus, prompting the search for an alternative material. Rigid expanded-polyurethane foam provided the answer and, as well as being cheaper to produce, it was stronger and lighter.

Left
Polypropylene chairs in a church, 1970s
Equally well suited for historic and modern interiors, the ubiquitous Polypropylene chair is to be found wherever stacking or linking chairs are needed, be it a school, a church, a village hall or a conference room. These chairs are fitted with hymn-book holders.

Below
Library, Milton Keynes College, 1980s
The Polypropylene chair has a timeless quality and, unlike other designs, it does not seem to date. It is seen here with white enamelled tubular steel skid bases.

Top
Centric chair, 1968
Like the Polypropylene chair, the upholstered Centric and Nimbus chairs could be mounted on a variety of different bases.

Above
Nimbus chair, 1965
The shell of this chair was originally made from polystyrene. Subsequently, polyurethane was used instead.

Polyurethane is shaped by means of a chemical reaction that causes the raw materials to expand and set. This means that the moulds can be made of fibreglass rather than metal, as they do not need to be able to withstand the type of heat and pressure used in the moulding of polystyrene and polypropylene. Leslie Julius later established a company called HIA Plastics (HIAP) where plastic shells were made. The formation of HIAP enabled the creation of a whole family of cheap, upholstered polyurethane shell designs, including the low-backed Centric chair, and the high-backed Kulminus armchair (also known as Cumulus), a precursor of the 4-4000 pedestal chair (1970), produced in ABS.

Robin Day: Storey's and Woodward Grosvenor

Reflecting on his career in 1964, Robin wrote: "I am sure that ideally one should avoid over-specialization, and that coming from one set of industrial problems to another makes for freshness, and a wider knowledge is an asset to each field of design concerned. I think, for instance, that the furniture designer must have a real knowledge of architectural developments and should know and meet architects. He should also have more than a passing familiarity with textiles, carpets, lighting and other elements of interior design." [13] Until the end of the 1950s, apart from his posters and exhibition graphics, Robin had largely confined his activities to three-dimensional design. However, his high profile in the design world meant that, as time went on, he was invited to collaborate with an increasingly wide range of clients, spurring him to experiment in new areas, notably pattern design.

During the late 1950s and early 1960s he was engaged as colour consultant by Storey's of Lancaster, having been recruited by the company's design director, Harry Spencer, who was a great admirer of his work.[14] Originally known as manufacturers of a type of cheap patterned floor and table coverings made of oilcloth, Storey's had recently expanded into the new field of flexible plastics, made using polyvinyl chloride (PVC). By the late 1950s their products included plastic curtains (Stor Decor), self-adhesive PVC sheeting (Con-Tact), fabric-backed vinyl wallcoverings (Stormur), and plastic-coated upholstery fabrics with embossed patterns, known as leathercloths. With his intimate knowledge of the furniture industry, Robin was ideally placed to choose the colours for Storey's leathercloth ranges, and it was in this area specifically that he was called upon to advise. His consultancy at Storey's also provided him with the opportunity to design his first pattern. Produced as an upholstery fabric for use on kitchen chairs, Pennant (1959) was composed of fine criss-crossing lines printed in black on a red, blue, yellow or white ground. As part of a joint initiative between Storey's and Formica, it was also manufactured in the form of a plastic laminate, intended for table tops and kitchen units.[15]

In 1952 Robin had been invited to judge a carpet design competition organized by *Furnishing* magazine.[16] Nine years later he was commissioned by the Kidderminster carpet manufacturer Woodward Grosvenor to design a range of modern Wilton carpets to complement their more traditional ranges. These carpets proved highly successful, and between 1961 and 1965 Robin created a substantial body of work amounting to more than thirty designs, some of which remained in production until the 1970s.[17] Abstract in character, they were geared specifically towards architects and intended primarily for contract use. Manufactured in three different grades, they were marketed initially with their own RD pattern numbers (standing for Robin Day) as part of the Akbar Saxony Wilton range. Later, after Woodward Grosvenor were taken over by Grays Carpets in 1967, they were included in the latter's Churchill Wilton and Project Wilton ranges, where they were promoted alongside patterns by in-house designers, some traditional, some modern.

Initially Robin's approach was similar to that of Lucienne in her early designs for Tomkinsons, and it is likely that, subconsciously, he was influenced in some respects by her style. His earliest carpets included tight linear patterns such as Elm and Delphic, the dynamic striped Iambic, and the mosaic-like Motley and Libra. Another early design, Cipher, was composed of tiny quasi-mathematical symbols, a theme to which Robin returned in a larger, bolder pattern called Cypher a few years later. With his instinctive understanding of the colour and pattern requirements of modern interiors, many of Robin's carpets were overtly architectural in character, particularly his multicoloured banded patterns, Sequence and Broken Stripe, with their strong lines and unusual colours. Flat geometric patterns formed the basis of much of his work, including the interlocking squares of Quadriga, and patterns such as Hexagonal, with more complex, intricate, subordinate motifs. Circle patterns were a recurrent feature, and formed the basis of some of his best-selling designs. They varied in size from the small spots of Abacus to the larger spheres of Discus, and culminated in more complex radiating patterns such as Aztec and Roundel.

Lucienne Day: Heal Fabrics

By 1960 Lucienne's furnishing fabric patterns were much freer and bolder than those of a decade earlier, the neatness and precision of the early 1950s having given way to looser and more open effects. A comparison between an early leaf pattern, Fall (1952), and a later variant, Linden (1960), highlights significant differences, the leaves in Linden being much more impressionistic and skeletal. Similarly, if one compares a typical early linear pattern such as Dandelion Clocks (1953) with the feathery grasses of Halcyon (1960), the latter is much more overtly expressive, and suggests an awareness of the paintings of Jackson Pollock. However, although Lucienne always acknowledged her debt to contemporary art, there were fundamental differences between her work and that of such artists as Harold Cohen, Cliff Holden, Louis Le Broquy and Donald Hamilton-Fraser, who were all producing painterly textiles for Heal's and David Whitehead at this date. They, along with a younger generation of designers trained during the post-war period, such as Doreen Dyall, reproduced the drips, splashes and brushstrokes of their paintings quite literally in their work, whereas Lucienne's designs, however free they seemed, were always highly controlled. The freer her patterns, the greater the skill required in handling the repeat in order to preserve a feeling of spontaneity. In fact, the looser they appeared, the more carefully structured they had to be from a design point of view.

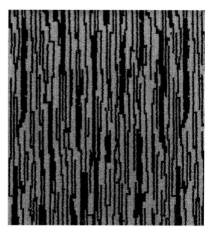

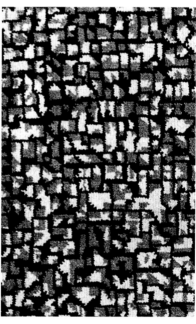

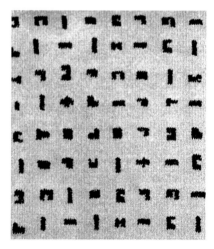

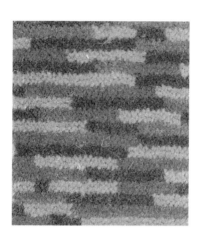

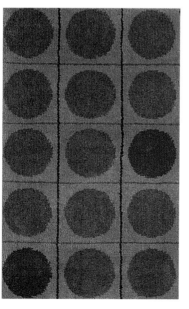

Carpets for Woodward Grosvenor, 1961–2
Although he mainly confined himself to three-dimensional design and graphics, Robin ventured into the field of pattern design during the early 1960s. The five carpets shown here were part of a substantial contract range he created for Woodward Grosvenor, some of which remained in production until the 1970s. Geared specifically towards architects, the patterns are: Elm (top left), Motley (centre left), Iambic (centre right), Cipher (bottom left) and Discus (bottom right). Discus was used in the study bedrooms at Churchill College, Cambridge (see pages 138–41).

Right
Rock Rose, Heal's, 1961
Lucienne developed a new
aesthetic during the 1960s
based on colour and texture
rather than line. The flowers in
this design were created from
cut coloured tissue paper
overprinted in black ink.

Below
Riga, Heal's, 1961
The artwork for this vibrant
pattern was created by means
of collage, using narrow strips
of coloured paper partly
overpainted in black.

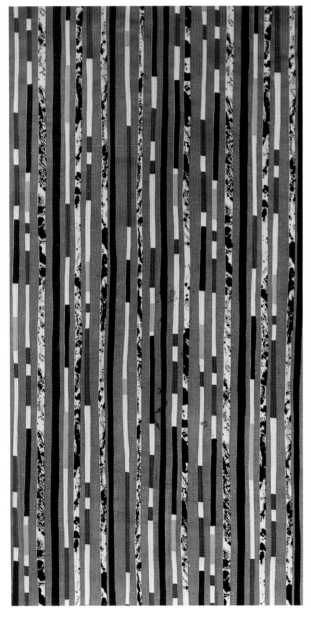

While accepting that she was influenced by the *Zeitgeist* to a certain extent, Lucienne's detached and thoughtful approach distinguished her from her more fashion-conscious contemporaries. There was a consistency and an internal logic to the development of her work during the 1960s, and her designs were much more subtle and considered than those of her younger colleagues. In 1968 she reflected: "Pattern of every kind is to some extent related to fashion, but I don't think I go along with fashion because this is the fashion this year, and so I must work in this particular way. I think it comes from within. I tend to use certain colours, or have a colour that I like very much at one period, which I use a lot throughout all the things I do. Then perhaps I suddenly get tired of it, or it doesn't seem right for a time, and so I use another set of colours." [18]

One thing that changed significantly during the 1960s was the way in which Lucienne created her artwork. Instead of drawing in pen and ink on a painted gouache ground, she employed a wider range of tools, and experimented with new techniques such as monoprinting and collage. The broken textural effects of Ducatoon (1959), Cadenza (1962) and Tekka (1962) were all produced by monoprinting, for example, while Riga (1961) and Fuego (1962), the latter inspired by a trip to Mexico, were created from strips of coloured paper. Rock Rose (1961) used simple cut-paper shapes to suggest a plant at various stages in its flowering cycle. Collage had a particularly liberating effect on Lucienne's style of pattern-making during this period, and in addition to coloured paper, she used materials such as transparent coloured plastic film and tissue paper.

A key difference between Lucienne and her younger contemporaries was that, whereas others sought to reproduce the effects of Op Art in a literal way through patterns that dazzled and confused the eye, to Lucienne, distortion and visual overload were anathema. Although there are obvious stylistic similarities between her geometric patterns and contemporary abstract art, minimalist American painters such as Ellsworth Kelly and Frank Stella come to mind rather than Op artists such as Bridget Riley and Victor Vasarely. It was never Lucienne's intention to create patterns that might be mistaken for paintings. Her primary concern was always with the impact of her fabrics within the context of an interior, and it was the interrelationship between her textiles and modern architecture to which she herself repeatedly drew attention. The two commissions she received in 1963 to design fabrics for specific buildings – Churchill College, Cambridge, and the Shell Centre in London – underline these parallels; and in both cases, significantly, she was invited to select the accompanying carpets as well. "Modern architecture and the ways in which textiles are used by good interior designers have had a great deal to do with their development," she explained. "Instead of being used as decorative strips or panels flanking window openings, they are often used as part of the interior architecture in the form of planes of colour, and texture from floor to ceiling, or perhaps covering a whole wall. In this way, the textile takes its own place in the balanced design of the interior, creating a foil for the harder surfaces of plaster, wood and other materials." [19]

Lucienne's flat geometric abstract patterns, such as Counterpoint (1964), Dovetail (1965), Causeway (1967) and

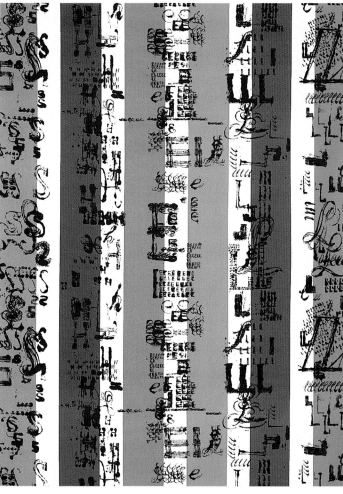

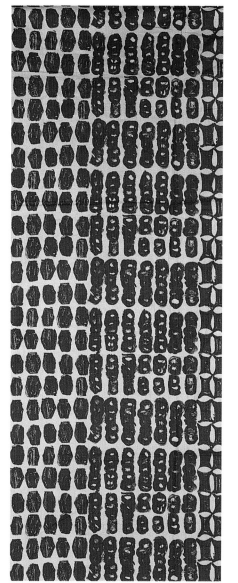

Left
Furnishing fabric for Shell Chemical Company, Heal's, 1963
This customized design for Shell was created for use in their company buildings. Although initially it appears abstract, the pattern incorporates the name of the firm, written across the fabric.

Below left
Cadenza, Heal's, 1962
Like the Shell fabric (left), the black motifs on this design were created using the technique of monoprinting, chosen because it produced interesting textural effects.

Below right
Cockaigne, Heal's, 1961
Cockaigne is decorated with three different monoprinted patterns. Across its full width the fabric is divided into two halves with contrasting background colours.

Simplicity (1968), complemented the clean lines and open spaces of modern interiors in the most obvious way. Like Robin, Lucienne regarded the home as a refuge from the frenetic pace of modern life, which is why her later designs, although stimulating, projected a greater feeling of calm. In Simplicity, for example, monochrome squares are interrupted at intervals by unlikely colour contrasts, which break up the otherwise monotonous grid pattern in a subtly subversive way. Similarly, in Counterpoint, unexpected structural deviations in the intersections between the horizontal and vertical stripes inject visual tension and depth into an otherwise flat geometric pattern. In Dovetail, the complexity lies less in the pattern than in the interaction between the juxtaposed colours, chosen to arouse but not to overwhelm. In Causeway, one of her most assured and intelligent designs, the subtle relationship between the thin coloured lines on the outer bands of the fabric and the dynamic patchwork running down the centre demonstrates Lucienne's mastery of pattern-making, her keen sense of rhythm, and her instinctive feeling for colour.

Although Lucienne continued to cater for modest domestic interiors as well as modern buildings with large picture windows, the exceptionally large scale of some of her 1960s patterns reflected the fashion for floor-to-ceiling drapes. Dividing the pattern vertically into two distinct halves, almost like two separate widths of fabric, was a ploy she had begun to explore a few years earlier to make her fabrics more architectural. First adopted in Sequoia (1959), this device was later used in Larch (1961) and Cockaigne (1961), and culminated in the divided structures and giant pattern repeats of the late 1960s, notably Apex (1967), Chevron (1968) and Sunrise (1969). Whatever their scale, however, her fabrics were always designed so that they made sense when drawn back in undulating folds as well as when fully extended and flat. This was why Lucienne used large V-shaped motifs in several designs, because they created an interesting secondary pattern when condensed. Chevron, which won a Design Centre Award in 1968, was particularly clever in the way it balanced broad diagonal stripes on the left with narrow stripes on the right, in a ratio of one to three.

Although Lucienne's dominant idiom during the 1960s was abstraction, she returned at intervals to her original source of creative stimulus, plants. "I'm always attracted by simple four-, five- or six-petalled flowers, like periwinkles, primroses and forget-me-nots," she observed in 1967. "I often use them for my designs, but never stick to exact botanical details." [20] In Periwinkle (1964), produced in two variants as a tablecloth and a tea-towel, she treated plants with mathematical precision. This design presaged the move towards increasing stylization and simplification, leading to her flat florals of the mid-1960s, made using coloured paper cutouts. High Noon (1965), composed entirely of flat petals and stems without any overlaid details or textures, signified the merger between abstraction and representation. Pennycress (1966) and Poinsettia (1966), although loosely based on flowers, served as a vehicle for controlled geometric patterns. The quatrefoil petals of Pennycress, for example, were overlaid with circles and squares, while the radiating flower heads of Poinsettia were arranged like wheels and cogs.[21]

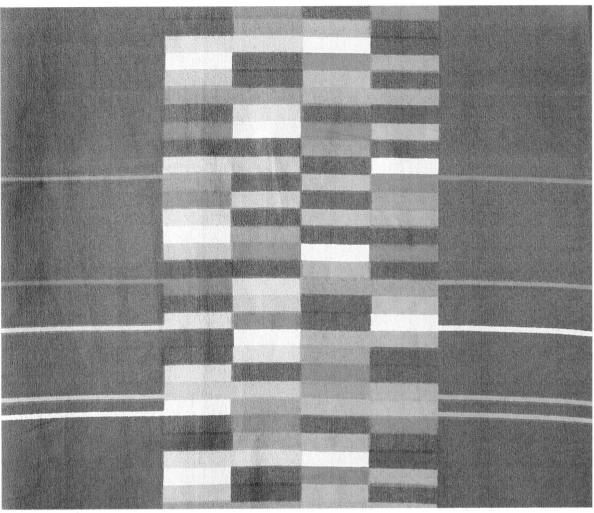

Opposite
Chevron, Heal's, 1968
The winner of a Design Centre Award in 1968, this fabric marked the culmination of a trend for large pattern repeats and for dividing the fabric into two distinct halves.

Left
Causeway, Heal's, 1967
This pattern provides a virtuoso demonstration of Lucienne's techniques as a colourist. Note how each of the colours in the central bands is picked out again in the narrow stripes in the borders.

Below
Apex, Heal's, 1967
Flat geometric abstract patterns characterized Lucienne's work during the mid- to late 1960s, while large pattern repeats reflected the prevailing fashion for floor-to-ceiling picture windows.

Lucienne Day: Carpets

As in the areas of furnishing fabrics and wallpapers, Lucienne's accomplishments as a carpet designer attracted interest both at home and abroad. Foreign clients included a Californian firm called Bigelow, which commissioned several designs during the late 1950s, and a Swiss manufacturer that invited Lucienne to design a group of Indian-made carpets in 1962.[22] Her main clients, however, were the two British firms with which she had entered into partnership during the late 1950s, Tomkinsons and the Wilton Royal Carpet Factory. In addition, she worked with the Banbury-based I. & C. Steele, a company taken over by Tomkinsons in 1959, which subsequently became their contract division.[23]

Developed in direct response to the needs of architects, Lucienne's carpets were intended to complement the spatial qualities of modern interiors. Consequently, geometric patterns became their defining characteristic, even more so than in her furnishing fabrics. The tone was set by two new carpets for Tomkinsons in 1960: Couplet, composed of isolated rectangular strips, and M1, a finely striped pattern suggesting motorway lanes.[24] Whereas Tomkinsons specialized in Axminster carpets for the domestic market, Steele produced tough hard-wearing Wilton carpets that could be produced in shorter runs for contract use. Responding to the opportunity to target her work at more adventurous clients, Lucienne's first pattern for Steele was Signum (1961), composed of circles, triangles, and minus and multiplication signs.[25] Crispness and precision were a key feature of her carpets at this date, and Signum was one of three patterns suggesting mathematical symbols, the others being Alpha (c.1962) for Tomkinsons, and New Day (1965) for Steele, both composed of small geometric motifs.

Another early carpet for Steele was Ramal (1961), an abstracted representation of the branches of leafless trees, atypical in being her only carpet design to draw on imagery from nature. Her boldest and most memorable design for Steele was Big Circle (1963), a dramatically enlarged variant of a pattern originally created the previous year as a knitted dress fabric design. The large-scale repeat of Big Circle, consisting of circles composed from smaller linear motifs, made it particularly suitable for public and commercial buildings. This design also appealed to the fashion for circular motifs, a trend paralleled in her Heal's fabric Zocalo (1963), and in several of Robin's carpets for Woodward Grosvenor. Big Circle, Signum and New Day, along with her reissued pattern Furrows (1957), were among the designs included in a new contract collection called Studio 3 launched jointly by Steele and Tomkinsons in 1965. The range was selected by the architect Helen Challen of Challen & Floyd, and other designers included Helen Dalby, Mary Yonge, Donald Harding and Hugh Mackinnon. The lasting success of Big Circle is indicated by the fact that, when a second edition of the Studio 3 range was issued in 1968 under the direction of Margaret Casson, this design was again included, five years after its original launch.[26]

Lucienne's relationship with Wilton Royal Carpets also flourished during the 1960s, with her input being channelled into two distinct areas. Until 1963 she acted exclusively as a colour

Opposite
Sunrise, Heal's, 1969
By the end of the 1960s the palette of colours upon which Lucienne was drawing had changed quite considerably from earlier in the decade, when olives, browns and earth tones had prevailed.

Far left
High Noon, Heal's, 1965
Although Lucienne embraced geometric abstraction during the 1960s, she continued to produce some stylized plant designs such as these, which were known as "flat florals".

Left
Poinsettia, Heal's, 1966
Although composed of flower heads, this pattern has a quasi-mechanistic character, and the flowers resemble small wheels and cogs.

Below
Pennycress, Heal's, 1966
In this design Lucienne uses quatrefoil floral motifs as a vehicle for a geometric pattern. Note the way the squares and circles alternate on the petals.

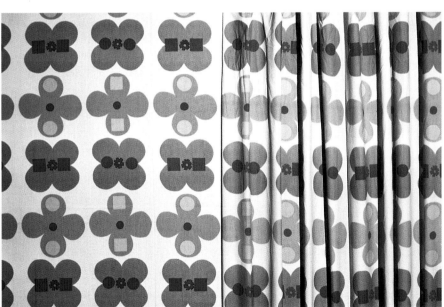

Right
**Big Circle carpet,
I. & C. Steele, 1963**
In this design Lucienne gives a
new twist to the popular early
1960s circle motif.

Centre left
**Octagon carpet, Wilton Royal,
1964**
In 1964 Lucienne designed a
new group of contract carpets
for Wilton Royal, marketed as
the Architects Nova collection.

Centre right
**Carpet (9310), Wilton Royal,
c.1964**
Shown here in three colourways,
this subtle pattern consists of
large squares sliced by fine lines.

Bottom left
**Signum carpet, I. & C. Steele,
1961**
The motifs in this pattern of
resemble mathematical symbols,
hence the Latin title Signum.

Bottom right
**Carpet (9307), Wilton Royal,
1964**
This carpet was used in the
foyer of the Curzon Cinema in
London's Leicester Square.

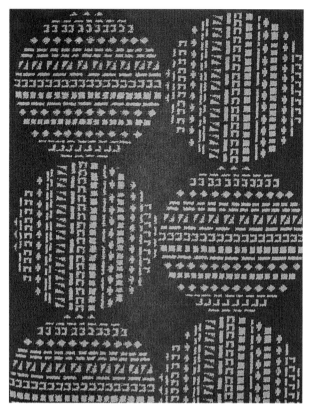

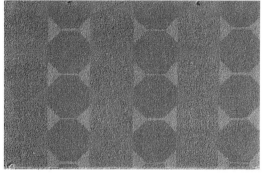

consultant, and in this capacity she was responsible for
colouring further patterns by the firm's in-house design team
for the Architects Collection, as well as a new range called
København, launched around 1961.[27] New designs introduced
into the Architects Collection (also produced as the Architects
Textured range) included a mottled pattern called Cobble
(1961) by Norman Runacres, and Cirrus (1959), a linear pattern
produced as a follow-up to Lamina, created by Philip Coombes.
By 1964 the collection also included two geometric patterns by
Pam Golding, one of which, Portcullis, was among the carpets
proposed by Lucienne for Churchill College.[28]

In 1964 Lucienne began to create patterns for a new
collection called Architects Nova, an advanced modern contract
range for large public and commercial interiors, characterized by
bold geometric designs such as Octagon and Planted Stripe.
Octagon was produced in bright colours such as oranges and
blues, whereas another design, composed of large squares
(pattern number 9310), was produced in more subtle earthy
hues. Another Nova carpet decorated with alternating diamonds
and squares (pattern number 9307) was similar to a ceramic
design of Lucienne's called Brokat, showing the continuing
cross-fertilization between different media. Although apparently
simple, this design was characteristically subtle and multilayered,
with each shape containing a smaller replica, and the basic
pattern overlaid by larger motifs.[29]

Lucienne Day: Rosenthal

Lucienne's involvement with Rosenthal took on a new dimension
in 1961 after she was invited to join their newly constituted
designers' panel, established at the initiative of Philip Rosenthal.
The panel brought together all the international designers who
contributed to the Studio Line range, and over the next few
years included Acton Bjørn, Bjørn Wiinblad and Sigvaard
Bernadotte from Denmark, Tapio Wirkkala from Finland,
Raymond Loewy and Richard Latham from the US, Raymond
Peynet from France, Claus Josef Riedel from Austria, and Hans
Theo Baumann, Cuno Fischer, Renate Rhein and Elsa Fischer-
Treyden from Germany. Hitherto Rosenthal's élite Studio Line
designers had occasionally met when visiting the factory at Selb,
but now they gathered together for two to three days at a time
once or twice a year. These meetings, which were partly social
and partly professional, gave them the chance to discuss their
current work, and provided a forum for an exchange of views on
wider issues affecting the future of the Studio Line range. Hosted
initially either by Philip Rosenthal at his country mansion, or by
other members of the panel in their native countries, meetings
were occasionally held in exotic locations, such as Lapland and
Granada in Spain, and one memorable gathering, in December
1963, took the form of a cruise on the Nile. Over time, an
increasingly important area of discussion was the Rosenthal
Studio Houses, a chain of retail outlets established by the
company in leading European cities during the early 1960s,
which by 1964 had grown to twenty in number. These shops
provided an important outlet for Rosenthal's Studio Line ranges,
but they also sold ceramics, glass, cutlery and kitchenware by
other design-led European firms. The designers' panel took an

increasingly keen interest in the choice of stock in the Studio Houses, and as a result, in 1964 it was decided for logistical reasons that future meetings would be held in Selb so that the panel could physically examine all the items under consideration. This led to the formation of Group 21, which included both Studio Line designers and other interested parties, where a formal voting system was adopted for reaching decisions on what stock was approved.

Some of Rosenthal's shops had temporary exhibition spaces, and it was the newly opened Studio House in Knightsbridge that provided the venue for Lucienne's second solo exhibition, which took place from 17 to 25 July 1963. In addition to her latest designs for Rosenthal, the exhibition featured a selection of her recent work for other manufacturers, complemented by several pieces of Robin's furniture. As with her previous show at Heal's in 1958, the exhibition highlighted the diversity of her output, and her skill in designing for a wide range of media. Alongside her ceramics the display included a selection of her recent furnishing fabrics for Heal's, glass towels and sheets for Thomas Somerset, handkerchiefs for ICI, knitted dress fabrics for Saint Joseph, and carpets for Tomkinsons and I. & C. Steele.

During the 1960s, on the advice of Rosenthal's art director, Heinrich Rank, most of Lucienne's tableware patterns were created in the form of bands or borders, rather than central motifs or all-over designs. Included in the 1963 exhibition was a stylized leaf pattern called Ivy; an intricate grid pattern called Brokat; and four small-scale geometric border patterns of various depths, Ilias, Windsor, Club and Delphi. The show also included a large group of experimental prototypes, specially produced in small quantities for the exhibition, which demonstrated how Lucienne was still actively striving to branch out in new directions in her work for Rosenthal. Among these pieces were some low circular ashtrays decorated with richly coloured abstract patterns resembling stained-glass windows, and a set of oval canister-shaped herb and spice jars, their contents identified by means of pictograms instead of lettering. Themed decoration of a more colourful and evocative kind was adopted for an hors d'oeuvres set and a dessert set, variously ornamented with fish, vegetables and cross-sections of fruit.

Very few of these experimental designs entered mass production as they were considered too expensive by Rosenthal, but a delayed spin-off from the show was the range of Flower Bricks produced by Bristol Pottery in 1966. After Rosenthal decided not to proceed with this design, Lucienne took it upon herself to find an English manufacturer. Initially she approached J.G. Green of Church Gresley, but eventually she ended up working with Bristol Pottery. Promoted as an updated version of an early 18th-century English delftware flower vase, these square and rectangular boxes, made in earthenware rather than porcelain, were decorated with three printed designs, all of which drew on, or led to, patterns in other media. One box was decorated with a mottled pink textural pattern similar to an earlier plastic fabric for Göppinger, for example. Another was decorated with a black and white Op-inspired pattern, originally evolved on her Triangles handkerchief (1962) for ICI,

Left
Lucienne Day with her daughter Paula, 1960
Six-year-old Paula is seen here watching her mother paint designs on porcelain blanks supplied by Rosenthal. Lucienne preferred to design ceramic patterns in this way rather than on paper.

Below
Rosenthal designers' panel, 1961
The designers are (from left to right) Renate Rhein, Raymond Peynet, Bjørn Wiinblad, Lucienne Day, Else Fischer-Treyden and (seated) Philip Rosenthal. On the table are ceramics, glass and cutlery for inspection.

while a third design, a pattern of ovals created from a collage of cut tissue paper, used a device from another handkerchief, Torn Circle (1962).

Lucienne's later tableware designs for Rosenthal were created for a wider range of services, including Medallion, Modulation, Variations and Composition. The only designs to enter production, however, were those for Hans Theo Baumann's Berlin service, notably Dreilinden, a stylized leaf pattern in black and green, and Ascot, decorated with fine coloured lines. In 1965 Lucienne broke fresh ground with her proposal for a group of rectangular vases decorated with simple large raised geometric motifs. This was her last recorded design to enter production, although she continued to supply a substantial group of patterns after this date. In 1968, however, her official partnership with Rosenthal was brought to a close by mutual agreement, and later that year the original Group 21 jury was disbanded, largely for economic reasons, as it had become too expensive to administer.

Lucienne Day: Table Linen and Handkerchiefs

Lucienne had begun to collaborate with the Irish firm Thomas Somerset in 1957, producing a series of designs for coordinated table linen. Further tablecloths followed during the early 1960s, including the minimalist geometric Maxim (1961), and others such as Pomegranate (1961), Daisy Belle (c.1963) and Periwinkle (1964) decorated with stylized fruit and plant motifs. A version of Periwinkle was also produced as a glass towel, and it was to this highly accessible area of household goods that Lucienne devoted most of her attention between 1959 and 1969. Designing glass towels provided light relief from her furnishing fabrics, and she particularly enjoyed the freedom of not having to put her patterns into repeat. Responding imaginatively to the compact rectangular format, she created at least seventeen vivid designs of a strikingly fresh and often witty character.

One of her most popular and entertaining designs was Too Many Cooks (1959), depicting rows of cooks of all ages, shapes and sizes. This design remained in production for about ten years, and made Lucienne into a household name. It was followed by a series of other designs on culinary themes, including Provençal, Bouquet Garni, Batterie de Cuisine, Good Food, and the quasi-historical Tudor Table, all dating from 1961–5. Too Many Cooks was also the first in a series of light-hearted figurative designs, including The Merry Makers, depicting friends sitting round the table at a Christmas party; and Many Hands Make Light Work, a special commission for Rosenthal, featuring cartoon sketches of Lucienne's colleagues on the designers' panel. Night and Day (c.1961–2) split the cloth into two, with a sun in one half, and an owl and a moon in the other. Butterflies (1960), sold to raise money for the Polio Research Fund, took motifs from her furnishing fabric Vanessa (1960), overlaid with flat brightly coloured flowers similar to Rock Rose (1961). Only two glass towels were abstract: an early pattern called Diabolo, which reused the familiar hourglass motif, and a late geometric pattern, Rose Diamond (1969), evoking kaleidoscopic effects. Her last designs, which included Tudor

Garden and the Art Nouveau-style Glass Towel (1969), were marketed by Nova Products. This was a new company established by Ron Crawford, her original contact at Thomas Somerset, whose designs had previously been sold under various trade names, including Fragonard and Best Linen.

Decorative kitchenwares were a growth area during the mid-1960s, and as a spin-off from her glass towels, Lucienne was commissioned to design a set of cheeseboards made from plastic laminate, decorated with stylized flowers.[30] Another minor project in 1962 was a group of handkerchiefs designed for ICI to use and promote their Procion dyes. In addition to Triangles and Torn Circle, mentioned above in relation to Lucienne's Flower Bricks, one design recycled flower motifs from Rock Rose, and another featured fruit from an earlier glass-cloth, Good Food. Lucienne's *Rosenthal Studio House* exhibition in 1963 also included several other domestic items, among which were a bathmat and towel for the Manchester firm Barlow and Jones, and a striped linen sheet set called Troubadour, made by Thomas Somerset.[31]

Lucienne Day: Mattress Tickings and Fashion Fabrics

As an offshoot of her work for Heal Fabrics, Lucienne was asked to design some woven mattress tickings for the bedding department at Heal's. Produced during the early 1960s, some patterns, such as Small Leaf (1960) were in the familiar "Contemporary" idiom, while others, such as Stripe (c.1961), were in a simpler, geometric style. Around this date she also designed another group of mattress tickings, this time printed, for a manufacturer called A.F. Buckingham, which were mentioned in the *Furniture Record* on 27 January 1961.[32]

Lucienne returned to the field of fashion fabrics on two occasions during the 1960s, although this time she worked with different sectors of the trade. One of her clients was a French manufacturer called Établissement Saint Joseph, for whom she created three knitted woollen jersey dress fabrics in 1962. Produced in muted colours, one design contained a miniaturized version of her Heal's fabric Runic, while another, composed of spherical and hemispherical forms, was a precursor of her later carpet Big Circle. A third pattern, produced in brighter colours, was more intentionally dynamic with its rows of squiggles and lines.

Lucienne's second fashion industry client was an organization called the West Indian Sea Island Cotton Association, which commissioned a group of printed shirt fabrics in 1969. Printed in zingy colours on extremely high-quality cotton, her designs included four tight-knit abstract patterns, Ribbon, Wave, Double Curve and Triangle, with small but vibrant motifs. A fifth pattern, Chrysanthemum, was rather different in character. Produced at a time when the Art Nouveau revival was at its height, it was composed of scrolling Beardsleyesque flowers.

Throughout her career, Lucienne had always striven to reach the mass market. "My aim is always to design for manufacturers who produce big, inexpensive ranges because I am interested in designing for young people who haven't very much money but want good things."[33] Designing everyday

Left
Rosenthal Studio House exhibition, July 1963
On the left are Lucienne's Night and Day glass towels for Thomas Somerset, and on the right her prototype storage jars (top two shelves) and a coffee set decorated with Brokat (bottom shelf).

Below left
Fruit Set, Rosenthal, 1963
Lucienne created several new designs for her Rosenthal exhibition, including this fruit set with each piece in a different colour. This design was made to order, rather than mass-produced.

Below
Ilias tableware, Rosenthal, 1962
This design was sold in two colourways, grey and olive, and remained in production until 1970. The motifs are similar to those in Lucienne's Signum carpet from 1961 (see page 132).

Bottom
Dreilinden tableware, Rosenthal, 1964
Most of Lucienne's tableware patterns were on Raymond Loewy's Service 2000, but this design was printed on Hans Theo Baumann's Berlin range.

Right
Pomegranate tablecloth, Thomas Somerset, 1961
Lucienne's relationship with the Irish linen manufacturer Thomas Somerset continued throughout the 1960s, encompassing tablecloths, glass towels and sheets.

Centre
Periwinkle tablecloth, Thomas Somerset, 1964
Sold under the trade name Best Linen, this tablecloth was complemented by a glass towel with similar motifs. The pattern reflects the fashion for what were known as "flat florals".

Bottom left
Provençal glass towel, Thomas Somerset, c.1961–2
Lucienne often used images of food and other culinary motifs on her glass towel designs.

Bottom right
Rose Diamond glass towel, Nova Products, 1969
This kaleidoscopic design derives from a handkerchief pattern called Triangles originally created for ICI as early as 1962.

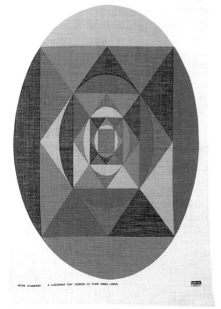

domestic goods and fashion fabrics, as well as furnishings, enabled her to achieve this goal, and gave her the opportunity to extend her creative range.

Robin and Lucienne Day: BOAC
Having both established a name for themselves independently, but being equally well-known as a husband and wife duo, during the 1960s Robin and Lucienne were invited by several clients to work together on particular projects, enabling them to pool their areas of complementary expertise. In 1961, for example, when Robin was appointed as a consultant designer to the British Overseas Airways Company (BOAC), it was announced that Lucienne would be associated with him in this work.[34] Although it was Robin who took the lead in the consultancy, Lucienne also attended design meetings and provided significant input behind the scenes. Their role was to advise on the decoration of aircraft interiors, with Robin drawing on his experience in seating, product design and interiors, and Lucienne contributing in the field of colour and the choice of textiles. "I am responsible for the colour and texture of all the surfaces that the public will see inside the new plane," explained Robin. "I am concerned with ambience, atmosphere, colour, mood and visual character as far as surfaces can create these things. When important questions of colour are involved, this is where I get support from Lucienne. When concerned with the cabin décor of an aircraft we spend a lot of time on the plane with rolls of material and colour samples."[35]

On taking up the consultancy, their initial task during September–October 1961 was to select the new décor for an existing airplane, the Comet 4. However, the main reason why they were engaged was to prepare a full interior scheme for a new plane, the Super VC10. BOAC had previously employed Gaby Schreiber as colour consultant for their Comets and VC10s, but by appointing the Days as her successor, they indicated a desire for a fresh approach. As Molly Neal noted in an article in *Flight* magazine in 1962, "Whereas Mrs Schreiber's philosophy has always included a large element of relaxation and restfulness, Mr Day intends to aim for a greater degree of stimulation and excitement, but at the same time providing a tasteful and distinguished effect as befits an international airline of BOAC's calibre." Because the Super VC10 was a new plane, this enabled Robin to have some input into the design of the seats, normally an area handled exclusively by specialist manufacturers. "Appearance-wise, he feels that the backs of the seats are far more important than the fronts, and he is working on the problem of cleaning up the lines of the seat back," noted Molly Neal. When *BOAC News* announced that the Days' interior scheme had been approved in March 1962, it explained how their theories had been carried through. "Robin Day's handling of colour provides a positive and cheerful impression inside the aircraft. Predominant are the seat backs; these are upholstered either in orange or in dark or light grey; the seats are grouped in the cabin so as to give a balanced colour pattern. Seat cushions are in dark grey, scatter cushions are lime green, and headrests are white. The patterned carpet is rust-brown, matching, in a lighter shade, the bulkheads which carry a design based on the projection lines of a map."

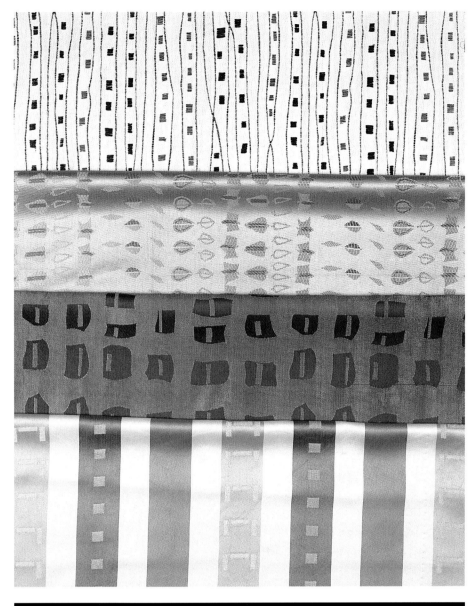

Left

Four mattress tickings, Heal's, 1960–61

These woven mattress tickings were commissioned by the Bedding Department at Heal's, and each design was produced in several colourways. Around this date Lucienne also designed some printed cotton mattress tickings for a firm called A.F. Buckingham.

Below

Wave and Ribbon shirt fabrics, West Indian Sea Island Cotton Association, 1970

At the end of the decade Lucienne designed a group of five cotton shirt fabrics. Swatches of two of these designs are shown here, each printed in three colourways. Tiny in scale, they are totally different in style from her furnishing fabrics.

Top
Refreshment tray for BOAC, 1968–9
Designed for use on Boeing 707 aircraft, this was one of Robin's last projects for BOAC and technically the most demanding. He designed not only the tray itself but the metal cutlery, the ceramic cup, and the plastic dishes and tumblers.

Above
Drawing of cutlery for BOAC refreshment tray, 1968–9
Robin's artistic skills are highlighted in this presentation drawing, which is so lifelike that it could easily be mistaken for a photograph. Various modifications were made before the design went into production, which is why the drawing differs from the finished cutlery (top).

At the same time as he was working on the Super VC10, Robin was asked to prepare a new decorative scheme for the Boeing 707 planes on BOAC's Eastern Line between New York and Hong Kong. The brief was to create an Oriental ambience and the final scheme included framed Chinese paintings in the cabin and Chinese dragons in the lounge, although the ornamental nature of this project was very much a one-off. In other interiors, decoration was limited to black and white reproductions of historical engravings on the bulkheads and line drawings of monuments or small-scale abstract patterns on the window surrounds. Subsequent interiors were all revamps, and included a series of facelifts to the VC10 in 1965 and 1967, and to the Boeing 707 in 1963, 1965 and 1966.

In 1967 BOAC took the decision to invest in a new plane, the Boeing 747, and because this came complete with interior design advice from the American industrial designer Walter Dorwin Teague, there was no need for the company to involve the Days. In 1968 the couple began work on a scheme for the interior of Concorde, although this never came to fruition. Robin's subsequent collaboration with BOAC centred on the design of a refreshment tray for economy class passengers, complete with cutlery, crockery and plastic drinking glasses. Work began in 1968 and continued for the next eighteen months. This proved to be an enormously complex and time-consuming project because of the number of components, each requiring numerous modifications, and each produced by a different supplier. "This was an interesting exercise in logistics," recalled Robin, "as economy of space and weight in even the smallest things are crucial to the economics of operating passenger aircraft. Relationships of dimensions and stacking were essential on several levels: firstly, the compact fitting of vessels and implements on trays; secondly, the exact accommodation of trays on mobile trolleys; and thirdly, the accommodation of this equipment on the galley, on the airfield and in the airport." [36]

After this there was a break of three years before Robin's next commission, when he was invited to prepare proposals for a combined interior and exterior scheme for BOAC's Gulf Aviation Aircraft in 1972. The following year he did some preliminary work on cabin equipment for Concorde, but after this his relationship with BOAC came to an end.

Robin and Lucienne Day: Churchill College

Sometimes a commission to one of the Days would lead to an invitation for related work from the other. This was the case with Churchill College, Cambridge, in which first Robin, then Lucienne, became involved. Built as a memorial to Sir Winston Churchill, the college was designed by Richard Sheppard, Robson and Partners, between 1959 and 1963. Building work was carried out in phases, with the main buildings and half the accommodation blocks being opened in 1964, and a library, theatre, chapel and the rest of the college's residential quarters being completed in 1967. The Days' involvement began in October 1962, when Robin was invited by the College Master, Sir John Cockcroft, to design the furniture for the main dining hall. This led to a series of commissions for furniture in other parts of the building, while Lucienne was invited to design some

Above left
Drawing of VC10 aircraft interior for BOAC, 1967
As well as designing the interiors of the BOAC's new Super VC10 aircraft (above and left), Robin and Lucienne designed a series of refurbishments for BOAC's existing fleet. This gouache by Robin shows a proposed facelift for a VC10 with a coordinated blue, orange and brown colour scheme. The bulkheads were to be decorated with an enlarged engraving of the *Celestial Planisphere* by Albrecht Dürer.

Left and above right
Interior of the Super VC10, 1961–2
Robin's expertise in seating design and Lucienne's knowledge of colour and textiles made them ideally suited to act as joint design consultants to BOAC. Their first project was an interior scheme for a new fleet of planes called the Super VC10 that went into service in 1962.

special curtains and to advise on carpets and upholstery fabrics for a suite of combination rooms. Thus, both Robin and Lucienne contributed to the college in tandem, and when Robin suffered a serious climbing accident in July 1963 which put him out of action for several months, Lucienne stepped in to deal with his affairs, ensuring that the project was not held up.[37]

Because of the phased development of the building programme and the fact that the furniture was commissioned by the college rather than the architect, Robin's design input was undertaken on a rather piecemeal basis over a period of four years from 1963 to 1967. His single most important contribution was the dining hall furniture, made by Heal's Contract Division, which included six long rows of sectionalized tables, 250 wooden stacking chairs, and a high table with a further sixty chairs, upholstered in tan leather. Made from oiled teak, the furniture was designed to complement the interior, which was characterized by large areas of wooden panelling, boarded concrete and rough exposed brick. Rich and dark in appearance, and rectilinear in form, the furniture was deliberately simple and plain, with elements of revealed construction on the table joints. "The furniture is excellent," commented *The Architect and Building News* on 9 September 1964. "Robust, solid teak tables and ample, comfortable chairs should make eating a pleasure and table talk a civilized leisurely pastime."

One of the peculiarities of the interior was that gifts of timber from Commonwealth countries were used for the floors and panelling. When Robin was asked to design a set of dining tables and chairs for the Senior Combination Dining Room in 1963, for example, he was specifically requested to use Australian black bean. Unfortunately, the wood turned out to have been inadequately seasoned, resulting in serious cracks. There were also problems with the Jamaican blue mahoe timber intended for the table and chairs that Robin designed for the Guest Dining Room in 1964, and after much labour and revision, this part of the project was eventually dropped. A satinwood desk and table made by Hille for Sir John Cockcroft's office were among the designs realized in 1964. These were followed by the black bean reading desks designed by Robin for the Bracken Library, and a group of tables for the Bevin Library, both made by Great Universal Stores in 1965. In addition, the college selected several of Robin's Hille production ranges to furnish the suite of combination rooms. Black leather-upholstered Club settees and armchairs, and black vinyl-covered Interplan desks and tables were installed in the Senior Combination Room. Studio armchairs made of Columbia pine were purchased for the Buttery Bar, and Form Group seating was installed in the Junior Combination Room.

In June 1963 Lucienne was invited by the architect, Richard Sheppard, to design a woven curtain fabric for the college, and the rooms in which this was eventually installed included the Club dining room, five combination rooms, and three adjacent TV and quiet rooms. The design was prepared over the next few months, and the fabric, later named Baldric, was woven by Edinburgh Weavers the following year. The rich, strong pattern consisted of broad vertical stripes, overlaid with a large irregular black abstract motif. Woven in three different

colourways, more than 600 yards (550m) of fabric was produced in all, with plum being used in the Club room, pink/orange in the Women's Combination Room and the Common Combination Room, and grey/brown for the other areas. Richard Sheppard was delighted with the results, which he thought were stunning and which perfectly complemented the restrained richness of the building itself.

As an offshoot of the original commission, Sheppard invited Lucienne to choose the carpets and upholstery fabrics for the suite of combination rooms in February 1964. Her carpet selection included designs by both herself and Robin, including Abacus for Woodward Grosvenor, and Signum for I. & C. Steele. She also chose three Wilton Royal patterns, Lamina, Cirrus and Portcullis, in various colourways, while other carpets by Robin, including Discus and Sequence, were chosen by the college for the study bedrooms.

Robin and Lucienne Day: John Lewis Partnership

The client with whom the Days worked most closely as a couple, and with whom their relationship was the most long-lasting and wide-ranging, was the John Lewis Partnership (JLP), for whom they acted as design consultants from 1962 to 1987. A quintessentially British institution with a unique structure and *modus operandi*, the Partnership had grown out of a small draper's shop established on Oxford Street in 1864. It was originally run on purely commercial lines; the founder's son, a Quaker called John Spedan Lewis, established the democratic principles by which the company came to operate. Motivated by strong moral convictions, he aimed as a retailer to be honest, to give good value, and to offer a wide assortment of stock. This became the credo of the John Lewis Partnership, established in 1929, which turned the company into a trust and transformed its employees into partners.

From 1950 onward the Partnership expanded rapidly, and in addition to its department stores, which numbered seventeen by 1973, it opened the first of many Waitrose supermarkets in 1955.[38] The larger the Partnership became, however, the greater the risk of its becoming fragmented and diluted. In 1961, therefore, Max Baker, Director of Trading, Department Stores, convinced the Chairman, Sir Bernard Miller, that the cohesive force of design was needed to assert identity and control. "Fired with the idea that any commercial organization needs a consistent visual character to show the world", it was he who instigated the appointment of Robin and Lucienne as design consultants in 1962.[39] The Partnership had taken the first steps towards introducing a house style during the mid-1950s by employing the respected graphic designer Jesse Collins to redesign its packaging.[40] By the 1960s Collins had retired, and the work required was by now far beyond the capabilities of one individual. With the appointment of the Days, the Partnership began to tackle corporate design issues on a much more ambitious scale, and although initially daunted by the immensity of the task, after twelve months the couple realized, "we were so deep into the Partnership and so much liked the people we met, that we felt a part of it. There was no question of giving it up."[41] Over the years the distinctive character of the Partnership and its

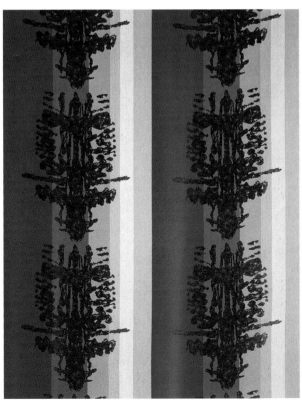

Above
Dining hall, Churchill College, Cambridge, 1964
Robin undertook a series of commissions to design furniture for this important new university building by Richard Sheppard, Robson and Partners during the mid-1960s. Shown here are his handsome oiled-teak dining tables and chairs made by Heal's.

Left
Baldric woven furnishing fabric, Edinburgh Weavers, 1964
Lucienne designed this bold abstract fabric for the suite of combination rooms at Churchill College. Woven by Edinburgh Weavers, it was produced in three different colourways.

deep-rooted concern with quality of service were clearly reflected in the Days' work, and in terms of outlook and ethos the designers and their clients were perfectly matched.

It was never the intention that the couple themselves would actually undertake design work, although during the 1970s Lucienne designed a group of furnishing fabrics, and Robin became increasingly involved with specific store interiors. Initially, their primary role was to develop a design strategy, to bring in specialists to implement this, and to exercise overall design control. "Part of the design consultants' problem will be to analyse the Partnership character and to consider whether it is appropriate to the present-day ideals and standing of the organization," Robin explained at the time of their appointment.[42] Their analysis, undertaken over the next six months, was presented as a report in 1963. This report, which covered every aspect of the Partnership's visual appearance, including architecture, interiors, signage, display, packaging, stationery, transport, publicity and publications, formed the basis of the programme of work that would be undertaken over the next decade. The report asserted the Days' belief that "the enterprising and enlightened ideas behind the Partnership can only be expressed in terms of really modern and uncompromising design."[43] It stressed that this could not be achieved overnight, and that the creation of a lasting Partnership image would require on-going design influence and control.

The first step towards implementing this radical programme was the appointment of a graphic designer. The person they chose was the distinguished Hans Schleger, and it was he who created the new JLP symbol, and who introduced a new crispness and rigour into the Partnership's graphics by abandoning their scrolling Baskerville typeface in favour of clean-lined Neue Haas. In 1967 Helvetica was adopted as the Partnership's standard typeface, favoured by the Days because it reflected the "straightforwardness, honesty, clarity and wholesomeness" of the organization itself.[44] The main problem the Days encountered was in raising design awareness and communicating the need for a standardized approach at root-and-branch level. "Twenty-five years ago the average Partner would not have known what the word 'design' meant. It was hard going to get the basic principles understood; for example, heads of department stores were used to having freedom in matters of design, and we had to insist that they keep to a policy," Robin recollected in 1987.[45]

In 1965 a Design Committee was established to coordinate all matters relating to design. It was this committee that prepared the John Lewis Partnership Design Manual, a comprehensive source of reference, issued in 1967, that codified every detail of the firm's house style. "House style" was the Days' preferred term, rather than "corporate identity". "It is very important to express the true rather than the wished-for character of the organization," declared Robin. "If this is not done, the picture presented, however smart or attractive, is merely a fancy dress without substance and is unlikely to stand the test of time. For this reason I do not like the term 'company image' which is used by some designers. It suggests a superficial mask, and 'house style' would seem a more appropriate term."[46]

The design manual's terms of reference covered all the areas in the Days' original report. "Although existing buildings must remain, any new exterior lettering is being done in a new standard form," Robin explained to Partners when the manual was launched. "Standard treatments of interior signs and lettering are also helping towards the clarity, order and simplicity which is our aim. The packaging of a great variety of John Lewis Partnership merchandise has been redesigned in a distinctive, modern and related style. Planned colour schemes have been introduced for offices and all non-selling areas, stationery redesigned and a new livery for all vehicles introduced. Certain visual elements have been agreed on and are applied wherever possible to strengthen the house style and the link between branches. These are the colours dark green with white, and sometimes a light green accent, a Partnership symbol, and the use of a particular type of lettering. Almost before anything else, we must, in designing for the Partnership, avoid fussiness, and work towards order, clarity and a modernity that will not tire."[47] The Days continued to advise on the appointment of design staff at John Lewis in later years, and among their recruits was Douglas Cooper, who set up the Partnership's highly successful in-house design department. "We cooperated fully with him, and watched the development of his department with great satisfaction," Lucienne recalled.[48]

By the time the design manual was finished, work was already under way on a similar guide for Waitrose. Here, the implementation of a coordinated design programme proved a lot easier because, unlike JLP's department stores, its supermarkets were mostly in new buildings where complete design control could be exercised. In addition, the high proportion of "own label" brands on the shelves made it easier to create a distinctive Waitrose look. Initially all Waitrose packaging was created by one freelance designer, Richard Daynes, whose artwork was submitted for approval to the Days, and it was because of this level of control that Waitrose was presented with a coveted Royal Society of Arts Design Management Award in 1971. The accompanying citation praised the Partnership – and by implication their design consultants – for their "deliberate and conscientious policy of maintaining decent standards of design, whether in building or lettering or packaging or display".

Robin and Lucienne's achievement in bringing about these fundamental changes at John Lewis and Waitrose was a direct consequence of the thoroughness and thoughtfulness of their original report. Robin described their approach as "evolutionary rather than revolutionary",[49] and their steady hand was crucial in guiding the Partnership in its gradual implementation of their design programme over a period of twenty-five years. Their design policy became as central to the ethos of the Partnership as its own principles of customer service and employee involvement. On their retirement as design consultants in 1987, Robin reflected: "What I am happy with is that although progress has been slow, any change that has been established seems to have been sufficiently well integrated to have been retained, and built on later. We have not simply followed fashion – so we have avoided the need to scrap things and start again."[50]

Left
Robin and Lucienne Day with Harry Legg, 1979
The Days enjoyed a long and productive relationship with the John Lewis Partnership between 1962 and 1987 in their capacity as joint design consultants. They are pictured here with Harry Legg, Director of Research and Expansion, with whom they worked closely. In the foreground is Robin's model of a proposed restaurant for the new John Lewis department store at Milton Keynes (see pages 164–5).

Centre
Drawing of proposed lounge for Peter Jones, c.1978
Robin and Lucienne advised on many interior schemes for John Lewis and Waitrose during the 1970s and 1980s. This gouache by Robin shows a proposal for a new lounge area near the lifts in the Peter Jones department store at Chelsea in London, incorporating banks of Polypropylene armchairs.

Bottom
Van liveries for the John Lewis Partnership, 1967
The Days appointed Hans Schleger as the Partnership's graphic designer in 1964, and it was he who created the new JLP logo. These images are taken from a Design Manual prepared by the Days, which standardized the Partnership's approach to all aspects of design from stationery to van liveries.

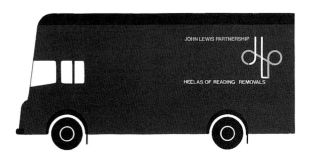

CHAPTER SIX

1970-93

LATER CAREERS

Robin Day: Series E and Polo Chairs

Having triumphantly pioneered the adoption of polypropylene in furniture design during the 1960s, Robin continued to investigate further applications for this resilient material during the ensuing decade, as well as experimenting with other forms of plastics. Since the early 1950s his two low-cost plywood stacking chairs, the Hillestak and the Q Stak, had been widely used in schools. In 1971, both these and the general purpose Polypropylene chair were superseded in the education sector by a new range of customized stacking chairs and stools entitled Series E. The polypropylene shells for these chairs were made on Hille's behalf by a firm called K.K.N. Sankey, who had one of the most highly automated injection-moulding plants in the country. Originally created as part of a coordinated range of school furniture for the Consortium of Local Authorities in Wales, the Series E package also consisted of four graduated stools and a range of heavy-duty circular, square, rectangular, hexagonal and trapezoid tables, along with specialist items such as screens, trolleys, benches, clay-modelling tables and clothes-hanging units.

Designed from a child's perspective, and conforming to BSI standards, the Series E chairs were produced in five sizes, originally colour-coded, A–E. The smallest chairs (A and B) were for infants, the medium chairs (C and D) for juniors, and the largest (E) for secondary-school use. In fact the shells of D and E were the same size; only the legs were a different height – a detail that greatly saved on tooling costs. Squarer in form than the Polypropylene chair, but with more curved corners at the top, the Series E chair included a novel feature: a rounded rectangular hole at the base of the seat back. As well as facilitating lifting, this made the chair lighter by reducing the amount of plastic in the shell. Like its predecessor, the Series E chair was aesthetically satisfying, ergonomically correct, phenomenally hard-wearing and remarkably cheap. This combination of advantages made it enormously popular with schools, and over the years, when times were hard for Hille, it was sales of the Series E that kept the company afloat. During the 1980s, tip-up variants were used in football stadia such as Coventry Football Club, and subsequently, during the early 1990s, the size A chair was sold by the global Swedish retailer IKEA.[1]

In 1975 another new model, the Polo chair, was added to the polypropylene group, and this, too, proved a resounding commercial success for Hille. The idea behind the Polo was to create a chair that would serve equally well both indoors and out. The Polypropylene chair was unsuited to being left outdoors because it had only limited resistance to ultraviolet light and its colour would fade over time, and when it rained, water

Opposite
Three Daughters of Mexico, silk mosaic, 1992–3
In her later career as a designer of one-off silk mosaics, Lucienne explored new themes and new forms of expression. This change of direction reinvigorated her creatively, and helped to keep her fresh.

Above
Polo chair, 1975
During the 1970s Robin added two new models to the Polypropylene chair family, the Series E school chair (see page 146) and the Polo. The Polo chair, seen here with a chromium-plated steel rod skid base, was designed for both indoor and outdoor use.

Right

Series E chair, 1971

A modified version of the
Polypropylene chair, the
Series E chair formed part of
a coordinated range of school
furniture originally created on
behalf of the Consortium of
Local Authorities in Wales.

Below

**Series E chairs in a
classroom**

Still in production today, the
Series E chair was designed
in five different sizes so that
it would be suitable for infant,
junior and secondary schools.

collected in the shell. To overcome these problems the Polo chair shell was produced in a specially formulated type of polypropylene containing anti-UV additives, and the shell was pierced by a series of holes, which facilitated both draining and ventilation.

Each member of the poly chair family has its own distinct character. The original Polypropylene side chair and armchair have a serious adult quality and are like the parents of the range. The Polo chair, by comparison, is a lively and energetic teenager, and the Series E chairs are the infant brood. The ebullient youthful character of the Polo chair was reflected in the fresh bright colours of its shell (originally white, black, yellow, red and emerald). The lower seat back made it more informal, and the holes in the seat, as well as being practical, had a playful quality. The Polo shell also differed from the Polypropylene chair in having a high gloss finish rather than a matt textural surface. As well as contributing to the freshness of its character, the sheen served the practical purpose of making the shell easier to clean. Like the Poly chair, the Polo was offered with a variety of bases, appearing at its jauntiest when mounted on a white enamelled steel rod skid base. Although many of Robin's designs are understated in the extreme, and anonymity was something to which he often aspired, there was another more upbeat side to his character, expressed through colour, pattern and sculptural line. It is this aspect of his personality that is embodied in the graduated rows of holes piercing the Polo shell, which inject a note of fun and make it one of his most endearing designs.

Robin Day: Propathene, Fibreglass and ABS

In 1973 Hille celebrated their achievement in the field of plastics by organizing an exhibition called *Furniture Takes to Technology* at London's Design Centre, which featured several new designs. Amongst these was the Obo chair (1972), made from propathene (ICI's version of polypropylene), and produced using a new technique, blow-moulding. In this process granules of raw material are fed into a long barrel containing a revolving screw. Heat turns the material into dough, which is forced through a die and extruded as a hollow cylinder. Sections of this soft material are then enclosed in a mould, and compressed air forces the plastic into shape. Blow-moulding is widely used to make cheap containers such as buckets and bottles, and tooling costs are much lower than for injection-moulding. The drawback is that both the extrusion marks and the mould lines are clearly visible and the standard of finish is rather poor. The most ingenious aspect of the Obo chair was that the mould produced two chairs in the form of one long cylinder, which was then sliced diagonally in half. The Obo was designed to make the most of the advantages of the blow-moulding process, but to minimize its drawbacks. To disguise the draw lines created during the extrusion process, for example, Robin used a strongly textured matt surface on the final mould. With its quartic form and recessed side handles, the Obo was one of his most unusual designs. A seat made from vacuum-formed polystyrene was inserted in the well, and the interior was then padded and upholstered, neatly covering the lip but leaving the white plastic exterior exposed.

Left and below
Polo chair, 1975
Originally produced in black, white, yellow, red and emerald green, the Polo chair is UV resistant. This, combined with the drainage and ventilation holes in the shell, made it ideal for outdoor use. Polo seating is seen here (left) in the Juba Cultural Centre, Sudan, and (below) installed in an outdoor stadium fixed directly to concrete terraces.

Another new form of plastic with which Robin experimented during the 1970s was injection-moulded ABS. ABS, or acrylonitrile butadiene styrene, is made by combining three polymers, each with a different character and strength. Although more difficult to mould than polypropylene, it has greater rigidity, which was why it was chosen for the shell of the 4-4000 reclining chair (1970), at that time the largest piece of injection-moulded furniture in the world. Lounge chairs are normally expensive to make, but the aim of the 4-4000 was to bring the price down by using high-volume production techniques. The generously proportioned seat was lined with large tailored cushions, complementing or contrasting with the white or buffalo-brown shell. The colour-coordinated enamelled steel swivel pedestal gave the chair a space-age quality, and its modernity made it particularly attractive to young people. Hence its inclusion in the youth-orientated Living Scene catalogue of 1972 – Hille's renewed venture into the domestic market – along with the Tote (1972) and Quadrille (1971) tables and the Obo chair.

Launched in the same year as the Obo chair, the Tote table adopted similar rounded square and circular forms, but, being made of ABS, it was finished with a smooth glossy sheen. Injection-moulded objects have to be designed so that they can be easily released from the mould, and it was this requirement that dictated the table's unusual shape, with its cylindrical hollow pedestal and central lift-off lid, produced in matching white or contrasting orange or brown. The well was large enough to hold a potted plant, but was mainly intended for storage. In advertisements it was illustrated as a drinks cabinet, with the lid doubling up as a tray.

Whereas the Living Scene range was directed at domestic consumers, the demountable stacking Toro chair (1971) was pitched at the contract market, and formed part of a wider range of café furniture, including the S290 table (1975) and the Ibex chair (1978). The Toro and the Ibex were both hybrids, made partly of plastic, partly of wood, partly of metal. The combined seat back and legs of the Toro were originally moulded in expanded polystyrene, with an upholstered wooden seat. In 1975, the frame was adapted so that it could be made of ABS. ABS was also considered for the seat back of the Ibex chair, but eventually polypropylene was chosen instead, combined with legs in tubular steel.

Another form of plastic with which Robin experimented in the 1970s was fibreglass-reinforced polyester resin, which was used for the cylindrical pedestal base of the Drum table (1973), combined with a white melamine-covered circular particleboard top. This design was unsuccessful, however, and a range of fibreglass shell Concourse Seating for airports (c.1974) similarly failed to progress beyond the prototype stage. By the end of the decade, the furniture industry's love affair with plastics was over, and styles were also changing fast. At the start of the 1980s Robin reflected: "We seem to be in a period of fragmentation as far as design directions go. One had always hoped that there would be a continuous modern development going on, getting better and better, but recently design has taken a lot of different directions – romantic perhaps, or very severe." [2]

Robin Day: Barbican Arts Centre

In July 1969 Robin was appointed as the Seating Design Consultant for the Barbican Arts Centre, the most extensive and lengthy design project of his career. Over the next twelve years he designed the seating for the foyer and the five auditoria, and through him, Hille secured substantial contracts to furnish large areas of this prestigious building. Designed by the architectural practice Chamberlin, Powell and Bon, the centre was part of a major 27-hectare (66-acre) housing and entertainment complex, originally conceived as early as 1955. The Barbican Centre for Arts and Conferences, as it eventually became known, did not finally open until 1981, and occupied a lot of Robin's time throughout the 1970s. Vast and multifaceted, it originally housed a concert hall for the London Symphony Orchestra, a theatre for the Royal Shakespeare Company, and extensive cinema, library, exhibition and conference facilities.

The building is characterized by bold use of bush-hammered concrete on both the interior and the exterior surfaces. This, combined with the vast monolithic scale of the complex, meant that the furniture had to be extremely robust in colour and form in order to make any impression. "The massive scale of the foyers with their high ceilings and open spaces demanded a range of furniture generous in scale and of an architectural character," Robin explained. The Hadrian range (1981), which he described as "large-scaled, chunky modular seating of strong simple geometric form, echoing the theme of the interior", was his characteristically bold response.[3] Aerial photographs of Hadrian confirm what a powerful impression it created when first installed. These images highlight its sinuous monumentality, and emphasize the associations with Hadrian's Wall. It could be arranged in innumerable formations, but worked best in carefully structured semicircular and U-shaped groups. Whereas previous lobby seating, such as Club (1962) and Dolce (1975), took the form of stand-alone settees, Hadrian was a flexible, curvilinear system, composed of straight, quarter-circle and wedge-shaped timber-framed units, upholstered in tan and bronze leather, and mounted on laminate plinths. Circular and rounded rectangular tables were created to complement the seating, and Robin also designed the cantilevered benches fixed to the massive concrete columns in the foyer, and the chunky timber-framed tables and chairs in the adjacent bars.

Robin's second major contribution to the Barbican was the seating for the five auditoria, which included three cinemas, a 1166-seat theatre, and a 2026-seat concert hall.[4] The visual and acoustic requirements of the theatre and concert hall made their seating layout particularly complex, and Robin's plans underwent numerous modifications during the 1970s as the auditoria themselves were redesigned. The Days' expertise in colour coordination is very much evident in these interiors. The theatre seats, with their dark-brown fabric upholstery and leather-covered arms, were deliberately subdued. The concert hall seating, by contrast, was rather more upbeat, with five different rich but mellow colours, alternating row by row.[5] The seating in these two auditoria and in Cinema 1 was fabricated by a specialist firm, Rank Audio Visual. An added technical complication was that, because the Barbican was intended

Far left

Obo chair, 1972
This photograph shows how two Obo chairs were created from one blow-moulded polypropylene drum (centre back), sliced diagonally across the middle. At the front is the vacuum-formed polystyrene shell that slotted into the drum to make the seat, which was then upholstered.

Left

Tote table, 1972
The distinctive feature of this low table is the fact that the hollow central drum can be used for storage. The white, orange or brown lid that covers the well doubles up as a tray.

Below

4-4000 armchair, 1970
Made from injection-moulded ABS plastic, this large pedestal armchair was produced in white or brown with matching or contrasting upholstery. Along with the Obo chair and the Tote table, it formed part of Hille's Living Scene collection, aimed at the youth market.

Right

Hadrian seating, Barbican Centre, 1981

In his capacity as seating consultant for the Barbican Centre, Robin designed all the seating for the foyers and auditoria. Shown here is a range of modular seating that he created for the foyers, complete with circular and oval tables. Originally it was arranged in snaking and hemispherical lines to complement the architecture of the interior.

Below

Bar tables and chairs, Barbican Centre, 1981

Whereas the Hadrian seating (right) subsequently entered the production range at Hille, these wooden tables and chairs were created as a one-off specifically for the Barbican.

Left

Concert hall, Barbican Centre, 1981
Robin designed the seating for all five auditoria in the Barbican. Renowned for its comfort, this seating is still in use thirty years after it was originally installed. The seating in the concert hall, made by Rank Audio Visual, is upholstered in a range of carefully chosen alternating colours.

Below

City seating, Barbican Centre, 1978
Shown here in one of the three cinemas at the Barbican Centre with its original multi-coloured upholstery, the City range was manufactured by Hille as one of their standard auditorium ranges.

Above
Director desk, 1962
Drawing on the skills of the firm's cabinetmakers, Hille continued to make executive office furniture. The rosewood veneered Director desk, shown here with two Nimbus chairs (right), was produced until at least 1974.

Opposite top and bottom left
Spectrum seating, 1983
Spectrum was a new range of tip-up polypropylene seating with a rust-proof frame launched shortly after Hille was taken over by Ergonom in 1983. Originally designed for sports stadia, it was also widely used in theatres and other indoor auditoria.

Opposite bottom right
Span auditorium seating, 1993
Robin's last major auditorium seating design, Span has die-cast aluminium arms and side frames, while the seat is made of moulded beech plywood.

as a major conference venue, all the cinema seats had to be equipped for simultaneous translation. The two smaller cinema/lecture rooms were fitted with Robin's City seating (1978), a standardized range of tip-up auditorium seating with an angular contoured profile, manufactured as a spin-off from the Barbican contract by Hille. A distinctive feature of the Barbican cinema seating was the vibrant polychrome upholstery, with individual seats being covered alternately in red, blue and green fabric, creating a lively and stimulating overall effect.

Robin Day: Hille

By 1972 Hille had adopted the name Hille International to reflect its rapidly expanding market abroad. However, although Robin's polypropylene ranges were extremely successful commercially, Hille, like all manufacturers, particularly those in plastics, was affected by the oil crisis and global recession of the 1970s, and eventually this began to take its toll. By this date several new designers, including Alan Turville, Fred Scott and Peter Murdoch, had entered the Hille fold. This, combined with the escalating size of the firm, meant that Robin, although still a major player, had less overall control. Whereas during the 1950s and 1960s, Hille's fortunes had been entirely dependent on the success or failure of his designs, by the 1970s the company had grown so large, and was branching out in so many directions, that its commercial well-being was increasingly out of his hands.

Although by this date Robin had largely ceased to design office furniture, Hille sought to maintain a lead in this market through the launch of the Hille Office System by Alan Turville, and Fred Scott's Supporto office chair. While the Supporto was a triumphant success, the Office System proved over-ambitious. By the early 1980s Hille were in serious financial difficulties, the combined effect of over-diversification in their product range, the loss of their lucrative Knoll licence, and increased competition. For a while the company put on a brave face, mounting a celebratory exhibition at the V&A in 1981 called *Hille – 75 Years of British Furniture*. However, 1982 did not bring the hoped-for improvements, and by the end of the year the writing was on the wall. The problems at Hille were compounded by the fact that by this date Leslie Julius, the managing director, was seriously ill. In October 1983, the situation came to a head, and the Hille family sold their controlling interest to one of their competitors, Ergonom.

This sudden change of ownership radically altered the direction and ethos of the company, which henceforth specialized in contract seating for schools, offices and auditoria. Since the mid-1980s Robin's designs for Hille have been much more sporadic, and following the departure of the Hille family, his relationship with the firm was never the same again. Although the Polypropylene, Polo and Series E ranges have remained in continuous production over the last two decades, Hille has changed hands on two further occasions and relocated several times.[6] Frequent personnel and policy changes over the last fifteen years have repeatedly interrupted the progress of Robin's designs, and although he has continued working with the company on and off, lack of continuity has made a creative relationship difficult to sustain.

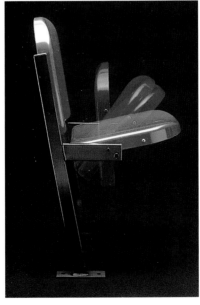

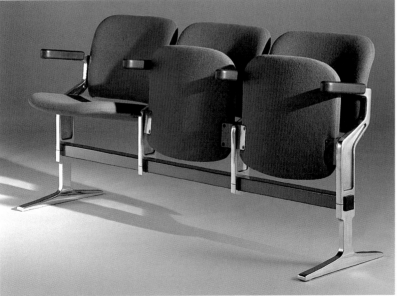

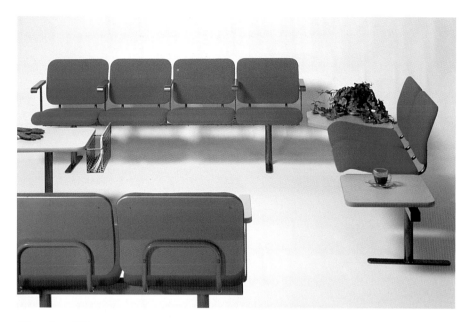

RD seating, 1984
This range of heavy-duty
beam-mounted seating was
originally designed for hospital
waiting rooms at the request
of a group of National Health
Service interior designers.
Made of sheet steel with
minimal padding, the seat
provides comfort and lumbar
support through its carefully
designed shape.

Robin Day: Stadium and Auditorium Seating

During the 1960s the Polypropylene chair revolutionized Hille,
opening up greatly increased domestic and worldwide markets.
As a result, from the 1970s onward, Robin's energies were
channelled mainly into designs for high-volume production, and
his work became increasingly focused on the specialized area
of stadium seating. As well as adapting the Polypropylene,
Series E and Polo shells for stadium use, he spent a lot of time
during the 1970s developing Arena, a new range of heavy-duty
tip-up seating. Designed for venues such as football and
athletics stadia, where limited space between rows precluded
the use of fixed shells, Arena seats were made of injection-
moulded polypropylene, formed in two parts and strengthened
on the underside by a series of ribs. Produced initially in two
versions, with U-shaped or linked steel frames, it was later
developed as a retractable system, and installed in sports stadia
throughout the country.

Development work on a second range of tip-up
polypropylene stadium seating called Spectrum (1983) was
already at an advanced stage when Hille were taken over.
This range, intended as a successor to Arena, was produced
in riser-fixed, tread-fixed, beam-mounted and retractable
versions, as well as in the form of individual linked folding chairs.
Distinguished by the simplicity of its rust-proof steel frame, and
by its use of nylon pivots and plastic stops, Spectrum eliminated
all metal-to-metal contact, and was made without screws or
bolts using a minimum of welds. It enjoyed great success
during the mid-1980s and was installed in numerous football
stadia and sports arenas, including Flushing Meadow Stadium
in New York, Cardiff Athletic Stadium, the Oval Cricket Club,
and Wembley Arena. In addition, the fact that it could also be
upholstered made it suitable for indoor venues, such as theatres
and lecture halls.

Because it was injection-moulded, the viability of Spectrum
was dependent on long runs. Blow-moulded plastics, by
contrast, although more expensive to manufacture, required
lower investment in terms of tooling and moulds, and the
process itself was also more flexible. This explains why Robin
subsequently designed another new range of tip-up auditorium
seating called Accord (1990), made from blow-moulded
polyethylene. Because polyethylene is not as strong as
polypropylene, the seat was strengthened by recessed ribs,
moulded within a double wall. Tamper-proof fixings, folding
arms, and a neat compact spring mechanism made Accord
ideal for sports stadia and, like Spectrum, it was produced in
vivid colours such as red, blue and green, while its textured
surface made it more scratch-resistant. Both ranges are still in
production in modified form, latterly manufactured by a specialist
stadium seating company called Link Seating, based at Pershore
in Worcestershire, England.

Shortly after the launch of Spectrum, Robin was asked to
develop a new range of upholstered indoor seating, which was
called Forum (1984). The brief was for an all-in-one system with
multiple applications, from lecture halls to courtrooms to waiting
rooms. Designed in the form of individual chairs and multiple
seating units, Forum combined a wider range of materials than

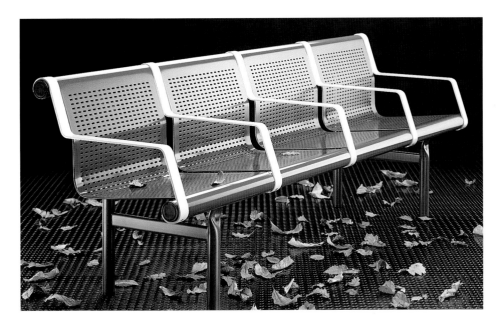

Left and centre
Toro seating, 1990
Widely used throughout the London Underground, this hard-wearing beam-mounted seating, fabricated entirely from metal, was designed to a stringent brief. Although made from pressed sheet steel, the seat is comfortable to sit on because of its angle and contours.

Bottom
Woodro seating, 1991
This is a variant of the Toro range (left and centre), made with a slatted hardwood seat instead of sheet steel. Like Toro it is distinguished by the elegant way in which the lip of the seat wraps around a cylindrical top and bottom rail.

Chest of drawers, 1982
This one-off cabinet, made of stained timber, was constructed by Robin to house Lucienne's sewing materials. Throughout his career Robin has always adopted a hands-on approach to design, and he particularly enjoys working with wood.

any of Robin's previous designs, including steel beams, cast-aluminium arm and back supports, moulded birch plywood seats, and expanded polyurethane foam arms. The compound curvature of the seat back was intended to provide comfort and lumbar support without the need for bulky upholstery. Initially this design failed to take off, but in recent years the beam-mounted version has been re-issued as Forum 2000.

Forum was succeeded by Span (1993), a new range of upholstered tip-up auditorium seating. Like its predecessor, it had a steel frame, cast-aluminium legs and arm units, and a padded and upholstered moulded plywood seat, but Span proved more successful at the time because it was directed to the needs of a more specific market.

Robin Day: Public Seating

In 1981 Robin stated: "I tend to lean towards the feeling that we have less and less justification for making and, therefore, designing highly prestigious manufactured artefacts which use a great deal of energy, time and material." [7] For this reason, apart from stadium and auditorium seating, Robin mainly focused during the 1980s and 1990s on heavy-duty public seating, which he felt to be a particularly worthwhile area of design. His RD range (1984), for example, arose out of a request from a consortium of National Health Service interior designers, led by John Haddock from South West Thames Regional Health Authority, for a beam-mounted seating system suitable for hospital waiting rooms. Set at a height to suit the elderly and infirm, the seats were characterized by their slim profile, and were made of pressed sheet steel with minimal padding and upholstery. The aim of the design was to achieve comfort and lumbar support through shape rather than deep padding. In addition, the design incorporated a number of important practical features, such as easily replaceable upholstery, clearance between the seat and back to prevent the accumulation of dirt, and widely spaced columns and flat floor plates to facilitate cleaning. Comparable with his British Rail bench of 1957, the RD range, which is still in production, demonstrates Robin's skill in responding to a tight and rigorous brief.

The most ubiquitous of Robin's later designs was his Toro seating (1990), widely used on London Underground stations, although originally designed for a wider range of applications, including casualty departments in hospitals. Unique in his *oeuvre* in being made entirely from metal, Toro is finished in brightly coloured enamels or polished steel, and is distinguished by the way its pierced seat curves upward and wraps round a cylindrical top and bottom rail. Tough, durable, yet visually attractive, it was supplemented by a hardwood version called Woodro (1991) the following year, and both are still in production, along with an upholstered variant, Exodus (1999).

Robin Day: Mines and West

Although Robin did not originally design furniture for John Lewis to sell, his consultancy work prompted occasional requests for short runs of customized items, including chairs for their shoe departments, and furniture for boardroom use. It was as a result of one such commission that he established contact

Left
**Solo reception seating,
Mines and West, 1987**
Originally designed for use in
John Lewis shoe departments,
this range of seating could be
constructed either as stand-
alone chairs or in multiple units
with shared arms. Visually Solo
is distinguished by its exposed
solid ash frame and its
upholstered flat side panels.

Below
**Accord stadium seating,
Hille, 1990**
The tip-up seats in this robust
range are made of blow-
moulded polyethylene. Because
this type of plastic is not as
strong as polypropylene, the
seats have a double wall,
strengthened by recessed ribs,
which can be seen on the
underside.

Top
Parkland, Heal's, 1974
This was Lucienne's last furnishing fabric design for Heal's. In it she returns to her favourite theme of trees, reinterpreted here in a completely fresh and original way.

Centre
Unity, Heal's, 1971
Lucienne's designs always contain more than meets the eye, which is one reason why they remain so satisfying. In this late furnishing fabric she creates variety out of uniformity by playing with the arrangement of identical motifs.

Bottom
Helix, Heal's, 1970
Multiple layers of pattern are a leitmotif running through Lucienne's abstract designs, exploited here with great dexterity in a furnishing fabric for Heal's.

in 1986 with a High Wycombe manufacturer, Mines and West, which produced high-quality furniture for office and commercial use. This acted as a catalyst for a liaison with the company, resulting in three new groups of seating entering production between 1987 and 1990. Mines and West specialized in timber furniture, and Robin's designs were all made of ash. As such they provide an interesting counterpoint to his high-volume production designs in metal and plastic, and reflect a different side to his character and his love of nature and natural materials. "More and more, I like things like trees and the way they're put together," he reflected in 1981.[8] In 2000 he observed: "A record of my design career seems to focus on machine-made things for quantity production, especially on plastic technology.... A less well known interest of mine is in organic materials and hand-work. I warm to wood, stone, leather, cane, etc., all of which improve and grow noble with time. It is not just an affection for their appearance and limitless variation of texture, but also the tactile enjoyment of touching and handling such hand-worked materials."

Robin's first design for Mines and West was a range of reception seating called Solo (1987). This was distinguished by its rounded square frame, made of solid ash, mounted on the exterior with upholstered panels in between. Solo was produced in bays of between two and four seats, as well as stand-alone chairs. Multiple units had shared sides, and square and rectangular tables, along with quadrant-shaped inserts, also formed part of the range.

Shortly after the launch of Solo, Robin began work on the Multo stacking armchair (1989), which was eventually produced in two versions, one made of bent ash, the other with an oval tubular steel frame. Because Mines and West did not have metalworking facilities, the frame of the steel version was fabricated by a specialist firm in Coventry called the Midland Repetition Company. The resulting chair was strong but elegant, and the metal version was chosen for the Vaults restaurant at the Royal Society of Arts. Robin's third production design for Mines and West, the ash-framed Downley boardroom chair (1990), was rather more traditional in character and construction, albeit deliberately so to suit a particular market.

By this date, however, Mines and West had fallen into debt, and in 1991 the company went into receivership, and was subsequently taken over. Robin's designs remained in production for several years, but he encountered increasing difficulties in extracting royalty payments from the new owners, and in 1995 the factory closed down. Coming on top of his problems at Hille, the Mines and West fiasco was a great disappointment, and underlined how unstable and unpredictable the British furniture industry had become since the 1970s.

Lucienne Day: Textiles for Heal Fabrics and John Lewis Partnership

Lucienne's career changed quite radically during the mid-1970s, partly due to external factors, partly at her own instigation. Over the previous twenty-five years she had enjoyed highly productive and stable relationships with her main clients, but during the early 1970s, three of her chief contacts – Tom Worthington,

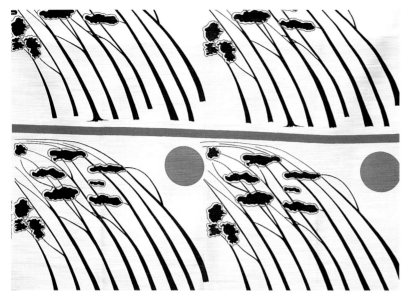

Top
Kyoto, Cavendish Textiles, 1975
The last mass-produced furnishing fabrics that Lucienne designed were for Cavendish Textiles, a division of the John Lewis Partnership. Stylistically they are unlike anything she had created before.

Centre
Halloween, Cavendish Textiles, 1975
In her late stylized patterns, Lucienne pares down tree forms to their essence – an outline or a silhouette. Unlike her earlier arboreal designs, these patterns are deliberately flat, and there are no textural effects.

Bottom
Lucienne, Cavendish Textiles, 1974
In this crisp abstract design Lucienne creates an illusion of three-dimensionality from the juxtaposition of flat geometric planes and graduated stripes.

Michael Tomkinson and Ron Crawford – all retired. Modern design had flourished in the field of home furnishings during the 1950s and 1960s, and design-led manufacturers had met with considerable commercial success. By the 1970s, however, the individuals who had headed the drive towards modernity twenty years earlier were disappearing from the scene, and this, combined with the worsening economic climate, triggered a loss of nerve in manufacturing which resulted in increasingly bland design. Lucienne found the prevailing fashions for ruralism and revivalism particularly hard to stomach, and as the decade progressed, she felt more and more out of sympathy with current trends

After 1970 she created only six more designs for Heal's, culminating in Parkland (1974), a pattern of stylized trees. At the start of decade, Helix (1970), with its dynamic spirals and overlaid squares, was as confident and accomplished as ever, and there was no hint that she might be thinking of giving up. However, her next four patterns, Hazy Daisy, Petal, Integration and Unity (1971), seemed to lack something of the visual spark of her earlier work, and from this date onward she became increasingly conscious that she was tiring of the demands of production design. In 1968, when asked about her future plans, she had answered: "My field is very much geared to fashion. Although I have no feelings about wanting to give up or retire now, this will obviously come, I think." [9] By the mid-1970s she realized it was time for a change, and she took the decision to withdraw from industrial design.

Before abandoning printed furnishing fabrics entirely, however, she created one last group of designs for John Lewis. Lucienne (1974), with its interplay between flat planes and three-dimensional perspective, reflected her old interest in architecture. Kyoto (1975), which contrasted red suns with black trees, and Halloween (1975), with its silhouettes of branches against the night sky, showed her exploring evocative new themes. Chestnut (1975) was witty and ingenious, with trees suggested by abstract clusters of diamonds and squares, while in Panama (1975) she played with overlaid shapes, a device executed with characteristic vigour. Spanning the full spectrum from stylization to abstraction, these late patterns for John Lewis marked a distinguished finale to an exceptional industrial design career.

Lucienne Day: Silk Mosaics

During the mid-1970s Lucienne was asked to design a pattern to decorate some metal fire shutters in a John Lewis department store at Newcastle-upon-Tyne. The pattern was broken down into horizontal rectangular strips, and a visitor to her studio, on seeing the design, suggested an analogy with embroidery. This triggered off the idea for Lucienne's silk mosaics, the new medium she pioneered during the second half of the 1970s, which provided an alternative avenue for her creative energies for the next twenty years, after her decision to withdraw from industry.

Although her activities fell loosely into what others categorized as art textiles, Lucienne was fiercely independent in technical and creative terms, and dissociated herself from patchwork. The term "silk mosaic" was chosen because the silk units were so small that they recalled the tesserae in Roman mosaics. Also, the word "mosaic" stressed correspondences with architecture rather than textiles, and thus highlighted the associations with interior design. Her silk mosaics were constructed from small squares or rectangles of coloured silk, sewn together, then supported on a stiffer fabric backing. This technique differed in several key respects from patchwork, notably in the shape of the elements (all created on a 1cm [0.4in] module), the choice of fabric (plain silks rather than printed cottons), and the fact that paper templates were not removed from the work. Also significant was the non-utilitarian nature of the finished hangings, conceived as works of art rather than coverings for domestic objects. In this way Lucienne made a decisive break, both from her own background as a designer of mass-produced furnishings for the home, and from the conventions of domestic handicraft traditions.

Initially, while developing her technique, Lucienne stitched the first few silk mosaics herself, and her first exhibition, at the Prestcote Gallery at Cropredy in Oxfordshire in 1979, consisted entirely of her own work. The hand-sewing process was extremely labour-intensive, however, and subsequently she employed two skilled seamstresses, her niece Karin Conradi from 1980, and Henrietta Brooks from 1988, so that she herself could concentrate on planning new designs. Although her decision to stop designing for industry coincided with the crafts revival of the 1970s, the idea of being a "maker" was not what attracted her to this medium, and her new work, although hand-made, was very much design-led. Her long experience as a designer played an important role in the way she conceived and planned her silk mosaics. For example, because of their geometric structure, and the juxtaposition of colour, they were composed using graph paper. Lucienne's background and outlook always set her apart from the mainstream crafts movement, and significantly, many of her new clients were former colleagues from the design world, while her commissions came from architects as well as collectors.

Nonetheless, although the adoption of the silk mosaic technique marked a radical step in her creative development, stylistically there was greater continuity between her production designs and her one-off pieces than might at first appear. The closest parallels are with her carpets, which were often strongly geometric and frequently composed of rectangular strips, as in Furrows (1957) and Couplet (1960). There are also similarities with some of Lucienne's abstract furnishing fabrics from the late 1960s, several of which, with hindsight, can be seen to have paved the way for her silk mosaics. Of these, Causeway (1967) is the most obvious, but rectilinear patterns were also central to Integration (1971), Lucienne (1974), and Panama (1975).

Although by comparison with her printed textiles, the silk mosaic technique might seem restrictive, Lucienne enjoyed the challenge of working within this self-imposed discipline, and responded to its limitations with characteristic ingenuity. She relished the chance to create one-off designs after so many years spent labouring over complex pattern repeats. Also, selecting silks (usually Thai or Indian) from the rich array on offer gave her the perfect opportunity to use her skills and indulge her pleasure in choosing and juxtaposing colour. She particularly

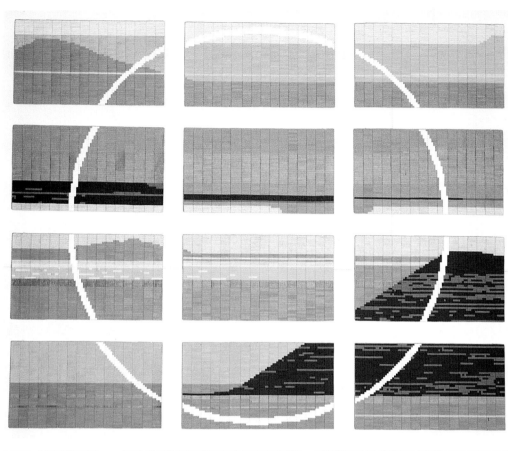

Left

Islands silk mosaic, 1991
This twelve-part composite silk mosaic was the second of the two monumental hangings that Lucienne created for the café in the new John Lewis department store at Kingston-upon-Thames designed by Ahrends, Burton and Koralek.

Below left and right

Aspects of the Sun silk mosaic, 1990
Lucienne is shown here installing her largest and most ambitious silk mosaic, Aspects of the Sun, created for the café in the new John Lewis department store at Kingston-upon-Thames. The six-part hanging was her single most important commission in this medium. The individual components are (anticlockwise from top): Partial Eclipse; Foggy Sun; Midnight Sun; Eclipse; Concentric Sun; Sun and Sea.

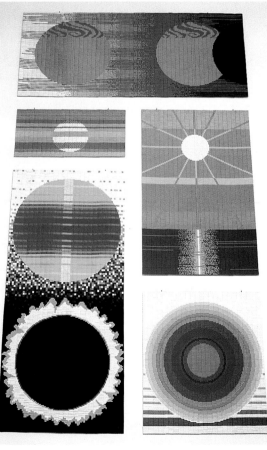

Their Exits and Their Entrances silk mosaic, 1981
In this work Lucienne explored variations on a theme, and the design as a whole consists of a number of distinct subsections.

enjoyed exploiting the slubbed textures of silk and used the two-tone iridescence of shot silks (woven from different coloured warp and weft) to bring an extra dimension to her designs. At this stage in her career, Lucienne felt that silk mosaics gave her greater freedom than industrial design. Also, working for herself meant that her choice of imagery was completely untrammelled, and she could go off at a tangent or explore new avenues whenever she chose. Moreover, because the making process was directly under her control, the quality of the end product was entirely in her hands. This was an ideal situation from Lucienne's point of view after years of indirect control.

Although relying on craft processes, Lucienne's silk mosaics were conceived from an architectural perspective. The figures in Standing (1981) and Meckanops (1982) loom like buildings, for example, and it is perhaps no coincidence that the strips of silk resemble bricks. Architecture recurred as a theme in several designs, from two of her earliest silk mosaics, Black Window and White Door, to Their Exits and Their Entrances (1981), and a more recent work, Museum (1990). The architectural context of her work was something that had always stimulated Lucienne, and through exhibitions held in venues such as Denys Lasdun's National Theatre, she was able to exploit these associations.

Some of her most notable works were prompted by commissions from architectural clients, who appreciated her ability to create works that harmonized with their interiors. Ronald Ward & Partners commissioned two sets of hangings – Board of Wisdom (1985), and Tangram Puzzle and Solution (1985) – for the headquarters of Shearman and Stirling, while The Window (1986) was created for the Queen Elizabeth Conference Centre at Westminster, designed by Powell and Moya. Lucienne's most impressive silk mosaics were the two large composite works commissioned by Ahrends Burton and Koralek for the café in their new John Lewis store at Kingston-on-Thames. The largest of the two, Aspects of the Sun (1990), was a six-part hanging measuring 4.9 metres (16 feet) in height, which used an earlier design, Midnight Sun, as a starting point for a series of variations on a solar theme. Although each section was distinctive, her careful choice of colours resulted in a balanced and unified whole. The success of this hanging led to a second commission for a work on an adjacent café wall, but instead of repeating her winning formula, Lucienne used this design, Islands (1991), to explore new structures and themes. Islands depicted a single scene rather than a series of contrasting images, and whereas the panels in Aspects of the Sun varied in scale, each of the twelve sections in Islands was the same size. Although Islands was representational, it had a strong abstract quality, with each section being locked together by the overlaid circle.

The titles of her silk mosaics often suggested a narrative or figurative content, and some, such as Summer Palace (c.1982) and Crowned Heads (1981–3), contained recognizable motifs. However, literal depictions of people and places were not the point of her work, and whatever their source of inspiration, her designs were always conceived in an abstract way. Mind play and lateral thinking had always been central to Lucienne's

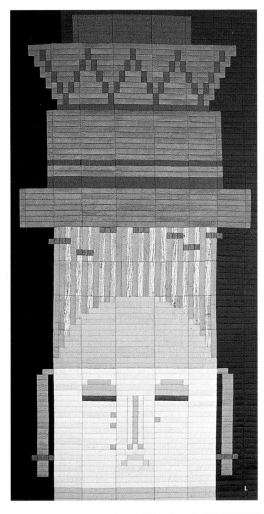

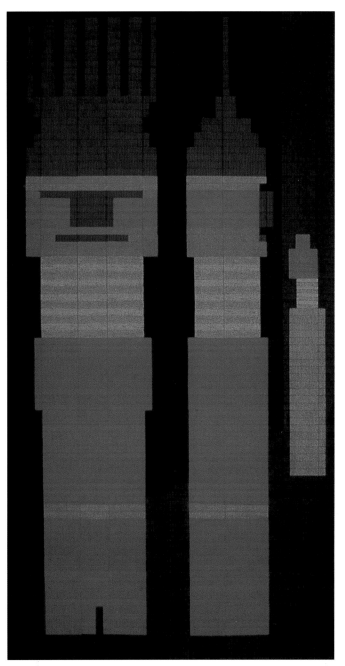

Far left
Sad Lady silk mosaic, 1983
This design was part of a series of four Crowned Heads created over a period of two years, which also included Trance, Chess King and The Queen.

Left
Meckanops silk mosaic, 1982
Lucienne's long-standing interest in architectural forms is evident both in this work and in Their Exits and Their Entrances (opposite).

Below
Circling the Square V silk mosaic, 1991
The last in a series of five panels, each a variation on a theme, this silk mosaic highlights the design dexterity in Lucienne's later work and her continuing interest in abstraction.

Robin Day, c.1973
Robin designed a series of
shop and café interiors for
the John Lewis Partnership
between 1973 and 1983. He is
shown here with a model of his
proposed restaurant for the
John Lewis department store
on Oxford Street in London,
completed in 1973.

approach to design, and the ingenious Enigma (1988) and Memory Game expressed her delight in visual tricks. Tangram, a Chinese puzzle in which a square is cut into seven pieces that fit together in different ways, prompted a series of hangings over many years, and creative virtuosity was also evident in the maze-like Koran (1986).

Structure was important, and many pieces were composite in form. Some, such as Enigma (1988) and Three Daughters of Mexico (1993), were created from separate panels. Others, such as The Castle and Other Stories (c.1979) and The Apple, consisted of self-contained elements, but were constructed as a unified whole. Sometimes a design initially conceived on a large scale might give rise to a series of smaller hangings. This aspect of her later work provides another parallel with her earlier approach to industrial design, when it was her custom to recycle personal leitmotifs from a common pool. Similarly, a group of works called Circling the Square (1991) demonstrates how, when she found an idea that particularly interested her, she returned to it periodically through a series of variations.

Lucienne organized regular exhibitions of her silk mosaics throughout the 1980s, including solo shows at the Footstool Gallery at St John's Smith Square in 1986, and the Lyttelton Gallery at the National Theatre in 1981 and 1991. In 1982 her work was shown in Japan at the National Museums of Modern Art in Tokyo and Kyoto, and the following year she held an important one-woman exhibition at the Röhsska Museum in Gothenburg. Her silk mosaics have been acquired by many leading museums at home and abroad, including the Victoria & Albert Museum, the Art Institute of Chicago, the Röhsska Museum, and the Whitworth Art Gallery in Manchester.[10]

Robin and Lucienne Day: John Lewis Partnership
The Days continued in their role as design consultants for the John Lewis Partnership until 1987, latterly becoming involved in specific projects, as well as steering the design direction of the organization as a whole. During the 1970s, for example, Lucienne designed a range of china for use in the Partnership's restaurants and cafés. The final chapter in her alliance with John Lewis – the two silk mosaics for the Kingston store – postdated her retirement as design consultant, indicating the high regard in which she was still held.

Robin's involvement with the Partnership increased significantly as time went on, and during the 1970s he became closely involved in interior design schemes for a series of John Lewis and Waitrose stores. Some of these were localized refurbishments of catering areas within existing buildings, such as the new restaurant and tea and coffee bar he designed for John Lewis store on Oxford Street in 1972–3.[11] In addition, he played an important role in the design of three flagship stores, each project spanning several years. In 1976 John Lewis opened a new branch in a gigantic shopping centre at Brent Cross near Hendon, the culmination of six years of work. The first new department store to be built by the Partnership since the war, its interior was designed by Harold Bennett, but with considerable input from Robin and Lucienne. Harry Legg, Director of Research and Expansion at John Lewis, noted

Left

Fashion floor, John Lewis, Milton Keynes, 1979
The John Lewis department store at Milton Keynes was the largest interior design scheme that Robin undertook for the Partnership. On completion Peter Lewis, the Partnership's chairman, praised Robin's work for being "admirably good in detail", and "thrillingly integrated, assured and powerful".

Below

Coffee shop, John Lewis, Milton Keynes, 1979
Circular forms are echoed in the shapes of the lamps, tables and stools that Robin designed for this café in the flagship John Lewis store at Milton Keynes.

Above
Auditorium seating, Mines and West, 1989
This range of tip-up upholstered auditorium seating was similar to that designed by Robin for the Durham Street auditorium at the Royal Society of Arts.

Right
Multo stacking chair, Mines and West, 1989
Intended for the restaurant and conference market, this chair was produced in two versions, one with a laminated wood frame, and the other with an oval tubular steel frame, as here.

Opposite
The Vaults Restaurant, Royal Society of Arts, 1989
Robin and Lucienne were both members of the design committee advising on the refurbishment of the vaults at the Royal Society of Arts, and it was they who suggested leaving the brickwork exposed. On completion, Robin's Multo chair for Mines and West (right) was chosen for the restaurant.

that the Days' influence "extended to almost every aspect of the design, including the elegant exterior." [12]

Following the success of Brent Cross, the Partnership decided to open a store at Milton Keynes. The location they chose was the stylish new shopping centre, a giant glass box designed by architects from the Milton Keynes Development Corporation, which provided accommodation for a hundred shops. This time Robin took the lead in designing the interior, again with input from Lucienne, working initially with Graham Heywood, the Partnership's Design Coordinator, until Heywood's death in 1977. Completed in 1979, the store was another success. One of its most popular features was the self-service restaurant, designed for high-volume throughput, where customers could select different types of food from alternative windows. "The entire scheme is confident, modern and straightforward," wrote Harry Legg when the store opened, and he praised Robin for "rising to an unusual challenge, responding to and respecting the objectives of the design of the shopping building, and of the new City as a whole." [13]

Robin's last major project for the Partnership was a Waitrose supermarket, which replaced a basement food hall in the John Barnes store at Hampstead. Opened on 20 October 1981, the interior was distinguished by its spaciousness and bold use of colour. Green was used behind the fruit and vegetable section, while the bakery walls were dark-blue wood. Special attention was paid to the design of the fish department, which was enlivened by a backdrop of decorative tiles. [14] The following year Robin was invited to design a mezzanine coffee shop within the same store, a project on which he collaborated during 1982–3 with Jonathan Pennington from the architectural practice Bennett and Pennington. These projects provided a satisfying outlet for Robin's creative energies, and enabled him to combine his skills as a furniture designer with his talents in graphics and interior design.

Robin and Lucienne Day: Royal Society of Arts
In 1987 Lucienne was appointed Master of the Faculty of Royal Designers for Industry, an honorary post she held for the next two years. This appointment brought her into closer contact with the Royal Society of Arts, and led to an invitation for her and Robin to join the RSA's design committee. The committee was set up during the late 1980s to advise on design matters relating to the redevelopment of the RSA's headquarters. This project, completed in 1990, involved the installation of a new restaurant and lecture theatre in the basement of the building, and provided two avenues for their creative input. First, they advised on interior design, and it was at the Days' suggestion that the impressive brick vaults were left undecorated, an interesting throwback to the exposed brickwork at Cheyne Walk. Secondly, Robin designed some of the seating, including the custom-made upholstered tip-up seating for the Durham Street Auditorium, and the steel-framed Multo stacking armchairs used in the restaurant, both produced by Mines and West. Subsequently Robin's Downley chairs and tables were chosen for the Fellows' Reading Room and in 1996, when the Great Hall was converted into a lecture theatre, his Span seating was installed in the auditorium.

CHAPTER SEVEN

1994-2010

FINAL YEARS

At the start of the 1990s Lucienne was at the height of her success with her silk mosaics, which she continued to exhibit throughout the decade. Her retrospective exhibition at the Whitworth Art Gallery in Manchester in 1993 included a large display of recent hangings, and she also held solo shows at the Brewery Arts Centre in Kendal in 1996 and Broughton House Gallery in Cambridge in 1998. Gradually, however, during the second half of the decade, she began to wind down her activities in the Cheyne Walk studio and devote more time to the study of plant life and horticulture.

'Since my early work I have been fascinated by the phenomenon of plant growth,' observed Lucienne in 2000. 'The decision to give up designing the silk mosaics gave me an opportunity to expand my knowledge in this field. Reading, attending lectures, studying plant families at the Chelsea Physic Garden, and, most useful of all, taking part in trips to plant-rich sites in Greece, Turkey and the Pyrenees and the Dolomites to study plants in their native habitats has proved such a valuable experience that I can begin to say "plants are the materials I design with now."'

By 1990 the Days had been practising as designers for so long that they had become almost legendary figures. This prompted the interest of design historians, and in 1991 I flagged up the couple's pivotal contribution to post-war design in my book *The New Look – Design in the Fifties*, which placed their achievements in an international context and identified their key role as pioneers of "Contemporary" design. This book accompanied a major exhibition at Manchester City Art Galleries, which the Days were jointly invited to open. In 1993 the Whitworth Art Gallery organized a solo show, *Lucienne Day – A Career in Design*, with a publication by curator Jennifer Harris. These books and exhibitions disseminated the Days' work to a wider audience and established their seminal position in the canon of 20th-century design.

As the Days began to be "rediscovered", there was growing interest in their work among collectors and dealers, triggering renewed attention from the media. A major joint *retrospective exhibition, Robin and Lucienne Day – Pioneers of Contemporary Design*, which I curated at the Barbican Art Gallery in 2001, marked the culmination of a decade of mounting appreciation. This exhibition, which examined the couple's evolution in parallel across the whole gamut of their astonishingly productive careers, was accompanied by the first edition of this book. By displaying their work side by side in tandem as it had been originally during the 1950s and 60s, the exhibition respected their independence but highlighted the complementary

Opposite
Robin and Lucienne Day, c.1995
In later years the Days witnessed a revival of interest in their earlier careers. They remained strongly committed to design and Robin continued to produce new work until shortly before his death.

Above
Polypropylene armchair, Habitat, 1999
Robin's Polypropylene chairs were given a new lease of life after being reissued by Habitat in a new range of translucent colours as part of the 20th Century Legends Collection.

Right

**Childsply chair,
Twentytwentyone, 1999**
Created from half a standard-sized sheet of birch-laminated plywood, this child's chair was designed by Robin for a charity auction organized by the London gallery Twentytwentyone.

Centre

**Avian lounge chair,
Twentytwentyone, 2000**
This prototype chair, with its distinctive moulded plywood arms and sledge-like flat steel-bar legs, was launched at *100% Design* in October 2000.

Bottom

**RD001 Sofa/Daybed, SCP,
2000**
From the late 1990s onwards Robin collaborated with several manufacturers, including the leading contemporary furniture company SCP. This sofa, launched at the Milan Furniture Fair in April 2000, is characteristically simple and understated.

nature of their designs and presented them on equal terms. The building itself – whose interiors and furnishings Robin had played such a vital role in designing during the 1970s – provided the perfect venue for the show.

Although Lucienne had retired by this date, Robin remained tireless in his interest and commitment to design. In 1968 he had predicted: "I tend to think I will keep working forever. In my field I still think my accumulated knowledge – technical knowledge apart from anything else – is of value and I reckon I will go on designing furniture for quite a few years." [1] True to his word, Robin was still hard at work until shortly before he died in 2010, his "accumulated knowledge" in demand from a host of manufacturers and retailers keen to produce his designs.

Tom Dixon, former Creative Director of Habitat, who was a great admirer of Robin's work, started the ball rolling by reintroducing the Polypropylene chair on to the domestic market. Launched in October 1999 as part of the 20th Century Legends Collection, the Polypropylene stacking chairs and armchairs were given a new lease of life with their translucent lemon, lime, blue and white shells, enthusing a new generation who missed them first time around. The 20th Century Legends Collection also included new versions of two of Lucienne's earlier designs. Her black and white Graphica fabric, originally created for Heal's in 1953, was converted into ready-made curtains, while the orange version of her Black Leaf glass-towel design, originally manufactured by Thomas Somerset in 1959, was enlarged on a duvet cover. Habitat also put Robin's handsome leather-upholstered Forum settee back into production, with an oak frame replacing the original afrormosia, as well as reissuing his personal favourite, the 675 dining chair.

Back in 1981 Robin had commented: "At one time, in the 1940s, anything modern was very exciting. Design, planning and new concepts of architectural design were going to be the salvation of mankind. It should be quite possible to have a high standard of design available to a great number of people by using modern materials and technology. But the 'modern style' has now become the familiar background to people, and this modern of a mediocre type has debased modern design in general. The idealism as well as the excitement behind the modern style seems to have faded." [2] After a dispiriting period during the 1980s when Robin felt "out of sync" with the furniture industry, he was happy to be back at the heart of things once more. In addition to his Polypropylene chairs, several of his other landmark designs are still in production, either by Hille or other firms, including his Series E school chairs, his Polo chair and the Toro and Woodro benches.

While Robin appreciated the enduring interest in his earlier work, his creative impulse remained as strong as ever, and he relished the opportunity to create new designs. The beech-framed RD001 Sofa / Daybed, commissioned by Sheridan Coakley for SCP, was launched at the Milan Furniture Fair in April 2000. Robin also worked closely with Simon Alderson at Twentytwentyone on a range of new and old designs. Reissues included the glass-topped Alpha table, originally produced by Hille in 1959, and an enlarged version of the moulded plywood Tricorne tray. These were launched at 100% Design in October 2000, along with the Avian lounge chair and settee. Novel features of this design were the moulded plywood arms, harking back to Robin's ground-breaking chairs for the Royal Festival Hall in 1951, and the sledge-like legs made of flat steel bars, a device first employed in his Single Convertible bed-settee in 1957.

Always responsive to positive initiatives, Robin was one of thirteen leading designers who were invited to design a piece of children's furniture for a project called Childsply, organized by Twentytwentyone in 1999. The brief stated that each object had to be made from a single sheet of birch-faced plywood. The resulting designs, manufactured by Windmill Furniture, were subsequently auctioned on behalf of the Children's Hope Foundation. Robin's contribution was a chair whose seat slotted neatly into a flat side frame. Typically, his design was so economical that not one but two chairs could be cut from a single sheet of wood. "Children are often interested in adult artefacts," Robin observed, recalling his own childhood. "I must have realized early on that everything had to be thought out and made." For Robin, imagination and discipline had always been inextricably combined. His later designs continued to reflect the ingenuity of an earlier, less affluent generation.

Robin's parallel interests in new and old technologies, and in both natural and man-made materials, remained equally significant in his later designs. In 2001 he designed four beautifully proportioned oak chairs with curved seat rails and turned legs for a project called Onetree. All the furniture and objects in this collection were made from a venerable 170-year old oak tree that had to be felled at Tatton Park in Cheshire. Robin's classic West Street armchair (2006), produced by Case for John Lewis, is also made of oak, with another variant in walnut.

At the opposite end of the technological spectrum is the Sussex bench (2003), a modular seating system made of air-moulded polypropylene, designed for the Italian company Magis. Intended for outdoor use, it consists of two units, one straight, the other curved, which can be run together to form crescents or long snaking lines. Visually it recalls traditional slatted wooden benches, but its materials and manufacturing processes are cutting edge.

It seemed that the Days would live forever, but Lucienne died on 30 January 2010 at the age of 93 and Robin passed away later that year on 9 November 2010 at the age of 95. His last public appearance was at the Royal Society of Arts for the premier of a film celebrating the couple's work: 'Contemporary Days: The Designs of Lucienne and Robin Day', directed by Murray Grigor for the American foundation, Design on Screen. Interest in the Days' careers continues to grow. Pallant House Museum in Chichester is hosting an exhibition called *Robin and Lucienne Day: Design and the Modern Interior in 2011*.

Throughout their long careers, the Days remained true to the ideals that originally inspired them. In their youth they witnessed the advent of the Modern Movement. After the war they were jointly responsible for popularizing "Contemporary" design, an accessible and optimistic school of modern design that was both practical and people-centred. Deploying their talents in a wide range of areas, the couple devoted their lives to developing and refining this idiom. Together they embody the whole history of British post-war design in microcosm. Their influence has been far-reaching, and their impact will resonate for many years to come.

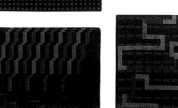

Above left
Tangram VI and VII silk mosaics, c.1992
A tangram is a Chinese puzzle in which a square is cut into seven pieces that fit together in different ways. Lucienne used this device as the basis for a series of silk mosaics during the 1980s and 1990s.

Above right
Black Leaf duvet cover, Habitat, 1999
This pattern was originally created as a glass towel for Thomas Somerset in 1959. It was reissued forty years later on a duvet cover for Habitat as part of their 20th Century Legends Collection.

Left
Enigma silk mosaic, 1988
This large composite work on the theme of water, now in the collection of the Whitworth Art Gallery in Manchester, reflects Lucienne's delight in visual puns. From top to bottom, working from left to right the twelve panels are as follows: Trident; Meander; Raindrops; Canal; Aquarius; Ripple; Reflexion; Torrent; Lake; Rain; Cascade; River.

CHAPTER 1

1 Where no other sources are quoted, information originates from conversations or correspondence with Robin and Lucienne Day.
2 Important design exhibitions held in London while Robin Day was at college included *British Industrial Art in Relation to the Home* at Dorland Hall in 1934, *British Art in Industry* at the Royal Academy in 1935 and the *Exhibition of Everyday Things* at the RIBA in 1936.
3 These were displayed alongside a hooked rug with a simple geometric Greek key pattern designed by Robin and made by his mother, which later formed part of the furnishings of Robin and Lucienne's apartment in Markham Square. *See* illustration on p.15.
4 Illustrated by Noel Carrington in "The Mantle of William Morris", *The Listener*, 17 November 1938, where it was contrasted with a painted cabinet by Philip Webb, 1861. The article is a review of the *Arts and Crafts Exhibition* at Burlington House, 1938, in which Robin's sideboard was featured.
5 Clients included Kitty Foster, who ran a boutique in Mayfair, for whom Robin produced showcards and advertisements. During the war, when luxury materials were in short supply, he designed some earrings carved from white plastic which were sold through this shop.
6 Robin's considerable skills in this area are demonstrated by the graphic panels he submitted to the Museum of Modern Art's Low-Cost Furniture Competion in 1948, and an illustration of a bar interior in "Designer: Robin Day" by Milner Gray, *Art and Industry*, May 1952, p.155.
7 Among his students at Beckenham was Frank Guille, later chief designer for Kandya.
8 It was Mrs Kinaston who introduced Lucienne to the work of the St Ives painters. For further information about Lucienne Day's early life and influences, see Lesley Jackson, "Sources of Inspiration", *Crafts*, May/June 1999, pp.46–9
9 Lucienne recalled that she created one design with birdcage motifs that may have entered production at Sanderson, although this has not been traced.
10 These quotations are taken from Maurice Richards, "SIA Profile: Lucienne Day", *SIA Journal*, no. 84, February 1960; and Russell Miller, "All in the Days' work", unidentified magazine article in Lucienne Day Press Cuttings Book, 1968.
11 This design is different from a later dress fabric, also called "Bushmen", produced by Cavendish Textiles in June 1946.
12 According to curators in the Textile Department at the V&A, this design was probably inspired by Sardinian embroideries. However, efforts to trace the precise objects in their collection that inspired Lucienne's early designs have proved inconclusive.
13 The chair with webbing is illustrated in *Designers in Britain*, no. 1, 1947, p.225, fig. 8, where it is described as a prototype. Lucienne's Signs of the Zodiac fabric is illustrated in *Designers in Britain*, no. 1, 1947, p.243, fig. 13.
14 Robin Day, "A Place of her Own", *Vogue*, August 1945, pp.50–51 and p.78.
15 Ingrid Etter, "Young Man in a Hurry – Artist in the Home", unidentified newspaper article in Robin Day Press Cuttings Book, 1949.
16 Quoted by Ingrid Etter, op. cit.

CHAPTER 2

1 All the lettering used on posters at this date had to be hand-drawn, as this was the era before the development of Letraset.
2 Conversation with the author.
3 Both are illustrated by Milner Gray in "Designer: Robin Day", *Art and Industry*, May 1952, p.158.
4 A photograph of the poster is among the Peter Moro Archives in the Royal Architectural Library at the RIBA.
5 The poster and the exhibition are both illustrated in "British Scientific Instruments Exhibition", *Architects' Journal*, 19 June 1947, p.527.
6 It recurs in several of his exhibition stands for ICI, for example, such as the stand for ICI Metals at the British Industries Fair (BIF) in 1948.
7 Illustrated in "Ladies – your evening gown is here", *Daily Graphic*, 19 January 1949.
8 Seven of these transport symbols are illustrated in Milner Gray, op. cit., p.154. Later, in 1954, Robin collaborated with John Reid on the design of some display cases housing models of vehicles for the British Transport Museum at Euston.
9 Robin's display in the *Whither Chemistry Exhibition* is illustrated in *Designers in Britain*, no. 1, 1947, p.143, fig. 9. His section of the ICI stand at the British Industries Fair in 1947 is illustrated in *Designers in Britain*, no. 2, 1949 p.109, fig. 4.
10 Milner Gray, op. cit., p.156.
11 He also designed a reception desk for Ekco's Vigo Street showrooms in London in 1951, illustrated by Milner Gray, op. cit., p.157. His work for Ekco is sparsely documented, however, and it is unclear whether he designed stands for the firm on an annual basis or more intermittently.
12 Illustrated in *Architects' Journal*, 4 September 1952, pp.278–9.
13 Illustrated in *Designers in Britain*, no. 1, 1947, p.224, figs 6 and 7.
14 See reports in *Furnishing World*, 21 January and 11 February 1949.
15 Robin Day and Clive Latimer, "The Day Latimer Storage Units", *Design*, May 1950, pp.17–19.
16 The Heal's exhibition was previewed in *The Cabinet Maker*, April 1950, with accompanying illustrations. The article mentions that it was hoped that the storage units would soon be mass-produced in Britain by a Middlesex manufacturer, although this never actually came about.
17 Several early dress fabrics and artwork for designs are illustrated in a Norwegian profile of the Days by Arne Remlov and Liv Schødt called "Two Outstanding English Designers", *Bonytt*, September 1951, pp.154–9.
18 Conversation with the author.

CHAPTER 3

1 Quoted by Marilyn Hoffman in "Simplicity of Robin Day's Elegant Modern Designs Widens U.S. Market for Old English Furniture Firm", *Christian Science Monitor*, 8 October 1951.
2 After being launched at the BIF in 1949, Robin's dining group was displayed at the *Furniture Trades Exhibitions* at Earls Court in 1950 and 1951, latterly made from mansonia with cherry inlaid with holly. *See Architects' Journal*, 22 February 1951, p.234.
3 Robin Day, "Designing for Hille", *Design and Industries Association Yearbook*, 1964–5, pp.88–91.
4 Quoted by Marilyn Hoffman, op. cit.
5 The modified chair is illustrated in a Hille Seating catalogue, 1956–7, and continues to appear in catalogues until 1967.
6 Illustrated in "These Suites are Today's Best-Sellers", *Furnishing*, May 1952, p.360.
7 Quoted by Sutherland Lyall in *Hille – 75 Years of British Furniture*, 1981, p.33.
8 Robin Day, op. cit.
9 Leslie Julius, "The Hille Story: Creating a Company 'Image'", *The Cabinet Maker and Complete House Furnisher*, 1 July 1960.
10 Ibid.
11 Robin Day, op. cit.
12 Foreword to *Royal Festival Hall – The Official Record*, 1951, p.7
13 Conversation with the author.
14 I am grateful to Mala Jones, Archivist at the Royal Festival Hall, for this and other information relating to the furnishing of the building.
15 Designed by Margaret Leischner and produced by Fothergill and Harvey.
16 Hille's new factory at Hainault was partially constructed when the company was hit by a financial crisis in 1950, and key loans were withdrawn. Subsequently they relocated to an old brewery in Watford, but delays in securing planning permission for this building to be extended made it impossible for them to fulfil their orders for the Royal Festival Hall. See Sutherland Lyall, op. cit., p.28 and p.39.
17 Seven of the twelve symbols, including Robin's, are illustrated in *Designers in Britain*, no. 3, 1951, pp.104–105. Information about the competition is recorded in the Design Council Archive, University of Brighton, ref. 5023, DD37.
18 Milner Gray, "Designer: Robin Day", *Art and Industry*, May 1952, p.154.
19 Festival of Britain Furniture Policy, Design Council Archive, ref. 5511, DD66, SB12a.
20 Ingrid Etter, "Young Man in a Hurry – Artist in the Home", unidentified newspaper article in Robin Day Press Cuttings Book, 1949.
21 Both interiors are illustrated in *Furnishings from Britain*, September 1951, p.69 and p.71.
22 Illustrated in *Design*, July 1951, p.18.
23 A copy of this is in the Heal's Archive in the National Archive of Art and Design at the V&A, ref. AAD/1994/16/2855.
24 Newly married architects Stuart and Beryl Sutcliffe bought Robin's D6553A Utility sideboard and D80 Utility bookcase from Heal's in September 1951 after seeing them on display at the Festival of Britain.
25 Festival of Britain Furniture Policy, Design Council Archive, ref. 5511, DD66.
26 Working drawings are illustrated in *Architects' Journal*, 30 August 1951, pp.9–10.
27 These units were displayed by Leslie and Rosamind Julius on a sales trip to the US in 1951. See Marilyn Hoffman, op. cit.
28 Strangely there appear to be no surviving photographs of it *in situ*.
29 Marilyn Hoffman, "Young Briton's Design Given Award in U.S.", *Christian Science Monitor*, April 1952.
30 The original name for what later became Heal Fabrics.
31 Press release in Lucienne Day Press Cuttings Book, March 1952.
32 Lucienne Day, "Plain or Fancy?", *Daily Mail Ideal Home Book*, 1957, pp.82–7.
33 Milner Gray, op. cit.
34 Robin Day, "At the Robin Days", *Daily Mail Ideal Home Book*, 1953, pp.34–9.
35 "A Day Dream Come True", unidentified newspaper article in Robin Day Press Cuttings Book, c.1953–4.
36 The original XU sofa (1952) was later replaced by two Forum settees (1964). Easy chairs evolved from the Reclining chair (1952) to the High, Wide and Handsome (1958) to the 4-4000 (1970). Dining chairs progressed from the 661 (1951) to the Q Stak (1953) to the Polypropylene chair (1964).
37 These curtains are illustrated in the American magazine *Interiors*, August 1953, p.75, along with a gauze room divider.
38 Quoted by Linda Charles in "At Home with Colour", *Everywoman*, August–September 1959, pp.48–51.
39 Lucienne Day, op. cit.
40 Quoted by Linda Charles, op. cit.
41 Robin Day, op. cit.
42 Ibid.
43 For a full list of articles in which the house was featured, *see* Bibliography.
44 22 September 1953.
45 27 December 1953.
46 The Days appeared in an advert for Smirnoff vodka in *House & Garden*, September 1955, p.113, illustrated in Jennifer Harris, *Lucienne Day – A Career in Design*, Whitworth Art Gallery, 1993, p.11. They are pictured with their baby daughter, Paula, in their Hillman convertible in *House & Garden*, November 1954, p.56.

CHAPTER 4

1 The Status catalogue was designed by June Fraser, the designer of this book.
2 Robin Day, "Designing for Hille", *Design and Industries Association Yearbook*, 1964–5, pp.88–91.
3 Working details are illustrated in *Architects' Journal*, 9 April 1953, along with designs for customized bookshelves and a cupboard that Robin designed for this office. Robin also designed an enamelled steel wall clock for the Time-Life building, manufactured by Gent's, illustrated in *Designers in Britain*, no. 4, 1954, p.50.
4 Quoted by Susan Hicklin in "What's the chair line for 1955", *Evening Standard*, 22 February 1955.
5 Quoted by Ross Percival in "Mr Day takes a tip from you", *Manchester Evening News*, 29 January 1957.
6 Vitrolite, a toughened opaque glass made by Pilkington of St Helens, was widely used in kitchens and bathrooms at this date.
7 Quoted in "Contemporary and so comfortable", unidentified magazine article in Robin Day Press Cuttings Book, 1959.
8 Robin Day, op. cit.
9 Quoted in *Sunday Express*, 27 December 1953.
10 Quoted in *Ideal Home*, June 1962, on the occasion of his Design Centre Award for the British Rail bench. In a profile of the Days in *House & Garden*, July 1952, there is a reference to Robin's having just returned from the US with a contract from an American manufacturer for hotel and office seating. Robin recalls that his 675 chair was originally designed for this company, but was subsequently manufactured by Hille instead, and sold in the US through Hille's American agent John Stuart.
11 *Everyday Art Quarterly*, Walker Art Center, Minneapolis, no. 28, 1953, p.18.
12 Robin was closely involved in selecting the upholstery fabrics for his furniture, and favoured manufacturers included Tibor, run by Tibor Reich in Straford-on-Avon, and Mourne Textiles, run by Gerd Hay-Edie in County Down, Northern Ireland.
13 Quoted in "Contemporary and so comfortable", op. cit.
14 This lecture was given jointly by Robin and Lucienne during the mid-1950s. A partial transcript survives among their archives, although the date and venue are unknown.
15 An Albemarle chair was among the photographs surmounting Robin's display at the Milan Triennale in 1954.
16 Hille became the British licensee for Herman Miller in 1957, and from 1970 acted in a similar capacity for Knoll International. In both cases the licences were eventually withdrawn because the products were so popular that the manufacturers decided to set up British operations of their own.
17 *Everyday Art Quarterly*, op. cit.
18 Quoted from a written account sent by June Yeatman (née Lyon) to the author, January 2000.
19 At the time of writing, Robin's Gatwick benches are still in use at the RIBA and the Tate Gallery.
20 The full range of British Rail furniture is illustrated in an advertisement in *Architectural Review* in July 1962, p.77. Robin subsequently designed several prototypes for litter bins for British Rail during 1957–8, which are recorded in his design drawings, although they were never produced.
21 *Designs of the Year 1958 and 1957*, Council of Industrial Design, 1958, p.38.
22 Letter to the author, 21 March 2000.
23 Partly quoted from "I Predict", an unidentified newspaper article in Robin Day Press Cuttings Book, December 1964; and partly quoted from *Design*, May 1966.
24 *Everyday Art Quarterly*, op. cit.
25 Conversation with the author.
26 Lucienne Day, "Plain or Fancy?", *Daily Mail Ideal Home Book*, 1957, pp.82–7.
27 Lucienne recalled that Flotilla was later used as an illustration on a record sleeve.
28 Marilyn Hoffman, "Young Briton's Design Given Award in U.S." *Christian Science Monitor*, April 1952.
29 Paul Reilly, "Tradition and Experiment", *Design*, July 1952, pp.18–21.
30 Illustrated in *House & Garden*, February 1952, p.45.
31 Illustrated in *Furnishings from Britain*, no. 2, 1953, p.57.
32 No images of Lucienne's work for this firm have yet been traced, but the company is mentioned as one of her clients in a press release issued at the time of her exhibition *Lucienne Day – Designs at Home and Abroad* at Heal's in May 1958.
33 *The Cabinet Maker*, 2 May 1953, refers to a group of contemporary bedspreads commissioned by Everwear Candlewick from Lucienne Day, Mary Baker, Marian Mahler and Ronald Grierson. Lucienne subsequently designed woven mattress tickings for Heal's and printed mattress tickings for A.F. Buckingham during the early 1960s, and a linen sheet set for Thomas Somerset in 1962.
34 Quoted by Russell Miller in "All in the Days' work", unidentified magazine article in Lucienne Day Press Cuttings Book, 1968.
35 Lucienne Day, op. cit.
36 Quoted in "Jewel Bright Colours for your Home", *Brides*, early spring 1967, pp.92–3.
37 Ibid.
38 Graphica was one of four fabrics that won a Gran Premio at the Milan Triennale in 1954, along with Linear, Ticker Tape and Spectators.

39 Heal's used Triad as the basis for a wool-faced woven moquette fabric called Berkley in 1956, apparently without consulting Lucienne herself. An example of this fabric is in the V&A Circ. 487-1956.
40 It was mischievously suggested by a columnist in the *Daily Telegraph* on 27 February 1953 that one of the figures in Spectators was intended as a caricature of Lady Prudence Maufe, the wife of the architect Sir Edward Maufe. Lady Maufe, who was one of Heal's directors, was a rather eccentric figure who wore round glasses and long skirts, and carried a shooting stick. Initially she failed to appreciate Lucienne's skills as a designer because her patterns looked so casual, but Lucienne's work proved so popular and successful that eventually she grudgingly accepted that she was wrong. Lucienne denied that any reference was intended, but apparently Lady Maufe herself interpreted the pattern in this way.
41 Dr Rasch first visited Lucienne in her studio at Motcombe Street in 1952, after being impressed by her textiles for Heal's. Later he wrote an article in a German magazine about the Days' new house at Cheyne Walk and their role in popularizing modern design in Britain. *See* "My visit to Lucienne Day in London", *Architektur und Wohnform*, October 1954, pp.40–42.
42 Three patterns, including Prisma and Spindel, are illustrated in an article by Paul Reilly called "German enterprise in wallpaper design", *Design*, July 1953, pp.16–19. It appears that the third design did not enter production. I am indebted to Gerrit Rasch and Kirsten Polkamp at Rasch for providing detailed information about the full range of Lucienne's work for Rasch.
43 Emil Rasch, "My visit to Lucienne Day in London", *Architektur und Wohnform*, no. 63, October 1954, pp.40–42.
44 The range is mentioned in *Tapeten Zeitung*, 20 August 1958, p.24.
45 Another unrealized prototype, created at the same time as Bond Street, showed a cross-section through a branch.
46 A translation of the quotation is as follows: "Red-haired Menelaus turned to the pair with a hospitable gesture and said: 'Fall to, and welcome. After you have dined we shall enquire who you may be. Your pedigree has left a stamp upon your looks that makes me take you for the sons of kings, those sceptred favourites of Zeus, for no mean folk could breed such men as you are.'" When sold as a complete service, a special plate was included, printed with this translation in the appropriate language, supplied in a leather-covered box.
47 Dan Johnston, "Future for Irish Linen", *Design*, August 1958, pp.36–7.
48 *The Design Centre Awards 1960*, Council of Industrial Design, 1960, p.17.
49 The manuscript, which is dated 1463, is held in the National Art Library, ref. MSL 354-1885. Heal's customers who bought 5 yards or more of the fabric were supplied with a translation of the text by Dr W. Arafat of the School of Oriental and African Studies: "Knowledge cannot be attained by one who prefers to follow his whim, or indulges in an easy life, or who can be turned from his quest, or who fears for himself, or worries about his living; but he must seek refuge with God, and prefer his religion to this world, and draw from the treasure of wisdom. The learned man who seeks knowledge must learn what he does not know, and teach what he already knows, and treat gently those of weak intelligence, and not express wonder at the slowness of the slow-witted."
50 Lucienne Day, op. cit.
51 These unnamed patterns are illustrated in *Contract Furnishing*, February 1958, and *Carpet Review*, April 1958, p.67.
52 Quoted by Linda Charles in "Fashion colours with White", *Everywoman*, August–September 1958, pp.48–51.
53 *Designs of the Year 1958 and 1957*, Council of Industrial Design, 1958, p.42.
54 Lucienne Day, op. cit.
55 All three are illustrated in an advertisment in *Furnishing*, September 1957, p.92.
56 *See* John E. Blake, "The Stream Revitalised", *Design*, April 1959, p.59: "Most significant is the large proportion of machine-printed designs – nine roller prints and fifteen mechanical screen prints – a strong re-affirmation of Heal's confidence in the rapidly expanding market for modern textiles at low prices."
57 Marilyn Hoffman, op.cit.
58 Judy Fallon, "These Contemporary Days", *The Sketch*, 6 April 1955, pp.298–9.
59 Quoted by Russell Miller in "All in the Days' work", unidentified magazine article in Lucienne Day Press Cuttings Book, 1968.
60 Ibid.
61 Illustrated in "On show in Norway", *Design*, July 1952, p.14.
62 Illustrated in *Furnishing*, September 1958, pp.52–5.
63 Gillian Naylor, "Profile of Robin and Lucienne Day", *Moebel + Decoration*, December 1960.

CHAPTER 5

1 Robin Day, "Designing for Hille", *Design and Industries Association Yearbook*, 1964–5, pp.88–91.
2 Quoted in *The Scotsman*, 31 December 1960.
3 Quoted in an unidentified newspaper article in Robin Day Press Cuttings Book, 1961.
4 According to a newspaper article in Robin Day Press Cuttings Book, a Club settee and a Director desk were among the furnishings purchased by the Chancellor of the Exchequer for 11 Downing Street shortly after they appeared on the market.
5 *See* advertisement in *Design*, February 1963.
6 *See* advertisement in *Design*, July 1965, headed "Leo works very well at work… is perfectly at home, at home".
7 The Studio Group is illustrated in *Architect and Building News*, 24 February 1965.
8 Quoted in "I Predict", an unidentified newspaper article in Robin Day Press Cuttings Book, December 1964.
9 Robin Day, op. cit.
10 Quoted by Russell Miller in "All in the Days' work", unidentified magazine article in Lucienne Day Press Cuttings Book, 1968.
11 *Architectural Review*, March 1967
12 Quoted in Hille Press Release, May 1963.
13 Robin Day, op. cit., p.91
14 Harry Spencer's widow, Elsie Spencer, recalls meeting Robin some time around 1957. According to Terry Gorman, a designer who joined Storey's in 1958 after leaving the RCA, Robin's appointment predated his arrival and lasted for about six years. A profile of Robin in *Modernes Wohnen*, Summer 1964, implies that he was still actively engaged as a consultant for Storey's at this date. Robin himself remembers very little about his involvement with the company, however, and there are no written records or illustrations among his archives. Storey's archives are in store at Lancashire County Records Office, but are currently uncatalogued and inaccessible.
15 This information is recorded in *The Cabinet Maker*, 30 October 1959, and *Northern Echo*, 5 November 1959, but no illustrations or samples have been traced, and it is unclear whether Pennant was a one-off or part of a wider range.
16 "'Furnishing' Carpet Design Competition 1952 – Review of Highly Commended Entries", *Furnishing*, January 1953, p.45.
17 Thirty-two designs have been identified with certainty, but it is possible there may be more. Robin's archives contain very little information, and the records held at Woodward Grosvenor are incomplete. Tracing his carpet designs is complicated by the fact that their pattern numbers were altered on at least two occasions during the course of the decade. Also, between 1967 and 1974 Robin's work was marketed under the name Grays Carpets, the parent company of Woodward Grosvenor during that period.
18 Quoted by Russell Miller, op. cit.
19 Quoted from an undated transcript of a lecture among Lucienne Day Archives.
20 Quoted in "My favourite flower", *Woman's Realm*, 26 August 1967, p.26.
21 Lucienne created another design for Heal's loosely based on flower heads in 1963, but it was withdrawn at her request before entering production, as she was unhappy with how it turned out. It was illustrated in an article by Anne Donaldson called "Woman with Designs on Many Products", *Glasgow Herald*, 16 December 1963.
22 Mentioned in *House & Garden*, May 1958, p.51, and *The Scotsman*, 26 June 1962.
23 There is a passing reference in Lucienne Day Archives to some kind of involvement with another company, Stoddart's, but it is unclear whether any carpets resulted from this.
24 Illustrated in "Quiet Contemporaries", *The Ambassador*, 1960, no. 7, p.111.
25 Illustrated in "British Floor Show", *The Ambassador*, 1961, no. 4, pp.109–124.
26 I am grateful to Helen Stubbs, chief designer at Steele's Carpets, for providing information about the Studio 3 collection.
27 Lucienne is referred to as the colourist of this range in *Carpet Review*, February 1962, p.93, which states: "These carpets are very suitable with contemporary furnishings, and have perfect background colours. The range has been well received in Denmark and Switzerland, as well as England, even though it has only been on the market for a short time."
28 I am grateful to Philip Coombes, formerly chief designer at Wilton Royal Carpets, for his assistance in clarifying the scope of Lucienne's work for this firm. I am also indebted to Pompi Parry, Archivist at the Wilton Carpet Factory, for checking company records.
29 In a letter to Rosenthal on 29 September 1967 Lucienne states that she was still designing a range of carpets for Wilton Royal each year, as well being their colour consultant. However, no patterns other than the four designs mentioned in this paragraph have been traced.
30 Some of the artwork for this project is among Lucienne Day Archives, although neither the manufacturer nor the date are recorded. Stylistically they would appear to date from c.1964–6, because of their similarity to Periwinkle and Poinsettia.
31 The sheet set is illustrated in *Sunday Times*, 24 March 1963, but no images of the towel have been traced, although there are records of it among the exhibition inventory in Lucienne Day Archives.
32 A few fragments of artwork and one small fabric sample survive for the Buckingham tickings, but there are no other substantial records.
33 Quoted by Margaret Moodie in "Modern design should be used with discretion", *The Scotsman*, 3 June 1963.
34 This statement was issued to the press at the time. During the late 1950s Robin had been responsible for redecorating the lounges of BOAC's Strato-cruisers, and it may have been this project that led to the subsequent design consultancy. Information about the Days' work with BOAC has been extracted from correspondence in Robin and Lucienne Day Archives.
35 Quoted in "All in the Days' work", unidentified magazine article in Lucienne Day Press Cuttings Book, 1968.
36 Letter to the author, 6 April 2000.
37 Information about the Days' work at Churchill College has been gleaned from correspondence in Robin and Lucienne Day Archives, and through a visit to the college in March 2000, which confirmed that much of the original furniture and some of the original carpets are still *in situ*. I am grateful to Joan Bullock-Anderson, the College Archivist, for her assistance with my research.
38 Waitrose was originally established as an independent grocer's shop by Messrs Waite, Rose and Taylor in 1904, adopting the name Waitrose in 1908. The shops were taken over by John Lewis in 1937, and the first supermarket was opened in Streatham in 1955. By 1973 there were 46 supermarkets; by the end of 2000, 137. I am grateful to Judy Faraday, Partnership Archivist, for this and other information relating to John Lewis.
39 Robin Day, quoted in "25 years of Partnership Design" by Catherine Dilke, *The Gazette*, 29 August 1987, pp.711–12. *The Gazette* is an in-house publication circulated to all the Partnership's staff.
40 Collins was Head of Book Production at the Central School, and formerly a member of the Design Research Unit. *See* "Developing a handwriting", *The Gazette*, 2 July 1960, pp.517–18.
41 Lucienne Day quoted by Catherine Dilke, op. cit. Their initial contract was for twelve months, but they eventually stayed for 25 years.
42 Quoted in "For Distinction in Design", *The Gazette*, 24 November 1962, pp.1067–8.
43 Quoted in "Design in the Partnership", *The Gazette*, 18 January 1964, pp.1248–9.
44 Letter from Robin Day to Ian Anderson, Director of Trading at JLP, dated 17 December 1984.
45 Quoted by Catherine Dilke, op. cit.
46 Robin Day, "Creating a house style", *The Gazette*, 29 April 1967, pp.307–8.
47 Ibid.
48 Letter to the author, 6 April 2000. At the date Cooper was still with the Partnership, and continued to play a very important role.
49 Robin Day, op. cit.
50 Quoted by Catherine Dilke, op. cit.

CHAPTER 6

1 Recorded in correspondence between Robin Day and Hille in 1991.
2 Quoted by Loyd Grossman in "Chair Persons", *Harpers & Queen*, July 1981, p.206. Robin's design for a prototype plastic easy chair with storage in the base is illustrated in *Designers in Britain*, no.7, 1971, p.180, but this design was never manufactured.
3 Quoted from a written description by Robin, among Robin Day Archives.
4 He also designed the orchestra chairs, which were adapted from his Festival Hall chairs from twenty years earlier.
5 Robin also designed an orange and brown check-patterned carpet for the Barbican, which was produced by a firm called Advanced Flooring Ltd of Middlesex. This is referred to in correspondence among Robin Day Archives dated 22 August 1979.
6 Hille International became part of the Hille Ergonom Group in November 1983. The following year the company sold Hille's office furniture interests to Barnes Office Systems, and announced that Hille would be concentrating on mass seating for schools and hospitals, arena seating, and office seating. By 1988 Hille International had become part of Wassall plc, and the company was split into two divisions. For the next few years Hille Auditorium Seating operated from Warrington in Cheshire, while Hille Polypropylene Products were based at Tredegar in Gwent. Hille was subsequently sold to IDEM, but they subsequently went into administration. Following a management buy-out, Hille is now owned by BKF Plastics (formerly Hille Propylene Products). The plastic shells are still made at Tredegar, while Hille Educational Products, as the company is now known, is based at Burnley. Hille Seating no longer exists (2011).
7 Quoted by Loyd Grossman, op. cit.
8 Ibid.
9 Quoted by Russell Miller in "All in the Days' work", unidentified magazine article in Lucienne Day Press Cuttings Book, 1968.
10 Robin's drawings for the Oxford Street restaurant, showing island seating units, screens and panels, are dated August 1972. Drawings for the tea and coffee bar are dated June–October 1973. He also designed a restaurant for the new Peterborough store in 1980.
11 Harry Legg, "A new concept in retailing", *The Gazette*, 13 March 1976, pp.124–5.
12 Harry Legg, "A promising start", *The Gazette*, 22 September 1979, pp.779–85.
13 For a description of the new store, *see* Brian Alford, "Waitrose John Barnes", *The Gazette*, 24 October 1981, p.843.

CHAPTER 7

1 Quoted by Russell Miller in "All in the Days' work", unidentified magazine article in Lucienne Day Press Cuttings Book, 1968.
2 Quoted by Loyd Grossman in "Chair Persons", *Harpers & Queen*, September 1981, p.202.

Robin Day

- Sections A1–A24 list production designs, grouped by manufacturer, producer or client.
- Sections A1–A3 are companies with whom Robin Day collaborated over a long period.
- Sections A4–A24 are other clients and contractors, arranged in chronological order.
- Section A25 lists exhibition and graphic design projects.
- Section A26 lists interior design projects.
- Unless otherwise indicated, designs are listed chronologically, then alphabetically or numerically by model number, year by year. Date given is first known or estimated year of production.
- Unless otherwise indicated, drawings are dated technical drawings in Robin Day Archives.
- Unless otherwise indicated, catalogues are dated Hille catalogues, leaflets and price lists in Robin Day Archives.
- Cross-references to illustrations in this book are italicized in bold. When objects are not illustrated, a contemporary published reference is cited wherever possible.
- Most dimensions are taken from factory catalogues, and are given in imperial until 1970, and thereafter in metric. Approximate conversions are also given. Minor alterations were sometimes made after a model had entered production.
- H = height, SH = seat height, D = depth, W = width, L = length, DI = diameter.

A1. HILLE: FURNITURE AND ACCESSORIES

Dining Group, 1949
Black-lacquered mansonia frames, with ash and cherry veneers, or cream-lacquered mansonia frames with cherry and holly veneers. Chairs are padded and upholstered. Sideboard has sliding glass doors and plate glass serving shelf. Brass fittings.
Note: Robin Day's first design for Hille, shown on Hille's stands at the British Industries Fair, 1949, and the *Furniture Trades Exhibitions*, Earl's Court, 1950 and 1951. Original chairs were upholstered in unborn Yemen calfskin and tan leather. Because of Utility regulations in Britain, this range was originally sold only in the US. Illustrated in *Architects' Journal*, 22 February 1951, p.234; and *Decorative Art Studio Yearbook, 1951–52*, p.32, fig. 1.
Illustrated p.35
Chairs: H 31in (79cm), D 22½in (57.5cm), W of side chair 20in (51cm), W of carver 24in (61cm). Table: H 29in (74cm), D 36in (91cm), W 72in (183cm) extending to 90in (229cm). Tall sideboard: H 49½in (126cm), W 73in (185cm), D 18½in (47.5cm). Low sideboard: H 36in (91cm), W 42in (107cm), D 21in (53cm)

Coffeestak Table, 1950
Solid beech frame with elm, cherry or walnut veneers, lipped with beech, or Warerite plastic laminate top.
Note: Low square version of the Hillestak table. Illustrated in *Furnishings from Britain*, no. 2, 1953, p.57
Catalogues: 1952–4. ***Illustrated p.59***
H 20in (51cm), W 24in (61cm), D 24in (61cm)

Hillestak Chair, 1950
Solid beech frame, laminated beech spine, seat and back of moulded plywood veneered in ash, beech, Nigerian cherry, mahogany or walnut.
Note: Original chairs from 1950 to 1955 had U-shaped leg structure. Chairs from 1956 onward had a modified V-shaped joint. Three variants produced: Hillestak A, with padded and upholstered seat; Hillestak B, with padded and upholstered seat and seat back; and a heavy-duty version with a riveted back. Ebonized version illustrated in *Decorative Art Studio Year Book*, 1955–6, p.48.
Catalogues: 1953–67. ***Illustrated pp.33, 35, 59 & 66***
H 29½in (75cm), SH 18in (46cm), D 19in (48cm), W 19½in (49.5cm)

Hillestak Table and Hillestak Desk, 1950
Solid beech frame with elm, Nigerian cherry, mahogany or walnut veneers, lipped with beech, or Warerite plastic laminate top.
Note: Desk was created by fitting a two-drawer unit to the underside of the Hillestak table.
Catalogues: 1952–66. ***Illustrated pp.35 & 59***
Hillestak table and desk: H 28½in (72cm), W 51in (130cm), D 24in (61cm).

Stickback Chair and Settee, 1950
Mansonia frame with sycamore spindles, or beech frame and spindles.
Note: An early design originated by Robin Day specifically to utilize the skills of the craftsmen at Hille. Displayed at *Furniture Trades Exhibition*, Earl's Court, January 1951. Illustrated in *Architects' Journal*, 22 February 1951, p.234.

652 Cocktail Unit and 653 Cupboard, 1950
Case veneered in sycamore, sliding glass doors.
Note: Tall storage cabinets, tapering towards the top. Sliding glass doors at top, hinged drop flap door in centre, horizontal beaded decoration on lower doors. Displayed at *Furniture Trades Exhibition*, Earl's Court, January 1951. Illustrated in *Architects' Journal*, 22 February 1951, p.234.

Occasional Table, 1950
Note: Three-legged rectangular low table, possibly made of mansonia with sycamore veneer. Tapering form suggests that the table also served as a magazine rack. Displayed at *Furniture Trades Exhibition*, Earl's Court, January 1951. Illustrated in *Architects' Journal*, 22 February 1951, p.234.

Butterfly Cocktail Cabinet, 1951
Note: Two-door drinks cabinet with copper-plated steel rod cross-bracing. Case decorated with rich hardwood veneers, including laurel. Right-hand door decorated with six inset butterflies mounted against cream silk, behind glass. Produced as a one-off display item for Hille's stand at the British Industries Fair, 1951, at the request of Ray Hille.
Illustrated p.35
H 47½in (120cm), W 46in (117cm), D16½in (42cm)

Hilleon Dining Group, 1951
Pencil-stripe walnut combined with beech, or mahogany combined with ash. Cabinet has sliding glass doors. Chair seats are padded and upholstered.
Note: Suite consists of extending dining table, chairs, sideboard and display cabinet.
Illustrated in *Furnishing*, May 1952, p.360.
Table extends to 90in (229cm)

658 Large Moulded Chair (Royal Festival Hall Lounge Chair), 1951
Moulded plywood seat back with ash, mahogany, rosewood or walnut veneer on interior and sycamore veneer on exterior. Grey stove-enamelled steel rod frame. Plywood seat and part of seat back padded and upholstered.
Note: Originally produced for the Royal Festival Hall with copper-plated legs and lemon upholstery. Subsequently manufactured commercially until c.1955, but replaced in 1956 by the 700 armchair.
Catalogues: 1953–4. ***Illustrated pp.40, 42, 51 & 66***
H 28in (71cm), SH 14in (35.5cm), W 35in (89cm), D 26in (66cm)

661 Small Moulded Chair (Royal Festival Hall Dining Chair), 1951
Moulded plywood seat back veneered in ash, mahogany or walnut. Black stove-enamelled steel rod legs. Moulded plywood seat, padded and upholstered.
Note: The original chairs made for the Royal Festival Hall were fabricated by Dare-Inglis of Harrow, Middlesex, with seat backs by Alesbury Brothers of Maidstone, Kent. These chairs were veneered on the inside in walnut and on the outside in birch, and had cream leather seats. The design was subsequently manufactured commercially by Hille with minor alterations.
Catalogues: 1953–62. ***Illustrated pp.40, 41, 47, 51, 57, 64 & 66.***
H 30in (76cm), SH 18in (46cm), W 23in (58cm), D 20½in (52cm)

661B, 661C and 661D Dining Chairs (Royal Festival Hall Orchestra Chair), 1951
Black or dark-grey stove-enamelled steel rod frame. Moulded plywood seat with beech, cherry, walnut or mahogany veneer. 661B has upholstered seat and seat back; 661C has plywood seat back and upholstered seat; 661D has beech plywood seat and seat back.
Note: The original Royal Festival Hall orchestra chairs (661C) were fabricated by Kingfisher Ltd, with tubular steel legs, and had a rail under the seat for holding the musicians' bows. Their seat backs were veneered in sapele mahogany, and their seats were upholstered in a woven plastic fabric called Tygan, designed by Margaret Leischner, and produced by Fothergill and Harvey. The design was subsequently manufactured commercially by Hille, who also produced the fully upholstered 661B, and the all-wood 661D.
Drawings: 1950. Catalogues: 1953–66. ***Illustrated pp.39, 46, 55, 57, 62, 64 & 66***
H 29in (74cm), SH 18in (46cm), W 18–19in (46–48cm), D 18–20in (46–51cm)

Royal Festival Hall Concert Hall Royal Box Chairs, 1951
Timber-framed chairs, padded, upholstered in leather.

Storage Units, 1951
White or black stove-enamelled square-section tubular steel frame. Cabinets and drawers made from mahogany, with yew, mahogany, macassar ebony or coromandel veneers.
Note: Storage system designed for the high-cost room setting in the Home Entertainment section of the Homes and Gardens Pavilion at the Festival of Britain, 1951. Also shown at the Milan Triennale in 1951 with a drop-flap door decorated with an engraving by Geoffrey Clarke bonded onto plastic. Because of Utility restrictions the range was subsequently sold exclusively in the US.
Illustrated pp.47 & 51

Desk Chair, c.1952
Moulded plywood seat back and arms, seat padded and upholstered, legs made of turned beech, mahogany or walnut. Also produced with a swivel base made from wood or dark-grey stove-enamelled tubular steel on castors.
Note: Similar to the Stamford chair, but with moulded plywood arms rather than solid wood arms.
Catalogues: 1953–7. ***Illustrated p.66***

Dressing Desk, c.1952
Solid beech frame. Lids veneered on exterior in walnut or Nigerian cherry. One lid lined with white melamine, the other fitted with a mirror.
Catalogues: 1953–4. ***Illustrated p.59***
H 29in (74cm), W 36in (91cm), D 18in (46cm)

Executive Desk, Cabinet and Table, 1952
Square-section tubular steel frame, stove-enamelled in dark grey, epoxy-coated in black, or chromium-plated. Desk, table and cabinet veneered in mahogany, walnut, elm or Rio rosewood. Desk top covered with grey leather.
Note: Junior desk has one pedestal, Senior desk has two pedestals, with optional centre panel. Pedestals contain drawers or filing units, and were produced separately on metal legs or castors as Executive Cabinet. Desk discontinued in 1980.
Catalogues: 1953–74. ***Illustrated: p.57***
H 29in (74cm), D 42in (107cm), W of Senior desk 72in (183cm), W of Junior desk 56in (142cm)

Hilleplan Dining Table, 1952
Solid beech frame, with fold-down top veneered in Nigerian cherry or walnut.
Note: Illustrated in *Decorative Art Studio Year Book, 1955–56*, p.59.
Catalogues: 1953–4. ***Illustrated p.59***
H 28½in (72cm), W 48in (122cm) folding to 24in (61cm), D 33in (84cm)

Hilleplan Desk, 1952
Solid mahogany carcass veneered with ash or rosewood. Top covered with black or grey linoleum, edged with mahogany. Turned wooden legs or dark-grey stove-enamelled square-section tubular steel legs, with aluminium alloy footrest.
Note: Hilleplan Junior desk has one pedestal, Hilleplan Senior desk has two pedestals. Pedestals fitted with drawers and filing units, originally produced with recessed handles, latterly with brass handles.
Catalogues: 1953–5. ***Illustrated p.55***
H 28½in (72cm), D 24in (61cm), W of Junior desk 48in (122cm), W of Senior desk 60in (152cm)

Hilleplan Storage Units, 1952
Solid agbar sides. Plywood back, doors and drawers, veneered with elm, Nigerian cherry or walnut, or made from black or light-grey vitrolite or clear glass. Turned wood or dark-grey stove-enamelled square-section tubular steel legs.
Note: Range of storage furniture created on an 18in (46cm) module.
Unit A: 54in (137cm) sideboard, sliding doors, two interior drawers and shelves.
Unit B: 54in (137cm) sideboard, sliding doors, two exterior top drawers, interior shelves.
Unit C: 36in (91cm) sideboard, sliding doors, four interior drawers and one shelf.
Unit D: 54in (137cm) bookcase, sliding glass doors, two adjustable shelves.
Unit E: 36in (91cm) sideboard, sliding doors, two shelves.
Unit F: 36in (91cm) chest of drawers with three drawers.
Unit G: 18in (46cm) chest of drawers with three drawers.
Unit H: 18in (46cm) cupboard, hinged drop-flap door, one shelf.
Unit J: 36in (91cm) writing desk, hinged drop-flap door above three exterior drawers.
Catalogues: 1953–4. ***Illustrated pp.52, 56 & 59***
H of legs 9in (23cm), H of Units A–H 20in (51cm), H of Unit J 35in (89cm), D 12in (30.5cm) or 18in (46cm), W 18in (46cm), 36in (91cm) or 54in (137cm)

Low Table, c.1952
Aluminium alloy legs with rubber feet. Top veneered in walnut, lipped with beech.
Note: Illustrated in *House Beautiful*, Summer 1954, p.20; and *Designers in Britain*, no. 4, 1954, p.1.
Catalogues: 1953–4. ***Illustrated p.59***
H 16in (41cm), W 48in (122cm), D 24in (61cm)

Occasional Table, c.1952
Moulded plywood frame, Derbyshire fossil stone top.
Note: Low rectangular table. Illustrated in *Decorative Art Studio Year Book, 1954–55*, p.20.

Reclining Chair, 1952
Black or dark-grey stove-enamelled steel rod frame, with ash or mahogany armrests. Hardwood frame with rubber webbing, padded and upholstered, with adjustable head cushion.
Catalogues: 1953–62. ***Illustrated pp.64, 66 & 67***
H 36in (91cm), SH 16in (41cm), W 35in (89cm), D 34in (86cm)

Slat Chair, 1952
Mahogany frame and beech legs. Beech slats support upholstered back cushion containing rubberized hair. Plastic-covered tension springs support upholstered seat cushion, containing coiled-spring unit embedded in rubberized hair.
Note: Latex foam cushions offered as an alternative. Illustrated in *Furnishing*, May 1952, p.378.
Catalogues: 1953–7. ***Illustrated p.66***
H 28in (71cm), SH 16in (41cm), W 21½in (54.5cm), D 28½in (72cm)

Stamford Chair, 1952
Moulded plywood seat back with solid hardwood armrests, seat with no-sag springing, both padded and upholstered. Black stove-enamelled or satin chrome tubular steel legs; or turned beech, teak or mahogany legs, either walnut colour or black. Alternatively, supplied with swivel base made of dark-grey stove-enamelled tubular steel, or walnut or black mahogany.
Note: Range of upholstered contract furniture, consisting of side chair, armchair, desk chair, and swivel chair with adjustable height and tilt mechanism. Originally called the Stafford chair, and illustrated as such in *Decorative Art Studio Year Book, 1957–58*, p.57.
Catalogues: 1953–70. ***Illustrated pp.57, 62–4, 66, 70 & 113***
H 32½in (82.5cm), SH 18½in (46cm). Armchair: W 26½in (67cm), D 22½in (57cm). Side chair: W 18½in (47cm), D 20in (51cm). Swivel chair: W 26½in (67cm), D 22½in (57cm)

Stool, c.1952
Black stove-enamelled tubular steel tripod legs with chromium-plated foot ring. Circular seat, padded and upholstered.
Note: Recorded in photograph in Robin Day Archives.

XU Easy Chair, Settee and Unit Seating, 1952
Hardwood frame and beech legs. Hand-tied coiled-spring seats and seat back. Cushions with coiled-spring units embedded in rubberized hair, upholstered.
Note: Monochrome or two-tone upholstery. Illustrated in *Decorative Art Studio Year Book, 1954–55*, p.20.
Catalogues: 1953–62. ***Illustrated pp.52, 64 & 66***
H 30in (76cm), SH 18in (46cm), D 31in (79cm), W of chair 18in (46cm), W of settee 72in (183cm). W of sectional units: 22in (56cm) for single seater armless unit, 44in (112cm) for two seater armless unit, 30in x 30in (76cm x 76cm) for corner seat unit, 25in (63.5cm) for single units with arms

675 Chair, 1952
Black or dark-grey stove-enamelled steel rod frame. Moulded plywood seat back and arms, veneered in beech, mahogany, American walnut, rosewood or ash. Seat padded and upholstered. Reissued by Habitat (2000) and Case (2009).
Catalogues: 1953–66. ***Illustrated pp.55, 64, 66, 71, 76 & 94***
H 31in (79cm), SH 18in (46cm), W 25in (63.5cm), D 21in (53cm)

676 Armchair, c.1952
Solid beech frame and legs, seat padded and upholstered.
Note: Demountable.
Catalogues: 1953–4. ***Illustrated p.66***
H 30in (76cm), SH 17¾in (45cm), W 20½in (52cm), D 20in (51cm)

677, 677A and 677B Tables, c.1952
Grey stove-enamelled tubular steel frame. Laminated wood top veneered in walnut, Nigerian cherry or elm.
Note: 677 is rectangular, 677A circular, 677B square. Illustrated in *House & Garden*, January 1954, p.1 and p.39; and *Designers in Britain*, no. 5, 1957, p.10.
Catalogues: c.1953–8. ***Illustrated p.59***
H 28½in (72cm). 677: W 60in (152cm), D 30in (76cm). 677A: DI 33in (84cm). 677B: 33in x 33in (84cm x 84cm)

678 Dining Chair, c.1952
Solid beech legs, laminated beech spine, padded and upholstered seat and seat back.
Note: Illustrated in *House & Garden*, January 1954, p.33.
Catalogues: 1953–4. ***Illustrated p.66***
H 30in (76cm), SH 18in (46cm), W 18½in (47cm), D 20½in (52cm)

Q Rod Chair, 1953
Moulded beech plywood seat, veneered in beech, Nigerian cherry or walnut, or padded and upholstered. Black stove-enamelled steel rod legs.
Note: Non-stacking version of the Q Stak chair with straight legs.
Catalogues: 1953–67. ***Illustrated pp.64 & 68***
H 31in (79cm), SH 17¾–18in (45–46cm), W 15½in (39cm), D 20in (51cm)

Q Stak Chair, 1953
Moulded beech plywood seat with beech, walnut or Nigerian cherry veneer, or with a grey, sand, light-green or light-blue melamine finish, or padded and upholstered. Beech legs, or grey or black stove-enamelled tubular steel legs.
Catalogues: 1953–67. ***Illustrated pp.58, 64, 68 & 69***
H 30½in (77cm), SH 17¾in (45cm), W 15½in (39cm), W 17¾in (45cm)

Q Stak Table, c.1953
Black stove-enamelled tubular steel frame and legs, top veneered in Nigerian cherry, walnut or covered in melamine, lipped in beech.
Catalogues: 1961–9.
H 28½in (72cm), W 48in (122cm), D of top 24in (61cm), D of frame 27in (68.5cm)

Telechair and Telesettee, 1953
Solid beech legs and laminated beech spine. Coiled hand-tied sprung seat, back padded with rubberized hair, both upholstered.
Note: Launched at *British Furniture Manufacturers Exhibition*, 1953. Illustrated in *Decorative Art Studio Year Book, 1954–55*, p.51.
Catalogues: 1953–9. ***Illustrated p.66***
H 28in (71cm), SH 16in (41cm), D 27in (68.5cm), W of chair 22in (56cm), W of settee 66in (168cm)

Albemarle Dining Group, 1954
Chair has mahogany frame, padded seat back secured with brass fixings, and reversible seat cushion supported on leather straps. Table made of mahogany with rosewood veneer. Sideboard made of mahogany with rosewood veneer on doors, maple veneer on interior, and green marble top.
Note: Chair exhibited at Milan Triennale in 1954.
Catalogues: 1956–9. ***Illustrated p.73***
Table: 72in x 39in (183cm x 99cm), extending to 108in (274cm). Chair: H 31½in (80cm), SH 18in (46cm), D 20in (51cm), W of side chairs 19¾in (50cm), W of carvers 24in (61cm). Sideboard: H 33½in (85cm), W 71½in (182cm), D 18in (46cm)

Interplan Storage Units, 1954
Solid mahogany carcass with plywood back. Doors and drawers veneered in rosewood or ash. Recessed or projecting right-angled metal handles. Turned wooden legs or black stove-enamelled tubular steel legs.
Note: Range of modular storage units, originally supported on legs or on Slatted Bench. Subsequently produced from 1958 as a wall-mounted system suspended on a tubular steel frame by brass bolts and collars. Exhibited at Milan Triennale in 1954.
Unit K: 54in (137cm) cabinet, sliding wooden doors, fixed interior shelves.
Unit L: 54in (137cm) cabinet, sliding wooden doors, four interior drawers, fixed shelves.
Unit M: 54in (137cm) cabinet, two hinged wooden doors, four exterior drawers.
Unit N: 36in (91cm) cabinet, sliding wooden doors, fixed shelves.
Unit P: 36in (91cm) chest of drawers with three drawers.
Unit O: 18in (46cm) chest of drawers with two drawers.
Unit R: 36in (91cm) cabinet, sliding wooden doors, four interior drawers, fixed shelf.
Unit T: 18in (46cm) cabinet, one hinged door, fixed shelf.
Unit U: 18in (46cm) chest of drawers with three drawers.
Unit V: 18in (46cm) cabinet, one exterior drawer, drop-flap door, interior filing unit.
Unit W: 36in (91cm) writing desk, drop-flap door with interior shelf and drawers, above three exterior drawers.
Unit X: 36in (91cm) double-height bookcase, sliding glass doors, adjustable shelves.
Unit Y: 54in (137cm) single-height bookcase, sliding glass doors, one adjustable shelf.
Unit Z: 36in (91cm) single-height bookcase, sliding glass doors, one adjustable shelf.
Catalogues: 1955–9. ***Illustrated pp.60–1 & 106***
H of legs: 10in (25cm). H of Unit W: 35in (89cm). H of other units: 20in (51cm). D 12in (30.5cm) or 18in (46cm), W 18in (46cm), 36in (91cm) or 54in (137cm)

Occasional Tables, 1954
Dark-grey stove-enamelled tubular steel legs. Blockboard top veneered in Nigerian cherry, Bombay rosewood, makore or walnut, with white or black PVC lipping.
Note: Produced in circular, oval and rectangular versions. Oval version exhibited at the Milan Triennale in 1954, and at the *H55* exhibition at Hälsingborg in Sweden in 1955. Illustrated in *Decorative Art Studio Year Book, 1956–57*, p.42; and *Decorative Art Studio Year Book, 1957–58*, p.22.
Catalogues: c.1958–63. ***Illustrated p.60***
H 14in (35.5cm). Circular table: DI 24in (61cm). Oval table: W 60in (152cm), D 20in (51cm). Rectangular tables: 60in x 20in (152cm x 51cm), and 30in x 20in (76cm x 51cm)

Q Swivel Chair, c.1954
Moulded beech plywood seat, padded and upholstered. Black stove-enamelled tubular steel swivel base with plastic feet.
Note: Q Stak variant, modified to create a typist's chair.
Catalogues: c.1954–8. ***Illustrated pp.62 & 69***
SH 16½–20in (42–51cm), W 15½in (39cm), D 19in (48cm)

Slatted Bench, 1954
Mahogany or makore slats. V-shaped black stove-enamelled steel rod frame.
Note: Exhibited at Milan Triennale in 1954. Intended as a bench, a low table, or a support for cabinets from the Interplan range.
Catalogues: 1955–63. ***Illustrated pp.60–61 & 106***
H 12½in (32cm), W 72in (183cm), D 18in (46cm)

Dover Dining Table and Chairs, c.1955
Beech frame. Table top and chair backs veneered in rosewood, cherry-mahogany or walnut. Chair seats padded and upholstered.
Note: Rectangular table marketed with Interplan Unit M as the Dover Group. Circular table marketed with Interplan Unit K/L as the Grafton Group. Illustrated in *Decorative Art Studio Year Book, 1956–57*, p.42
Catalogue: c.1958.
Rectangular table top: 45in x 33in (114cm x 84cm), extending to 60in (152cm), or 54in x 33in (137cm x 84cm), extending to 72in (183cm). Circular table top: DI 33in (84cm)

Tricorne Tray, c.1955
Veneered moulded plywood.
Note: Rounded triangular tray with up-curved rims, decorated with a range of different veneers. Originally designed as a promotional gift for Hille's clients, it proved so popular that it remained in production well into the 1960s. Robin Day also designed the packaging for the triangular box. Illustrated in *Designers in Britain*, no. 5, 1957, p.90.

682 Tub Chair and Settee, c.1955
Turned beech legs. Moulded plywood seat back, padded with rubber and rubberized hair, with buttoned fabric upholstery. Upholstered foam cushion supported on rubber webbing.
Note: Similar in style to the Stamford Armchair, but the shape of the seat back is closer to the 700 chair. Settee produced as a two-seater and a three-seater. Illustrated in *Decorative Art Studio Year Book, 1957–58*, p.22.
Catalogues: 1956–62. ***Illustrated pp.60, 64 & 74***
Chair: H 30½in (77cm), SH 16in (41cm), W 30in (76cm), D 27in (68.5cm). Settee: H 31in (79cm), D 28in (71cm), W 52in (132cm) and 75in (190.5cm)

690 Dining Table and Chairs, c.1955
Chair and table legs made of turned beech. Chair frame and seat made of mahogany, seat padded and upholstered.
Note: Chair produced with and without arms. Table has rounded rectangular top, with extension flap stored underneath.
Catalogues: 1956–7 (chair), 1962 (table).
Chair: H 31½in (80cm), SH 17½in (44.5cm), W 18½in (47cm), D 19½in (49.5cm). Table: H 29in (74cm); D 33in (84cm), W 57in (145cm) extending to 72in (183cm)

British Rail Bench, Chair and Table, 1956
Seats were produced in three versions: moulded beech plywood, padded and upholstered; veneered moulded plywood; solid makore slats. Seating and tables have rust-proof black stove-enamelled tubular steel frames with stainless steel spats and rubber feet.
Table has solid makore top.
Note: Originally commissioned by the Eastern Division of British Rail, 1955. Design Centre Award, 1962.
Drawings: 1955. Catalogues: c.1959–63. ***Illustrated p.75***
Chair: H 28in (71cm), W 26in (66cm), D 25in (63.5cm). Bench: H 28in (71cm), D 24in (61cm), W 40in (102cm), 60in (152cm) and 80in (203cm). Table: H 17½in (44.5cm), W 48in (122cm), D 18in (46cm)

700 Armchair, c.1956
Grey stove-enamelled steel rod frame. Moulded plywood seat back and arms, veneered in ash, mahogany or walnut. Seat and part of seat back padded and upholstered.
Drawings: 1956. Catalogues: 1956–62. ***Illustrated p.64***
H: 26½in (67cm); SH 14½in (37cm), W 34½in (87.5cm), D 26in (66cm)

President Boardroom Table, c.1957
Mahogany or walnut colour legs, top veneered in mahogany, rosewood or walnut.
Note: Custom-designed boardroom table, a precursor of standardized boat-shaped tables introduced in 1962.
Catalogue: c.1958.

President Chair, c.1957
Mahogany or makore frame. Moulded plywood seat, padded and upholstered.
Note: High-quality boardroom chair in the Danish style. Used in the Aston Webb Room at the RIBA; and in the boardroom at the Bowater Paper Company.
Catalogues: c.1958–67. ***Illustrated pp.64 & 73***
H 32in (81cm), SH 18in (46cm), W 23½in (60cm), D 23½in (60cm)

Single and Double Convertible Bed-Settee, 1957
Mahogany or black stove-enamelled flat steel legs. Mahogany end panels. Upholstered Dunlopillo foam mattress supported on rubber webbing.
Note: The back of the Single Convertible drops down vertically. The back of the Double Convertible drops down horizontally to extend the width of the bed. Design Centre Award, 1957.
Drawings: 1956 (Single), 1958 (Double). Catalogues: 1958–67. ***Illustrated p.71***
Single Convertible: H 27½in (70cm), SH 16½in (42cm), W 76½in (194cm), D (closed) 33½in (85cm), D (open) 38½in (98cm). Single mattress: L 74in (188cm), W 33in (84cm), D 4in (10cm). Double Convertible: H 30in (76cm), SH 25½in (65cm), W 76½in (194cm), D (closed) 37in (94cm), D (open) 48in (122cm). Double mattress: L 74in (188cm), W 48in (122cm), D 5in (13cm)

Albany Dining Group, 1958
Sideboard, table and chairs all have mahogany legs. Table top, chair seats and sideboard have mahogany or Bombay rosewood veneer. Sideboard doors covered in cream leather with brass fittings.
Note: Table produced in two sizes with a fixed top or extending leaf stored underneath.
Drawings: 1958, revised 1963. Catalogues: 1958–62. ***Illustrated p.64 (chair)***
Table: H 31½in (80.5cm), L 64in (162.5cm) or 84in (213cm). Carvers: H 31½in (80.5cm), W 19in (48cm), D 20½in (52cm). Side chairs: H 32¾in (83cm), SH 17¾in (45cm), W 22¾in (57.5cm), D 21½in (54.5cm). Sideboard: H 30in (76cm), W 72in (183cm), D 18in (46cm)

Cane Back Armchair and Settee, 1958
Mahogany frame with woven cane seat back. Reversible upholstered foam cushions supported on rubber webbing.
Note: Settee produced in two-seater and three-seater versions.
Catalogues: 1958–63. ***Illustrated pp.64 & 72***
H 29in (74cm), SH 15¾in (40cm), D 31in (79cm), W of chair 28in (71cm), W of settee 48½in (123cm) and 69½in (176.5cm)

Gatwick Chair and Bench, 1958
Square-section stainless steel frame with satin chrome finish. Chair has upholstered foam cushions supported on rubber webbing. Bench padded and upholstered over base board.
Note: Originally designed as concourse seating for Gatwick Airport. Reissued by Keen, 2000.
Drawings: 1958. Catalogues: 1959–69. ***Illustrated pp.64, 75 & 111***
Chair: H 28in (71cm), SH 17in (43cm), W 29in (74cm), D 30in (76cm). Bench: H 16½in (42cm), W 81in (206cm), D 30in (76cm)

Gatwick Table, 1958
Square-section stainless steel or black stove-enamelled steel frame, with black or white melamine laminate top lipped with solid mahogany.
Note: Designed to complement the Gatwick chair and bench.
Drawings: 1957. Catalogues: 1965–8.
H 15in. Rectangular table top: 60in x 20in (152cm x 51cm). Square table top: 24in x 24in (61cm x 61cm)

High, Wide and Handsome Armchair, 1958
Two-part moulded plywood seat, padded and upholstered, supported on chromium-plated or black stove-enamelled steel rod skid base.
Note: Illustrated in *Decorative Art Studio Year Book, 1958–59*, p.36.
Catalogues: 1958–62. ***Illustrated pp.64 & 106***
H 33in (84cm), SH 16in (41cm), W 43in (109cm), D 37½in (95cm)

680 Dining Group, c.1958
Note: Composite suite consisting of Interplan storage units, Q Stak chairs, and a rectangular dining table veneered with cherry mahogany or rosewood.
Catalogue: c.1958.
Table top: 60in (152.5cm) x 30in (76cm)

Alpha Table, 1959
Tops made of marble or clear, bronze or grey plate glass. Black epoxy-coated steel underframe with bright or satin chromium-plated flat steel legs.
Note: Range of circular, square and rectangular tables for commercial and domestic use. Later reissued by twentytwentyone.
Drawings: 1959–60. Catalogues: 1965–75.
Illustrated pp.107 & 111
H 14½in (37cm) or 15in (38cm). Circular table: DI 33in (84cm) or 39in (99cm). Rectangular table: W 48in (122cm), D 18in (46cm) or 21in (53cm). Square table 30in (76cm)

Chevron Chair, 1959
Mahogany, makore or teak frame and arms. Chromium-plated or black stove-enamelled steel rod legs. Upholstered reversible foam cushions supported by rubber webbing.
Note: Produced with and without arms.
Drawings: 1959. Catalogues: c.1963–7. ***Illustrated pp.64–5 & 70***
H 29in (74cm), SH 16in (41cm), W with arms 26½in (67cm), W without arms 24in (61cm), D 28in (71cm)

Cheyne Chair, 1959
Black stove-enamelled square-section tubular steel frame, padded and upholstered seat, mahogany armrests.
Note: Chair was produced with and without arms. Robin Day also designed a two-seater settee in 1960, but this appears not to have been produced.
Drawings: 1959–61. Catalogues: 1961–8. ***Illustrated p.64***
H 27in (68.5cm), SH 15in (38cm), D 27in (68.5cm), W of chair 22in (56cm), W of armchair 27in (68.5cm)

Cheyne Table, 1959
Black stove-enamelled or nylon-coated square-section tubular steel frame. Blockboard top covered with white melamine or mahogany veneer, with mahogany lipping.
Note: Square or rectangular occasional table, designed to complement Cheyne chair.
Drawings: 1959. Catalogues: c.1963–8. ***Illustrated p.65***
H 15¼in. Square table tops: 24in (61cm), 27in (68.5cm) or 30in (76cm). Rectangular tops: 42in x 18in (107cm x 46cm)

Clifford Armchair and Settee, 1959
Hardwood frame, padded, with upholstered foam cushions. Mahogany or square-section tubular steel legs, black stove-enamelled or satin chromium-plated.
Note: Chair produced in low-back and high-back versions. Settee produced as a two-seater and a three-seater. Chairs used on the SS *Oriana* in 1960.
Catalogues: 1961–8. ***Illustrated p.64***
High-back chair: H 37½in (95cm), SH 15in (38cm), W 29in (74cm), D 25in (63.5cm). Low-back chair: H 28in (71cm), SH 15in (38cm), W 29in (74cm), D 33in (84cm). Settee: H 28in (71cm), SH 15in (38cm), D 33in (84cm), W 50in (127cm) and 72in (183cm)

H.L. Unit Seating, 1959
Hardwood frame, with mahogany or black stove-enamelled square-section tubular steel or satin chrome legs. Seat has steel springs, padded and upholstered.
Note: Modular seating system produced in single, double and triple units, and corner seats, with optional armrests. Illustrated in *Ideal Home*, February 1959.
Catalogues: 1960–62. ***Illustrated pp.64 & 66***
H 29½in (75cm), SH 15in (38cm), D 30½in (77cm), W 22in (56cm), 44in (112cm), and 66in (168cm)

London Sideboard, 1959
Carcass veneered in rosewood, with black leather-covered sliding doors. Satin chromium-plated square-section tubular steel legs.
Note: Similar to the SKP and SLP sideboards, but the materials and dimensions are different.
Drawings: 1959. Catalogues: 1962–3.
H 30in (76cm), W 72in (183cm), D 18in (46cm)

London Table, 1959
Square-section tubular steel legs with bright or satin chrome finish. Top veneered in Bombay or Rio rosewood or teak.
Note: Domestic or boardroom table, produced in various sizes with four, six or eight legs.
Drawings: 1958–9. Catalogues: c.1959–67.
H 28in (71cm); D 42in (107cm); W 84–240in (213–610cm), increasing at 12in (30cm) intervals

Occasional Table, c.1959
Square-section tubular steel frame with satin chrome finish. Plate-glass or marble top.
Catalogue: 1960 (line drawing)

Office Accessories, c.1959–63
Blotting pad, filing trays and desk set made of pressed anodized aluminium with a black or silver finish. Waste-paper bins made of spun anodized aluminium with a black or silver finish. Coat stand has black stove-enamelled tubular steel column, with bright chrome steel bar base and racks. Pedestal ashtrays have either black stove-enamelled steel rod column with spun aluminium tray, or bright chrome tubular steel column with china tray; both with nylon-coated cast-iron base. Umbrella stand has chromium-plated steel rod column and ring, set into a nylon-coated cast-iron base.
Note: Blotting pad (RD1 and RD2) and filing trays (RD11–14) were produced initially from c.1959. Hand blotter, single and double pen stand (RD3 and RD4), letter rack (RD6), desk ashtray (RD7), waste-paper bin, coat stand, pedestal ashtray and umbrella stand were produced from c.1963. The aluminium components range was manufactured initially by Acorn Products on behalf of Hille, and later by Lesco Aluminium Products until at least 1989.
Drawings: 1957 (filing tray), 1961–2. Catalogues: 1966–7 (full range), 1969 (coat stand only). ***Illustrated pp.63 & 112–13***
Blotting pad: 17½in x 11in (44.5cm x 28cm), and 17½in x 22in (44.5cm x 56cm). Waste-paper bin: H 10in (25cm), 12½in (32cm) and 14in (35.5cm). Coat stand: H 66¼in (168cm), DI 24in (61cm). Pedestal ashtrays: H 22¼in (56.5cm) and 23in (58cm), DI 7½in (19cm) and 8in (20cm). Umbrella stand: H 21in (53cm), DI 6in (15cm).

SKP and SLP Sideboard, c.1959
Mahogany, with black or white leathercloth sliding doors. Black stove-enamelled square-section tubular steel legs.
Note: Similar to the London sideboard, but dimensions and materials are different.
Catalogue: 1962.
H 23¾in (60cm), W 54in (137cm), D 18in (46cm)

Status Bookcases and Cabinets, 1959
Units have mahogany veneer on interior, and mahogany, teak or walnut veneers on exterior. Black stove-enamelled or satin chrome square-section tubular steel legs. Recessed finger grips or projecting right-angled handles in silver or black anodized aluminium. Bookcase has sliding glass doors.
Note: Range of modular office storage furniture designed as part of the Status Group.
Drawings: 1959 and 1962. Catalogues: 1959–65. ***Illustrated pp.62–3***
H of legs 7¾in (19.5cm), H of cabinets 20in (51cm), H of bookcase 17½in (44.5cm). Units: D 18in (46cm), W 36in (91cm), 54in (137cm), 72in (183cm)

Status Desk, 1959
Mahogany carcass, veneered with mahogany, Pacific walnut, oiled or polished teak, or Bombay rosewood. Alternatively, tops covered with light-grey, black or white melamine, lipped with matching hardwood. Square-section black stove-enamelled tubular steel legs. Projecting right-angled handles in silver or black anodized aluminium.
Note: Range of single and double pedestal desks with rectangular or angled tops, and optional veneered front panels. Pedestals included: DA, 27in (68.5cm) unit with three drawers; DB, 27in (68.5cm) unit with one drawer and one filing drawer; DC, 27in (68.5cm) cupboard with adjustable shelf; DD, 27in (68.5cm) typewriter cupboard with spring-balanced typewriter platform; DE, 18in (46cm) unit with three drawers; DF, 18in (46cm) cupboard with adjustable shelf.
Drawings: 1958–62. Catalogues: 1959–65. ***Illustrated pp.62–3***
Single pedestal desk top sizes: 45in x 18in (114cm x 46cm), 45in x 27in (114cm x 68.5cm), 54in x 27in (137cm x 68.5cm), 63in x 27in (160cm x 68.5cm), 63in x 33in (160cm x 84cm), 72in x 36in (183cm x 91cm), 84in x 36in (213cm x 91cm). Double pedestal desk top sizes: 63in x 27in (160cm x 68.5cm), 63in x 33in (160cm x 84cm), 72in x 36in (183cm x 91cm), 84in x 36in (213cm x 91cm). Pedestals: H 20in (51cm), W 18in (46cm), D 18in (46cm) and 27in (68.5cm)

Status Table, 1959
Top veneered in mahogany, Pacific walnut, rosewood or teak, or covered in white melamine. Satin chrome or black stove-enamelled square-section tubular steel frame.
Note: Office tables in a wide range of sizes, designed as part of the Status Group of office furniture.
Drawings: 1958–62. Catalogues: 1959–66.
H 29in (74cm), except typing tables, H 27 (68.5cm). Model 4404: 63in x 27in (160cm x 68.5cm); Model 4409: 72in x 36in (183cm x 91cm). Other sizes: 45in x 18in (114cm x 46cm), 45in x 27in (114cm x 68.5cm), 54in x 27in (137cm x 68.5cm), 63in x 33in (160cm x 84cm) and 84in x 36in (213cm x 91cm).

Wolfson Institute Auditorium Seating, c.1959
Note: The Wolfson Institute, designed by Lyons, Israel and Ellis, was a postgraduate medical school attached to Hammersmith Hospital. Robin Day designed the seating for three lecture theatres.

Curzon Table and Sideboard, 1960
Oiled teak. Sideboard has brass fittings. Table has black-enamelled steel pedestal with cruciform wooden base and adjustable brass feet.
Note: Marketed with Marson chairs as the Curzon Group. Fixed and extending tables produced, with loose leaf stored under sideboard.
Drawings: 1960. Catalogue: 1962.
Table: DI 48in (122cm), extending to 64in (162.5cm). Sideboard: H 33in (84cm), W 72in (183cm), D 18in (46cm)

Form Group, 1960
Black stove-enamelled or chromium-plated square-section tubular steel underframe and legs. Seat frames made from solid makore or oiled teak. Upholstered foam cushions supported by rubber webbing. Tables and drinks cabinet veneered with mahogany or teak, or covered with black or white melamine.
Note: Flexible seating system, originally known as Modulus, designed on a 28in module. Produced in two, three or four bay units, with optional tables and drinks cabinet with lift-up lid. Seats supplied with or without backrests and arms. Design Centre Award, 1961.
Catalogues: 1960–74. ***Illustrated p.65***
H 28½in (72cm), SH 15in (38cm), D 28in (71cm), W 56in (142cm), 84in (213cm) or 112in (285.5)

Oakley Chair, c.1960
Mahogany frame, seat padded and upholstered.
Note: Produced with or without arms. Armless version could be used as continuous seating.
Catalogues: 1961–2. ***Illustrated p.64***
H 27in (68.5cm), SH 15in (38cm). D 28½–29in (72–74cm). W of armless chair 22in (56cm), W of armchair 27in (68.5cm)

Dinner Wagon, 1961
Frame made from square-section bright chromium-plated tubular steel, or satin-finished stainless steel, with black steel cross members. White melamine top edged with makore.
Drawings: 1961. Catalogues: 1961–7.
H 30in (76cm), W 33in (84cm), D 18in (46cm)

Marson Dining Group, 1961
Bombay rosewood or teak, with brass fittings on sideboard. Rosewood chairs upholstered in tan leather, teak chairs upholstered in black leather.
Note: Illustrated in *Daily Telegraph*, 31 January 1961.
Drawings: 1961. Catalogues: 1961–2.
Table: H 29in (74cm), W 84in (213cm), D 39in (99cm). Chairs: H 32½in (82.5cm), SH 18in (46cm), D 19½in (49.5cm), W of side chair 20in (51cm), W of carver 22½in (57cm). Sideboard: H 30in (76cm), W 72in (183cm), D 18in (46cm)

Bedford Dining Group, 1962
Note: Composite suite consisting of SKP or SLP sideboard, Status table and 675 chairs.
Catalogue: 1962.

Boat-shaped Boardroom Tables, 1962
Turned timber legs or tubular steel legs with bright or satin chrome finish. Top veneered in Rio or Santos rosewood, teak or oak, with solid wood lippings.
Note: Range of tables with four, six or eight legs.
Drawings: 1962. Catalogues: 1966–84.
H 28in (71cm). W 96in (244cm), 120in (305cm), 168in (427cm), 192in (488cm), 216in (549cm), 240in (610cm). D 45in (114cm), 51in (130cm), 57in (145cm), 63in (160cm), 65in (165cm), 72in (183cm)

Club Armchair and Settee, 1962
Teak or square-section stainless steel legs. Foam cushions supported on rubber webbing, buttoned upholstery. Reissued by Loft International, currently manufactured (2011).
Note: Settee is a three-seater.
Drawings: 1962. Catalogues: 1962–82. ***Illustrated p.111***
Chair: H 24in (61cm) or 28½in (72cm), SH 16½in (42cm) or 17in (43cm), W 33in (84cm), D 32in (81cm). Settee: H 24in (61cm) or 28¼in (72cm), SH 16½in (42cm) or 17in (43cm), W 81¼in (21cm), D 32in (81cm)

Club Table, c.1962
Square-section tubular steel legs with bright chrome finish. White melamine or Rio rosewood veneered top.
Catalogue: 1972.
H 14in (35.5cm). Rectangular table: W 48in (122cm), D 21in (53cm). Square table: 30in x 30in (76cm x 76cm)

DH 62 Armchair, Ottoman and Table, 1962
Upholstered foam cushions supported on rubber webbing. Seat back upholstered in PVC, arms upholstered in leather. Black nylon-coated steel swivel base.
Note: Illustrated in *Sunday Telegraph*, 28 January 1962.
Catalogue: 1962.
Chair: H 33in (84cm), SH 17in (43cm), W 35in (89cm), D 31in (79cm). Ottoman: H 12½in (32cm), W 23in (58cm), D 23in (58cm). Table: H 29in (74cm), DI 36in (91cm)

Director Desk and Cabinet, 1962
Rectangular-section stainless steel or bright chrome tubular steel legs, with black stove-enamelled steel crossframe. Desk and cabinet veneered in Rio rosewood veneer. Desk top covered with leather.
Note: Single or double pedestal desk, with or without front panel and extension leaf. Four-door cabinet fitted with trays, shelves and filing units. Outer doors are side-hinged, inner doors are drop-down flaps.
Drawings: 1962 (desk), 1963 (cabinet). Catalogues: 1965–74.
Illustrated pp.113 & 152
Desk: H 29in (74cm), W 78in (198cm), D 36in (91cm), D with extension leaf 51in (130cm)

Interplan Desk and Table, 1962
Solid afrormosia or black stove-enamelled square-section tubular steel legs. Solid and veneered afromosia carcass with black vinyl-covered top.
Note: Low-priced knock-down desk, produced in single or double pedestal versions, with optional typing extension. Table similar in style but without the pedestals.
Drawings: 1962–3 (desk). Catalogues: c.1964–9 (desk), 1966 (table). ***Illustrated pp.113 (desk) & 117 (table)***
H 28in. Metal-legged tops: 48in x 24in (122cm x 61cm), 54in x 24in (137cm x 61cm), 60in x 30in (152cm x 76cm),

72in x 30in (183cm x 76cm). Wooden-legged tops: 73¾in x 24in (187cm x 61cm), 55¾in x 24in (141.5cm x 61cm), 61¾in x 30in (157cm x 76cm), 73¾in x 30in (187cm x 76cm)

Plan Chair, 1962
Black stove-enamelled or chromium-plated square-section tubular steel frame, with optional teak or mahogany arm rests. Seat padded and upholstered, supported by rubber webbing.
Note: Produced with and without arms. Illustrated in Hille showroom in *Architectural Review*, January 1963, p.254.
Drawings: 1961. Catalogues: 1962–7.
H 30in (76cm), SH 18in (46cm), D 20in (51cm), W of side chair 16½in (42cm), W of armchair 22½in (57cm)

President Occasional Tables, c.1962
Solid makore frame, top made of high-density particleboard with makore veneer and solid mahogany lipping.
Catalogue: 1963.
H 18in (46cm) or 22in (56cm). Rectangular table: W 48in (122cm), D 20in (56cm). Circular table: Dl 30in (76cm)

Scimitar Chair, 1962
Moulded plywood seat back, solid beech-framed seat with no-sag springing, both padded and upholstered. Bases include satin chrome or black stove-enamelled tubular steel legs, and various steel pedestal cruciform bases with adjustable height and swivel mechanisms.
Drawings: 1961–2. Catalogues: 1962–70. ***Illustrated p.117***
H 29in (74cm), SH 18in (46cm), W 22in (56cm), D 20in (56cm)

Shelley Dining Group, 1962
Note: Composite suite consisting of Q Stak chairs, Interplan Unit K/L and 677 Table.
Catalogue: 1962.

Single Convertible Bed Settee Mark II and Armchair, 1962
Afrormosia frame with black enamelled-steel seat frame. Upholstered foam cushions and mattress supported on rubber webbing.
Note: Settee is complemented by an armchair in a similar style.
Drawings: 1962. Catalogues: 1963–9. ***Illustrated p.115***
Settee: H 28in (71cm), SH 15¼in (38.5cm), W 79½in (202cm), D (open) 35½in (90cm), D (closed) 30in (76cm). Mattress: L 76in (193cm), W 30in (76cm), D 4in (10cm)

Status Desk Chair, 1962
Moulded plywood seat, padded and upholstered, with optional fixed or reclining back. Supported on pedestal column with swivel, tilt and adjustable height mechanisms, on chromium-plated steel or teak, mahogany or stained-beech cruciform base with castors.
Note: Designed to complement the desks in the Status Group, 1959.
Drawings: 1961–2. Catalogues: 1964–70.
H: 32¼-35¼in (82–89.5cm), SH 18¼-21¼in (46–54cm), W 27in (68.5cm), D 24½in (62cm)

Welbeck Dining Group, 1962
Note: Composite suite consisting of Status Table, 661B chairs and SKP or SLP sideboard.
Catalogue: 1962.

Weymouth Dining Group, 1962
Note: Composite suite consisting of 690 table, Albany chairs and Interplan Unit K or L.
Catalogue: 1962.

Wigmore Dining Group, 1962
Note: Composite suite consisting of 690 table, Albany chairs and Interplan Unit M.
Catalogue: 1962.

41 Chair, 1962
Bright chrome tubular steel or stainless steel legs. Solid rosewood or ash seat back, seat padded and upholstered.
Catalogues: 1964–70. ***Illustrated p.117***
H 29in (74cm), SH 18in (46cm), W 22½in (57cm), D 18¾in (48cm)

41 Sideboard and Table, 1962
Bright chromium-plated tubular steel legs, and ebonized wood under-frame. Table veneered in ash or rosewood with solid wood lippings.
Note: Circular table has knock-down construction. Table and sideboard form part of the 41 Group with the 41 chairs.
Drawings: 1962 (table). Catalogues: 1966–7 (sideboard and table), 1969 (table). ***Illustrated p.117***
Table: H 28in (71cm), Dl 48in (122cm)

Captain's Chair and Table, 1963
Chair frame made of turned afrormosia, makore, mahogany or teak. Seat and seat back made of moulded plywood, padded and upholstered.
Note: Illustrated in *Architectural Review*, January 1963, p.254
Catalogues: 1964–6.
H 29in (74cm), SH 18in (46cm), W 22in (56cm), D 20in (51cm)

Churchill College Furniture, 1963–4
Note: Custom-designed furniture for Churchill College, Cambridge, made by various manufacturers. Items made by Hille included the black bean dining table and chairs for the Senior Combination Dining Room, 1963; and the satinwood desk and table for the Master's Office, 1964.

Interplan Desk Chair, 1963
Moulded plywood seat, padded and upholstered. Seat back supported on steel spine. Swivel and adjustable-height seat mechanism. Black stove-enamelled, nylon-coated or chromium-plated steel pedestal with cruciform base, fitted with plastic glides or castors.
Drawings: 1963. Catalogue: 1964.
H 29½–34in (75–86cm), SH 18½–23in (47–58cm), W 22¾in (57.5cm), D 22¾in (57.5cm)

London Chair, 1963
Bright chrome square-section tubular steel frame, with teak, rosewood or mahogany armrests. Beech-framed seat with no-sag springing, padded and upholstered.
Note: Produced with or without arms. Designed to complement the London table and sideboard. Illustrated in *Architects' Journal*, 6 February 1963, p.284.
Drawings: 1963. Catalogues: 1964–7.
H 31in (79cm), SH 18in (46cm), D 21–21½in (53–54.5cm)

Nottingham Theatre Seating, 1963
Moulded plywood tip-up seat. Curved seat back and armrest, either left plain or padded and upholstered. Epoxy-coated steel frame.
Note: Originally designed for Nottingham Playhouse. Subsequently produced commercially with optional swivel bases and fold-away writing tablets.
Drawings: 1963. Catalogues: 1965–77. ***Illustrated p.119***
H 29½in (75cm), SH 18in (46cm), W 20¾ –22½in (52.5–57cm), D 26½in (67cm)

Polypropylene Chair, 1963
Injection-moulded polypropylene shell. Produced with a variety of bases, including enamelled or chromium-plated tubular steel legs in stacking or non-stacking versions, wooden legs, steel rod skid base, and steel pedestal cruciform or five-branch base with plastic glides or orbital castors.
Note: Mark I version of side chair introduced in 1963, Mark II in 1964, and the armchair in 1967. Both were subsequently adapted for auditorium and concourse use. Original colours were charcoal, light grey and flame red. Dark blue was introduced in 1968, white in 1970. Cambrelle version, made using ICI's propathene, was introduced in 1978; this had a melded non-woven nylon fabric with a tweed-like houndstooth pattern moulded to the shell. Fire-retardant bracken-brown version introduced in 1980. Polyspex version, made using recycled polypropylene, introduced in 1990. Mark II won a Design Centre Award, 1965. Both currently manufactured by Hille Educational Products, armchair to order; armchair also produced as Poly chair by Loft International (2011).
Catalogues: 1964–present. ***Illustrated pp.6, 108, 120–23***
Mark II side chair: H 29½in (75cm), SH 17¼in (44cm), W 21in (53cm), D 21in (53cm). Armchair: H 29½in (75cm), SH 17¼in (44cm), W 23½in (60cm), D 21½in (54.5cm)

Forum Armchair and Settee, 1964
Square-section solid steel legs with bright chrome finish. Solid rosewood or afrormosia frame with comb joints, padded and upholstered on interior. Upholstered feather and down cushions supported on rubber webbing. Reissued by Habitat (1999).
Drawings: 1964 (chair), 1968 (three-seater settee). Catalogues: 1966–76. ***Illustrated pp.53 & 111***
H 27in (68.5cm), SH 15½in (39cm), D 32in (81cm), W of chair 37in (94cm), W of settee 83in (211cm)

Rectangular Boardroom Tables, 1964
Square-section tubular steel or turned wood legs. Veneered top with solid wood lippings.
Note: Standardized boardroom table, produced in graduated sizes in various veneers, with four, six or eight legs.
Drawings: 1964. Catalogues: 1966–9.
4-legged tables 90in–132in (229–335cm); 6-legged tables 132in–192in (335–488cm); 8-legged tables 192in–240in (488–610cm)

Studio Cabinets, 1964
Solid afrormosia with teak veneer, or solid pine with pine veneer.
Note: Part of the Studio Group of living room-dining room furniture. Units could be combined in a variety of configurations. The full range consisted of a cabinet with two hinged doors and interior shelves; a four-drawer chest of drawers; a drop-flap cabinet suitable as a writing desk; and an open shelving unit.
Catalogue: 1965.
W of each unit: 32in (81cm)

Studio Easy Chair, Settee and Coffee Table, 1964
Seating has afrormosia frames, with seat backs of teak-veneered moulded plywood, and upholstered foam cushions supported on rubber webbing. Coffee table has solid afrormosia frame with veneered afrormosia top.
Note: Part of the Studio Group of living room-dining room furniture launched at the *International Furniture Show* in 1965. Settee is a three-seater. Seating produced with or without arms.
Catalogues: 1965–8.
Armchair: H 27¾in (70.5cm), SH 15in (38cm), W 28¾in (73cm), D 30½in (76cm). Settee with arms: H 27¾in (70.5cm), SH 15in (38cm), W 75in (190.5cm), D 25½in (65cm). Coffee table: H 13in (33cm), W 48in (122cm), D 20in (51cm)

Studio Dining Group, 1964
All furniture made of solid afrormosia. Dining chairs have stretched PVC seats and seat backs. Sideboard has woven rattan cane panels on sliding doors. Trolley has white melamine shelves, PVC-covered metal handles, and castors.
Note: Part of the Studio Group of living room-dining room furniture launched at the *International Furniture Show* in 1965. Dining table had extension flap stored underneath. In 1966 the range was supplemented by an alternative modified range of dining chairs called Durham.
Drawings: 1964. Catalogues: 1965–6 (whole group), 1967–9 (trolley). ***Illustrated p.116***
Table: H 28in (71cm), table top 60in x 36in (152cm x 91cm) extending to 76in (193cm). Sideboard: H 28in (71cm), W 84in (213cm), D 18in (46cm). Chair: H 19in (48cm), SH 17½in (44.5cm), W of side chair 18¼in (46cm), W of armchair 20in (51cm). Trolley: H 28in (71cm), W 30in (76cm), D 18in (46cm)

Concourse Armchair, Settee and Table, 1965
Seating and tables have tubular steel frame with bright chrome finish. Upholstered seats padded with foam over zig-zag springing, seat backs padded with foam over moulded plywood. Tables have black or white melamine tops, lipped with black PVC.
Note: Originally designed for Gatwick Airport.
Drawings: 1964–5. Catalogues: 1966–8. ***Illustrated p.117***
H 25½in (65cm), SH 15in (38cm), D 28½in (72cm), W of chair 30in (76cm), W of settee 78in (198cm). Circular table: Dl 48in (122cm). Square table: 30in (76cm) or 36in (91cm). Rectangular table 30in x 52in (76cm x 132cm) or 30in x 54in (76cm x 137cm)

Leo Armchair, Ottoman, Desk Chair and Settee, 1965
Timber-framed seat, padded and upholstered. Chair produced with a variety of bases, including teak legs; bright chrome flat steel bar legs; five-branch or cruciform bright chrome steel swivel pedestal; or gunmetal nylon-coated circular swivel base.
Note: Desk chair version had swivel, tilt and adjustable-height seat. Settee was a three-seater.
Drawings: 1965. Catalogues: 1965–70. ***Illustrated p.113***
Armchair: H 33in (84cm), SH 15in (38cm), W 29½in (75cm), D 22in (56cm). Ottoman: H 15in (38cm), W 29½in (75cm), D 22in (56cm). Desk chair: H 39–42in (99–107cm), SH 18¼ –21¼in (46–54cm), W 27½in (70cm), D 28in (71cm). Settee: H 36in (91cm), SH 15in (38cm), W 74in (188cm), D 33in (84cm)

Nimbus Chair, 1965
Shell originally produced in expanded polystyrene, subsequently in rigid expanded polyurethane foam, padded and upholstered. Chromium-plated, black stove-enamelled or epoxy-coated tubular steel legs, or chromium-plated steel pedestal on cruciform or five-branch base with plastic glides or orbital castors.
Note: Originally described as the Polystyrene Chair. Produced in high-back and low-back versions. Discontinued in 1980.
Catalogues: 1966–76. ***Illustrated pp.113, 124 & 152***
H 31½in (80cm) or 35in (89cm), SH 15½in (39cm) or 20½in (52cm), W 25 (63.5cm) or 25½in (65cm), D 25in (63.5cm)

Plus Group, 1965
Base frames made of either African walnut or pine, or black stove-enamelled square-section tubular steel. Upholstered padded sprung seats and foam cushions. Table tops veneered in African walnut.
Note: Flexible seating system designed on a 24in (61cm) module, produced in units of two, three and four, with high or low seat backs, and matching tables. Stand-alone easy chairs also produced.
Drawings: 1965. Catalogues: 1966–9. ***Illustrated p.116***
Base frames: H 10in (25cm), D 24in (61cm), W 48in (122cm), 72in (183cm) and 96in (244cm). Table tops: 24in x 24in (61cm x 62cm). Chairs: H 26in (66cm) or 38in (96.5cm), W 24in (61cm), D 28in (71cm)

Plus Table, 1965
African walnut or pine frame with combed joints. Top covered in black PVC.
Note: Square or rectangular occasional tables designed to complement the Plus Group. Illustrated in *Design*, April 1965.
Catalogues: 1965–9.
H 14in. Square table 24in x 24in (61cm x 62cm). Rectangular table 48in x 21in (122cm x 53cm)

Taurus Chair and Ottoman, 1965
Bright chrome square-section tubular steel legs with rosewood rails. Seat padded, with buttoned upholstery.
Note: Wing-backed easy chair.
Catalogues: 1965–6.
Chair: H 37½in (95cm), SH 16½in (42cm), W 32½in (82.5cm), D 32½in (82.5cm)

Audley Storage Unit, c.1966
Bright chrome steel legs. Carcass veneered in Santos or Rio rosewood.
Note: Four-door unit resembling a sideboard, but described in catalogue as a storage unit or credenza. Designed to match the Audley table, and suitable for either domestic or office use.
Catalogues: 1969–74. ***Illustrated p.113***
H 28in (71cm), W 84in (213cm), D 17½in (44.5cm)

Audley Table, 1966
Top veneered in Santos or Rio rosewood with solid rosewood lipping. Adjustable-height pedestals have black columns and chromium-plated cruciform bases.
Note: Circular tables with single pedestal, and rounded rectangular tables with single, double or triple pedestals, intended for commercial or domestic use. Circular table has radial veneers.
Drawings: 1964–5. Catalogues: 1966–74. ***Illustrated p.113***
Circular table: H 28in (71cm), Dl 72in (183cm). Rounded rectangular table: single pedestal L 84in (213cm), 96in (244cm), 108in (274cm), W 44–48in (112–122cm); double pedestal L 120in (305cm), 132in (335cm), 144in (366cm), 156in (396cm), 168in (427cm), W 48–56in (122–142cm); triple pedestal L 180in (457cm), 192in (488cm), 204in (518cm), 216in (549cm), 228in (579cm) and 240in (610cm),

W 58–68in (147–173cm)

Axis Chair, 1966
Die-cast polished aluminium frame. Moulded plywood seat with rosewood or teak veneer, or padded and upholstered seat supported on rubber webbing. Tables have white melamine tops, or rosewood or teak veneers.
Note: Demountable stand-alone chair, or multiple unit seating, produced with and without arms.
Drawings: 1965. Catalogues: 1966–9. *Illustrated p.118*
Wooden armchair: H 26¼in (66.5cm), SH 15¼in (38.5cm), W 25½in (65cm), D 26in (66cm). Upholstered armchair: H 27½in (70cm), SH 16½in (42cm), W 26in (66cm), D 28in (71cm). Table top: 22in x 22in (56cm x 56cm)

BT Pedestal Table, 1966
Bright chrome or black stove-enamelled tubular steel pedestal on black cast-iron base. Top made of terrazzo, marble, or timber covered with mahogany veneer or melamine, with solid lippings.
Note: Heavy-duty circular table for contract use.
Catalogues: 1966–7.
H 18in (46cm), DI 27in (68.5cm)

Carlton Table, 1966
Black stove-enamelled, nylon-coated, or bright chrome square-section tubular steel legs and steel angle underframe. White melamine or walnut, teak or mahogany top.
Note: Square or rectangular table for contract use.
Catalogue: 1966.
H 29in (74cm). Rectangular table top: 48in x 24in (122cm x 61cm). Square table top: 33in x 33in (84cm x 84cm)

Disque Table, 1966
White melamine or teak-veneered top with black PVC lipping. Black stove-enamelled or epoxy-coated pedestal with bright chrome steel tripod base.
Note: Demountable table for commercial use. Illustrated in *Design*, April 1967, p.56.
Catalogues: 1966–75.
H 27in (68.5cm), DI 24in (61cm)

Durham Chair, 1966
Solid afrormosia rectangular-section frame. Seat padded and upholstered.
Note: Variant of the earlier Studio dining chair, with back rail added behind seat back, and side rail omitted at the foot. Produced with and without arms.
Catalogues: 1966–7.
H 29in (74cm), SH 17in (43cm), W 18¾in (47.5cm), D 18¾in (47.5cm)

Forum Table, 1966
Square-section solid stainless steel legs. Solid afrormosia or veneered rosewood sides. Plate-glass top suspended above magazine shelf covered in black PVC
Note: Designed to complement the Forum armchair and settee. Illustrated in *Design*, August 1967, p.56. Temporarily reissued by Habitat (c. 2002).
Catalogues: 1966–75.
H 14½in (37cm), W 34¾in (88cm), D 37in (94cm)

339 Table, 1966
Top veneered with teak, mahogany or rosewood, or covered with white melamine with black PVC lipping. Black stove-enamelled tubular steel pedestal with bright chrome cruciform flat steel base.
Note: Dining table for contract market.
Catalogues: 1966–7.
H 28in (71cm). Circular table: DI 36in (91cm). Square table: 36in x 36in (91cm x 91cm)

Chesterfield Settee, c.1967
Beech frame on castors. Seat back padded with foam, seat padded with rubberized hair. Buttoned upholstery and feather cushions.
Catalogues: 1967–74.
H 25in (63.5cm), SH 20in (51cm), W 96in (244cm), D 37in (94cm)

Centric Chair, 1968
Rigid expanded polyurethane foam shell, padded and upholstered. Steel rod skid base or chromium-plated steel pedestal cruciform base.
Catalogues: 1968–9. *Illustrated p.124*
H 36½in (93cm), SH 16in (41cm), W 32½in (82.5cm), D 38in (96.5cm)

City Chair, 1968
Moulded plywood seat, padded and upholstered. Wooden or upholstered armrests. Mounted on a variety of bases, including mahogany, afrormosia or teak legs; square-section tubular steel legs; bright chrome steel pedestal cruciform base; or aluminium-framed multiple seating units.
Note: Contract seating, produced as a stand-alone chair or in multiple seating units, with or without arms. Illustrated in *The Cabinet Maker and Retail Furnisher*, 20 December 1968, p.572.
Drawings: 1967. Catalogues: 1969–76.
Basic side chair: H 32in (81cm), SH 19in (48cm), W 19½in (49.5cm), D 32in (81cm)

Delphi Chairs, Table and Sideboard, 1968
Chairs and table have inverted T-shaped frames made from flat chromium-plated steel. Chairs also produced with afrormosia, mahogany or rosewood legs. Chairs have padded seat with buttoned

upholstery. Table veneered in Rio rosewood or teak, with solid wood lipping. Sideboard veneered in rosewood.
Note: Luxury range of boardroom furniture. Four-door sideboard has interior trays and adjustable shelves.
Drawings: 1968–9. Catalogues: 1969–76. *Illustrated p.115*
Steel chair: H 33in (84cm), SH 19in (48cm), W 25in (63.5cm), D 21½in (54.5cm). Wood chair: H 33½in (85cm), SH 19in (48cm), W 25½in (65cm), D 24½in (62cm). Table: H 28in (71cm), W 96in (244cm), D 45in (114cm). Sideboard: H 28in (71cm), W 84in (213cm), D 18in (46cm)

Kulminus Armchair, 1968
Rigid expanded polyurethane foam shell, padded and upholstered, with fitted cushions. Five-branch chromium-plated steel pedestal base.
Note: High-backed easy chair set at a reclining angle, also known as Cumulus. Similar in form to the 4-4000.
Drawings: 1967. Catalogues: 1968–74.
H 36½in (93cm), SH 16in (41cm), W 32½in (82.5cm), D 38in (96.5cm)

Brutus Armchair, 1969
Solid beech frame with combed joints. Upholstered foam cushions supported on rubber platform.
Drawings: 1968. Catalogue: 1969.
H 27½in (70cm), SH 17in (43cm), W 31in (79cm), D 33in (84cm)

Interseating, 1969
Bright chrome tubular steel legs. Beech-framed seats with no-sag springing, padded and upholstered. Table covered in white melamine.
Note: Modular seating system for heavy-duty contract use, produced in two-, three- or four-seat units, combining benches, chairs and tables.
Drawings: 1967–9. Catalogue: 1969.
Seating: H 27in (68.5cm), SH 16in (41cm), D 28in (71cm), W 28in (71cm), 56in (142cm), 84in (213cm), 112in (285.5)

Lancaster Chair, 1969
Moulded plywood seat and seat back, padded and upholstered. Bright chrome tubular steel legs.
Note: Stacking armchair for contract market, with optional writing tablet, linking device and floor fixing bar.
Catalogue: 1969.

P280, P281 and P282 Tables, 1969
White melamine or teak-veneered tops with black PVC lipping. Circular P280 and square P281 tables mounted on black stove-enamelled pedestal with chromium-plated cruciform steel base. Rectangular P282 table has inverted T-shaped legs with black columns and chromium-plated steel bases.
Note: Range of tables for contract use, produced in two heights.
Catalogues: 1969–75. *Illustrated p.115*
H 17in (43cm) and 28in (71cm). P280: DI 36in (91cm) and 44in (112cm). P281: 30in x 30in (76cm x 76cm). P282: 24in x 48in (61cm x 122cm), 30in x 48in (76cm x 122cm), 27in x 72in (68.5cm x 183cm)

Reclining Chair, 1969
Solid beech frame. Polyester sleeve with stitched vinyl upholstery zipped over a tubular steel framework. Fabric-covered headrest.
Drawings: 1967–9. Catalogue: 1969.
H 37in (94cm), SH 14in (35.5cm), W 26in (66cm), D 37in (94cm)

Stratford Auditorium Seating, 1969
Wooden seat frame, with optional wooden arms. Seat fitted with no-sag springing, padded and upholstered. Epoxy-coated steel frame.
Note: Originally designed for the refurbishment of the Shakespeare Memorial Theatre in Stratford-upon-Avon.
Drawings: 1968–9. Catalogues: 1977–81.
H: 29½in (75cm), D 26in (66cm), W 19in (48cm), 20in (51cm) and 21in (53cm)

4-4000 Armchair and Ottoman, 1970
Injection-moulded ABS plastic shell in white or buffalo brown, padded and upholstered, with tailored cushions and optional arm pads. Colour-coordinated bases include steel swivel disc base, five-branch swivel base, and cruciform tubular steel anchor base.
Drawings: 1969–70. Catalogues: 1971–6. *Illustrated pp.53 & 149*
Chair: H 92cm (36¼in), SH 40cm (15¾in), W 70cm (27½in), D 92cm (36¼in). Ottoman: H 38cm (15in), W 53cm (21in), D 53cm (21in)

Executive Desk Chair, 1971
Bright chrome steel arms, with upholstered armrest. Padded seat and seat back upholstered in leather. Black epoxy-coated steel pedestal column with bright chrome five-branch base on castors.
Note: High- or low-back chair with swivel and tilt mechanism. Illustrated in *The Cabinet Maker and Retail Furnisher*, 25 March 1977.
Drawings: 1971. Catalogues: 1974–6.
H 111cm (43¾in), SH 52cm (20½in), W 67cm (26¼in), D 72cm (28½in)

Quadrille Table, 1971
White melamine top with black PVC lipping. Black or white epoxy-coated tubular steel base.
Note: Circular demountable table for café use, also known as the Diabolo table.
Drawings: 1971. Catalogue: 1972.
H 71cm (28in), DI 91cm (35¾in)

Senator Group, 1971–81
Table top, desk and storage unit veneered in Santos or Rio rosewood. Stainless steel plinth bases and trim, with anodized aluminium finger grips on desk.
Note: Luxury range of executive furniture designed over a period of ten years. Full range consisted of double pedestal desk, four-door storage unit, and meeting table, together described as the Senator Group.
Drawings: 1971 (desk), 1977 (storage unit), 1981 (table).
Catalogues: 1984–6.
Desk: H 74.5cm (29¼in), W 190cm (74¾in), D 91.5cm (36in). Storage unit: H 71cm (28in), W 213cm (83¾in), D 46cm (18in). Table: H 72.5cm (28½in), W 274.5cm (108in), D 116.5cm (45¾in)

Series E School Chairs, 1971
Polypropylene shell. Epoxy-coated tubular steel legs.
Note: Range of heavy-duty school chairs produced in five sizes. Originally commissioned by the Consortium of Local Authorities for Wales. Currently produced by Hille Educational Products (2011).
Drawings: 1971. Catalogues: 1971–present. *Illustrated p.146*
Chair A: H 52cm (20½in), SH 28cm (11in), W 31cm (12¼in), D 52cm (20½in). Chair B: H 59cm (23¼in), SH 32cm (12½in), W 37cm (14½in), D 38cm (15in). Chair C: H 64.8cm (25½in), SH 35.5cm (14in), W 41cm (16in), D 42cm (16½in). Chair D: H 71cm (28in), SH 39cm (15½in), W 47cm (18½in), D 50cm (19½in). Chair E: H 75cm (29½in), SH 43cm (17in), W 47cm (18½in), D 50cm (19½in)

Series E School Stools, 1971
Polypropylene seat. Epoxy-coated tubular steel legs.
Note: Produced in two versions, with footrests (eight sizes) and without footrests (four sizes). Currently produced by Hille Educational Products (2011).
Stools without footrests – Stool 1: H 43cm (17in), W 41cm (16in), D 38.5cm (15¼in). Stool 2: H 39.5cm (15½in), W 41cm (16in), D 37cm (14½in). Stool 3: H 28cm (14½in), W 41cm (16in), D 32cm (12½in). Stool 4: H 23cm (9in), W 41cm (16in), D 34cm (13¾in)
Stools with footrests – Stool A: H 43cm (17in), W 41cm (16in), D 38.5cm (15¼in). Stool B: H 45cm (17¾in), W 41cm (16in), D 39cm (15½in). Stool C: H 52.5cm (20¾in), W 41cm (16in), D 43cm (17in). Stool D: H 57.5cm (22½in), W 41cm (16in), D 39.5cm (15½in). Stool E: H 61cm (24in), W 41cm (16in), D 41cm (16in). Stool F: H 66cm (26in), W 41cm (16in), D 43cm (17in). Stool G: H 68.5cm (27in), W 41cm (16in), D 44cm (17¼in). Stool H: H 71cm (28in), W 41cm (16in), D 45cm (17¾in)

Series E School Tables, 1971
Black or brown epoxy-coated tubular steel frame. Doeskin-coloured laminate tops edged with grey PVC.
Note: Heavy-duty square, rectangular, hexagonal and trapezoid tables, which form part of the Series E range of school furniture. The range also includes specialist items such as screens, trolleys, benches, clay-modelling tables and clothes hanger units.
Rectangular tables – PA01: H 45cm (17¾in), W 90cm (35½in), D 45cm (17¾in). PA02: H 50cm (19½in), W 90cm (35½in), D 45cm (17¾in). PA03: H 55cm (21¾in), W 110cm (43¼in), D 55cm (21¾in). PA04: H 60cm (23½in), W 110cm (43¼in), D 55cm (21¾in). PA05 (for teachers): H 70cm (27½in), W 110cm (43¼in), D 55cm (21¾in). PA29: H 65cm (25½in), W 110cm (43¼in), D 55cm (21¾in). SA12 (for teachers): H 70cm (27½in), W 120cm (47in), D 60cm (23½in). Trapezoid tables – PA17: H 50cm (19½in), W 110cm (43¼in), D 55cm (21¾in). PA18: H 55cm (21¾in), W 110cm (43¼in), D 55cm (21¾in)

Toro Chair, 1971
Beech seat, padded and upholstered. Legs and seat back originally made of expanded polystyrene, and subsequently of white or black ABS plastic.
Note: Partially upholstered stacking chair for restaurant use. ABS variant introduced in 1976.
Drawings: 1971, revised 1975. Catalogues: 1975–6.
H 74cm (29in), W 51cm (20in), D 48cm (18¾in)

Arena Seating, 1972
Polypropylene seats. Heavy-gauge mild steel frames, nylon-coated or epoxy-coated.
Note: Initially produced in two versions with individual U-frame seats or linked frame units. Subsequently produced as tread-fixed, beam-mounted, free-standing or retractable seating.
Drawings: 1969–79. Catalogues: 1975–81.
H: 76cm (30in), SH 39cm (15½in), W 42.5cm (16¾in), D 50.5cm (19¾in)

Obo Chair, 1972
Blow-moulded white polypropylene drum, with vacuum-formed polystyrene seat, padded and upholstered.
Note: Made using ICI's propathene.
Drawings: 1972. Catalogues: 1972–3. *Illustrated p.149*
H 68cm (26¾in), SH 43cm (17in), W 56cm (22in), D 68cm (26¾in)

Tote Table, 1972
Injection-moulded ABS.
Note: Table is white. Removable central lid covers well intended for storage. Lid, which doubles up as a tray, produced in white, brown and orange.
Drawings: 1972. Catalogues: 1972–5. *Illustrated p.149*
H 34cm (13¼in), W 61cm (24in), D 61cm (24in)

Drum Table, 1973
Particleboard top covered and lipped with white melamine. Drum-shaped white fibreglass pedestal.

Drawings: 1973–4. Catalogue: 1974.
H 72cm (28½in), Dl 91cm (35¾in) or 112cm (44in)

Concourse Seating, c.1974
Fibreglass shell mounted on black steel beam, with legs of polished aluminium.
Note: Designed for public areas such as airports. Produced in units of two, three, four or five seats, with or without upholstered pads.
Catalogues: 1974–80.
H 75cm (29½in), SH 35cm (13¾in), D 62cm (24½in), W 110.5cm (43½in), 167.5cm (66in), 225cm (88½in), 282cm (111in)

Dolce Seating and Table, 1975
Seating has timber frame, padded with fire-retardant foam and upholstered. Glass-topped table has matching upholstery on sides.
Note: Modular seating system for foyers, complemented by a stand-alone armchair and low table.
Drawings: 1975 (seating), 1979 (table). Catalogues: 1982–6.
Seating: H 70cm (27½in), SH 39cm (15½in), D 78cm (30¾in), W of corner unit 78cm (30¾in), W of armless unit 71cm (28in), W of armchair 107cm (42in). Table: H 28cm (11in), W 78cm (30¾in), D 78cm (30¾in)

Polo Chair, 1975
Polypropylene shell with high-gloss finish. Produced with various metal bases, including nylon-coated or chromium-plated tubular steel legs, and steel rod skid base.
Note: Range includes stacking chairs, with and without arms; skid and sledge chairs; bar stools; multiple beam-mounted seating; and riser, tread or strap-fixed stadium seating. Originally produced in white, flame, yellow, emerald green and black. Later produced in blue. Currently manufactured by Loft International (2011).
Drawings: 1974–5. Catalogues: 1975 onwards. ***Illustrated pp.145 & 147***
Stacking chair: H 71cm (28in), SH 44cm (17¼in), W 53.4cm (21in), D 53cm (21in)

S290 Tables, c.1975
White melamine or teak-veneered tops. Black-enamelled or chromium-plated square-section tubular steel frame and legs.
Note: Dining tables for the contract market, designed to link together and stack spirally. Produced in five sizes.
Catalogue: 1975.
H 71cm (28in), W 122cm (48in), 152cm (59¾in) and 183cm (72in), D 61cm (24in) and 76cm (30in)

City Auditorium Seating, 1978
Epoxy-coated steel frame. Moulded plywood seat back. Hardwood-framed seat with no-sag springing, padded and upholstered. Hardwood arms.
Note: Mass-produced variant of tip-up seating originally designed for Cinemas 2 and 3 at the Barbican Centre in 1978. Seats could be fitted with simultaneous translation equipment, wired through tubular supports.
Drawings: 1978. Catalogues: 1981–5. ***Illustrated p.151***
H 96.5cm (38in), SH 45cm (17¾in), W 53.3cm (21in), D 67.5cm (26½in)

Ibex Chair, 1978
Chromium-plated or epoxy-coated tubular steel legs and frame. Polypropylene seat back. Polyurethane foam seat, padded and upholstered.
Note: Moderately priced stacking chair for the contract market, intended for dining or conference use. Also produced with arms, writing tablet and linking device.
Drawings: 1978–80. Catalogues: 1980–86.
H 76cm (30in), SH 45cm (17¾in), W 50cm (19½in), D 49cm (19in)

Maroc Settee, c.1980
Timber frame, padded and upholstered. Cushions supported on rubber webbing.
Note: Foyer seating.

Barbican Bar Tables and Chairs, 1981
Square pedestal tables with timber tops. Timber-framed armchairs with upholstered seats.
Note: Designed for the foyer of the Barbican Centre, but not produced commercially.
Illustrated p.150

Hadrian Seating and Tables, 1981
Timber-framed seating, padded and upholstered in leather, raised on a laminate plinth. Circular and rounded rectangular tables with timber tops mounted on steel pedestal bases.
Note: Large-scale modular seating range originally designed for the foyer of the Barbican Centre, consisting of straight, concave and corner seat units.
Drawings: 1980. Catalogues: 1982–6. ***Illustrated p.150***
H 71cm (28in), SH 40cm (15¾in), D 86cm (33¾in), W of straight unit 86cm (33¾in), W of concave unit 87.5cm (34½in), W of corner unit 121.5cm (47¾in)

Spectrum Seating, 1983
Steel frame. Red or blue polypropylene seat.
Note: Tip-up seating produced in riser-fixed, tread-fixed, beam-mounted and retractable versions. Originally developed for sports arenas, but could also be upholstered for lecture hall and theatre use. Currently manufactured in modified form by Link Seating (2011).
Drawings: 1982. Catalogues: 1983–9. ***Illustrated p.153***
SH 44.5cm (17½in), D 52cm (20½in), W with arms 49cm (19in), W without arms 46cm (18in)

RD Seating, 1984
Nylon-coated steel frame. Sheet steel seat, padded and upholstered.
Note: Heavy-duty beam-mounted seating, produced in two-, three- or four-seat units, originally designed for hospital waiting rooms, with optional tables and magazine racks. Metal coated in beige, brown, black, grey, gunmetal, white, yellow, green or red. Not currently manufactured (2011).
Catalogues: 1984 onwards. ***Illustrated p.154***
Seating: H 77cm (30¼in), SH 45.5cm (17½in), D 58cm (22¾in), W without arms 102cm (40in), 153cm (60in), 204cm (80¼in), W with arms 112cm (44in), 163cm (64in), 214cm. Corner table: 61cm x 61cm (24in x 24in). Free-standing tables: H 50cm (19½in), D 48cm (18¾in), W 48cm (18¾in) or 121cm (47½in)

Forum Seating, 1986
Moulded birch plywood seats, padded and upholstered. Epoxy-coated or nylon-coated steel beam units with cast-aluminium arm and back supports, and optional polyurethane foam arms.
Note: Flexible seating system for auditorium, waiting room and courtroom use. Produced in the form of beam-mounted and free-standing chairs. Later produced as Forum 2000 but no longer manufactured (2011).
Drawings: 1984–6. Catalogue: 1986.

Accord Seating, 1990
Blow-moulded polyethylene seat. Steel supports or tubular steel legs.
Note: Range of tread-fixed, riser-fixed or beam-mounted tip-up stadium and auditorium seating. Produced in various widths, plain or upholstered, with tamper-proof fixings and folding arms. Also made as individual stacking chairs. Currently manufactured by Link Trading. Currently manufactured using air-assisted moulding by Link Seating (2011).
Drawings: 1988–9. Catalogue: 1990. ***Illustrated p.157***
H 78.5cm (31in), D 57cm (22¼in), W 46cm (18in), 48cm (18¾in), 50cm (19½in) and 52cm (20½in)

Toro Seating, 1990
Nylon-coated steel beam frame, perforated sheet seat.
Note: Heavy-duty beam-mounted public seating system, produced in two- to six-seat units, with optional armrests and tables. Produced in polished steel, and in twelve colours: white, beige, light grey, gunmetal, black, brown, yellow, green, blue, red, midnight blue and racing green. Used extensively on London Underground. Upholstered variant introduced in 1999, marketed under the name Exodus. Toro currently manufactured by Hille Educational Products, but not Exodus (2011).
Drawings: 1990 and 1992. Catalogues: 1990–present. ***Illustrated p.155***
H 76.5cm (30in), SH 44.5cm (17½in), D 60cm (23½in), W without arms 112.5cm (44¼in), 170.5cm (67in), 228.5cm (90in), 286.5cm (112¾in), 344.5cm (135½in), W with arms 122.5cm (48¼in), 180.5cm (71in), 238.5cm (93¾in), 296.5cm (116¾in), 354.5cm (139½in)

Woodro Seating, 1991
Steel frame. Slatted hardwood seat.
Note: Wooden variant of the Toro heavy-duty beam-mounted public seating system, produced in two- to six-seat units, with or without arms. Currently manufactured by Hille Educational Products (2011).
Catalogues: 1991–present. ***Illustrated p.155***
H 76.5cm (30in), SH 47cm (18½in), D 65cm (25½in), W without arms 112.5cm (44¼in), 170.5cm (67in), 228.5cm (90in), 286.5cm (112¾in), 344.5cm (135½in), W with arms 1225.cm (48¼in), 180.5cm (71in), 238.5cm (93¾in), 296.5cm (116¾in), 354.5cm (139½in)

Span Auditorium Seating, 1993
Tubular steel frame, aluminium legs and arms. Beech plywood seat, padded and upholstered.
Note: Tip-up auditorium seating, produced in beam-mounted and individual floor-fixed versions, and as a free-standing chair, with or without arms.
Drawings: 1991–3. Catalogue: 1993. ***Illustrated p.153***
H 84.5cm (33¼in), SH 44cm (17¼in), D 56cm (22in), W with arms 57.5cm (22½iin), W without arms 54.5cm (21½iin)

A2. PYE: PRODUCT DESIGN

Radiogramophone, c.1948
Veneered timber case, with plastic dials.
Note: Large console model. Illustrated in *Designers in Britain*, no. 2, 1949, p.14, fig. 2.

Table Radio, c.1948
Veneered timber case, with plastic dials.
Note: Small table model. Illustrated in *Designers in Britain*, no. 2, 1949, p.14, fig. 3.

Radio (Model PE60), 1952
Lacquered wood case, white plastic speaker grill, glass control panel, black plastic knobs.
Illustrated in *The Setmakers*, p.301.
H 15in (38cm), W 21in (53cm), D at base 14in (35.5cm), D at top 6in (15cm)

Television (Models CW17, CW17C, CS17 and CS17C), 1957
Japanese sen or French walnut veneered cabinet. Black plastic control panel. Table model supplied with black stove-enamelled tubular steel stand with rubber feet.
Note: Valve-operated television, with technical design by J.E. Cope. Produced as a console version with a built-in speaker panel in walnut (CW17C) or sen (CS17C), and as a table model with optional metal stand (CW17 and CS17). Design Centre Award, 1957.
Pye catalogue: 1957. ***Illustrated pp.76 & 106***
Table model: H 21in (53cm), W 18½iin (47cm), D 21¼in (54cm). Stand: H 18in (46cm); W 17in (43cm); D 16in (41cm). Console model: H 34in (86cm), W 18¾in (47.5cm), D 21¼in (54cm)

Transistor Radio (Model 444), c.1958
Ribbed pressed aluminium case. Grey and orange plastic knobs. Gold grill.
Note: This rounded rectangular radio was one of the earliest transistorized models.
H 7¾in (19.5cm), W 12⅞in (33cm), D 3½in (9cm)

Stereogram (Model 1207), 1964
Teak cabinet. Black or white vinyl-covered front with anodized aluminium edge. Grey linen speaker covers.
Note: Illustrated in *Designers in Britain*, no. 6, 1964, p.197; *Design*, September, 1965, pp.36–7.
Illustrated p.77
H 21¾in (55cm), W 50in (127cm), D 17¼in (44cm)

Radio (Mono Model 1108, Stereo Model 1111), 1965
Teak-veneered cabinet with satin-finished anodized aluminium control panel, black plastic speaker grill, and grey plastic knobs.
Note: Designed by Robin Day in association with Douglas Jones, head of Pye's advanced development department. Design Centre Award, 1966. Illustrated in *Design*, September 1965, pp.36–7; and *Design*, May 1966.
Illustrated p.77
Radio: H 8in (20cm); W 26in (66cm), D 7in (18cm). Speaker: H 8in (20cm), W 9½in (24cm), D 7in (18cm)

Television (Model 24), 1965
Teak cabinet with black anodized aluminium control panel. Optional black stove-enamelled tubular steel stand.
Note: Illustrated in *Design*, September 1965, pp.36–7.
Illustrated p.77
H 16½in (42cm), W 29in (74cm), D 13¼in (33.5cm)

A3. WOODWARD GROSVENOR: CARPETS

Note: Robin Day designed carpets for the Kidderminster manufacturer Woodward, Grosvenor & Co. between c.1960 and 1966. Some of his designs remained in production until the 1970s, and between 1967 and 1974 they were marketed under the name of Woodward Grosvenor's parent company, Grays Carpets, of Ayr, Scotland.

Woodward Grosvenor Saxony Wilton all-wool carpet was produced in three qualities: Akbar (medium duty), Super Akbar (heavy duty) and Extra Super Akbar (very heavy duty). Grays Project Wilton carpet was made from 80% wool and 20% nylon, and was produced in three qualities: Project and Project Minor (heavy domestic and medium contract use), and Project Major (luxury domestic and heavy contract use). Robin Day's designs were originally allocated their own RD pattern numbers, starting at RD 11. RD 50–52 appear to have been designed out of sequence, however. Subsequently, standard Woodward Grosvenor four-digit pattern numbers were allocated. Some designs just have RD pattern numbers; some designs have one or two Woodward Grosvenor four-digit pattern numbers; and some have both. They are listed below in pattern number order, along with their pattern names where they exist. Where patterns are not illustrated, a brief description is given. Drawings and catalogues refer to material held in Woodward Grosvenor Archives.

Delphic (RD 11)
Akbar Saxony Wilton range.
Note: Pattern of fine lines broken by rows of dots. 15in (38cm) repeat. Produced in five colourways. Illustrated in *Architectural Review*, April 1962, p.121.
Drawings: Woodward Grosvenor Design Papers. Catalogues: Modern Group leaflet.

Sequence (RD 12)
Akbar Saxony Wilton range.
Note: Pattern of even three-colour stripes. 18in (46cm) repeat. Produced in five colourways. Illustrated in *Architectural Review*, June 1962, p.130, and February 1963, p.52.
Drawings: Woodward Grosvenor Design Papers. Catalogues: Modern Group leaflet.

RD 13
Note: Mosiac-like pattern of random small rectangles.
Drawings: Woodward Grosvenor Design Papers.

Cipher (RD 14)
Akbar Saxony Wilton range.
Note: 11½in (29cm) repeat. Produced in four colourways. Illustrated in *Architectural Review*, February 1962, p.131.
Drawings: Woodward Grosvenor Design Papers. Catalogues: Modern Group leaflet. ***Illustrated p.125***

Iambic (RD 15)
Akbar Saxony Wilton range.
Note: 12in (30.5cm) repeat. Produced in two colourways. Illustrated in *The Ambassador*, 1961 no. 7, pp.74–89; *Architectural Review*,

September 1962, p.103.
Drawings: Woodward Grosvenor Design Papers. Catalogues: Modern Group leaflet. ***Illustrated p.125***

RD 16
Note: Pattern of rectangles with overlaid blotches.
Drawings: Woodward Grosvenor Design Papers.

Motley (RD 17 and Woodward Grosvenor pattern nos 7126 and 7681)
Akbar Saxony Wilton and Project Wilton range.
Note: 19in (48cm), 20½in (52cm) or 22⅝in (57.5cm) repeat. Originally produced in four colourways. Illustrated in *The Ambassador*, 1961 no. 7, pp.74–89; *Architectural Review*, December 1961, p.113, and October 1962, p.149.
Catalogues: Woodward Grosvenor Modern Group leaflet; Grays Carpets Contract Wiltons. ***Illustrated p.125***

RD 18
Note: Pattern of squares with circles, dots, squares, stars and other motifs inside.
Drawings: RD artwork (dated 1962), and Woodward Grosvenor Design Papers.

Abacus (RD 19 and Woodward Grosvenor pattern no. 7127)
Akbar Saxony Wilton range.
Note: Pattern of rows of small circles. 3½in (9cm) repeat. Produced in four colourways.
Drawings: RD artwork, and Woodward Grosvenor Design Papers.
Catalogues: Grays Carpets Contract Wiltons.

RD 20
Note: Abstract linear pattern, similar to Elm (RD 52).
Drawings: Woodward Grosvenor Design Papers.

Discus (RD 21)
Akbar Saxony Wilton range.
Note: Another variation of Discus (RD 51), produced in three colourways on a different scale with a 24in (61cm) repeat.
Drawings: RD artwork, and Woodward Grosvenor Design Papers.
Catalogues: Grays Carpets Contract Wiltons.
Illustrated p.125

RD 22
Note: Grid pattern of broken squares.
Drawings: RD artwork, and Woodward Grosvenor Design Papers.

RD 23
Note: Pattern of broad fragmented stripes.
Drawings: RD artwork, and Woodward Grosvenor Design Papers.

RD 24
Note: Triangular lattice pattern.
Drawings: RD artwork, and Woodward Grosvenor Design Papers.

RD 25
Note: Pattern of small crosses.
Drawings: RD artwork, and Woodward Grosvenor Design Papers.

Aztec (RD 26 and Woodward Grosvenor pattern nos 7129 and 7679)
Akbar Saxony Wilton and Project Wilton range.
Note: Pattern of large circles, composed of concentic rings of geometric motifs. 18½in (47cm) repeat. Produced in seven colourways.
Drawings: RD artwork, and Woodward Grosvenor Design Papers.
Catalogues: Grays Carpets Contract Wiltons.

Libra (RD 27 and Woodward Grosvenor pattern nos 7130 and 7683)
Akbar Saxony Wilton and Project Wilton range.
Note: Mosaic-like mottled pattern. 9in (23cm) repeat. Produced in three colourways.
Drawings: RD artwork (dated 1965), and Woodward Grosvenor Design Papers. Catalogues: Grays Carpets Contract Wiltons.

Leo (RD 28 and Woodward Grosvenor pattern nos 7131 and 7682)
Akbar Saxony Wilton and Project Wilton range.
Note: Pattern of small irregular squares. 10½in (27cm) repeat. Produced in four colourways.
Drawings: Woodward Grosvenor Design Papers. Catalogues: Grays Carpets Contract Wiltons.

RD 30
Note: Pattern of rectangles with broken edges.
Drawings: Woodward Grosvenor Design Papers.

RD 31
Note: Pattern of interlocking geometric lines.
Drawings: Woodward Grosvenor Design Papers.

Roundel (RD 32 and Woodward Grosvenor pattern no. 7132)
Churchill Wilton range.
Note: Pattern of large radiating circular motifs. 13½in (34cm) repeat. Drawings: Woodward Grosvenor Design Papers.
Catalogues: Grays Carpets Contract Wiltons.

Hexagon (RD 33 and Woodward Grosvenor pattern no. 7133)
Churchill Wilton range.
Note: Pattern of small hexagons containing triangles, stars, dots and other geometric motifs. 23in (58cm) repeat.
Drawings: Woodward Grosvenor Design Papers. Catalogues: Grays Carpets Contract Wiltons.

RD 50
Note: Pattern of irregular bands of stripes.
Drawings: RD artwork, and Woodward Grosvenor Design Papers.

Discus (RD 51 and Woodward Grosvenor pattern nos 7128 and 7680)
Project Wilton range.
Note: 27in (68.5cm) or 26½in (66cm) repeat. Originally produced in three colourways. Illustrated in *The Ambassador*, 1962 no.7, p.103; *Architectural Review*, August 1963, p.84, and May 1966, p.41.
Drawings: RD artwork, and Woodward Grosvenor Design Papers.
Catalogues: Modern Group leaflet (Trend range); Grays Carpets Contract Wiltons. ***Illustrated p.125***

Elm (RD52)
Akbar Saxony Wilton range.
Drawings: RD artwork, and Woodward Grosvenor Design Papers.
Catalogues: Modern Group leaflet (Trend range). ***Illustrated p.125***

Discus Variation (Woodward Grosvenor pattern no. 7685)
Project Wilton range.
Note: Another variation of Discus (RD 51), produced on a much smaller scale with a 4½in (11.5cm) repeat.
Drawings: RD artwork, and Woodward Grosvenor Design Papers.
Catalogues: Grays Carpets Contract Wiltons.

Broken Stripe (Woodward Grosvenor pattern no. 7686)
Project Wilton range.
Note: Irregular five-colour stripe pattern. 18in (46cm) repeat. Produced in two colourways.
Catalogues: Grays Carpets Contract Wiltons.

Cypher (Woodward Grosvenor pattern no. 7694)
Project Wilton range.
Note: Grid pattern composed of various small geometric motifs. 8½in (21.5cm) repeat.
Catalogues: Grays Carpets Contract Wiltons.

Quadriga (Woodward Grosvenor pattern no. 7695)
Project Wilton range.
Note: Grid pattern of squares linked by lines. 2½in (7.5cm) repeat. Produced in two colourways.
Catalogues: Grays Carpets Contract Wiltons.

Meridian (Woodward Grosvenor pattern no. 7696)
Project Wilton range.
Note: Pattern of rectangles overlaid with irregular fine lines. 24in (61cm) repeat.
Catalogues: Grays Carpets Contract Wiltons.

Isis (Woodward Grosvenor pattern no. 7699)
Project Wilton range.
Note: Mazelike pattern of irregular interweaving lines. 13½in (34cm) repeat. Produced in three colourways.
Catalogues: Grays Carpets Contract Wiltons.

A4. PRESTON DESIGNS: FURNITURE

Demountable Chair, c.1946
Cast-aluminium frame. Seat padded and upholstered.
Note: Illustrated in *Designers in Britain*, no. 1, 1947, pp.224–5, figs 6–7.

A5. HEAL'S: FURNITURE

Low-Cost Furniture Competition Storage Units, 1950
Birch-veneered moulded plywood shells with solid mahogany ends. Sliding glass doors run in aluminium grooves. Tubular aluminium alloy legs.
Note: In 1948 Robin Day and Clive Latimer won the storage section of Museum of Modern Art's International Low-Cost Furniture Competition. Two years later Heal's made a set of prototypes. These were exhibited at their Tottenham Court Road store in May 1950.
Illustrated p.25–7

D6553A Utility Sideboard and D80 Utility Bookcase, 1951
Sideboard made of mahogany and ash. Bookcase made of mahogany, with sliding glass doors. Steel rod legs.
Note: Part of a range of storage furniture designed for the low-cost room setting designed by Robin Day for the Home Entertainment section of the Homes and Gardens Pavilion at the Festival of Britain in 1951. Originally produced by Heal's for the Festival, and subsequently manufactured and sold by Heal's under the Utility scheme.
Illustrated p.46
H 28in (71cm), W 54in (137cm); D of sideboard 18in (46cm); D of bookcase 10in (25cm)

Dining Tables and Chairs for Churchill College, Cambridge, 1964
Oiled teak. High-table chairs upholstered in leather.
Note: Hille made the prototypes for this design, but Heal's Contract Division won the contract after it was put out to tender. The full range of furniture included a high table and sixty upholstered chairs for the Master and Fellows, and six rows of sectionalized dining tables and 250 stacking chairs for the students. See *Architect and Building News*, 9 September 1964.
Drawings: 1963. ***Illustrated p.141***

A6. COX AND CO.: AUDITORIUM SEATING

Royal Festival Hall Concert Hall Seating, 1951
Stove-enamelled elliptical tubular steel frame. Seat frame made of pressed steel, padded with foam rubber and upholstered in ribbed moquette. Additional glass fibre padding behind pierced acoustic panel on underside of tip-up seat. Leather-covered armrests veneered on the side with sapele mahogany.
Drawings: 1950. ***Illustrated pp.37–8***

A7. KINGFISHER LTD: FURNITURE

Royal Festival Hall Dining Tables, 1951
Black stove-enamelled tubular steel legs with steel rod supports. Plywood top with walnut veneer and birch lipping.
Note: Circular tables produced for the restaurant at the Royal Festival Hall, square tables for the terraces.
Illustrated pp.41–3

Royal Festival Hall Orchestra Chair, 1951
See entry for 661C Dining Chair by Hille, 1951.

Royal Festival Hall Terrace Chair, 1951
Black stove-enamelled steel rod legs and flat bar frame. Seat made of wooden slats painted white.
Note: Produced for the terraces at the Royal Festival Hall.
Illustrated p.43

A8. HAMPTON & SONS: FURNITURE

Royal Festival Hall Dumb Waiter, 1951
Timber frame, veneered with sapele mahogany. Cutlery tray made of anodized aluminium.
Note: Produced for the restaurant at the Royal Festival Hall, and designed to complement Robin Day's dining tables and chairs. Illustrated in *Architectural Review*, June 1951.

A9. THORN ELECTRICAL INDUSTRIES: LIGHTING

Floor Lamp, 1951
Black or white stove-enamelled tubular steel and steel rod stand, with mahogany hand grip. Spun aluminium shade.
Note: Co-designed by Robin Day and John Reid. Used in the high-cost room setting in the Home Entertainment section of the Homes and Gardens Pavilion at the Festival of Britain, and in Robin Day's display at the Milan Triennale, 1951. Illustrated in *Decorative Art Studio Yearbook, 1952–53*, p.112
Illustrated pp.42 & 51

A10. GENT & CO.: CLOCK

Wall Clock, 1952
Steel, with black and white enamel face, yellow and blue enamel hands, and brass rim.
Note: Designed for the London headquarters of Time-Life International, and installed in an executive office designed by Robin Day. Illustrated in *Designers in Britain*, no. 4, 1954.
Illustrated p.50
Dl 9in (23cm)

A11. STOREY'S OF LANCASTER: UPHOLSTERY FABRICS

Pennant Upholstery Vinyl, 1959
PVC-coated fabric.
Note: Robin Day was engaged as colour consultant for Storey's c.1957–64. This is his only recorded pattern design. It was also produced as a plastic laminate by Formica. See *The Cabinet Maker*, 30 October 1959, and *Northern Echo*, 5 November 1959.

A12. MARCONI: PRODUCT DESIGN

Cabinet for Myriad Computer, 1964–5
Drawings: 1964–5.

A13. GREAT UNIVERSAL STORES: FURNITURE

Library Tables for Churchill College, Cambridge, 1965
Black bean.
Note: The tables were for the Bracken Library and the Bevin Library. GUS won the contract after it was put out to tender. Other furniture for Churchill College was made by Hille and Heal's during 1963–4.
Drawings: 1965.

A14. BOAC: AIRCRAFT INTERIORS AND PRODUCT DESIGN

BOAC Boeing 707, 1961–6
Note: Robin and Lucienne Day were responsible for the refurbishment of BOAC's Boeing 707 aircraft interiors in 1961–2, 1963, 1965 and 1966.
Illustrated p.139

BOAC Super VC10 and VC10, 1961–7
Note: Robin and Lucienne Day designed the interiors for BOAC's Super VC10 aircraft during 1961–2, and were responsible for the refurbishment of BOAC's Super VC10 aircraft interiors in 1965 and 1967.
Illustrated p.139

Refreshment Tray, 1968–9
Plastic tray; EPNS cutlery; ceramic bowls and coffee cup; clear

plastic drinking glass.
Note: Robin Day was commissioned to design this set of catering equipment for the economy class cabins of BOAC's Boeing 707 aircraft, after seven years redesigning cabin interiors for BOAC. Illustrated in *Designers in Britain*, no. 7, 1971, p.217.
Drawings : 1968–9. ***Illustrated p.138***

A15. RANK AUDIO VISUAL: AUDITORIUM SEATING

Barbican Concert Hall, Theatre and Cinema Seating, 1981
Solid beech frame with plywood skin, padded and upholstered.
Note: Fixed seating designed for the three main auditoria at the Barbican Centre, made by a specialist firm based in Warrington. These designs were subject to frequent revisions throughout the 1970s.
Drawings: 1970–78. ***Illustrated p.151***

A16. MINES AND WEST: FURNITURE

Solo Reception Chair, Conference Chair and Table, 1987
Chairs have exposed solid ash frame with natural or stained finish. Sides and seat padded and upholstered. Table made of solid ash.
Note: Range of reception seating designed to be used singly or in multiple units, originally created for John Lewis shoe departments.
Illustrated: p.157
Reception chair: H 75cm (29½in), SH 45cm (17¾in), W 69cm (27in), D 66cm (26in). Conference chair: H 83.5cm (32¾in), SH 45cm (17¾in), W 61cm (24in), D 62cm (24½in). Quadrant table top: radius 66cm (26in). Square and rectangular tables: H 40cm (15¾in), D 64cm (25in), W 100cm (39¼in) and 64cm (25in)

Multo Stacking Armchair and Maximo Conference Chair, 1989
Moulded laminated ash or walnut frame, or oval tubular steel frame. Seat and seat back padded and upholstered.
Note: Seat back of Maximo chair extends down to the rear of the seat, and has different mechanism for attaching back of arm to top of back leg. Steel-framed chair was used in the Vaults Restaurant at the Royal Society of Arts.
Illustrated pp.166–7

Royal Society of Arts: Durham Street Auditorium Seating, 1989
Note: Custom-designed auditorium seating for new basement auditorium.
Illustrated p.166

Downley Boardroom Chair, 1990
Solid ash frame with natural or stained finish. Padded and upholstered seat and seat back.
Note: Used in the Fellows Reading Room at Royal Society of Arts with specially designed accompanying tables.

A17. TWENTYTWENTYONE: FURNITURE AND ACCESSORIES

Childsply Chair, 1999
Birch-veneered plywood.
Note: Children's chair, designed so that two units can be cut from a single sheet of plywood. Created as a one-off design to be auctioned for charity in September 1999; fabricated by Windmill Furniture.
Illustrated p.170

Alpha Table, 2000
Clear glass or reversible laminate top in three colours. Satin chrome flat steel legs with powder-coated steel underframe.
Note: Temporary reissue of modified design originally dating from 1959.
H 40cm. Circular table: DI 100cm. Rectangular table tops: 140cm x 60cm, and 60cm x 40cm.

Avian Lounge Chair and Settee, 2000
Moulded plywood arms veneered in oak or bubinga. Sledgelike satin chrome flat bar legs with "snake-eye" fixings. Seat padded with multi-density polyurethane foam and upholstered in leather or woven fabric made by Bute.
Note: Seating system composed of an armchair and two sizes of settee. Launched at *100% Design* in October 2000.
Illustrated p.170
H 65.5cm, SH 40cm, D 77cm, W of chair 85cm, W of settees 140cm and 195cm

Tricorne Tray, 2000
Moulded plywood, produced with a variety of veneers.
Note: Reissue of design dating from c. 1955; larger than the original. Currently manufactured (2011).
Table: H 47cm. Tray and table top: 50cm x 50cm x 50cm.

A18. HABITAT: FURNITURE

Forum Settee, 1999
Note: Reissue of design dating from 1964, made with oak frame instead of afrofmosia. Currently manufactured (2011).

Polypropylene Chair and Armchair, 1999
Translucent blue, white, lemon and lime injection-moulded polypropylene shells. White enamelled tubular steel legs.
Note: Reissue of designs dating from 1964 and 1967; produced for Habitat by Hille.
Catalogues: 1999–2000. ***Illustrated p.169***

CV Bed-Settee, 2000
Note: Temporary reissue of Single Convertible bed-settee, originally dating from 1957.

675 Chair, 2000
Note: Reissue of design dating from 1952. Currently manufactured (2011).

A19. CHARLES KEEN: FURNITURE

Day Chair, 2000
Note: Reissue of Gatwick chair, 1958.

A20. SCP: FURNITURE

RD001 Sofa/Daybed, 2000
Solid beech frame with lacquered side and back panels. Polished chrome tubular steel legs. Multi-density foam seat and back cushions, upholstered.
Note: Launched at Milan Furniture Fair, April 2000.
Catalogue: 2000. ***Illustrated p.170***
H 67.4cm (26½in), W 205cm (80¾in), D 84cm (33in)

A21. ONETREE: FURNITURE

Oak Chair, 2001
Note: Four side chairs with curved seat rails and turned legs; made from a 170-year old oak tree, produced as a one-off for Onetree project. Illustrated in *Onetree*, 2001, p.61

A22. MAGIS: FURNITURE

Sussex Bench, 2003
Air-moulded polypropylene seat, galvanised steel plate base.
Note: Modular seating suitable for outdoor use; two units: straight and curved. Currently manufactured (2011).
H 76cm (30in), L of straight bench 17.5cm (70¼in), W of curved bench 144.5cm (57in).

Sussex Table, 2005
Slate top, galvanised steel plate base.
Note: Suitable for outdoor use, produced in two sizes. Currently manufactured (2011).
H 71.5cm (28in), W 66cm (26¼in), L 159cm (62½in) and 200cm (78¾in).

A23. CASE: FURNITURE

West Street Armchair, 2006
Oak or walnut frame, padded leather seat and seat back.
Note: Sold in the UK through John Lewis. Currently manufactured (2011).
H 72cm (28¼in) W 52.4cm (20¾in), D 46cm (18in)

675 Chair, 2009
Note: Reissue of design dating from 1952. Currently manufactured (2011).

A24. LOFT INTERNATIONAL

Club Armchair and Settee
Note: Reissue of designs dating from 1962; currently manufactured (2011).

Polo Chair
Note: Reissue of design dating from 1975; currently manufactured (2011).

Poly Chair
Note: Reissue of Polypropylene Armchair, 1967; currently manufactured (2011).

A25. EXHIBITIONS AND GRAPHIC DESIGN
Note: All designs are for exhibitions, unless otherwise indicated.

Exhibition Stands for ICI, c.1946–62
Note: Robin Day designed numerous exhibition stands for ICI over a period of about sixteen years. Documented stands and their sources, including photographs in Robin Day Archives, include the following:
ICI, *Whither Chemistry Exhibition*, c.1946 (illustrated in *Designers in Britain*, no. 1, 1947, p.143 fig. 9).
ICI, British Industries Fair, Birmingham, 1947 (illustrated in *Designers in Britain*, no. 2, 1949, p.109, fig. 4; photographs in Robin Day Archives).
ICI Metals Division, British Industries Fair, 1948 (photographs in Robin Day Archives).
ICI Metals Division, British Industries Fair, 1949 (photographs in Robin Day Archives).
ICI General Chemicals Division, British Industries Fair, 1949 (photographs in Robin Day Archives).
ICI General Chemicals Division, British Industries Fair, 1950 (photographs in Robin Day Archives).
ICI Metals Division, British Industries Fair, 1950 (photographs in Robin Day Archives).
ICI Metals Division, British Industries Fair, 1951 (photographs in Robin Day Archives).
ICI Leathercloth, Metals and Plastics Divisions, *National Building Exhibition*, 1951 (photographs in Robin Day Archives).
ICI Leathercloth, Metals and Plastics Divisions, *National Building Exhibition*, c.1952 (photographs in Robin Day Archives).
ICI Agriculture Division, *Royal Show*, 1952–62 (illustrated in *Designers in Britain*, no. 5, 1957, p.79; photographs and drawings in Robin Day Archives). ***Illustrated p.23***
ICI Metals Division, British Industries Fair, 1952 (photographs in Robin Day Archives).
ICI Metals Division, British Industries Fair, 1953 (photographs in Robin Day Archives).
ICI Plastics Division, British Industries Fair, Birmingham, 1953 (photographs in Robin Day Archives). ***Illustrated p.21***
ICI Metals Division, British Industries Fair, c.1955 (photographs in Robin Day Archives).
ICI Metals Division, British Industries Fair, c.1956 (photographs in Robin Day Archives).
Undated stands include the following:
ICI Paints Division, British Industries Fair (two stands recorded in photographs in Robin Day Archives).
ICI Plastics Division (unidentified stand recorded in photograph in Robin Day Archives).
ICI Exhibition, Finland (drawings and photographs of drawings in Robin Day Archives).
Illustrated pp.21–3

***Jet*, 1946**
Poster designed by Robin Day; exhibition co-designed by Robin Day and Peter Moro for Ministry of Supply, Charing Cross Underground station, London.
Note: Exhibition dates were 16 December 1946 – 3 January 1947. Illustrated in *Designers in Britain*, no. 1, 1947, p.38, fig. 4 and p.138, figs 4 and 5.
Illustrated pp.17 (exhibition) and 18 (poster)

***Precisely Yours* – British Scientific Instruments, 1947**
Co-designed by Robin Day and Peter Moro for Ministry of Supply, Charing Cross Underground station, London.
Illustrated p.20

Exhibition Stand for GPO, 1947
Co-designed by Robin Day and Peter Moro for Radiolympia.
Note: Recorded in photographs in Robin Day Archives.

Poster for *Building Science Exhibition*, 1947
Exhibition organized by the Incorporated Association of Architects and Surveyors / Department of Scientific and Industrial Research, Caxton Hall, Westminster, London, 13–18 January 1947.
Note: For an account of the exhibition, see *Architects' Journal*, 6 March 1947, p.180. Poster recorded in a photograph in Peter Moro Archives in RIBA Photograph Collection.

***The Miner Comes to Town*, 1947**
Exhibition organized by the National Coal Board and the Ministry of Fuel and Power at the Exhibition Centre, Marble Arch, London. Byproducts section co-designed by Robin Day and Peter Moro for the Central Office of Information.
Note: See *Architects' Journal*, 2 October 1947, pp.299–300. Recorded in photographs in Robin Day Archives.

***Atomic Energy*, 1948**
Co-designed by Robin Day and Peter Moro for the Atomic Energy Research Establishment / Atomic Scientists Association.
Note: Displayed on a train that toured Britain during 1948–9. See *Architects' Journal*, 13 November 1947, p.434.
Illustrated p.20

RAF Recruitment Posters, 1948–9
Note: Seven posters were displayed on 7,400 hoardings around Britain during 1948–50. Illustrated in *Royal Air Force Review*, April 1949. Titles and dates of display were as follows:
Look to the future in the RAF, 1948.
My aircraft in the RAF, 1948.
They rely on me in the RAF, August 1948–October 1949.
Overseas in the RAF, September 1948–October 1949.
Join now – learn a trade in the Royal Air Force, May–October 1949.
Join the Women's Royal Air Force and give your ambition wings, October 1949–November 1950.
Do a grand job in your spare time in the RAF, November 1949–November 1950.
Illustrated p.16

***British Transport*, 1949**
Exhibition at Charing Cross Underground station, London. Main display designed by Peter Moro for Design Research Unit; one subsection by Robin Day.
Note: See *Architects' Journal*, 22 September 1949, pp.301 & 305.
Illustrated p.22

Sculpture for Rayon Design Centre, 1949
Note: Demountable sculptural feature commissioned by the British Rayon Federation, made from aluminium rod, perspex sheet and rayon thread. Illustrated in *Daily Graphic*, 19 January 1949; and *Designers in Britain*, no. 2, 1949, p.113, fig. 6.
Illustrated p.21

Posters for Royal Society for the Prevention of Accidents, c. 1949-54
Note:Two posters: Wait Till It Stops, warning people not to jump off buses; and Let The Electrician Do It, warning about the dangers of faulty wiring. Copies in the Wellcome Library (3254 and 3255), both dated c. 1954, but may be earlier.

Exhibition Stands for EKCO Plastics, c.1949–61
Note: Robin Day designed a series of exhibition stands for Ekco over

a period of at least twelve years. Documented stands and their sources include the following:
Radiolympia, 1949 (illustrated in *Architects' Journal*, 13 October 1949, p.394; and *Designers in Britain*, no. 2, 1951, pp.19 & 25). ***Illustrated p.23***
National Radio Show, Earl's Court, c.1950–51. ***Illustrated p.23***
National Radio Show, Earl's Court, 1952 (illustrated in *Architects' Journal*, 4 September 1952).
National Radio Show, Earl's Court, 1953 (recorded in photograph in Robin Day Archives).
National Radio Show, Earl's Court, 1956 (illustrated in *The Setmakers*, p.354).
British Plastics Exhibition, 1957 (drawings in Robin Day Archives).
British Plastics Exhibition, 1959 (drawings in Robin Day Archives).
Interplas Exhibition, 1961 (drawings in Robin Day Archives).

Hille Graphics, 1949–1970s
Note: In 1949 Robin Day designed a new logo for Hille, and c.1950–62 he designed most of the firm's catalogues and advertisements. He continued to undertake miscellaneous graphic design for Hille until the 1970s, including their van livery and party invitation cards.
Illustrated pp.59, 61, 64 & 109

Hille Exhibition Stands, 1950s–1970s
Note: Robin Day designed many exhibition stands for Hille. Stands documented in Robin Day Archives include:
British Furniture Manufacturers Fair, 1964 (drawings).
British Furniture Manufacturers Fair, 1965 (drawings).
Milan Furniture Fair, c.1970 (photograph).

Festival of Britain Logo, 1950
Note: Design submitted in response to an invitation from the Festival organizers. Illustrated in *Designers in Britain*, no. 3, 1951, pp.104–105.
Illustrated p.44

Home Entertainment Section of Homes and Gardens Pavilion, Festival of Britain, 1951
Note: Robin Day designed three room settings: one low-cost room, one high-cost room, and one room featuring different forms of lighting. Illustrated in *Design*, July 1951, p.18; *Furnishings from Britain*, September 1951, p.69 and p.71.
Illustrated pp.46–47

Signage for Festival of Britain, 1951
Co-designed by Robin Day and Milner Gray, with their associates Kenneth Lamble, John Messenger, Sylvia Reid and Peter Werner.
Note: The scheme included service pictograms, free-standing signposts, pavilion directional signs, upstream and downstream pointers. Recorded in photographs in Robin Day Archives.
Illustrated p.45

Poster for *Exhibition of Science*, Festival of Britain, 1951
Science Museum, South Kensington, London, 3 May – 30 September 1951.
Illustrated p.44

Milan Triennale, 1951
Note: Room setting designed and furnished by Robin Day, awarded a Gold Medal.
Illustrated p.51

Book Jacket for *Ardil – The Protein Fibre*, c.1952
Note: Promotional book produced by ICI. Illustrated in *Art and Industry*, May 1952, p.158.

***Design from Britain*, 1952**
Exhibition organized by the Society of Industrial Artists, held in Oslo, Bergen and Stavanger in Norway. Illustrated in *Design*, July 1952, p.14.

Magazine Cover for *Furnishings from Britain*, c.1952
Note: Illustrated in *Art and Industry*, May 1952, p.158.

British Transport Museum, 1954
Note: Display cases for transport models co-designed by Robin Day and John Reid for museum at Euston station, London. Recorded in photographs in Robin Day Archives.
Drawings: 1954.

Milan Triennale, 1954
Note: Room setting designed and furnished by Robin Day. Illustrated in *Furnishings from Britain*, no. 1, 1955.

Exhibition Stand for British Trades Fair, Helsinki, 1957
Designed by Challen & Floyd in association with Robin Day, on behalf of Board of Trade and the Council of Industrial Design.
Drawings: 1957.

***British Design Today*, 1958**
Göppinger Galerie, Frankfurt-am-Main, Germany.
Note: Illustrated in *Furnishing*, September 1958, pp.52–5.
Illustrated p.106

Exhibition Stand for Woodward Grosvenor Carpets, 1963
Harrogate Fair.
Drawings: 1963.

***British Furniture and Furnishings*, 1967**
Exhibition in Brussels.
Drawings: 1967.

Exhibition Stand for Grays Carpets, c.1967–70
Note: Recorded in undated photographs and drawings in Robin

Day Archives.

Graphics for British Mountaineering Council and Climbers' Club, c.1970s
Note: Robin Day was an experienced mountaineer. He designed a number of logos, letterheads and instructional diagrams for these two specialist climbing organizations.

A26. INTERIOR DESIGN
Note: Many of the following interiors were co-designed by Robin and Lucienne Day.

Day Residence, 33 Markham Square, Chelsea, London, 1942
Illustrated p.15

Day Residence, 49 Cheyne Walk, Chelsea, London, 1952
Illustrated pp.52–3

Executive Office, Time-Life Building, London, 1952
Note: The architect for the building was Michael Rosenauer, and the interiors were designed by Sir Hugh Casson in association with Misha Black of the Design Research Unit. Robin Day designed and furnished an office for the Editorial Bureau Chief. Illustrated in *Furnishings from Britain*, no. 2, 1953, pp.32–5; *Architects' Journal*, 9 April 1953; and *Designers in Britain*, no. 4, 1954, p.50.
Illustrated p.57

Hille Showroom, 39 Albemarle Street, London, 1952
Note: Interior designed by Robin Day. Used for ten years until the opening of a new showroom at 41 Albemarle Street.

Hille Showroom, 41 Albemarle Street, London, 1962
Interior designed by Peter Moro & Partners in association with Robin Day.
Drawings: 10 August 1961 and 9 February 1962 (spiral staircase).
Illustrated pp.110–11

Hille Showroom, Geneva, 1967
Drawings: 1967.

Hille Showroom, Whittington House, 19–30 Alfred Place, London, 1973
Drawings: 1973–4 (various fittings).

Restaurant and Café, John Lewis, Oxford Street, London, 1973
Drawings: 1972–3. ***Illustrated p.164***

John Lewis, Brent Cross, 1976
Note: Interior was designed by Harold Bennett with input from Robin and Lucienne Day. Illustrated in *The Gazette*, 13 March 1976, pp.124–6.

John Lewis, Milton Keynes, 1979
Note: Interior was designed by Robin Day with input from Graham Heywood until the latter's death in 1977. Illustrated in *The Gazette*, 22 September 1979, pp. 779–85.
Drawings: 1977. ***Illustrated pp.143 & 165***

Restaurant, John Lewis, Peterborough, 1980
Drawings: 1980.

Waitrose, John Barnes (John Lewis Partnership), Hampstead, London, 1981
Note: See *The Gazette*, 24 October 1981, p.843.

Coffee Shop, John Barnes (John Lewis Partnership), Hampstead, London, 1983
Co-designed by Robin Day and Jonathan Pennington from Bennett and Pennington, 1982–3.
Drawings: 1983.

Vaults Restaurant, Royal Society of Arts, John Adam Street, London, 1990
Note: Robin and Lucienne Day served on the RSA's Design Committee during 1989–90 and advised on the refurbishment of the basement of the RSA's headquarters.
Illustrated p.167

Lucienne Day

• Designs are grouped by manufacturer, with individual designs listed chronologically, then alphabetically.
• Sections B1–B9 list designs for major clients with whom Lucienne Day collaborated over a period of several years.
• Sections B11–B36 list designs for minor clients with whom Lucienne Day collaborated for shorter periods, arranged in chronological order.
• Section B37 lists silk mosaics.
• Only production designs are listed, except in the case of silk mosaics.
• Dates given are first known or estimated year of production.
• Cross references to illustrations in the book are italicized in bold. Where items are not illustrated, brief descriptions and cross-references to other published sources or collections are given wherever possible.

B1. CAVENDISH TEXTILES (JOHN LEWIS PARTNERSHIP): PRINTED DRESS AND FURNISHING FABRICS

Bushmen, June 1946
Printed dress fabric.
Recorded in photograph in Lucienne Day Archives.

Chiltern Meadow, 1946
Printed furnishing fabric.
Note: Pattern of sprigs of flowers. Illustrated in *Designers in Britain*, no. 1, 1947, p.242, fig. 10.

Greek Wave, 1947
Printed cotton satin furnishing fabric.
Note: Pattern of Greek helmets and vases, in wavy borders. Designed in 1944. Illustrated in *Designers in Britain*, no. 1, 1947, p.248, fig. 1.

Dress fabric (pattern number HC 6236), 1954
Printed cotton dress fabric.
Note: Pattern of triangular and diamond shapes strung on lines. Illustrated in *Design*, October 1954, p.50.
Illustrated p.99

Dress fabric (pattern number HC 6237), c.1954
Printed cotton dress fabric.
Note: Pattern of triangular leaves and stalks.
Illustrated p.99

Dress fabric (pattern number HC 6239), c.1954
Printed cotton dress fabric.
Note: Pattern of diamond shapes joined by fine lines.
Illustrated p.99

Sequence (pattern number HC 6238), 1954
Printed cotton dress fabric.
Note: Pattern of rows of figures. Illustrated in *Design*, October 1954, p.50; *House & Garden*, August 1956, p.41.
Illustrated p.99

Serenade (pattern number HC 6241), c.1954
Printed cotton dress fabric.
Note: Pattern of rows of small leaves. Samples in Whitworth Art Gallery (T1998.67).

Symphony (pattern number HC 6240), 1954
Printed cotton dress fabric.
Note: Pattern of skeletal leaves.
Illustrated p.99

Lucienne, 1974
Screen-printed cotton furnishing fabric.
Illustrated p.159

Chestnut, 1975
Screen-printed cotton furnishing fabric.
Note: Pattern of stylized trees composed of geometric motifs. Recorded in photograph in Cavendish Textiles Archives.

Halloween, 1975
Screen-printed cotton furnishing fabric.
Illustrated p.159

Kyoto, 1975
Screen-printed cotton furnishing fabric.
Illustrated p.159

Panama, 1975
Screen-printed cotton furnishing fabric.
Note: Geometric diamond pattern. Recorded in photograph in Cavendish Textiles Archives.

B2. EDINBURGH WEAVERS AND MORTON SUNDOUR FABRICS: PRINTED AND WOVEN FURNISHING FABRICS

Martlet, 1945
Jacquard-woven furnishing fabric.
Note: Pattern of small birds and chevrons. Recorded in photograph in Lucienne Day Archives as Edinburgh Weavers, but probably Morton Sundour Fabrics.

Elysian, 1949
Screen-printed linen.
Note: Stylized floral sprig pattern. Designed in 1948. Illustrated in *Designers in Britain*, no. 2, 1949, p.55, fig. 55; *Decorative Art Studio Year Book, 1951–52*, p.54; *Furnishings from Britain*, 1952, no. 2, p.47; and *Lucienne Day – A Career in Design*, p.17, fig. 9.

Florimel, 1949
Screen-printed cotton.
Note: Designed in 1948.
Illustrated p.30

Telekinema fabric, 1951
Jacquard-woven upholstery fabric.
Note: Designed for seats in Telekinema auditorium at Festival of Britain. Produced in dark blue and grey with brown horizontal lines by Morton Sundour Fabrics.
Illustrated p.48

Acres, 1952
Screen-printed cotton crepe.
Illustrated p.82

Cocktail, 1952
Screen-printed cotton.
Note: Linear abstract pattern, loosely based on a grid. Illustrated in *House & Garden*, February 1952, p.45; and *Designers in Britain*, no.4, 1954, p.37.
Illustrated p.35 (in situ at US Airforce Officers Club)

Fall, 1952
Screen-printed cotton.
Illustrated p.82

Foreshore, 1952
Screen-printed cotton.
Illustrated p.82

Baldric, 1964
Jacquard-woven mercerized cotton.
Note: Designed in 1963 as a special commission for the suite of Combination Rooms in Churchill College, Cambridge. Produced in three colourways: grey/brown, plum and pink.
Illustrated p.141

B3. HEAL FABRICS: PRINTED FURNISHING FABRICS
Note: All fabrics are 48in (122cm) wide, excluding selvedge.

Fluellin, 1950
Screen-printed linen.
Illustrated p.30

Calyx, 1951
Screen-printed linen or rayon.
Note: Exhibited in the Home Entertainment section of the Homes and Gardens Pavilion at the Festival of Britain, 1951, and at the Milan Triennale, where it won a Gold Medal. Citation of Merit from American Institute of Decorators, 1952. Reissued as digital print by twentytwentyone.
Illustrated pp.32, 48 & 51

Allegro, 1952
Screen-printed linen.
Note: Abstract pattern with horizontal strings of kite-like motifs. Illustrated in *Lucienne Day – A Career in Design*, p.34, fig. 34.

Flotilla, 1952
Screen-printed linen, cotton or rayon.
Note: Reissued as digital print by twentytwentyone..
Illustrated p.79

Rig, 1952
Screen-printed cotton or linen.
Illustrated p.79

Small Hours, 1952
Screen-printed cotton.
Illustrated p.79

Strata, 1952
Screen-printed cotton.
Note: Pattern of oval motifs in layers. Illustrated in *Furnishings from Britain*, no. 2, 1953, p.54.

Lapis, 1953
Screen-printed cotton.
Illustrated p.86

Dandelion Clocks, 1953
Screen-printed linen and cotton.
Note: Reissued as digital print by twentytwentyone.
Illustrated p.84

Graphica, 1953
Screen-printed cotton.
Note: Gran Premio, Milan Triennale, 1954. Reissued as digital print by twentytwentyone.
Illustrated p.85

Linear, 1953
Screen-printed cotton.
Note: Gran Premio, Milan Triennale, 1954.
Illustrated p.85

Spectators, 1953
Screen-printed cotton, linen and rayon.
Note: Gran Premio, Milan Triennale, 1954. Reissued as digital print by twentytwentyone.
Illustrated p.54

Ticker Tape, 1953
Screen-printed cotton.
Note: Gran Premio, Milan Triennale, 1954.
Illustrated pp.86 & 105

Chequers, 1954
Screen-printed cotton satin.
Illustrated p.107

Flower Show, 1954
Roller-printed cotton.
Note: Pattern of attenuated linear flowers. Illustrated in *Decorative Art Studio Year Book 1954–55*, p.83; and *Lucienne Day – A Career in*

Design, p.37, fig. 37.

Springboard, 1954
Screen-printed cotton, cotton satin and linen.
Illustrated p.87

Trio, 1954
Screen-printed cotton.
Reissued as digital print by twentytwentyone.
Illustrated p.89

Isosceles, 1955
Screen-printed cotton or satin crepe.
Note: Abstract pattern composed of flat triangular motifs. Illustrated in *Design*, August 1955, p.18.

Triad, 1955
Screen-printed cotton or cotton satin crepe.
Illustrated p.89

Herb Antony, 1956
Screen-printed cotton.
Illustrated p.84

Highway, 1956
Roller-printed cotton.
Illustrated p.88

Perpendicular, 1956
Roller-printed cotton.
Illustrated p.88

Script, 1956
Roller-printed cotton.
Illustrated pp.100 & 105

Magnetic, 1957
Roller-printed cotton.
Note: Reissued as digital print by twentytwentyone.
Illustrated p.101

Cedar, 1958
Roller-printed cotton.
Note: Pattern of triangles against a textured ground.

Mezzanine, 1958
Screen-printed glazed cotton, cotton crepe or viscose satin.
Note: Pattern of horizontal strips and cross-bracing. Illustrated in *Lucienne Day – A Career in Design*, p.40, fig. 41.
Illustrated p.105

Plantation, 1958
Screen-printed cotton crepe.
Illustrated p.102

Silver Birch, 1958
Screen-printed glazed cotton, viscose satin or cotton crepe.
Illustrated p.101

Tarn, 1958
Roller-printed cotton.
Illustrated p.101

Ducatoon, 1959
Roller-printed cotton.
Note: Gold Medal, California State Fair, 1959. Also produced as a plastic laminate by Heal's. Illustrated on kitchen tops in Christopher Heal's kitchen in *Everywoman*, May 1959, pp.51–2.
Illustrated p.105

Forest, 1959
Roller-printed cotton.
Note: Pattern of tree trunks. Sample in V&A (Circ.37-1959).

Maquis, 1959
Roller-printed cotton.
Illustrated p.102

Runic, 1959
Roller-printed cotton.
Illustrated p.101

Sequoia, 1959
Screen-printed cotton crepe.
Note: Reissued as digital print by twentytwentyone.
Illustrated p.103

Talisman, 1959
Roller-printed cotton.
Illustrated p.98

Halcyon, 1960
Screen-printed cotton.
Note: Pattern of feathery plants. Sample in Whitworth Art Gallery (T10558).

Linden, 1960
Roller-printed cotton.
Note: Gold Medal, California State Fair, 1960.
Illustrated p.103

Quarto, 1960
Screen-printed cotton crepe.
Illustrated p.107

Vanessa, 1960
Roller-printed cotton.
Note: Pattern of sketchy butterflies. Illustrated in *Lucienne Day – A Career in Design*, p.30, fig. 31.

Banderol, 1961
Screen-printed cotton.
Note: Abstract pattern of overlapping rectangular strips. Illustrated in *Furniture Record*, 30 December 1960; and *The Ambassador*, no. 3, 1961.

Brushwood, 1961
Screen-printed cotton crepe.
Note: Dense abstract pattern of criss-crossing lines. Illustrated in *The Ambassador*, April 1961.

Cockaigne, 1961
Roller-printed cotton.
Illustrated pp.53 (on cushions near hearth) & 127

Larch, 1961
Screen-printed cotton crepe.
Note: Reissued as digital print by twentytwentyone.
Illustrated p.103

Riga, 1961
Roller-printed cotton.
Note: Reissued as digital print by twentytwentyone.
Illustrated p.126

Rock Rose, 1961
Roller-printed cotton.
Illustrated p.126

Cadenza, 1962
Roller-printed cotton.
Illustrated p.127

Fuego, 1962
Roller-printed cotton.
Note: Pattern of coloured stripes, inspired by a visit to Mexico in 1961. Illustrated in *Bonytt*, March 1964, p.69.

Tekka, 1962
Screen-printed cotton.
Textural abstract pattern resembling tree bark. Sample in V&A (Circ.4-1962).

Apollo, 1963
Screen-printed cotton.
Note: Pattern of oval motifs overlaid with other patterns. Illustrated in *Glasgow Herald*, 16 December 1963; and *Designing Women*, 2008.

Furnishing Fabric for Shell Chemical Company, 1963
Screen-printed cotton.
Note: Designed for the offices of the Shell Chemical Company.
Illustrated p.127

Zocalo, 1963
Roller-printed cotton.
Note: Pattern of rows of small circles and squares, inspired by visit to Mexico in 1961. Sample in V&A Textile Department (T.330:1&2-1999).

Counterpoint, 1964
Screen-printed cotton.
Note: Geometric grid pattern. Sample in Whitworth Art Gallery (T1998.24).

Dovetail, 1965
Screen-printed cotton.
Note: Pattern of dovetail joint-shaped forms. Sample in Whitworth Art Gallery (T1998.31). Illustrated in *Designing Women*, 2008.

High Noon, 1965
Screen-printed cotton crepe.
Illustrated p.131

Pennycress, 1966
Screen-printed cotton.
Illustrated p.131

Poinsettia, 1966
Screen-printed cotton.
Illustrated p.131

Apex, 1967
Screen-printed cotton.
Note: Reissued as digital print by twentytwentyone.
Illustrated p.129

Causeway, 1967
Screen-printed cotton crepe.
Illustrated p.129

Chevron, 1968
Screen-printed cotton.
Note: Design Centre Award, 1968.
Illustrated p.128

Simplicity, 1968
Screen-printed cotton.
Note: Abstract geometric grid pattern. Illustrated in *Lucienne Day – A Career in Design*, p.61, fig. 65.

Celtic Cross, 1969
Screen-printed cotton.
Note: Pattern of interlocking crosses. Sample in V&A (Circ.32-1969). Illustrated in *Designing Women*, 2008.

Sunrise, 1969
Screen-printed cotton.
Illustrated p.130

Helix, 1970
Screen-printed cotton.
Illustrated p.158

Hazy Daisy, 1971
Screen-printed cotton.
Note: Pattern of rows of small flower heads in a chevron formation. Sample in Whitworth Art Gallery (T1998.23).

Integration, 1971
Screen-printed cotton.
Note: Herringbone-like geometric pattern. Sample in Whitworth Art Gallery (T1998.36).

Petal, 1971
Screen-printed cotton.
Note: Pattern of large stylized flower heads. Illustrated in *Designing Women*, 2008.

Unity, 1971
Screen-printed cotton.
Illustrated p.158

Parkland, 1974
Screen-printed cotton.
Illustrated p.158

B4. RASCH: WALLPAPERS

Prisma, 1954
Machine-printed wallpaper.
Note: Linear abstract geometric pattern designed in 1953, similar to Heal's fabric Graphica (1953). Rasch Kollektion 1954/55 and 1956/57. Originally produced in nine colourways, four on a rough ground and five on a smooth ground; subsequently produced in four colourways with gold lines instead of white. Illustrated in *Design*, July 1953, p.17; and *Lucienne Day – A Career in Design*, p.47, fig. 45.

Chelsea, 1956
Machine-printed wallpaper.
Note: Rasch Kollektion 1956/57 and Bauhaus-Kollektion 1958/59. Originally produced in four colourways, subsequently in five. Illustrated in *Tapeten Zeitung*, 26 March 1956, p.28; *Designers in Britain*, no. 5, 1957, p.38.
Illustrated p.93

City, 1956
Machine-printed wallpaper.
Note: Rasch Kollektion 1956/57, and Bauhaus-Kollektion 1958/59. Illustrated in *Designers in Britain*, no. 5, 1957, p.38; *Künstlerisches Schaffen – Industrielles Gestalten*, Städtisches Museum Osnabrück, July – September 1956, cats 76 and 77.
Illustrated p.92

Lotura, 1956
Machine-printed wallpaper.
Note: Abstract pattern composed of feathery attenuated motifs against a striped ground, produced in three colourways. Rasch Kollektion 1956/57. Illustrated in *Tapeten Zeitung*, 26 March 1956, p.28.

Picadelli, 1956
Machine-printed wallpaper.
Note: Abstract pattern composed of attenuated vertical dashes, produced in three colourways. Rasch Kollektion 1956/57. Sample in Rasch Archives.

Spindel, 1956
Machine-printed wallpaper.
Note: Pattern of spindle-like motifs. Designed in 1953. Rasch Kollektion 1956/57. Produced in three colourways. Illustrated in *Design*, July 1953, p.17; and *Tapeten Zeitung*, 20 March 1956, p.28.

Kleinmuster-Motiv, 1958
Machine-printed wallpaper.
Note: Bauhaus-Kollektion 1958/59, produced with small motifs in ten colourways, including one in reverse. Rasch Kollektion 1958/59, produced in variants with enlarged motifs in six colourways, and with background stripes in two colourways (see Waterloo, below).
Illustrated pp.93 & 106.

Waterloo, 1958
Machine-printed wallpaper.
Note: Version of Kleinmuster-Motiv with striped background. Illustrated in *The Cabinet Maker and Complete House Furnisher*, 23 May 1958.

Westminster, 1958
Machine-printed wallpaper.
Note: Rasch Kollektion 1958/59; produced in six colourways.
Illustrated pp.93 & 105

Bristol, 1960
Machine-printed wallpaper.
Note: Abstract pattern composed of fibre-like strands, produced in two versions, one in beige and white, the other with additional horizontal stripes in red, yellow and blue. Rasch Kollektion 1960/61. Sample in Rasch Archives.

B5. LIGHTBOWN ASPINALL BRANCH OF THE WALL PAPER MANUFACTURERS LTD (CROWN): WALLPAPERS

C-Stripe (Crown pattern numbers C649 and C650), 1954
Machine-printed wallpaper.
Note: *Architects' Book of One Hundred Wallpapers*, 1954.
Illustrated p.91

Wallpaper (WPM pattern number 93495, Crown pattern numbers C691, C692 and C693), 1954
Machine-printed wallpaper.
Note: Pattern of dotted ovals, included in *Architects' Book of One Hundred Wallpapers*, 1954. Illustrated in *Design*, January 1954.
Illustrated p.90

Yokohama Times (WPM pattern numbers L46724 and L46725, Crown pattern numbers C761 and C762), c.1956
Machine-printed wallpaper.
Note: Lightbown Aspinall, Crown Wallpapers Pattern Book, and *Architects' Book of One Hundred Wallpapers*, c.1956.
Illustrated p.91

Serif (Modus pattern numbers M1031, M1032 and M1033), c.1957
Machine-printed wallpaper.
Note: Modus First Collection. Sample in Whitworth Art Gallery (W1998.25).

Wallpaper (Crown pattern numbers C868 and C689), c.1958
Machine-printed wallpaper.
Note: Pattern of bands of stripes and broken lines, included in *Architects' Book of One Hundred Wallpapers*, 1958–9.
Illustrated p.90

B6. TOMKINSONS AND I. & C. STEELE: CARPETS
Note: I. & C. Steele were taken over by Tomkinsons in 1959, and became their contract division. Lucienne Day designed for Tomkinsons from 1957 to 1962, and for Steele from 1961 to 1965, with some overlap between the two.

B6A. TOMKINSONS
Crossways (pattern number 9623), 1957
Imperial Axminster carpet, width 27in (68.5cm) or 12ft (3.6m) broadloom.
Note: Abstract geometric rectangular grid pattern. Illustrated in *Furniture Record*, 30 May 1958; and *Carpet Annual*, 1958–9, p.86.

Fandango (pattern number 9602), 1957
Imperial Axminster carpet, width 27in (68.5cm) or 12ft (3.6m) broadloom.
Note: Pattern of notched lines, displayed at Brussels Expo, 1958. Illustrated in *Furnishing*, September 1957, p.92; *House Beautiful*, September 1957; *Carpet Review*, November 1957, p.69; *Furnishing*, January 1958, p.59; *Carpet Review*, March 1958, p.114 and pp.77–9; and *Furniture Record*, 30 May 1958.

Furrows (pattern number 9622), 1957
Imperial Axminster carpet.
Note: Reissued by I. & C. Steele as part of their Studio 3 collection in 1965 (pattern number 1003).
Illustrated p.104

Strada (pattern number 9601), 1957
Imperial Axminster carpet, width 27in (68.5cm) or 12ft (3.6m) broadloom.
Note: Illustrated in *Birmingham Post*, 20 March 1957; *Furnishing*, September 1957, p.92; *Carpet Review*, November 1957, p.69. Exhibited at the Brussels Expo, 1958.
Illustrated p.104

Tesserae (pattern number 9600), 1957
Imperial Axminster carpet, width 27in (68.5cm) or 12ft (3.6m) broadloom.
Note: Design Centre Award, 1957.
Illustrated p.104

Pennant, 1958
Royal Gobelin Axminster carpet.
Note: Pattern of stylized pennants, some upright, some inverted. Illustrated in *Carpet Review*, February 1958, p.50.

Forum (pattern number 9656), 1959
Imperial Axminster carpet.
Note: Illustrated in *Carpet Review*, April 1959, p.93.
Illustrated p.104

Couplet (pattern number 9680), 1960
Imperial Axminster carpet.
Note: Pattern of horizontal strips, launched at the International Carpet Fair, February 1960. Illustrated in *Birmingham Mail*, 26 February 1960; *The Cabinet Maker*, 27 February 1960; *Carpet Review*, March 1960, p.87; and *The Ambassador*, no. 7, 1960, p.111.

M1 (pattern number 9681), 1960
Imperial Axminster carpet.
Note: Pattern of fine vertical stripes broken at intervals by short horizontal lines. Launched at the International Carpet Fair in February 1960. Illustrated in *Carpet Review*, March 1960; *The Ambassador*, no. 7, 1960, p.111.

Alpha, c.1962
Royal Gobelin Axminster carpet, width 27in (68.5cm).
Note: Pattern of square motifs, illustrated in an unidentified newspaper clipping in Lucienne Day Press Cuttings Book, c.1962–3. Shown in Rosenthal Studio House exhibition, July 1963.

B6B. I. & C. STEELE

Ramal, 1961
Wilton Maire carpet, width 27in (68.5cm).
Note: Linear pattern depicting stylized branches. Illustrated in *Carpet Review*, February 1961, p.115 (dark on light), and March 1962, p.72 (light on dark).

Signum (pattern number 1006), 1961
Banbury Wilton carpet, Studio 3 collection, width 27in (68.5cm).
Note: Geometric pattern of triangles, circles, dashes and crosses. Illustrated in *Carpet Review*, February 1961, p.115; *Carpet Annual*, 1961–2, p.106; *The Ambassador*, 1961 no. 4, pp.109–124.
Illustrated p.132

Big Circle (pattern number 1005), 1963
Banbury Wilton carpet, Studio 3 collection, width 27in (68.5cm).
Illustrated p.132

Furrows (pattern number 1003), 1965
Imperial Axminster carpet, width 27in (68.5cm).
Note: Originally produced by Tomkinsons in 1957. Reissued by I. & C. Steele as part of their Studio 3 collection in 1965.
Illustrated p.104

New Day (pattern number 1007), 1965
Wilton and Axminster carpet, Studio 3 collection, widths 27in (68.5cm) and 36in (91cm).
Note: Pattern of rows of small crosses. Recorded in Design Council Slide Library (4877).

B7. WILTON ROYAL: CARPETS
Note: From 1957 to 1963 Lucienne Day selected and coloured carpets for the Architects Collection and København Range. From 1964 she designed carpets for the Architects Nova range.

Fiord (pattern number 9054), 1957
Designed by Norman Runacres, coloured by Lucienne Day.
Wilton carpet, Architects Collection, widths 27in (68.5cm) and 36in (91cm).
Note: Pattern of rows of small irregular motifs, launched at the National Carpet Show in February 1958. Illustrated in Carpet Review, April 1958, p.67; Contract Furnishing, February 1958. Illustrated in Wilton catalogue, October 1964, in one colourway.

Lamina (pattern number 9118), 1957
Designed by Philip Coombes, coloured by Lucienne Day.
Wilton carpet, Architects Collection, widths 27in (68.5cm) and 36in (91cm).
Note: Launched at the National Carpet Show in February 1958. Illustrated in Carpet Review, April 1958, p.67. Illustrated in Wilton catalogue, October 1964, in four colourways. Used by the Days on the stairs in their house at Cheyne Walk. Fourteen different colour samples in V&A (T.528:1–14).
Illustrated p.104

Lilliput (pattern number 9119), 1957
Designed by Wilton Royal Carpets Design Studio, coloured by Lucienne Day.
Wilton carpet, Architects Collection, widths 27in (68.5cm) and 36in (91cm).
Note: Pattern of small random dashes, launched at the National Carpet Show in February 1958. Illustrated in Contract Furnishing, February 1958. Discontinued in 1962. Sample in Whitworth Art Gallery (T1999.118).

Carpet (pattern number 9120), 1957
Designed by Wilton Royal Carpets Design Studio, coloured by Lucienne Day.
Wilton carpet, Architects Collection, widths 27in (68.5cm) and 36in (91cm).
Note: Pattern of horizontal bars of different lengths, some with linear patterning, launched at the National Carpet Show in February 1958. Illustrated in Carpet Review, April 1958, p.67; and Contract

Furnishing, February 1958. Sample in Whitworth Art Gallery (T1999.117)

Cirrus (pattern number 9142), c.1958
Designed by Philip Coombes, coloured by Lucienne Day.
Wilton carpet, Architects Collection, widths 27in (68.5cm) and 36in (91cm).
Note: Illustrated in Wilton catalogue, October 1964, and Council of Industrial Design Index sheet, 1967–8. Sample in Lucienne Day Archives (2000).
Illustrated p.104

Cobble (pattern number 9199), 1959
Designed by Norman Runacres, coloured by Lucienne Day.
Wilton carpet, Architects Collection, widths 27in (68.5cm) and 36in (91cm).
Note: Irregular mottled pattern. Illustrated in Ideal Home, April 1960, p.84; Wilton catalogue, October 1964, and Council of Industrial Design Index sheet 1967–8. Sample in Whitworth Art Gallery (T1999.120).

Københaven Range, c.1961
Designed by Wilton Royal Carpets Design Studio, coloured by Lucienne Day.
Axminster (width 27in/68.5cm) and Wilton Wylye (36in/91cm) carpets.
Note: *Carpet Review*, February 1962, p.93, states that Wilton will show this recent range at the International Carpet Fair in March 1962. Four patterns illustrated in Wilton catalogue, October 1964: 92482, 92491, 92654, 92670.

Portcullis (pattern number 9238), 1961
Designed by Pam Golding, coloured by Lucienne Day.
Wilton carpet, Architects Collection, widths 27in (68.5cm) and 36in (91cm).
Note: Pattern of small square portcullis-like motifs. Illustrated in Wilton catalogue, October 1964, in five colourways. Sample in Whitworth Art Gallery (T1999.111).

Carpet (pattern number 9274), c.1963
Designed by Pam Golding, coloured by Lucienne Day.
Wilton carpet, Architects Collection, widths 27in (68.5cm) and 36in (91cm).
Note: Illustrated in Wilton catalogue, October 1964, in three colourways.

Octagon (pattern number 9291), 1964
Designed by Lucienne Day.
Wilton carpet, Architects Nova range.
Illustrated p.132

Carpet (pattern number 9307), c.1964
Designed by Lucienne Day.
Wilton carpet, Architects Nova range.
Note: Pattern of squares and diamonds.
Illustrated p.132

Planted Stripe (pattern number 9308), 1964
Designed by Lucienne Day.
Wilton carpet, Architects Nova range.
Note: Pattern of columns of small squares. A sample in Whitworth Art Gallery (T1999.108), donated by the factory, is documented as by Lucienne Day, but the designer queried this attribution.

Carpet (pattern number 9310), c.1964
Designed by Lucienne Day.
Wilton carpet, Architects Nova range.
Note: Pattern of parallel lines in large squares.
Illustrated p.132

B8. ROSENTHAL: CERAMICS
Note: Lucienne Day designed approximately four to eight patterns annually for Rosenthal between 1957 and 1968. The tableware patterns listed below are the ones that entered production. Also listed are the prototypes shown at Lucienne's exhibition at Rosenthal's London Studio House in July 1963, which were produced to order.

Bond Street, 1957
Service 2000. Porcelain, printed in black and brown enamels.
Illustrated pp.95 & 106

Columbine (pattern number 3736), 1958
Service 2000. Porcelain, printed in grey, complemented by bands of yellow or pink enamel.
Note: Also known as Piccadilly.
Illustrated p.95

Four Seasons (pattern number 3769), 1958
Service 2000. Porcelain, printed in tobacco, grey-blue, lime and pink enamels.
Note: Displayed at Heal's exhibition, May 1958. Produced 1959–63. Applied to shape number 2000 designed by Raymond Loewy. Complementary embroidered place mats produced by Thomas Somerset.
Illustrated pp.96 & 105

Odyssey (pattern number 3770), 1958
Service 2000. Porcelain, with etched gold border.
Note: Displayed at Heal's exhibition, May 1958.
Illustrated pp.97 & 105

Regent Street (pattern number 3768), 1958
Service 2000. Porcelain, printed in grey and red enamels.
Note: Originally called Grey Line. Shown at Heal's exhibition, May 1958, and manufactured from 1959. Complementary table linen produced by Thomas Somerset under the name Mitre. Illustrated in *The Cabinet Maker and Complete House Furnisher*, 23 May 1958.
Illustrated p.97

Esplanade (pattern number 4012), 1960
Service 3000. Porcelain, printed in white and red on pale grey ground.
Note: Geometric abstract pattern of rectangles, dashes and dots, produced until December 1970. Recorded in Rosenthal Archives and Lucienne Day Archives.

Brokat (pattern number 3908), c.1962
Service 2000. Porcelain, printed in black over matt olive-green enamel.
Note: Shown at Rosenthal Studio House exhibition, July 1963, but not manufactured until 1966. Recorded in Rosenthal Archives and photograph in Lucienne Day Archives.
Illustrated p.135

Club (pattern number 3785), c.1962
Service 2000. Porcelain, printed with gold circles on a caramel-glazed border.
Note: Shown at Rosenthal Studio House exhibition, July 1963. Illustrated in *The Observer*, July 1963.

Delphi (pattern number 3820), 1962
Service 2000. Porcelain, printed in red-brown enamel over gilt border.
Note: Produced until 1970.
Illustrated p.97

Ilias (pattern number 3821), 1962
Service 2000. Porcelain, printed in gold over matt grey or olive enamel.
Note: Produced until 1970.
Illustrated p.135

Ivy, c.1962
Service 2000. Porcelain printed in enamel with ivy leaves.
Note: Prototype pattern shown at Rosenthal Studio House exhibition, July 1963, illustrated in *The Observer*, July 1963.

Poliergoldband mit Goldornamenten (pattern number 3818), 1962
Service 2000. Porcelain, printed in black over gold border.
Note: Geometric pattern of crosses and lines, produced until 1970. Recorded in Rosenthal Archives and Lucienne Day Archives.

Windsor (pattern number 3768), c.1962
Service 2000. Porcelain, printed in grey with small circles and lines.
Note: Shown at Rosenthal Studio House exhibition, July 1963. Recorded in Lucienne Day Archives.

Ashtrays, c.1963
Note: Nest of prototype circular ashtrays decorated with pattern similar to Torn Circle motif on ICI handkerchief. Shown at Rosenthal Studio House exhibition, July 1963. Recorded in photograph in Lucienne Day Archives.

Flower Bricks, c.1963
Note: Porcelain prototypes shown at Rosenthal Studio House exhibition, July 1963. Subsequently manufactured commercially by Bristol Pottery. Illustrated in *Bonytt*, March 1964, p.70; and *Lucienne Day – A Career in Design*, p.51, fig. 54.

Hors d'Oeuvres Dishes and Fruit Set, c.1963
Note: Prototype fish, meat and salad dishes, decorated with images of different types of food. Shown at Rosenthal Studio House exhibition, July 1963; produced to order. Fruit set illustrated in *Sunday Times*, 11 August 1963; and *Bonytt*, March 1964, p.70.
Illustrated p.135

Herb, Spice and Storage Jars, c.1963
Porcelain, printed in black enamel with flame, olive or curry-brown lids.
Note: Prototype storage jars decorated with universal food symbols. Shown at Rosenthal Studio House exhibition, July 1963. Illustrated in *Bonytt*, March 1964, p.70.
Illustrated p.135

Dreilinden (pattern number 4086), 1964
Service 3000. Porcelain, printed in green and black enamels.
Note: Produced until December 1965.
Illustrated p.135

Ascot (pattern number 4095), 1965
Service 3000.
Note: Pattern of fine horizontal lines produced April–December 1965. Recorded in Rosenthal Archives.

Four vases (pattern number 1730), 1965
Vase numbers 2907, 2908, 2909 and 2910.
Note: Raised geometric motifs applied to a group of rectangular vases. Recorded in Rosenthal Archives.

B9. THOMAS SOMERSET: TABLE LINEN, GLASS TOWELS AND SHEETS
Note: All items are made of linen. The trade name of the manufacturer is given on the line following the title.

Motley Place Mats and Napkins, 1957
Note: Place mats printed with irregular abstract motifs; napkins plain. Illustrated in *Furniture Record*, 30 May 1958; and *Design*, August 1958.

Mitre Tablecloth and Napkins, 1958
Tablecloth: 52in x 52in (132cm x 132cm).
Note: Decorated with a column of geometric motifs, designed to complement the Regent Street tableware by Rosenthal. Illustrated in *Design*, August 1958.
Illustrated p.97

Black Leaf Glass Towel, 1959
Fragonard.
Note: Design Centre Award, 1960. Gold Medal, California State Fair, 1960.
Illustrated p.98

Bouquet Garni Glass Towel, 1959
Fragonard.
Note: Design Centre Award, 1960. Gold Medal, California State Fair, 1960.
Illustrated p.98

Jack Sprat, c. 1959
Fragonard.
Note: Pattern of tall thin husband and small round wife. Illustrated in *Designing Women*, 2008.

Too Many Cooks Glass Towel, 1959
Fragonard. Reissued by twentytwentyone.
Note: Design Centre Award, 1960. Gold Medal, California State Fair, 1960.
Illustrated p.98

Four Seasons Place Mats and Napkins, c.1959
Note: Decorated with four different linear motifs, designed to complement the Four Seasons tableware by Rosenthal. Place mats made of black linen, embroidered in white; napkins plain.
Illustrated p.96

Butterflies Glass Towel, 1960
Fragonard, sold on behalf of Polio Research Fund.
Note: Pattern of butterfly motifs similar to Heal's fabric Vanessa (1960). Mentioned in *The Drapers' Record*, 16 July 1960. Sample in Lucienne Day collection (2001).

Maxim Tablecloth, 1961
Note: Decorated with rectangular shapes in grey and yellow on white. Illustrated in *The Ambassador*, 1961, no. 2, p.65.

Pomegranate Tablecloth and Napkins, 1961
Fragonard, 52in x 52in (132cm x 132cm).
Illustrated p.136

Batterie de Cuisine Glass Towel, c.1961–2
Fragonard. Reissued by twentytwentyone.
Illustrated p.136

Good Food Glass Towel, c.1961–2
Fragonard.
Note: Pattern of rows of fruit and vegetables. Shown at Rosenthal Studio House exhibition, July 1963. Sample in Whitworth Art Gallery (T1998.47). Illustrated in *Designing Women*, 2008.

Night and Day Glass Towel, c.1961–2
Fragonard. Reissued by twentytwentyone.
Note: Pattern depicts a sun on one half and an owl and the moon on the other. Shown at Rosenthal Studio House exhibition, July 1963.
Illustrated p.135

Provençal Glass Towel, c.1961–2
Fragonard. Reissued by twentytwentyone.
Note: Shown at Rosenthal Studio House exhibition, July 1963. Illustrated in *Bonytt*, March 1964, p.69.
Illustrated p.136

Diabolo Glass Towel, c.1962–3
Fragonard.
Note: Pattern composed of hourglass-shaped abstract motifs. Produced in four colourways. Recorded in photograph in Lucienne Day Archives. Illustrated in *Designing Women*, 2008.

Merry Makers Glass Towel, c.1962–3
Fragonard.
Note: Pattern shows an overhead view of figures around a Christmas dinner table. Shown at Rosenthal Studio House exhibition, July 1963. Recorded in photograph in Lucienne Day Archives.

Daisy Belle Tablecloth, c.1963
Fragonard.
Note: Depicts stylized flowers. Shown at Rosenthal Studio House exhibition, July 1963. Recorded in Lucienne Day Archives.

Troubadour Sheet Set, 1963
70in x 108in (178cm x 274cm) and 90in x 108in (229cm x 274cm).
Note: Mustard-brown border with handkerchief stripes of black, mustard and orange on white. Illustrated in *Sunday Times*, 24 March 1963. Shown at Rosenthal Studio House exhibition, July 1963.

Many Hands Make Light Work Glass Towel, c.1964
Bedford Street, produced on behalf of Rosenthal.
Note: Pattern depicts figures based on members of the Rosenthal
Designers' Panel. Samples in Lucienne Day collection (2001).

Periwinkle Glass Towel, 1964
Best Linen.
Note: Pattern of flat stylized flowers similar to Periwinkle tablecloth.
Sample in Whitworth Art Gallery (T1998.52).

Periwinkle Tablecloth, 1964
Best Linen.
Illustrated p.136

Tudor Table Glass Towel, c.1964
Best Linen.
Note: Pattern depicts boar's head and fish. Sample in Whitworth Art
Gallery (T1998.47).

Glass Towel, 1969
Nova Products.
Note: Pattern consists of the words "Glass Towel" in Art Nouveau-style
lettering. Illustrated in *Lucienne Day – A Career in Design*, p.57, fig. 62.

Rose Diamond Glass Towel, 1969
Nova Products.
Note: Kaleidoscopic abstract geometric pattern. Illustrated
in *Designers in Britain*, no. 7, 1971, p.263; and *Lucienne Day –
A Career in Design*, p.57, fig. 62.

Tudor Garden Glass Towel, 1969
Nova Products.
Note: Pattern of aerial view of a garden. Illustrated in *Lucienne Day –
A Career in Design*, p.57, fig. 62.

B10. STEVENSON & SON: PRINTED DRESS FABRICS

English Summer, 1945
Printed rayon moygashel.
Note: Pattern of sun and rain motifs. Illustrated in *Designers in Britain*,
no. 1, 1947, p.243, fig. 11; and *Lucienne Day – A Career in Design*,
p.16, fig. 6.

Toro, 1945
Printed rayon moygashel.
Note: Illustrated in *Designers in Britain*, no. 1, 1947, p.243, fig. 12.
Illustrated p.28

Toyshop, 1946
Printed rayon moygashel.
Note: Pattern of small objects resembling toys. Recorded
in photograph in Lucienne Day Archives.

Jet, c.1947
Printed rayon moygashel.
Note: Produced shortly after Robin Day's poster design
for the *Jet* exhibition.
Illustrated p.28

B11. J.H. BIRTWISTLE: PRINTED DRESS FABRICS

Dress fabric, 1948
Note: Abstract pattern of double figure of eight motifs. Illustrated
in *Designers in Britain*, no. 2, 1949, p.54, fig. 2.

Dress fabric, c.1948
Note: Pattern of pebble and fossil motifs. Recorded in photograph
in Lucienne Day Archives.

B12. PASMAN FABRICS: PRINTED DRESS FABRIC

Dress fabric, c.1948
Note: Pattern of typographic motifs. Recorded in photograph
in Lucienne Day Archives.
Illustrated p.29

B13. SILKELLA: PRINTED DRESS FABRICS

Dress fabric, 1948
Note: Screen-printed Utility fabric with pattern of wavy abstract
motifs. Illustrated in *Designers in Britain*, no. 2, 1949.
Illustrated p.29

Dress fabric, c.1948
Note: Pattern of leaves and butterflies. Illustrated in *Designers
in Britain*, no. 2, 1949, p.54, fig. 3.

Dress fabric, 1948
Note: Pattern of bands of broken stripes. Recorded in photograph
in Lucienne Day Archives.

B14. MARKS & SPENCER: PRINTED DRESS FABRIC

Dress fabric, 1949
Note: Pattern of elongated wavy leaves. Recorded in photograph
in Lucienne Day Archives.

B15. HORROCKSES: PRINTED DRESS FABRIC

Dress fabric, 1949

Note: Pattern of birds, ferns and leaves, originally designed in May
1946. Recorded in photograph in Lucienne Day Archives.

Dress fabric, 1949
Note: Pattern of sketchy spirals. Illustrated in *The Ambassador*, 1950,
no.1, p.110.

**B16. RAYON INDUSTRY DESIGN CENTRE: PRINTED DRESS
FABRIC**

Owls, 1949
Printed rayon
Note: Pattern of rows of stylized owls. Illustrated in *Designers
in Britain*, no. 3, 1951; and *Lucienne Day – A Career in Design*,
p.16, fig. 7.

B17. ARGAND LTD: PRINTED DRESS FABRICS

Dress fabric, 1950
Note: Pattern of bands of serrated stripes, with a black ground,
and tan and yellow detail. Recorded in photograph in Lucienne
Day Archives. Illustrated in *The Ambassador*, 1950, no.1, p.109.

Dress fabric, 1950
Note: Pattern of stylized windows. Recorded in photograph
in Lucienne Day Archives. Illustrated in *The Ambassador*, 1950,
no.1, p.111.

Dress fabric, 1950
Note: Abstract pattern of attenuated diamond-shaped motifs
in lime green and black.
Illustrated p.30

B18. PENNY MASON MODELS: PRINTED DRESS FABRIC

Festival of Britain, 1950
Printed rayon.
Note: Abstract pattern incorporating the words "festival",
"fete", "fiesta" etc. Recorded in photograph in Lucienne Day
Archives.

B19. COLE & SON: WALLPAPERS

Diabolo, 1951
Screen-printed wallpaper.
Note: Used in the Kitchens Section of the Homes and Gardens
Pavilion at the Festival of Britain, 1951. Initial colourway was slate
grey/beige/lemon yellow.
Illustrated p.50

Stella, 1951
Screen-printed wallpaper.
Note: Used in the Kitchens Section (Country Farmer's Dining
Room) of the Homes and Gardens Pavilion at the Festival of Britain,
1951. Initial colourways were white/blue-grey/dark brown, and
white/mushroom pink/dark brown.
Illustrated p.50

B20. JOHN LINE: WALLPAPER

Provence, 1951
Hand block-printed wallpaper.
Note: Used in low-cost room setting designed by Robin Day for
the Home Entertainment section of the Homes and Gardens Pavilion
at the Festival of Britain, 1951.
Illustrated pp.44 & 49

B21. PRIMAVERA: PRINTED FURNISHING FABRIC

Printed Furnishing Fabric, 1952
Screen-printed cotton.
Note: Designed in January 1948. Produced in two colourways:
mushroom/black and green/black.
Illustrated p.31

B22. MÖLNLYCKE: PRINTED FURNISHING FABRICS

Four Printed Furnishing Fabrics, 1952
Screen-printed cotton.
Note: Two patterns showing stylized plant motifs recorded
in photographs in Lucienne Day Archives.
Illustrated p.83

B23. VALLØ TAPETENFABRIK: WALLPAPER

Wallpaper, c.1952
Note: Norwegian manufacturer cited as a client on a press release
for Lucienne Day's solo exhibition at Heal's, May 1958.

B24. BRITISH CELANESE: PRINTED FURNISHING FABRICS

Miscellany, 1952
Screen-printed acetate rayon taffeta and Travacel glazed slub rayon
chintz.
Illustrated p.81

Palisade, 1952
Screen-printed acetate rayon taffeta and Travacel glazed slub rayon

chintz.
Illustrated p.80

Quadrille, 1952
Screen-printed acetate rayon taffeta and Travacel glazed slub rayon
chintz.
Note: Abstract pattern composed of rounded rectangular motifs.
Illustrated in *Fifties Furnishing Fabrics*, pl. 2.

Climbing Trees, 1953
Screen-printed acetate rayon taffeta and Travacel glazed slub rayon
chintz.
Illustrated p.80

Perpetua, 1953
Screen-printed acetate rayon taffeta and Travacel glazed slub rayon
chintz.
Illustrated p.81

Travelogue, 1953
Screen-printed acetate rayon taffeta and Travacel glazed slub rayon
chintz.
Note: Pattern of triangles joined by fine diagonal lines. Illustrated in
Fifties Furnishing Fabrics, pl. 17.

B25. EVERWEAR CANDLEWICK: BEDSPREAD

Bedspread, 1953
Note: Referred to in *The Cabinet Maker*, 2 May 1953.

B26. HILLE: PRINTED UPHOLSTERY FABRIC

Eclipse, 1953
Screen-printed linen.
Note: A one-off abstract pattern for Hille composed of rounded
square motifs, used to upholster Robin Day's Telechair. Illustrated in
Furnishings from Britain, no. 2, 1953, p.57; and *Designers in Britain*,
no. 4, 1954, p.1.
Illustrated p.66

B27. LIBERTY: PRINTED DRESS AND FURNISHING FABRICS

Coronation Rose, 1953
Screen-printed linen dress fabric.
Note: Pattern composed of stylized linear rose motifs, designed for
the coronation of Elizabeth II in 1953. Also known as Tudor Rose.
Recorded in Liberty Archives. Strike-off illustrated in *Liberty and Co. in
the Fifties and Sixties*, p.40.

Fritillary, 1954
Screen-printed cotton or linen furnishing fabric.
Illustrated p.83

**B28. GÖPPINGER KALIKO- UND KUNSTLERDERWERKE
GMBH: PRINTED PLASTIC FABRICS**

Plastic fabric (pattern number 0327), 1958
Note: Mottled pattern.
Illustrated p.94

Plastic fabric, 1958
Note: Pattern of stylized dandelions and grasses. Sample in
Whitworth Art Gallery (T1998.73).**Plastic fabric, 1958**
Note: Pattern of coloured leaves against fine black twigs. Illustrated in
Lucienne Day – A Career in Design, p.52, fig. 55.
Illustrated p.94

**B29. HEAL'S (BEDDING DEPARTMENT): WOVEN MATTRESS
TICKINGS**

Small Leaf Mattress Ticking, 1960
Note: Pattern of rows of small leaves. Produced in three
colourways, charcoal, grey and peach. Illustrated in *Furniture
Record*, 4 March 1960.
Illustrated p.137

Mattress Ticking, 1960
Note: Pattern of fine lines and small squares. Produced in
ivory/black/lime, ivory/blue/green and pink/charcoal. Illustrated
in *Furniture Record*, 4 March 1960.
Illustrated p.137

Mattress Ticking, c.1960
Note: Rough tracing of pattern of circles and squares in Lucienne
Day Archives.

Mattress Ticking, c.1960
Note: Pattern of irregular blocks.
Illustrated p.137

Stripe Mattress Ticking, c.1961
Note: Pattern of coloured stripes. Illustrated in BBC booklet called
Looking at Things, 8 March 1962, covering school broadcasts from
January to March.
Illustrated p.137

Check Mattress Ticking, 1963
Note: Identified from dated artwork in Lucienne Day Archives.
Produced in four colourways.

B30. A.F. BUCKINGHAM: PRINTED MATTRESS TICKINGS

Mattress Tickings, 1960–61
Printed cotton.
Note: Collaboration between Lucienne Day and A.F. Buckingham mentioned in *The Cabinet Maker*, 23 December 1960 (which mentions a pattern of "wild roses presented in a medallion form") and *Furniture Record*, 27 January 1961. Two designs identified from artwork and samples in Lucienne Day Archives: pattern of triangles and squares in two colourways; pattern of oval motifs (similar to torn circle design for Flower Bricks) in four colourways – gold, green, pink and blue-grey, dated 1961.

B31. ICI: HANDKERCHIEFS
Note: Screen-printed cotton handkerchiefs produced to promote ICI Dyestuff Division's Procion dyes. Dated from artwork in Lucienne Day Archives. Shown at Rosenthal Studio House exhibition, July 1963.

Apple and Pear Handkerchief, c.1962
Note: Apple and pear motifs, similar to those on Good Food glass towel. Sample in Whitworth Art Gallery (T1998.55).

Floral Handkerchief, 1962
Note: Pattern of flower motifs similar to Heal's Rock Rose fabric (1961). Sample in Lucienne Day collection (2001).

Torn Circle Handkerchief, 1962
Note: Pattern of mottled circles resembling stained glass, similar to design on Bristol Pottery flower brick. Sample in Whitworth Art Gallery (T1998.56).

Triangles Handkerchief, 1962
Note: Abstract geometric pattern, similar to Rose Diamond glass towel. Sample in Whitworth Art Gallery (T1998.54).

B32. ETABLISSEMENT SAINT JOSEPH, BORDEAUX: KNITTED DRESS FABRICS
Note: Knitted woollen jersey dress fabrics. Dated from artwork in Lucienne Day Archives. Shown at Rosenthal Studio House exhibition, July 1963.

Big Circle, 1962
Note: Pattern of half circles, similar to Big Circle carpet for I. & C. Steele. Mentioned in "Modern design should be used with discretion", *The Scotsman*, 3 June 1963. Shown at Rosenthal Studio House exhibition, July 1963. Samples in Whitworth Art Gallery (T1998.68).

Knitted Jersey Dress Fabric, 1962
Note: Linear pattern similar to Heal's fabric Runic (1959). Recorded in artwork in Lucienne Day Archives.

Knitted Jersey Dress Fabric, 1962
Note: Pattern of small rectangles and scrolls, alternating with vertical dashes. Recorded in artwork in Lucienne Day Archives.

Knitted Jersey Dress Fabric, 1962
Note: Pattern suggests stylized flower heads. Recorded in artwork in Lucienne Day Archives.

B33. BARLOW AND JONES: BATH MAT AND TOWELS

Sherwood Bath Mat and Towels (refs 0691 and 0692), c.1963
Terry cotton.
Towel: 30in x 55in (76cm x 140cm). Bath mat: 22in x 32in (56cm x 81cm).
Note: Shown at Rosenthal Studio House exhibition, July 1963. Recorded in Lucienne Day Archives.

B34. BRISTOL POTTERY: CERAMICS

Flower Bricks, 1966
Earthenware, printed in coloured enamels, with black glazed lids.
Note: Originally designed for Rosenthal and shown at Rosenthal Studio House exhibition, July 1963. Subsequently manufactured commercially in earthenware by Bristol Pottery. Range consists of rectangular and square bricks, decorated with three patterns: black and white diamonds; mottled pink pattern; and fragmented blue/green/black circles and ovals. Illustrated in "The Robin Days", *Home Furnishings Daily*, 29 March 1966; and *Lucienne Day – A Career in Design*, p.51, fig. 54.

B35. WEST INDIAN SEA ISLAND COTTON ASSOCIATION: PRINTED SHIRT FABRICS
Note: The West Indian Sea Island Cotton Association was a group of manufacturers producing very fine cottons for the fashion trade and for sheeting. Lucienne Day's commission to design shirt fabrics and sheets was announced in *West Indian Sea Island Cotton News*, 1 November 1969. Completed range of shirt fabrics mentioned in *The Lady*, 9 July 1970.

Chrysanthemum, 1970
Printed cotton.
Note: Pattern of stylized flowers in Art Nouveau style. Sample in Whitworth Art Gallery (T1998.57).

Double Curve, 1970
Printed cotton.
Note: Pattern of small ovals and spots. Sample in Whitworth Art Gallery (T1998.61).

Ribbon, 1970
Printed cotton.
Illustrated p.137

Triangle, 1970
Printed cotton.
Note: Pattern of multicoloured triangles. Sample in Whitworth Art Gallery (T1998.59).

Wave, 1970
Printed cotton.
Illustrated p.137

B36. HABITAT: CURTAINS AND DUVET COVER

Black Leaf Duvet Cover, 1999
Note: Adaptation of design originally produced as a Glass Towel by Thomas Somerset, 1959.
Illustrated p.171

Graphica Curtains, 1999
Note: Adaptation of design originally produced as a furnishing fabric for Heal's, 1953.
Illustrated p.85

B37. SILK MOSAICS
Note: Listed in the order they are recorded in Lucienne Day Archives, which is roughly the order in which they were produced. Dates and sizes are only given where known. Specially commissioned works and pieces in public collections are indicated.

1. Circle
2. Black Window
3. White Door
4. Toutes Directions
5. Three Blue Shapes
6. Summer Tree
7. Autumn Tree
8. The Castle and Other Stories, 1979 (136cm x 162cm / 54in x 64in)
9. Tangram I (28cm x 134cm / 11in x 53in)
10. Tangram II (28cm x 134cm / 11in x 53in)
11. Tangram III
12. Faerie Castle (33cm x 33cm / 13in x 13in)
13. Midnight Sun
14. Reflection
15. Stage Set
16. Shape and Outline
17. Plan of Peking I (96cm x 105cm / 38in x 41in)
18. Plan of Peking II (96cm x 105cm / 38in x 41in)
19. Striped Hills
20. Green Tower
21. The Apple
22. Flying
23. New Hexagon
24. Plan of Peking III (96cm x 105cm / 38in x 41in)
25. Bookmark, Black and Pink
26. Bookmark, Serpent
27. Bookmark, Shapes
28. The Howgills
29. Noah's Flood (96cm x 107cm / 38in x 42in)
30. Mexico (50cm x 95cm / 19½in x 37½in)
31. Castle Terrace
32. Flying in Blue, 1981 (56cm x 123cm / 22in x 48½in)
    Note: Owned by the Victoria & Albert Museum. Illustrated in *Lucienne Day – A Career in Design*, p.62, fig. 68.
33. Ivory Tower
34. Standing, 1981 (56cm x 123cm / 22in x 48½in)
    Note: Owned by the Röhsska Museum, Gothenburg.
35. Their Exits and Their Entrances, 1981 (136cm x 162cm / 53½in x 63½in)
    Illustrated p.162
36. Green Man
37. Red Mask
38. Meckanops, 1982
    Illustrated p.163
39. Crowned Heads Series: Trance (50cm x 95cm / 19½in x 37½in)
40. Copper Mask (33cm x 33cm / 13in x 13in)
41. Boat House (33cm x 33cm / 13in x 13in)
42. The Island (35cm x 63cm / 14in x 25in)
43. Pavilion
44. Attica
45. Whirligig I
46. Whirligig II
47. Whirligig III (38cm x 38cm / 15in x 15in)
48. Whirligig IV (38cm x 38cm / 15in x 15in)
49. Whirligig V
50. Whirligig VI
51. Whirligig VII
52. Whirligig VIII
53. Decoy and Pond 1, 1983 (53cm x 45cm / 21in x 17½in)
54. Decoy and Pond 2, 1983 (53cm x 45cm / 21in x 17½in)
55. Decoy and Pond 3, 1983 (51cm x 45cm / 20in x 17½in)
56. Decoy and Pond 4, 1983 (50cm x 45cm / 19½in x 17½in)
57. Decoy and Pond 5, 1983 (56cm x 45cm / 22in x 17½in)
58. Decoy and Pond 6, 1983 (51cm x 45cm / 20in x 17½in)
59. Summer Palace (78cm x 107cm / 30½in x 42in)
60. Crowned Heads Series: Chess King, 1982 (50cm x 95cm / 19½in x 37½in)
61. Crowned Heads Series: The Queen (50cm x 95cm / 19½in x 37½in)
62. Boat House, Pink
63. Crowned Heads Series: Sad Lady, 1983 (50cm x 95cm / 19½in x 37½in)
    Illustrated p.163
64. Tea House (35cm x 63cm / 13½in x 25in)
65. Astrid
66. Eagle Owl I
67. Eagle Owl II
68. Little Owl
69. Barn Owl I
70. Barn Owl II
71. Tangram, Black and White I, 1985
72. Tangram, Black and White II, 1985
    Illustrated p.171
73. Genesis I (130cm x 161cm / 51in x 63in)
74. Little Tangram, Red
75. Little Tangram, Blue
76. Little Tangram, Yellow
77. Art Gallery (80cm x 94cm / 31½in x 37in)
78. Gemini (45cm x 40cm / 17½in x 15½in)
79. Signs of the Zodiac: Libra I (45cm x 40cm / 17½in x 15½in)
80. Signs of the Zodiac: Capricorn I (45cm x 40cm / 17½in x 15½in)
81. Signs of the Zodiac: Pisces (45cm x 40cm / 17½in x 15½in)
82. Tangram Puzzle, 1985 (28cm x 134cm / 11in x 5½in)
83. Tangram Solution, 1985 (28cm x 134cm / 11in x 5½in)
84. Board of Wisdom, 1985
    Note: Above three works commissioned by Ronald Ward & Partners for the headquarters of Shearman and Stirling.
85. Koran, 1986 (78cm x 82cm / 30½in x 32in)
86. Signs of the Zodiac: Aquarius (45cm x 40cm / 17½in x 15½in)
87. Signs of the Zodiac: Taurus (45cm x 40cm / 17½in x 15½in)
88. Signs of the Zodiac: Libra II (45cm x 40cm / 17½in x 15½in)
89. Signs of the Zodiac: Capricorn II (45cm x 40cm / 17½in x 15½in)
90. Little Tangram, Green
91. Little Tangram, Turquoise
92. Little Tangram, Red
93. Little Tangram, Pink
94. Little Tangram, Orange
95. Kyoto, 1986 (78cm x 78cm / 30½in x 30½in)
96. The Window, 1986 (135cm x 160cm / 53in x 63in)
    Note: Commissioned by Powell & Moya for the Queen Elizabeth Conference Centre, Westminster, London.
97. Enigma: Trident, 1988
98. Enigma: Meander, 1988
99. Enigma: Raindrops, 1988
100. Enigma: Canal, 1988
101. Enigma: Aquarius, 1988
102. Enigma: Ripple, 1988
103. Enigma: Reflexion, 1988
104. Enigma: Torrent, 1988
105. Enigma: Lake, 1988
106. Enigma: Rain, 1988
107. Enigma: Cascade, 1988
108. Enigma: River, 1988
    Note: Enigma is a twelve-part composite silk mosaic on the theme of water, measuring 129cm x 177cm (50½in x 69½in) overall. Owned by the Whitworth Art Gallery.
    Illustrated p.171
109. Aspects of the Sun: Partial Eclipse, 1990
110. Aspects of the Sun: Foggy Sun, 1990
111. Aspects of the Sun: Midnight Sun, 1990
112. Aspects of the Sun: Eclipse, 1990
113. Aspects of the Sun: Sun and Sea, 1990
114. Aspects of the Sun: Concentric Sun, 1990
    Note: Aspects of the Sun is a six-part silk mosaic commissioned by Ahrends, Burton and Koralek for the John Lewis department store at Kingston-on-Thames. It measures approximately 285cm x 480cm (112in x 189in) overall.
    Illustrated p.161
115. Meander I (39cm x 39cm / 15in x 15in)
116. Meander II (37cm x 27cm / 14½in x 10½in)
117. Meander III (37cm x 37cm / 14½in x 14½in)
118. Museum I (51cm x 41cm / 20in x 16in)
119. Museum II, 1990 (51cm x 41cm / 20in x 16in)
120. Purple Shadow, 1990
121. Islands, 1991
    Note: Islands is a twelve-part silk mosaic commissioned by Ahrends, Burton and Koralek for the John Lewis department store at Kingston-on-Thames.
    Illustrated p.161
122. Circling the Square I, 1991 (55cm x 56cm / 21½in x 22in)
123. Circling the Square II, 1991 (55cm x 56cm / 21½in x 22in)
124. Circling the Square III, 1991 (55cm x 56cm / 21½in x 22in)
125. Circling the Square IV, 1991 (55cm x 56cm / 21½in x 22in)
126. Circling the Square V, 1991 (55cm x 56cm / 21½in x 22in)
    Illustrated p.163
127. Three Daughters of Mexico, 1992–3 (180cm x 140cm / 71in x 55in)
    Illustrated p.144
128. Tangram IV, 1990–91 (148cm x 32cm / 58in x 12½in)
    Note: Owned by the Art Institute of Chicago.
129. Ripple
130. Tangram V
131. Tangram VI
132. Tangram VII

Bibliography

• RD relates to Robin Day; LD relates to Lucienne Day; RD/LD relates to Robin and Lucienne Day.

Selected Articles

Listed in chronological order. Where articles are written by RD or LD, their names are highlighted in bold.

Noel Carrington, "The mantle of William Morris", *The Listener*, 17 November 1938 (RD)
Robin Day, "A place of her own", *Vogue*, August 1945, pp.50–51 and p.78 (RD)
"Jets on exhibition", *Architects' Journal*, 6 March 1947, pp.410–11 (RD)
"British Scientific Instruments exhibition", *Architects' Journal*, 19 June 1947, p.527 (RD)
"Atom train", *Architects' Journal*, 13 November 1947, p.434 (RD)
"Mining exhibition", *Architects' Journal*, 2 October 1947, pp.299–300 (RD)
"Recent exhibitions designed by Peter Moro and Robin Day", *The Architect and Building News*, 13 February 1948, pp.138 & 140 (RD)
"Ladies – your evening gown is here", *Daily Graphic*, 19 January 1949 (RD)
"British designs win international award", *The Furnishing World*, 21 January 1949 (RD)
"He's drawing the recruits", *Royal Air Force Review*, April 1949 (RD)
"British talent shapes a sensible trend", *Furnishing*, Spring 1949 (RD)
Robin Day, "Make room for television", *House & Garden*, Spring 1949, pp.52–3 (RD)
"British Transport", *Architects' Journal*, 22 September 1949, p.305 (RD)
"S.I.A. Designs", The Ambassador, 1950, no.1, pp.109-13 (LD)
"American success for British designers", *Design*, January 1950, p.12 (RD)
"Day-Latimer storage furniture", *The Cabinet Maker*, April 1950 (RD)
Robin Day and Clive Latimer, "The Day-Latimer storage units", *Design*, May 1950, pp.17–19 (RD)
Lucienne Day, "Making patterns in line and colour" and "All over patterns", *Looking at Things – BBC Broadcasts to Schools*, 13–27 October 1950, pp.14–21 (LD)
"Furniture exhibition", *Architects' Journal*, 22 February 1951, pp.234–5 (RD)
"Royal Festival Hall", *Architectural Review*, June 1951, pp.363–76 & 386–7 (RD)
"Homes and Gardens", *Design*, July 1951, p.18 (RD)
"British furniture at Triennale", *Architects' Journal*, 5 July 1951, p.13 (RD/LD)
Robin Day, "Milan 1951", *Design*, August 1951, pp.20–21 (RD)
"Chairs from the Royal Festival Hall", *Architects' Journal*, 23 August 1951, p.239 (RD)
"Glass shelves: Homes and Gardens Pavilion, South Bank Exhibition", *Architects' Journal*, 30 August 1951, p.262 (RD)
"Focus on the Festival", *Furnishings from Britain*, September 1951, pp.67–74 (RD/LD)
Arne Remlov and Liv Schøldt, "Two outstanding English designers", *Bonytt*, no. 9, September 1951, pp.154–9 (RD/LD)
Robin Day and Olive Shapley, "Tables and chairs", *Looking at Things – BBC Broadcasts to Schools*, 26 October 1951 (RD)
"Wallpaper and textile designs by Lucienne Day", *Architectural Design*, November 1951, p.343 (LD)
Marilyn Hoffman, "Simplicity of Robin Day's elegant modern designs widens U.S. market for old English furniture firm", *Christian Science Monitor*, 8 October 1951 (RD)
"Limited Editions", *Design*, December 1951, pp.10–11 (LD)
"News in print", *House & Garden*, February 1952, pp.42–5 (LD)
"British furnishing fabric wins international award", *Furniture Record*, 28 March 1952 (LD)
"Lucienne Day is first to bring coveted American prize to Britain", *The Cabinet Maker*, 29 March 1952 (LD)
"Young Briton's design given award in U.S.", *Christian Science Monitor*, April 1952 (LD)
Ann Ruggles, "Decorating homes problem for Britons", *New York World-Telegraph and Sun*, April 1952 (RD/LD)
Milner Gray, "Designer: Robin Day", *Art and Industry*, May 1952, pp.154–9 (RD)
"These suites are today's best-sellers", *Furnishing*, May 1952, pp.360–63 (RD)
"British designer wins coveted US award", *Design*, May 1952, p.32 (LD)
"American honour for British designer", *Skinners Silk and Rayon Record*, May 1952 (LD)
"On show in Norway", *Design*, July 1952, p.14 (RD/LD)
Paul Reilly, "Tradition and experiment", *Design*, July 1952, pp.18–21 (LD)
"Lucienne and Robin Day – two talented prize-winning designers", *House & Garden*, July 1952, pp.42–3 & 86 (RD/LD)
"Autumn furnishing and decoration ideas", and "You need colour in winter", *House & Garden*, September 1952, pp.8–15 and pp.36–45 (LD)
"Exhibition stands at the National Radio Show, Earls Court, London", *Architects' Journal*, 4 September 1952, pp.278–9 (RD)
Judith Simons, "Homemaking ideas", *Aberdeen Evening Express*, 20 September 1952 (RD/LD)
Lucienne Day, "Making patterns in line and colour", and "All over patterns", *Looking at Things – BBC Broadcasts to Schools*, Autumn 1952, pp.20–23 (LD)
"First printed taffeta furnishings shortly", *Furniture Record*, 10 October 1952 (LD)
Robin Day, "Robin Day", *Everyday Art Quarterly*, no. 28, 1953, pp.18–22 (RD)
"New Time-Life Office in London", and "Fabrics by Lucienne Day", *Furnishings from Britain*, no. 2, 1953, pp.32–5 and p.54 (RD/LD)
James de Holden Stone, "Curtains in the breeze", *The Studio*, February 1953, pp.44–53 (LD)
"Modern art in the home", *Times Weekly Review*, 26 March 1953 (LD)
"Picture of advanced fabric trends", *Furnishing World*, 3 April 1953 (LD)
"Textile Group's new work", *The Cabinet Maker*, 4 April 1953 (LD)
"Offices in Time-Life International', *Architects' Journal*, 5 March 1953, pp.312–7
"Bookshelves and cupboard: Offices in London W1" and "Executive's desk: Offices in London W1", *Architects' Journal*, 26 March 1953 and 9 April 1953 (RD)
"New fabrics from Heal's", *The Cabinet Maker*, 11 April 1953 (LD)
Paul Reilly, "German enterprise in wallpaper design", *Design*, July 1953, pp.16–19 (LD)
"The year's work", *Interiors*, August 1953, p.75 (RD/LD)
"Transformation of the hall", *Daily Telegraph*, 19 September 1953 (RD/LD)
Audrey Werge, "Get warm for winter now", *Daily Telegraph*, 29 September 1953 (RD/LD)
"Dressing for dinner – the changing scene", *Vogue*, November 1953, pp.134–7 (RD/LD)
"Brightening up… is going to be fun", *Sunday Express*, 27 December 1953 (RD/LD)
Robin Day, "At the Robin Days", *Daily Mail Ideal Home Book*, 1953–4, pp.34–9 (RD/LD)
Marie-Jaqueline Lancaster, "Ideas from an office", *Daily Mail Ideal Home Book*, 1953–4, pp.69–75 (RD)
"Designers at home", *House & Garden*, January 1954, pp.28–31 (RD/LD)
"Young designers come in pairs", *House Beautiful*, Summer 1954, pp.20–21 (RD/LD)
"Meet the ladies", *Furniture Record*, 3 September 1954 (LD)
Dr Emil Rasch, "Mein Besuch bei Lucienne Day in London" *Architektur und Wohnform*, October 1954, pp.40–42 (LD)
"Points from the Triennale", and "Furnishings into dress", *Design*, October 1954, p.8 and p.50 (RD/LD)
"Your kind of car", *House & Garden*, November 1954, pp.54–7 (RD/LD)
"Britain's triumph at Milan", *Furnishings from Britain*, no. 1, 1955 (RD/LD)
"Bold colours and textures at Cotton Board's SIA show", *Furnishing*, Feburary 1955, pp.170–171 (LD)
Robin Day, "Steel rod in furniture", *Urbanism – Journal of the University of Manchester*, no. 3, spring 1955, pp.16–18 (RD)
Judy Fallon, "These contemporary Days", *The Sketch*, 6 April 1955, pp.298–9 (RD/LD)
"Award to Lucienne Day", *Skinners Silk and Rayon Record*, April 1955, p.414 (LD)
"A survey of textiles", *Design*, August 1955, pp.16–31 (LD)
Misha Black, "1930–1955 – A quarter century of design: Lucienne Day", *The Ambassador*, December 1955, p.81 (LD)
"Lucienne Day" and "Robin Day", *Design Quarterly*, no. 36, 1956, pp.9–13 (RD/LD)
"Lucienne Day", *Tapeten Zeitung*, 20 March 1956, pp.28–9 (LD)
"Künstlerisches Schaffen – Industrielles Gestalten", *Tapeten Zeitung*, 20 July 1956, pp.6–10 (LD)
"Children in their own rooms", *House & Garden*, August 1956, pp.38–41 (RD/LD)
"Modernised waiting room, King's Cross Station", *Architects' Journal*, 23 August 1956 (RD)
Edith Teague, "Round-the-clock marriage", *Evening News*, 1 October 1956 (RD/LD)
"Lucienne Day", *Der Regenbogen*, November 1956, pp.14–15 (LD)
"10 years of outspoken and sound design", *The Ambassador*, November 1956, pp.108–109 (LD)
Lucienne Day, "Plain or Fancy?", *Daily Mail Ideal Home Book*, 1957, pp.82–7 (LD)
Robin Day, "Storage", *Daily Mail Ideal Home Book*, 1957, pp.103–107 (RD)
Ross Percival, "Mr Day takes a tip from you", *Manchester Evening News*, 29 January 1957 (RD)
"Italian night-scene – in carpets", *Birmingham Post*, 20 March 1957 (LD)
Robert Harling, "Designs of the Year – Would you have chosen these?", *Sunday Times*, 12 May 1957 (RD/LD)
"Designers win recognition – for manufacturers", *Architects' Journal*, 16 May 1957, p.724 (RD/LD)
Designs of the Year 1958 and 1957, Council of Industrial Design, 1958, p.36, p.38 and p.42 (RD/LD)
"Robin Day awarded SIA Medal", *SIA Journal*, February 1958, p.1 (RD)
"Designed for architects', *Contract Furnishing*, February 1958 (LD)
"Impressions: Lucienne Day", *House & Garden*, May 1958, p.51 (LD)
Alice Hope, "Designers want a neutral background", *Daily Telegraph*, 20 May 1958, p.78 (RD/LD)
"Heal's exhibition of Lucienne Day's work", *The Cabinet Maker and Complete House Furnisher*, 23 May 1958, p.550 (LD)
"Furniture men set up UNESCO Gift Room Committee", and "Lucienne Day designs at Heal's", *Furniture Record and International Furnisher*, 30 May 1958, p.858 and p.863 (RD/LD)
"Exhibition for designer", *Design*, no. 114, June 1958, p.67 (LD)
Paul Reilly, "Englische Dekostoffe von Heute", *Heimtex*, July 1958, pp.39–40 (LD)
Dan Johnston, "Future for Irish linen", *Design*, August 1958, pp.36–7 (LD)
"Die Neue 'Göppinger Plastics'", *Tapeten Zeitung*, 20 August 1958, p.24 (LD)
"Britische Formgebung – 'British Design' in der Göppinger Galerie in Frankfurt", *Haus und Heim*, August 1958, pp.6–13 (RD/LD)
"British furniture at Frankfurt", *Furnishing*, September 1958, pp.52–5 (RD/LD)
"Die 'Göppinger Galerie' zeigte Englische Entwürfe", *Tapeten Zeitung*, 5 October 1958, pp.8–9 (RD/LD)
Ingeborg Meinecke, "Lucienne Day", *Gebrauchsgraphik*, January 1959, pp.50–55 (LD)
"Four for your money", *Daily Express*, 28 January 1959 (RD/LD)
"Close-up", *Ideal Home*, February 1959, pp.52–6 (RD/LD)
John E. Blake, "The stream revitalised," *Design*, April 1959, p.48 (LD)
"Collaboration", *Design*, May 1959, p.59 (RD)
Dennis Barker, "Britain's design is not different enough", *Express and Star*, 10 June 1959 (RD)
Dennis Barker, "Going all 'modern', and on a moderate income", *Express and Star*, 17 June 1959 (RD)
Linda Charles, "At home with colour" and "Fashion colours with white", *Everywoman*, August–September 1959, pp.48–51 (LD)
"New textile designs for Heal Fabrics Ltd. London", *Moebel + Decoration*, September 1959, pp.463–6 (LD)
"Storey's new PVC designs", *The Cabinet Maker*, October 1959 (RD)
"Rosenthal's new pattern", *Pottery Gazette and Glass Trade Review*, November 1959, p.1320 (LD)
"Prettier plastics are on the way", *Northern Echo*, 5 November 1959 (RD)
"Introducing the Status Group", *The Cabinet Maker*, 20 November 1959 (RD)
"New furniture and ideas for family living", *Ideal Home*, February 1960, pp.29–31 (RD)
Maurice Richards, "SIA Profile: Lucienne Day", *SIA Journal*, no. 84, Feburary 1960 (LD)
"Heal's, the sure touch", *The Ambassador*, March 1960 (LD)
Lucienne Day, "Ich Sage Designer", *ITA 60 – Katalog der Internationalen Tapetenausstellung*, Haus der Kunst, Munich, 25 April – 13 May 1960 (LD)
Joan Whitney, "Designed for better living", *Northern Echo*, 19 May 1960 (RD/LD)
"Irish linen glass towels", *Design Centre Awards 1960*, Council of Industrial Design, 1960, p.17 (LD)
"Fourteen days of grace for furnishing wisely and well… with adaptability in mind", *Ideal Home*, May 1960 (RD)
"Status Group", *Industrial Architecture*, May–June 1960, p.199 (RD)
"So wohne ich – Entwerferin Lucienne Day", *Schöner Wohnen*, April 1960, pp.41–4 (LD)
Leslie Julius, "The Hille story: Creating a company 'image'", *The Cabinet Maker and Complete House Furnisher*, 1 July 1960 (RD)
"Comfort of good lighting", *Home*, September–October 1960, pp.62–3 (RD/LD)
Gillian Naylor, "Profile of Robin and Lucienne Day", *Moebel + Decoration*, December 1960, pp.19–20 (RD/LD)
"Buckingham in 1961 – Top designers working on new beds", *The Cabinet Maker*, 23 December 1960 (LD)
"Unwilling to predict", *The Scotsman*, 31 December 1960 (RD)
"Furniture showrooms", *Architects' Journal*, 16 March 1961 (RD)
"Young school with design", *The Ambassador*, April 1961, pp.67–70 (LD)
"'Form' unit furniture", *Design*, June 1961, p.58 (RD)
"Ekco Plastics Ltd.", *Advertiser's Weekly*, 23 June 1961 (RD)
Vivien Hislop, "All in the Days' work", *Evening News*, 5 September 1961 (RD/LD)
"Two busy Days meet Jet Age challenge", *Scandinavian Times*, October 1961 (RD/LD)
"The 'Studio House' policy", *Pottery and Glass*, October 1961, pp.811–13 and p.835 (LD)
Vivien Hislop, "Home of the past: now it's way ahead", *Manchester Evening News*, 7 October 1961 (RD/LD)
Lucienne Day, "Pattern on fabrics", *Looking at Things – BBC Broadcasts to Schools*, 8 March 1962, pp.28–31 (LD)
"BR heavy duty upholstered settee", *Design Centre Awards 1962*, Council of Industrial Design, 1962 (RD)
"New designs in china", *The Scotsman*, 14 July 1962 (LD)
"It's news to us", *The Lady*, 9 August 1962 (LD)
O.B. Miller, "For distinction in design", *The Gazette of the John Lewis Partnership*, 24 November 1962, pp.1067–1068 (RD/LD)
"Furniture showrooms and offices, Albemarle Street, London", *Architectural Review*, January 1963, pp.250–54 (RD)
"Hille looks forward", *The Cabinet Maker and Retail Furnisher*, 19 January 1963 (RD)
"House that Hille built", *Sunday Times*, 20 January 1963 (RD)
"Clean and shapely", *Architects' Journal*, 23 January 1963 (RD)
"It's the Hille touch – and it's spreading", *West Herts Post*, 21 February 1963 (RD)
"Counsels of perfection", *Tatler*, 20 March 1963, pp.604–605 (RD/LD)
R.F. Salmons, "Polypropylene chair", *British Plastics*, May 1963, pp.2–4 (RD)
"Unique plastic chairs", *Financial Times*, 2 May 1963 (RD)
"Revolutionary Hille chair", *The Cabinet Maker*, 3 May 1963 (RD)

"Story behind Hille's new polypropylene shell chair", *The Cabinet Maker*, 10 May 1963 (RD)
Brian Henderson, "Polypropylene chairs", *Architects' Journal*, 15 May 1963, p.1024 (RD)
Elizabeth Good, "In all directions", *Sunday Times*, 19 May 1963 (RD)
Margaret Moodie, "Modern design should be used with discretion", *The Scotsman*, 3 June 1963 (LD)
"Lucienne Day show", *Tableware*, August 1963, pp.562–63 (LD)
"Lucienne Day exhibition at Studio House", *Pottery Gazette and Glass Trade Review*, August 1963, p.868 (LD)
Anne Donaldson, "Woman with designs on many products", *Glasgow Herald*, 16 December 1963 (LD)
O.B. Miller, "Design in the Partnership", *The Gazette of the John Lewis Partnership*, 18 January 1964, pp.1248–1249 (RD/LD)
Liv Schøldt, "Profiler i britisk brukskunst: Robin Day", *Bonytt*, February 1964, pp.35–7 (RD)
Liv Schøldt, "Profiler i britisk brukskunst: Lucienne Day, *Bonytt*, March 1964, pp.68–70 (LD)
"Lucienne Day" and "Robin Day", *Modernes Wohnen*, Summer 1964, pp.16–17 (RD/LD)
"Hille sales plans for new polypropylene chair", *The Cabinet Maker and Retail Furnisher*, 20 July 1964 (RD)
N. Keith Scott, "Churchill College, Cambridge", *The Architect and Building News*, 9 September 1964, pp.493–505 (RD)
Robin Day, "Designing for Hille", *Design and Industries Association Yearbook*, 1964–5, pp.88–91 (RD)
Richard Carr, "Polypropylene chair", *Design*, February 1965, pp.32–7 (RD)
"Furniture show", *The Architect and Building News*, 24 February 1965 (RD)
O.B. Miller, "Establishment of a Partnership Design Committee", *The Gazette of the John Lewis Partnership*, 17 April 1965, p.260 (RD/LD)
"Polypropylene stacking chair, 1964 model", *Design*, June 1965, p.30 (RD)
"Carpets", *Architectural Review*, August 1965, pp.137–8 (LD)
"Oxbridge builds", *Interior Design and Contract Furnishing*, September–October 1965, pp.253–60 (RD)
Linda Charles, "Homes of the future", *Everywoman*, November 1965 (LD)
Mary Neale, "The Robin Days", *Home Furnishings Daily*, 29 March 1966, pp.7–9 (RD/LD)
"'Starfish' seating", *Design*, August 1966, p.48 (RD)
"Churchill College, Cambridge", *Architectural Design*, December 1966, pp.593–4 (RD)
Jacqueline Smith, "Jewel bright colours for your home", *Brides*, Early Spring 1967, pp.92–3 (LD)
Robin Day, "Creating a house style", *The Gazette of the John Lewis Partnership*, 29 April 1967, pp.307–308 (RD)
Violet Stevenson, "My favourite flower", *Woman's Realm*, 26 August 1967, p.26 (LD)
"Take it easy", *Shell Magazine*, no. 721, January 1968, pp.12–13 (RD)
"Furnishing fabrics: Heal's Chevron, Complex and Extension", *Design*, May 1968, pp.42–3 (LD)
"Heal's Win It", *The Ambassador*, October 1968, pp.92–3 (LD)
Eila Saarinen and Penny Tweedie, "Robin Day & Finn Fuurn", *Hopeapeili*, 27 March 1969, pp.20–23 (RD)
"Building revisited: Churchill College, Cambridge", *Architects' Journal*, July 1971, pp.141–50 (RD)
"A Design Management Award for Waitrose", *The Gazette of the John Lewis Partnership*, 18 September 1971, pp.832–3 (RD/LD)
"Plastiscene", *Building Design*, 6 April 1973, p.4 (RD)
"Up Hille all the way", *The Guardian*, 31 January 1974 (RD)
Harry Legg, "A new concept in retailing", *The Gazette of the John Lewis Partnership*, 13 March 1976, pp.124–6 (RD)
Jane Cooper, "Problems of a packed house", *Design*, January 1977, pp.36–41 (RD)
"Robin Day London", *Bauen + Wohnen*, June 1979, p.228 (RD)
Harry Legg, "A promising start", *The Gazette of the John Lewis Partnership*, 22 September 1979, pp.779–785 (RD)
Robin Day, "Not even reindeer", *The Gazette of the John Lewis Partnership*, 5 January 1980, pp.1112–1113 (RD)
Loyd Grossman, "Storming the Barbican", *Harpers & Queen*, July 1981, pp.150–54 (RD)
Psyche Pirie, "Designing women", *Woman's Journal*, August 1981, pp.74–9 (LD)
Loyd Grossman, "Chair persons", *Harpers & Queen*, September 1981, pp.200–214 (RD)
Lance Knobel, "Barbican Arts Centre, London", *Architectural Review*, October 1981, pp.239–54 (RD)
Brian Alford, "Waitrose John Barnes", *The Gazette of the John Lewis Partnership*, 24 October 1981, p.843 (RD)
Victor Glasstone, "A triumph of theatre", *Architects' Journal*, 18 August 1982, pp.31–44 (RD)
"The most ubiquitous chair in modern Britain", *House & Garden*, September 1982, pp.128–9 (RD)
Graham Hughes, "Lucienne and Robin Day", *Arts Review*, 29 April 1983, pp.230–31 (RD/LD)
José Manser, "Top British designers", *Illustrated London News*, November 1983, pp.64–6 (RD)
"Hille plays the game to win", *What's New in Interiors*, June 1984, pp.4–5 (RD)
Caroline Dilke, "25 years of Partnership design", *The Gazette of the John Lewis Partnership*, 29 August 1987, pp.711–12 (RD/LD)
Natalie Cairnes, "The coffee shop gets weaving", *The Gazette of the John Lewis Partnership*, 15 September 1990, p.817 (LD)
"Kingston repair is tall order", *The Gazette of the John Lewis Partnership*, 30 November 1991, p.112 (LD)
Jennifer Harris, "Fabric of society", *Design Review*, Spring 1992, pp.44–9 (LD)
Jonathan Glancey, "Adding colour to a material world", *The Independent*, 24 April 1993 (LD)
José Manser, "Modern Day", *Design Week*, 21 May 1993, pp.16–17 (RD)
Fay Sweet, "Material girl", *Design Week*, February–March 1994 (LD)
Hugh Pearman, "Design classic: the Polyprop chair", *Sunday Times*, 20 March 1994, p.19 (RD)
David Redhead, "The stacking man", *Blueprint*, November 1994, pp.48–50 (RD)
Robin Day, "The brave old 1950s", *Design Review*, no. 14, 1995, pp.5–6 (RD/LD)
Jane Withers, "What's new?", *Independent Magazine*, 19 March 1996, pp.24–8 (RD)
David Redhead, "Design for life", *Elle Decoration*, October 1996, pp.40–45 (RD/LD)
David Etchells, "Clothing walls in subtle silks", *Cambridge Evening News*, 7 May 1998 (LD)
"Times of Day", *Contract Furnishing*, September 1998, pp.14–15 (RD)
David Redhead, "In a Day's work", *Space (Guardian)*, 18 September 1998, pp.6–8 (RD/LD)
Magdalen Vanstone, "Wedded to their vision", *Independent*, 2 October 1998, p.12 (RD/LD)
Charlotte Abrahams, "The people's chair", *Guardian Weekend*, 13 March 1999, pp.56–9 (RD)
Tamsin Blanchard, "Happy Days", *Observer*, 2 May 1999, pp.64–7 (RD/LD)
Lesley Jackson, "Sources of inspiration: Lucienne Day", *Crafts*, May–June 1999, pp.46–9 (LD)
Tamsin Blanchard, "Playtime", *Observer*, 19 September 1999, p.84 (RD)
Lesley Jackson, "Ply and the family home", *Independent*, 25 September 1999, p.18 (RD)
Lesley Jackson, "Robin and Lucienne Day", Design in Britain, Design Museum, 2004 (http://designmuseum.org/design/robin-lucienne-day)
Fiona MacCarthy, "Lucienne Day", Guardian, 3 February 2010 (obituary)
Lesley Jackson, "Lucienne Day", Independent, 13 February 2010 (obituary)
Lesley Jackson, "Lucienne Day", Crafts, April 2010 (obituary)
Fiona MacCarthy, "Robin Day", Guardian, 18 November 2010 (obituary)
Lesley Jackson, "Lucienne Day", Independent, 19 November 2010 (obituary)

Selected Books

Listed in alphabetical order by author or title.

Isabelle Anscombe, *A Woman's Touch – Women in Design from 1860 to the Present*, Virago, London, 1984 (LD)
Mary Banham and Bevis Hillier, eds, *A Tonic to the Nation – The Festival of Britain 1951*, Thames and Hudson, London, 1976 (RD/LD)
Anna Buruma, Note: Liberty and Co. in the Fifties and Sixties, ACC, Suffolk, 2009
Colorado Springs Fine Arts Center, Designing Women of Postwar Britain, Denver, 2008 (LD)
Gordon Bussey and Keith Geddes, *The Setmakers – A History of the Radio and Television Industry*, British Radio and Electronic Equipment Manufacturers Association, London, 1991 (RD)
Terence Conran, *Printed Textile Design*, Studio Publications, London, 1957 (LD)
Decorative Art Studio Year Book, vols 41–50, The Studio, London, 1951–60 (RD/LD)
Designers in Britain, vols 1–7, Society of Industrial Artists / Allan Wingate (vols 1–4), André Deutsch (vols 5–7), London, 1947–71 (RD/LD)
Fine Art Society, *Austerity to Affluence: British Art and Design 1945–1962*, Merrell Hoberton, London, 1997 (RD/LD)
Susanna Goodden, *A History of Heal's*, Heal & Son Ltd, London, 1984 (RD/LD)
Jennifer Harris, *Lucienne Day – A Career in Design*, Whitworth Art Gallery, Manchester, 1993 (LD)
Kathryn Hiesinger and George Marcus, *Design Since 1945*, Philadelphia Museum of Art, 1983 (RD/LD)
Frances Hinchliffe, *Fifties Furnishing Fabrics*, V&A, London, 1989 (LD)
Ngozi Ikoku, British Textile Design from 1940 to the Present, V&A, London, 1999 (LD)
Ngozi Ikoku, ed., *Post-War British Textiles*, Francesca Galloway, London, 2006 (LD)
Lesley Jackson, *The New Look – Design in the Fifties*, Thames and Hudson, London, 1991 (RD/LD)
Lesley Jackson, *"Contemporary" Architecture and Interiors of the 1950s*, Phaidon, London, 1994 (RD/LD)
Lesley Jackson, *The Sixties – Decade of Design Revolution*, Phaidon, London, 1998 (RD/LD)
Lesley Jackson, 20th Century Pattern Design – Textile & Wallpaper Pioneers, Mitchell Beazley, London, 2002 (LD)
Lesley Jackson, From Atoms to Patterns – Crystal Structure Designs from the 1951 Festival of Britain, Richard Dennis, Somerset, 2008 (LD)
Lesley Jackson, Alastair Morton and Edinburgh Weavers, V&A, London, 2012 (LD)
Edgar Kaufmann Jr, *Prize Designs for Modern Furniture from the International Competition for Low-Cost Furniture Design*, Museum of Modern Art, New York, 1950 (RD)
Sue Kerry, Twentieth Century Textiles, Francesca Galloway, London, 2007 (LD)
Sutherland Lyall, *Hille – 75 Years of British Furniture*, Elron Press / Victoria and Albert Museum, London, 1981 (RD)
Fiona MacCarthy and Patrick Nuttgens, *Eye for Industry – Royal Designers for Industry 1936–1986*, Lund Humphries, London, 1986 (RD/LD)
John McKean, *Royal Festival Hall London 1948–1951*, Phaidon, London, 1992 (RD)
Garry Olson and Peter Toaig, Onetree, Merrell, London, 2001 (RD)
Paul Rennie, Festival of Britain – Design 1951, ACC, Suffolk, 2007 (RD)
Royal Festival Hall – The Official Record, Max Parrish / London County Council, London, 1951 (RD)
Mary Schoeser, *Fabrics and Wallpapers – Twentieth Century Design*, Bell & Hyman, London, 1986 (LD)
Klaus-Jürgen Sembach, *Contemporary Furniture*, Design Council, London, 1982 (RD)
Penny Sparke, *A Century of Design – Design Pioneers of the 20th Century*, Mitchell Beazley, London, 1998 (RD/LD)
Whitechapel Art Gallery, *Modern Chairs 1918–1970*, London, 1970 (RD)

Author acknowledgments

This book would not have been possible without the kind cooperation of Robin and Lucienne Day. I would like to express my special thanks to them for all the time and effort they have devoted to this project, and for their generous hospitality during the long months of my research. Their archives have been an invaluable resource, and it is reassuring to know that these will be accessible in future through the Archive of Art and Design at the Victoria and Albert Museum.

A large debt of gratitude is also due to the staff at the Whitworth Art Gallery at the University of Manchester. As the guardians of a major collection of work by Lucienne Day (much of which was donated by the designer herself), they have photographed a substantial quantity of textiles and wallpapers for the book, and lent a large amount of material to the exhibition. All this has been very time-consuming, and I would particularly like to thank Dr Jennifer Harris, Frances Pritchard and Ann Tullo in the Textile Department, and Christine Woods and Nicola McNeff in the Wallpapers Department, for their kindness and patience. I am also indebted to Jennifer Harris for allowing me to draw on the research undertaken for her earlier book *Lucienne Day – A Career in Design*, published at the time of the Whitworth Art Gallery's exhibition in 1993.

My research into the Days' multi-faceted careers has taken me in many different directions, and many people have responded to my requests for information and loans. I would particularly like to thank the following individuals and organizations for the help they have provided during the course of my research for the book and the accompanying exhibition at the Barbican Art Gallery: Leo Armitage; David Attwood; Alan Bednall; Helen Berresford; Howard Coutts (Bowes Museum); Mary Bowring; Paul James Brewer; Karin Walton (Bristol Museum and Art Gallery); Peter Cornish (Buckinghamshire Chilterns University College); Joan Bullock-Anderson and Gillian Dickinson (Churchill College, Cambridge); Jim Clayton; Philip Coombes; Carolyn Aram (Courtaulds Textiles); Andrew Cox; Gerhardt Knodel (Cranbrook Academy of Art); John Davies; Dr Catherine Moriarty and Dr Lesley Whitworth (Design Council Archive, University of Brighton); John Davis (Design Council Slide Collection, Manchester Metropolitan University); James Peto (Design Museum, London); Petra Werner (Deutsches Porzellan Museum); Joanna Smith (English Heritage); Marianne Erikson; Eleanor Gawne; Simon Carter and Louise Woodford (Geffrye Museum); Terry Gorman; Lorna Green; Karen Hay-Edie; Andrew Dakin and Bill Maunder (Hille); Geoffrey Howard; Brian Mackey (Irish Linen Centre); Judy Faraday (John Lewis Partnership); Andew and Laura Jones; Rosamind Julius; Charles Keen; Graham Kneen; Barbara Mundt (Kunstgewerbemuseum, Berlin); Andrew Thynne (Lancashire Record Office); Susan Ashworth (Lancaster City Museum); Brian Law; Anna Buruma (Liberty plc); John Cooper (Link Trading); Keith Pille (The Minneapolis Institute of Arts); Gail Cleverly (Moygashel Ltd); Zoe Hendon and Lesley Hoskins (Museum of Domestic Design and Architecture, University of Middlesex); Michelle Harvey and Pierre Adler (Museum of Modern Art, New York); Jacqueline Welsh (Nordenfjeldske Kunstindustrimuseum); Vivienne Metcalfe (Pilkington Automotive UK Ltd); Margaret Pollard; Rosalinda Hardiman (Portsmouth City Museum and Records Office); Gerrit Rasch and Kirsten Pollkamp (Tapetenfabrik Gebr. Rasch GmbH); Shirley Roberts; Inger Cavallius (Röhsska Museet, Gothenburg); Astrid Kühn (Rosenthal); Henry Rothschild; Vernon Creek (Royal Air Force Museum, Hendon); Eugene Rae (Royal College of Art); Mala Jones (Royal Festival Hall); Dr Neil Bingham and Robert Elwall (Royal Institute of British Architects); Susan Bennett (Royal Society of Arts); Cherrill and Ian Scheer; Mary Schoeser; Sheridan Coakley (SCP); Stanley Sellers; Brian Smith; Elsie Spencer; Helen Stubbs (Steeles Carpets); Beryl and Stuart Sutcliffe; Richard Chamberlain and Geoff Rayner (Target Gallery); Frederika Launert (Sanderson); David Tong; Simon Alderson (Twentytwentyone); Caroline Imlah and Andrew Greg (Tyne and Wear Museums); Guy Baxter, Shaun Cole, Sorrel Herschberg, Ngozi Ikoku, Serena Kelly, Justine Lewis, Linda Parry, Nick Ross, Jennifer Wearden and Eva White (Victoria and Albert Museum); Gerry Wells (Vintage Wireless Museum); Mavis Watney; Pompi Parry (Wilton Carpet Factory); Yvonne Smith (Woodward Grosvenor); June Yeatman.

At Mitchell Beazley my managing editor Anthea Snow has acted as a linchpin, and I am extremely grateful to her for the patience and efficiency with which she has managed this demanding project. My picture researcher Christine Crawshaw has made a vital contribution to the book by securing all the images that were needed, and Kirsty Seymour-Ure has taken great care with the copy-editing and proofreading. Special thanks are also due to freelance graphic designer June Fraser, an old friend and colleague of the Days, for her superb work in designing the book. The contribution of Tony Mann, who took many of the original photographs in the Days' archives, and who has undertaken some new photography for the book, also deserves special acknowledgment. I would also like to thank Alison Starling, my original commissioning editor at Mitchell Beazley, for getting the ball rolling on this project, and to executive editor Mark Fletcher, deputy art director Vivienne Brar, and managing director Jane Aspden for seeing it through to fruition.

Thanks are also due to all the staff at the Barbican Art Gallery who have worked on the accompanying exhibition. I am particularly grateful to director John Hoole for his support and enthusiasm for the project, and to curator Conrad Bodman and exhibition organizer Louise Vaughan, for all their dedication and hard work.

Picture acknowledgments

KEY: fc: front cover; **bc:** back cover; **t:** top; **b:** bottom; **r:** right; **l:** left; **c:** centre;

AJ: Property of Andrew Jones; **BC:** Courtesy of Barbican Centre, London; **BM:** The Bowes Museum, Barnard Castle, Co. Durham, UK; **CL:** Country Life Picture Library; **CR:** Cracknell, photographer; **CW:** Chris Wood, photographer; **DCMM:** Design Council Slide Library at The Manchester Metropolitan University; **DCUB:** Design Council/DHRC, University of Brighton; **DH:** Dennis Hooker, photographer; **EM:** Emap Construct; **ES:** Egon G. Schleinitz, photographer; **FAS:** The Fine Art Society, London; **GG:** Guy Gravett, photographer; **GS:** Gunter Senfft, photographer; **HA:** Habitat UK Ltd.; **HAM:** courtesy of Hamptons International; **HB:** Henry Bourne, photographer; **HI:** Hille Ltd.; **HS:** Henk Snoek, photographer; **IT:** Ian Thomas, photographer; **JG:** John Garner, photographer; **JNG:** John Gay, photographer; **JL:** The John Lewis Partnership Archive Collection; **JRJD:** John Rose & John Dyble, photographers; **JRP:** John R. Pantlin, photographer; **JV:** John Vickers, photographer; **LK:** Luke Kirwan, photographer; **LS:** L. Schröder, photographer; **MC:** Martin Charles, photographer; **MD:** Michael Dunne Studio Ltd., photographer; **MO:** Photographic panel for the exhibition "Prize Designs for Modern Furniture." Photograph © 2000 The Museum of Modern Art, New York; **OPG:** Octopus Publishing Group Ltd.; **PB:** Peter Bloomfield, photographer; **RA:** Tapetenfabrik Gebr. Rasch GmbH & Co., Bramsche, Germany; **RF:** The Royal Festival Hall; **RI:** British Architectural Library, RIBA, London; **RLDA:** Robin and Lucienne Day archive; **RO:** Rosenthal-Porzellan A.G.; **ROY:** Royal Air Force Museum Hendon; **RSA:** The Royal Society of Arts; **RY:** Rylee, photographer; **SB:** Studio Briggs, photographer; **SCP:** SCP Ltd.; **SN:** Sydney W. Newbery, photographer; **SS:** Studio Sun Ltd., photographer; **ST:** Steve Tanner, photographer; **STU:** Studio 2; **TF:** Trevor Fry, photographer; **TM:** Tony Mann, photographer; **TG:** courtesy of The Target Gallery, London; **TGL:** The Target Gallery, London;**TW:** Twentytwentyone; **VA:** V&A Picture Library; **WG:** Woodward, Grosvenor & Co. Ltd.; **WDM:** Willy de Mayo; **WH:** The Whitworth Art Gallery, University of Manchester.

fcl HI; **fcr** WH; **bc** RLDA; **2** RLDA; **6** RLDA/HI; **7** RLDA/TM; **8t** RLDA; **8bl** RLDA; **8br** RLDA; **9** RLDA; **11tl** RLDA; **11tr** RLDA; **11b** RLDA; **13t** RLDA; **13bl** RLDA; **13br** VA; **15t** RLDA/JV; **15b** RLDA/JV; **16tl** ROY/ref. FA 10321; **16tr** ROY/ref. FA 10320; **16bl** ROY/ref. FA 11061; **16ct** ROY/ref. FA 10543; **16cb** ROY/ref. FA 10277; **16cr** ROY/ref. FA 10548; **16br** ROY/ref. FA 10544; **18t** RLDA/TM; **18b** RLDA/TM; **19** ROY/ref. FA 10771; **20t** RLDA/EM; **20b** RI; **21t** RLDA; **21b** RLDA/RY; **22t** RLDA/CR; **22b** OPG/TM; **23t** RLDA/JRP; **23b** OPG/TM; **25t** RLDA/TM; **25b** RLDA/TM; **26** MO; **27** MO; **28t** RLDA; **28b** RLDA; **29t** RLDA; **29b** RLDA/SS; **30tl** RLDA; **30tr** RLDA; **30b** VA; **31** RLDA; **32** WH; **33** OPG/TG/ST; **35t** RLDA/JRJD; **35cr** OPG/TG/ST; **35cl** DCMM; **35b** RLDA; **37tl** RLDA/JRP; **37tr** RLDA; **37b** RLDA; **38** RLDA/EM; **39** RLDA/SN; **40t** OPG/TG/ST; **40b** OPG/TG/ST; **41** RLDA/RF; **42** RLDA; **43** RLDA/SN; **44t** OPG/TM; **44b** VA; **45** RLDA/CR; **46** VA; **47t** RLDA; **47b** RLDA; **48t** RLDA/SB; **48b** RLDA; **49** WH; **50t** WH; **50b** WH; **51** RLDA; **52t** RLDA/HAM/CW; **52b** OPG/TM; **53t** RLDA/GG; **53b** RLDA/HAM/CW; **54** WH; **55** RLDA/TM; **56t** RLDA/TM; **56b** RLDA/TM; **57t** RLDA/DCUB; **57b** RLDA/TM; **58** RLDA; **59** OPG/TM; **60t** RLDA/TM; **60bl** RLDA/TM; **60br** RLDA/TM; **61** OPG/TM; **62** RLDA/TM; **63** RLDA/TM; **64** OPG/TM; **65t** CL; **65b** RLDA; **66** OPG/TM; **67** TGL/FAS; **68t** RLDA/TM; **68b** RLDA/TM; **69t** RLDA/TM; **69b** RLDA; **70t** OPG/TG/ST; **70b** RLDA/TM; **71tl** RLDA/TM; **71tr** RLDA/TM; **71b** DCMM; **72** RLDA/TM; **73t** RLDA; **73b** RLDA; **74** DCMM; **75t** HI; **75b** RLDA/TM; **76** RLDA; **77t** RLDA/TM; **77c** DCMM; **77bl** RLDA/TM; **77br** RLDA/TM; **79tl** OPG/TG/ST; **79tr** RLDA/JNG; **79bl** VA/IT; **79br** OPG/TG/ST; **80t** VA; **80b** VA; **81t** OPG/TG/ST; **81b** VA; **82t** WH; **82bl** VA; **82br** OPG/TG/ST; **83t** RLDA/TM; **83b** VA; **84t** WH; **84b** WH; **85t** OPG/TG/ST; **85b** WH; **86tl** RLDA; **86tr** WH; **86b** OPG/TG/ST; **87** OPG/TG/ST; **88t** OPG/TG/ST; **88b** OPG/TG/ST; **89t** OPG/TG/ST; **89b** OPG/TG/ST; **90t** WH; **90b** WH; **91t** WH; **91b** WH; **92** RA; **93t** RLDA/ES; **93cl** RA; **93bl** RA; **93br** WH; **94t** WH; **94b** RLDA/GS; **95t** RLDA/RO; **95b** RLDA/RO; **96t** OPG/TG/ST; **96b** RLDA/RO; **97t** RLDA/RO; **97b** OPG/TG/ST; **98t** RLDA/TM; **98c** RLDA/TM; **98b** DCMM; **99tl** WH; **99tcl** WH; **99tr** WH; **99cb** WH; **99b** WH; **100** WH; **101tl** OPG/TG/ST; **101tr** RLDA; **101bl** WH; **101br** WH; **102t** OPG/TG/ST; **102b** WH; **103t** WH; **103bl** OPG/TG/ST; **103br** OPG/TG/ST; **104tl** OPG/TM; **104tr** OPG/TM; **104ct** WH; **104cb** BM; **104bl** RLDA; **104br** RLDA; **105t** RLDA/TM; **105b** OPG/TG/ST; **106t** RLDA; **106b** RLDA/GS; **107t** DCMM/HI; **107bl** VA; **107br** OPG/TG/ST; **108** RLDA/HI; **109** RLDA/TM; **110** RLDA/HS; **111t** RLDA/TM; **111cl** RLDA/SB; **111bl** RLDA/DH; **111br** HI; **112** RLDA/HI; **113tl** RLDA/TM; **113tr** RLDA/DH; **113cl** RLDA/TM; **113cr** RLDA/DH; **113b** RLDA/HI; **115t** RLDA/HI; **115bl** RLDA/DH; **115br** RLDA/TM; **116t** RLDA/TM; **116b** RLDA/DH; **117tl** OPG/TG/ST; **117tr** RLDA/TM; **117bl** RLDA/TM; **117br** RLDA/TM; **118t** RLDA; **118c** RLDA; **118b** RLDA/TM; **119** RLDA; **120t** RLDA/TM; **120b** RLDA/HI; **121t** HI; **121b** RLDA/HI; **122t** RLDA/HI; **122b** RLDA/WDM; **123t** RLDA/HI; **123b** HI; **124t** RLDA/DH; **124b** HI; **125t** WG; **125cl** WG; **125cr** OPG/TM; **125bl** WG; **125br** OPG/TM; **126t** WH; **126b** RLDA; **127tl** WH; **127bl** OPG/TG/ST; **127r** VA; **128** WH; **129t** OPG/TG/ST; **129b** WH; **130** VA; **131tl** WH; **131tr** WH; **131b** RLDA; **132t** WH; **132cl** WH; **132cr** WH; **132bl** OPG/TM; **132br** WH; **133t** RLDA; **133b** RLDA/LS; **135tl** RLDA/MD; **135tr** OPG/TG/ST; **135bl** RLDA/TM; **135br** OPG/TG/ST; **136t** DCMM; **136c** WH; **136bl** WH; **136br** WH; **137t** WH; **137b** WH; **138t** OPG/TM; **138b** OPG/TM; **139tl** OPG/TM; **139tr** RLDA; **139b** RLDA/JG; **141t** RLDA; **141b** WH; **143t** RLDA/TF; **143c** OPG/TM; **143b** RLDA; **144** RLDA/TM; **145** HI; **146t** RLDA/HI/STU; **146b** RLDA/HI; **147t** RLDA/HI; **147b** HI; **149tl** RLDA/HI; **149tr** DCMM; **149b** OPG/TG/ST; **150t** HI; **150b** HI; **151t** BC/PB; **151b** EM/MC; **152** HI; **153t** RLDA/HI; **153bl** RLDA/HI; **153br** RLDA/HI; **154** RLDA/HI; **155t** RLDA/HI; **155c** RLDA/HI; **155b** HI; **156** OPG/TG/ST; **157t** RLDA; **157b** RLDA/HI; **158t** WH; **158c** WH; **158b** WH; **159t** WH; **159c** WH; **159b** WH; **161t** JL; **161bl** RLDA/JL; **161br** JL; **162** RLDA/TM; **163tl** RLDA/TM; **163bl** OPG/TG/ST; **163r** RLDA/TM; **164** RLDA; **165t** JL; **165b** JL; **166t** RLDA; **166b** RLDA; **167** RSA; **168** HB; **169** HA; **170t** TW/LK/AJ; **170c** TW; **170b** SCP; **171tl** RLDA/TM; **171tr** HA; **171b** RLDA/TM.